RENEWALS 458-4574
DATE DUE

WITHDRAWN
UTSA Libraries

The Riverscape and the River

The study of water in the landscape is a new and rapidly expanding field Rivers make riverscapes (even if the rivers are frozen) and riverscapes then determine the rivers: except for the ever-increasing human impact. Dr Haslam examines how the quantity, function and ecology of water changes as it moves from watershed to river. The development of river and riverscape, their ecology, the effect of human activities (such as water abstractions, flood control and management for recreational use) and water resources are described both in principle and using case histories. Contrasting examples are given from across the world, including Iceland, Hungary, Malta, Britain and the USA, which enables understanding of how water and riverscape interact with each other, and with human impact. The study, development and loss of water resources is also described, including the extreme example of Malta, whose clean water now depends solely on oil imports. This innovative book is aimed at undergraduate and graduate students and professionals, but is also accessible to anyone interested in how water and riverscape interact.

DR S. M. HASLAM is a fresh water ecologist in the Department of Plant Sciences at Cambridge University.

The Riverscape
and the River

S. M. Haslam,
M.A., Sc.D.
Department of Plant Sciences
University of Cambridge, England

CAMBRIDGE UNIVERSITY PRESS
Cambridge, New York, Melbourne, Madrid, Cape Town, Singapore, São Paulo

Cambridge University Press
The Edinburgh Building, Cambridge CB2 8RU, UK

Published in the United States of America by Cambridge University Press, New York

www.cambridge.org
Information on this title: www.cambridge.org/9780521839785

© S. M. Haslam 2008

This publication is in copyright. Subject to statutory exception
and to the provisions of relevant collective licensing agreements,
no reproduction of any part may take place without
the written permission of Cambridge University Press.

First published 2008

Printed in the United Kingdom at the University Press, Cambridge

A catalogue record for this publication is available from the British Library

ISBN 978-0-521-83978-5 hardback

Library
University of Texas
at San Antonio

Cambridge University Press has no responsibility for the persistence or accuracy of URLs for external or third-party internet websites referred to in this publication, and does not guarantee that any content on such websites is, or will remain, accurate or appropriate.

To: Mr H. W. Haslam and Mrs J. M. Psaila who (more than others) drove the author hither and drove her thither, in England and Malta, respectively, so that she could study the riverscapes.

*Thou makest springs gush forth in the valleys,
they flow between the hills,
they give drink to every beast of the field; . . .
the earth is satisfied with the fruit of Thy work.*

Ps.104

Contents

List of tables xi
Preface xiii
Acknowledgements xv

1 Introduction 1
Introduction 1
Interpretation 3
A working entity 4
Riverscape elements 5
Catchments and their diversity 6
Natural capital 8
Intangible values of riverscapes 8
Values 15

2 The natural river and its destruction 16
The concept of naturalness 16
Human impact 19
River vegetation 22
River animals 41
Connections and mosaics 42
Skewing and loss of vegetation from human impact 47
Restoration and rehabilitation 50

3 The natural riverscape and its modification 53
Introduction 53
The layers of the riverscape 54
History 55

Case studies 56
1 Waccasassa River, Florida, USA 56
2 R. Cam, Cambridgeshire, England 58
3 River Kbir, Malta 67
4 R. Golo, Corsica 77
5 R. Don (Aberdeen) Scotland 81
6 R. San Gorg, Malta 84
Discussion 84

4 **Resources I. Water resources and their loss** 86
Introduction 86
The European Union Water Framework Directive 87
The functioning river and riverscape 89
The example of Malta 94
Loss in temperate Europe 99
Discussion 105

5 **Development and variation of rivers** 107
Upstream – Downstream 107
Downstream variation in vegetation 127
Case studies: R. Wylye, England 136
                R. Itchen, England 137
                Brief case studies 139
Connectivity and mosaics 139

6 **Development and variation of riverscapes** 141
Introduction 141
Sense of place 144
Patterns 147
Riverscape construction 149
Recent floods 155
Discussion 156

7 **Building blocks of river vegetation** 157
River architecture 157
Examining architecture 161
The building blocks and their habitats 165
Animals and structure 174
Water-supported vegetation 175
Conclusions 177

8 Building blocks of flood plain vegetation 179
Introduction 179
The building blocks 180
Traditional vegetation types 194
Building blocks of river plain vegetation 197
Case studies 200
Discussion 209

9 Resources II. Plants and animals, cleaning and minerals 217
Introduction 217
Resources of rivers and other fresh waters 217
Birds 221
Mammals 224
Other animals 225
Wetlands 226
Materials 235
Recreation 236

10 Building blocks of the riverscape 237
Introduction 237
Case study: Malta 240
Riverscape description 243
Building blocks which drive riverscape development 245
The effect of land use changes 248
Trees 250
Building blocks for individual species 251
Buffer strips and beetle banks 254
Historical examples 255
Discussion 256

11 Patterns, boundaries and fragmentation 260
Introduction 260
Scale 260
Mosaics 262
Community size and fragmentation 264
Fragments 265
Communication 267
Fragmentation and destruction of habitat: case study, Malta 268
Cultural fragmentation 269
Change over two decades: Gozo, Maltese Islands 270
Pattern in relation to habitat, Icklingham Poors' Fen, Suffolk 274
The Scottish Cairngorms, change over millennia 276

x   Contents

Dartmoor, England, over millennia   276
Sensitivity and resistance   276
Discussion   278

12   **Resources III. Settlements and constructions**   281
Settlements   281
Different types of riverscape   291
Sacred riverscapes   295

13   **The harsh riverscape**   307
Introduction   308
Case studies   309
Summary   332

14   **The tempered or smiling riverscape**   333
Introduction   334
River trade   335
R. Thames   336
R. Tapio   351
Old edge of Cambridge, R. Cam   354
Pond landscape   354
Discussion   357

15   **Envoi**   359
The water features in the riverscape   359

Bibliography   367
Index to plant and animal vernacular and taxonomic names   394
General subject index   398

Tables

1.1	Lower riverscape values	page 12
2.1	Climate and geomorphic changes of the post-glacial era in Britain	18
2.2	Significant river species of west and central Europe, with their habits	31
2.3	Changeless change	37
2.4	Species particularly tolerant to different types of damage	40
2.5	Geographic distributions of European river plants.	46
3.1	Loss of aquatic species in Malta	75
4.1	Damage to some East Anglian fens	95
5.1	Riverscape elements in the Maltese Islands	108
5.2	Species distribution in relation to stream width and slope	120
5.3	Interpretation of habitat from species lists	130
5.4	Cover-Diversity, CoDi, values in relation to habitat	131
5.5	Change over 40 years with shallowing in River Dove, Peak District, England	133
6.1	Riverscape elements in the Eger catchment, Hungary	142
6.2	Characteristics that give rise to landscape organisation	150
6.3	Effects of heterogeneity on landscapes	152
7.1	Building blocks of river vegetation	162
7.2	Habitat of emergent building blocks	163
7.3	Habitat preferences within the one building block of tall monocotyledons	164
7.4	Comparison of the importance of some building blocks in Europe and (E. and Central) North America	168
7.5	European and North American plant similarities	169
7.6	Bank Vegetation	172

8.1 (a)	Habitat features formed by different water sources	182
8.1 (b)	Water regimes of different wetland types	183
8.1 (c)	The effect of water level fluctuations	184
8.1 (d)	Management for some types of fen and marsh herbaceous vegetation, in similar water regimes	185
8.2	Outline of CORINE Wetland Classification	189
8.3	Water Quality comments	197
8.4	English Broadland change and deterioration	214
9.1	Values of riparian ecosystems	218
9.2	Major habitat requirements for some animals	222
9.3	Commercial value of wetlands	226
9.4	Examples of chemical removal in constructed wetlands	232
9.5	Selecting best management practices by pollutant: rules of thumb	233
9.6	Recreation sites, rivers and wetlands	236
10.1	Ancient and planned countryside	246
10.2	Building blocks of riverscapes	257
11.1	Environmental flows in Gozo	270
11.2	Socio-economic forces causing change in Gozo	271
11.3	Environmental effects of socio-economic forces in Gozo	272
11.4	Past and futures of Icklingham Poors' Fen, England	275
11.5	Peat histories, England (representative of numerous sites investigated)	277
12.1	Some river uses for people	282
14.1	Some origins of ponds	356

Preface

The study of landscape ecology has developed rapidly in the past two decades, though the limited area of riverscape has not received great attention as such. This book attempts to link river and riverscape in an integrated whole. It has more ecology (natural, cultural and historical) and less mathematics and modelling than is currently usual: reflecting my interests, and my preference for observation and synthesis.

I have worked for over 35 years on rivers, mostly on their vegetation, waters, channels and other contents. More recently I realised the interest of the wider ecosystem, of the river and the riverscape being inextricably joined, both by the water they share, and by the human impact (some interesting, most destructive) inflicted upon them. Changes have been made to allow people to survive, and indeed to live pleasantly. Great changes have also been made from ignorance or greed to remove and contaminate both water and natural heritage. *The Riverscape and the River* tries to reflect the interest and diversity of that natural heritage, and what has been done to it down the ages.

The book is primarily about Europe (with a little on North America).

S. M. H.
September 2006

Acknowledgements

I am most grateful to the many people who have helped with this book. I would single out particularly those driving me on field work, Mrs T. Bone, Artist and Desktop Publisher, for the preparation of the manuscript and turning sketches into publishable figures, and Mrs P. A. Wolseley and Mrs Y. Bower for permission to use figures drawn previously. My debt to Mrs Bone is even greater than usual, because my injuries left me, for a long time, writing even worse than before. Typing this script required uncommon skill and patience. The list of those who have helped with references, information permissions and in the field is long: my most grateful thanks go to all. Ms A. Imlash (RSPB, Farsinard) most kindly provided the photographs. Some picture postcards, several or many decades old, have been reproduced.

Finally, I would like to thank the publishers for their patience, waiting for me to recover from concussion caused by a continental lorry driver not knowing he had a 'blind spot' on English motorways.

Every effort has been made to secure necessary permissions to reproduce copyright material in this work, though in some cases it has proved impossible to trace copyright holders. If any omissions are brought to our notice, we will be happy to include appropriate acknowledgements on reprinting (in any subsequent edition).

1

Introduction

We belong to a time as well as a landscape

(Storey, 1993)

We seek order out of chaos.
The more we discern, the less we seem to know.

(Bell, 1997)

Rivers . . . were made for wise men to contemplate, and for fools to pass by without consideration.

(cited in Walton, 1653)

Introduction

The riverscape and the river share the sheet of water which covers the land: in whole or part, permanently or intermittently. The river is a stream of water flowing along a bed in the earth, to the sea (lake or river). The riverscape is that part of landscape which has (or had) a watercourse as its focus. Rain falls upon the riverscape. Some evaporates, some sinks below, gradually emerging as springs or flushes, and (usually) most runs down the slope, gradually collecting into the rivers and finally the seas. The hydrological cycle is finished by the evaporation of sea (and fresh) water into the air, and its precipitation back on the earth's surface.

Seeing that life on earth is based on water, and life on land, on fresh water, the river is essential to land life, as well as river life. The riverscape and, to a considerable extent all that grows on it or is put on it, depends on the river, since the river (or the ice-river of a precursor glacier) first formed the riverscape. The two are interdependent, both are modified by human impact (even in Antarctica, e.g. air and sea pollution, and climate change), and both are natural capital, hence natural resources for people. They thus come from the interaction of natural elements such as flowing water and rising hills, and the interaction with these and the cultural dimension and its diversity. They are live archives, demonstrating the management of natural resources such as water and soil (Andressen & Curado, 2001).

The valley, according to *Chambers Dictionary*, is a stretch of country watered by a river, an elongated hollow between hills. How much can be seen, what is seen, and how it is seen, varies with the point of observation. From the river, looking out, the riverside grades up the slope, giving a fairly enclosed view, from large (to hills beyond) to small (the riverside bushes). The viewpoint can move anywhere up slope to the hill top, where the view is generally wide and open, and the overall pattern (not the river detail) can be seen better. Aerial photographs, of course, give a yet different view of the river basin. All are equally true, all showing different facets of the riverscape and river.

Riverscapes have three characters: structure, function and change.

Structure

Passing from centre outwards, first the size, shape, pattern of:

- the river and of what grows in it;
- the riverside, narrow or wide, what grows on it (e.g. wood, flooded wetland, grass, crops) and what has been put on it (e.g. houses, mills, wharfs, roads, towns, telephone wires);
- the land beyond, which may usually rise to well-marked hills or continuing lowland, or even flood plain for the extent of the riverscape view. This also has much put upon it, both vegetation and the associated animals. These may be native plants, varying from large, like trees and forests of oak, pine and so on, to small, like daisies or mosses. They may be meadow or pastures of traditional, rather than of native species. They may be agricultural crops, like cabbage or barley.

The underlying structure of topography and geology, soil and water has on it (and in it) the natural structure of vegetation, and the imposed structures of people, from isolated farms nestling in valleys to great port towns, from pilgrims' ways to radio-lines for mobile telephone masts, from canals to deep abstraction boreholes and sewage treatment works.

Function

The river and riverscape function in their own right, in the hydrological cycle and in the consequent perpetual erosion of the land and sedimentation of the sea: until the next earth movements! In the course of this, water, wetland, damp and dryland habitats appear, in which plants – and animals and micro-organisms – can grow, spread and develop. For the past 800,000 years they have also functioned for people, to provide food, shelter, clothing, communications and much more (Table 1.1).

The river and riverscape are the basis of the human environment. They bear the plants and animals needed by people, and these are in communities influenced by people (e.g. Vink, 1983). They are working entities, places of many processes.

Change

Nothing on earth is permanent, but the scale of change varies from the long-term erosion of mountains to the short-term flood.

Interpretation

Nature, culture and history are complex, complex in themselves, and complex in their inter-relations. Few people can see and understand all, at one time. This author can visit a riverscape to look at one of (say):

river plants and channel
wetlands near rivers
river cultural patterns, past and present
settlement patterns
landscape elements
communications, for biota and people
heritage, visible and invisible.

These and more can be studied and (often) understood. But this author's head has difficulty in seeing and assessing two of these on one visit, and finds it impossible to see and interpret all. The same site yields quite different material, depending on the purpose of the visit. This factor underlies all such field study. The human brain is limited, while nature, culture and history are not – in the present state of knowledge.

Many different aspects and perceptions of river and riverscape can be, and have been, developed. Each brings out or enhances a different facet. Difficulties arise only when like is not compared with like, or when someone asserts there is only one method right and true. Looking at connectivity, for instance, that for surface water and that for the movement of herons may overlap, since both include shallow water, but the two patterns differ in content, in solidity, in time and, of course, in purpose. To call either or indeed both *the* connectivity of the riverscape is incorrect (what about hedges, woods, deer, badgers, otters, dragonflies, water lilies, roads, telephone lines . . .?) To use any to interpret part of the surface pattern is valuable. It would take a lifetime to work out total communication lines in one place (anaerobic bacteria? nematodes? dispersion of wind-borne seeds? and to do so by species, topography, land use and season with the components thereof, winds, strength, direction; time of day; temperatures, etc. And so on, including the bird which arrives but once a century with alien seeds on its feet, and the people who walk at least 10 m from the path).

Consequently, when looking at a river and riverscape, what is seen is confusion of these and many more elements. To understand, one thread is disentangled, then another... But those doing the interpreting should be quick to explain these threads and how they relate to the whole riverscape: they should be very slow to condemn others working in a different way. It is better to discuss how using a different method sheds new light.

A working entity

The riverscape is a working entity, generally managed for the welfare of those living on or near it. This cultural identity has made the riverscape fascinating in its variety, pattern and processes, or dreary, in their loss. Conservators need to claim and arrange to leave the old unless a new good (not a new greed!) cannot be met without change. Then change blends with the old, the past moulding the present, and the present exhibiting the past, say:

- the village wharf, where once boats came with coals, candles and luxuries, and left with malt and vegetables;
- the holy well up the hill with the deep-set path worn by thousands of pilgrims;
- and the old wood, now belonging to the Wildlife Trust, once the source of timber for ship and manor, of charcoal, withies and fuel, and of food for pigs and deer.

Unfortunately, the destruction of the old after 1945, the Second World War, has been extreme. England has been one of the worst-damaged countries. The land has been drained, water has been abstracted, rivers and ponds have been lost, hedges and woods have been removed, wild flowers and song birds have diminished greatly under the still-increasing pressure (including Directives) to Grow More, Grow More, Grow More, More Cheaply. While conservation organisations thrive, damage thrives more and faster. Indeed, Rackham (1986) finds more destruction, in England, between 1945 and 1986 than in the previous thousand years. Malta has moved to destruction even faster, since wealth came in around 1980. Rackham & Moody (1996) consider wealth more pernicious to the country and landscape than war or earthquake. A chilling, though true, observation. For two millennia it has been written that the love of money is the root of all evil (1. Tim., 6:10). Certainly, money is at the root of most destruction of natural and cultural heritage: the love of it, the gaining of it, and the spending of it without knowledge.

Population increases have not helped. Since 1800, Britain has increased from about 16 to nearly 60 million, Malta from 100,000 to 400,000 (including much emigration).

Riverscape elements

Landscape, riverscape, can be divided (Countryside Commission, Swanwick, 2002) into:

1. The natural: geology, land form, water, air and climate, soils, flora and fauna.
2. The cultural and social, which are superimposed on the natural; land use, from fisheries and grouse moors to huge mono-specific regions of grain, from paths to trains and motorways, from isolated farms to great dormitory suburbs. People need food, clothing and shelter, but want infinitely more than that: a never-ending stream of luxuries from baths to computers, crockery to cars (and the petrol to run them), food from half way across the globe. . . The combination of a huge population and its never-ending wants places intolerable and unsustainable pressure on the water and on the land, and degradation ensues.
3. Perceptual and aesthetic, the invisible heritage and causes of patterning. This is the history associated with the place, from a famous battle to 'I picnicked here as a child', the birthplace of great people, the inspiration for painting or writing; and love, often love enduring for centuries, for a landscape, sounds, smells and touches; farming patterns of texture and colour. It is perceptions that turn land into landscape, and so give Sense of Place. Riverscapes are distinctive parts of landscapes.

Various terms describe different scales or perceptions. One group is *Character*, a consistent pattern of elements that make a riverscape distinctive, e.g. Alpine valleys. A *Characteristic* is an element or combination making a particular contribution to the whole, e.g. Alpine meadows. *Elements* are components which make up the landscape, e.g. little valleys and woody features outlining the meadows. *Features* are prominent and eye-catching, e.g. mountains on the skyline, villages clustered round churches in the valley. *Types* occur in many broadly similar parts, e.g. flat valley bottoms with former wetland, roads and development. (Similar ties are in geology, topography, drainage, vegetation, history, settlement pattern and land use.) Finally, *Areas* are discrete geographical areas of a particular landscape type, e.g. the chalet-farm areas of various different mountains.

Patterns in the riverscape are separated, so defined, firstly by what can be seen. It is the eye, which looks for pattern, which seeks unity and order, and finds it by omission as much as by presence. The eye recognises and categorises distinctiveness before the brain defines it. The eye flows across skylines, and notes the lines of visual force, such as hedge patterns, before the brain has recognised 'field shapes and their boundaries'. For instance:

- land form, vertical form (sheer cliff, rolling lowland to horizon), horizontal form, altitude;
- land pattern; mosaics, connections, corridors, matrix, scale, shapes random, organised, repeating, or formal;
- structural pattern, scale (small-large), enclosure (exposed, open, tight pattern, scattered), diversity (uniform, complex), texture (smooth, rugged), unity (all fields with dry stone walls, only the hill tops with these, complete jumble of field and settlement types);
- local form; shapes and patterns of fields, streams, woods, hedges, roads, settlements;
- diversity; uniform to complex (sub-divided into the above);
- line (straight, angular, curved, braided, sinuous);
- special separation; isolation, rarity, crowded, confused; it is possible to define these, but more difficult for:
- colour; monochrome, muted colours, bright ones, contrasts (e.g., conifer wood, white-stoned village, oilseed rape in flower);
- beauty, pretty, attractive, sublime, majestic, dreary, etc.;
- sound and movement; noisiness, tranquillity, calmness, busyness;
- coherence, mystery; remembrance of past fact or fiction influencing interpretation of the present (e.g. Dracula country, Transylvania; Battlefield of Waterloo, Belgium; the filmed valleys of *The Lord of the Rings*, New Zealand; Saga country, Iceland; Black Forest, Grimms' fairy tales, Germany; Yorkshire Dales, Herriot (Vet.) country, England;
- balance; harmonious, disruptive;
- holiness; sacred feature, history, building.

All of these, and more, make up the Sense of Place, more, the *Genius loci*, which is so easily recognised, so difficult to define (after Bell, 1999; Swanwick, 2002).

Catchments and their diversity

The catchment or river basin is a unit of area down which the run-off from its rain flows (or once flowed), gathering together to leave the basin at (usually) a single point. This flow ends in the sea, but for some purposes parts of basins may be treated separately, e.g. catchments of tributaries, reaching their mouths when flowing into the main river or into a lake. A riverscape is part or all of a catchment.

Catchments vary greatly, and in a goodly diversity of features, from scale (e.g. R. Armier, Malta, 0.25 km to, say, the mighty Mississippi, USA, 15 000 km and more, even excluding tributaries) to human impact (e.g. R. Fleet, London, completely built-over and a river near Thingvellir, Iceland, with only minor alterations). Catchments vary in type. Streams may gather run-off in flowery meadows, and run through gorges. All, by definition, have (or had) a stream running through. That is their unifying characteristic.

The 'bones' of the riverscape are its rocks, underneath, or also outcropping. The jagged peaks of the Alps are outcropping rock. The gentle agricultural lowlands have their rock padded/upholstered by soil and subsoil, on which tall vegetation (not just lichens, mosses, etc.) can grow. Catchments can be Alpine or near-plain, large or small, moderately uniform to highly diverse (mountains, torrents, gorges, lowland, plateau, plain; forested, agricultural, urban). Rivers may be in a traditional state with minor or major management of them, even with them put underground; 'streams' can resemble those of a millennium ago, or can be greatly polluted or dried. More detailed culture is superimposed, the particular way of altering streams is characteristic of the country and can indicate history: the Danish dyke patterns of now-German Schleswig Holstein, for instance. The shape of *Salix alba* riverside bands varies from east to west across Europe. Neolithic field patterns may still be traced or may indeed have been incorporated into a later field pattern (re-arranged anything up to the twenty-first century).

> Still round the corner we may meet
> A sudden tree or standing stone
> That none have seen but we alone
> Hill and water under sky
> Pass them by! Pass them by!
> (J. R. R. Tolkien)

Round the corner the riverscape may differ sharply, in topography, land use, settlement and water use: or it may be very similar.

Where rocks outcrop, these may be vertical or craggy (e.g. some hard limestone, dolomite) or non-obtrusive or smooth, not obstructing part of the general hilly structure (e.g. Scottish gneiss). Where the rock is blanketed (soil, peat, alluvium, etc.), the blanket softens and smooths the riverscape, it may be from a few cm to many metres deep. The vegetation or buildings above add diversity, in their shape, colour, position, height, etc., and illustrate not just present, but often past cultural, religious and social land use patterns also.

Natural capital

The term 'natural' was used a century ago, to describe habitats and ecosystems untouched, unaffected by human impact. At that time human impact was less, and, more importantly, the extent of this impact was unknown. Ancient woodlands could be described as natural, despite being originally planted and having centuries of human use. The 'natural' river Rhine had borne boats for at least two millennia. The Somerset Levels (England) wetlands were 'natural' before drainage, despite having Neolithic villages and continuous use. Although such places, if not greatly degraded, are now better described as 'traditional', the concept remains in Natural Capital. This is what the riverscape originally provided, and most, some or hardly any may now remain. The riverscape provides potential energy, the energy of the water, sediment and debris flowing down. This may be unused, lessened by drainage and drying, or harnessed for human use (e.g. water, hydropower, fisheries). The riverscape provides a surface, a space, which vegetation and buildings may use. The choice of vegetation may be, say, forest, traditional wetlands, wildflower (nutritious and sustainable) grassland, ley grass, arable and of buildings, e.g. old, fitted to landscape, bridges, wharfs; or new, ignoring past patterns. The natural capital of the medieval town (historical interest, tourism, culture, beauty, etc.) can be all too easily lost: and lost to future generations. We hold the past in trust for the future. Loss of riverscape productivity may take decades or centuries to replace. Soil may take millennia to develop. Polluted groundwater could take millennia to clean. Polluted soil and surface water is probably quicker, being on a shorter hydrological cycle. But pollution removes sensitive biota. Lost biota may be irreplaceable. For human use, the cost of cleaning increasingly dirty water for mains supply constantly increases.

The natural capital also includes the clean air, the wind, its energy and its environmental effects.

The European Union Water Framework Directive is intended to alter the thinking of all authorities and agencies dealing with river basins. If this succeeds, the idea of sustaining, while using, natural capital may also be part of maintenance and planning.

Intangible values of riverscapes

These may well also have commercial and economic value, it all depends how they are seen. Culture is the hidden hand of land use planning, it marks boundaries, selects the valued and the useless, leads to maps, place names, artists. Something is more valuable in a cultural or historic context – the whole is more than the sum of its parts. There are traces of different eras, overlapping layers, local and regional values, written in age-old spiritual and symbolic meaning (One person's home is another's discovery) (Alumäe et al., 2001).

The English early nineteenth-century painter, John Constable, painted countryside river and riverscape pictures, particularly in the Dedham part of Essex. This is now marketed as 'Constable Country', and those living there are now profiting by the vision and talent of a great man. They do so while continuing to degrade the original riverscape, losing the non-enduring natural capital. The same applies in many areas: and those areas where tourists will pay because a great person lived there are (a little) more likely to preserve that which people will pay to see.

> Man's wonder-making hand had everywhere
> subdued all circumstance of stubborn soil
> Of fen and moor reclaimed, rich gardens smiled
> And prosperous hamlets rose, amidst the wild.
> (R. Southey)

Every riverscape settled by people becomes a blend of the natural and the human. There is a surface fabric made by people, and this book attempts to analyse the materials of the construction and the patterns of its design (after Williams, 1970).

Riverscapes, rural and urban, private and public, are and were and have been designed for human life, comfort, convenience, prosperity and delight. Old-settled riverscapes developed over centuries (and the few quick-growing towns had far fewer people than now), and developed in relation to the natural features on which they depended. These were likely to be 'good' riverscapes. In recently developed riverscapes, where dependence on natural features is less or absent, and – as often – design is absent, the environment develops for short-term, perhaps greedy purposes (see, for instance, the 'industrial farmland' fringing Milan, new housing estates by rivers in Malta and nineteenth-century towns elsewhere). This can be said to be uncivilised, and the term 'progress' merely means loss. As with government, society shall have the environment it deserves (Edwards, 1962).

Places come into being through being named, and the name encloses a place. Hence countries, mountain passes, lakes and rivers (Feld & Basso, 1996). The limits of the name enclose a place. Artistic appreciation may need only paint and canvas, but for others, words are needed, words to describe, interpret and illuminate. They may also (Feld & Basso, 1996) give a poetic overlay, geography, above the literal meaning (e.g. Altnacealgach, the burn of the deceivers, R. Rihana, the river of the myrtle tree).

The intangible can be classed as (Baker 1992):

> nature (humanity insignificant)
> habitat (people adjusted to nature)
> artefacts (from shops to telephone wires)
> systems (interacting processes from erosion and sedimentation, to food production and sustainability)
> problems (from making better roads to making their effects on ecology minimal)
> wealth (from the quality of farming and ownership of land, to the architecture of the old centre of the river port town and of the modern bridge)
> places (mountains, historic trees, villages and fields of different ages, and their names and meanings)
> history (dating and changes – and features visible or findable – from twentieth century backwards, and historical 'blocks', from different periods of history, as a Mediaeval village with ex-open field system of pasture and arable and a modern village independent of the land around, except for roads in and out)
> aesthetics (artistic quality, or the 'good feel' from just looking at riverscapes, and the extreme variety, from green and pleasant lowland with winding streams, to mountains with raging torrents, to Rhine barges, to beauties of Amsterdam)
> ideology (cultural values and social philosophy. This is where Monet painted the water lilies. These are the valleys worked by the vet known by the fictional name of James Herriot. Here, in the marshes of Maldon, the Saxons, defeated by the Danes, gained a moral victory and an undying poem. This Gozo cave valley and river mouth is (perhaps) Calypso's cave in the *Odyssey*. This defunct railway above Huy is the last remains of the once-thriving iron valley town. This riverscape shows settlement and farming by independent farmers, that, by local social patterns, the other, dictated by central government.
> That land is sacred, from the lives of the saints who lived here.

Ideas and feelings come from within (Peterken, 1996) are evoked differently by different people. The same view can bring 'Look at that church on the horizon with its ray of light.' and 'What a long walk home.' The future of the riverscape may depend on temperament and luck evoking the first, if a new housing estate is proposed.

Yet all these integrate, and no one perspective is 'better' or 'truer' in itself,. Those who plan the maintenance and change of riverscapes do well to remember all, however, since now change can so easily destroy the value created by centuries of culture, and the unique habitats of the riverscape resulting from this, superimposed on the natural.

Riverscapes have been the inspiration of artists, e.g. Beaumont, Boudin, Constable, Cuyp, Matisse, Millais, Monet, Ninham, Pissarro, Rembrandt, Renoir, Rossetti, Symoens, Turner, van Ruysdael, Siberechts, Watteau, and of the innumerable 'ordinary people' who understand beauty similarly, but who are not great painters.

Poets also have been inspired, though rather less often, e.g. Arany, Blake, both Brownings, Jukasz, Petöfi, Swift and Wordsworth.

Composers, perhaps pre-eminently Grieg, have been inspired to high art by landscapes (but, unlike artists, these have tended to have, and compose for, city life). The two can combine, e.g. Handel's Water Music, composed for a royal procession on the Thames.

Prose authors have not been missing. Many in the English-speaking world have their first encounter with the cultural value of water with Jeremy Fisher (Beatrix Potter), following it with *The Wind in the Willows* (K. Grahame), the watery adventures of Arthur Ransome's children and others. Adult fiction is more likely to include riverscapes in passing, from Shakespeare and Spenser onwards, though the Arthurian cycle has water scenes of primary importance. Dickens in *Our Mutual Friend* used the Thames to good effect, as did George Eliot, for a country river in *The Mill on the Floss*.

In view of the amount of great culture given to humanity from riverscapes, they surely deserve protection and enhancement! Surely as much and more can come in the future: provided the source of inspiration is not destroyed.

For the less talented, riverscapes can appeal for beauty, artistic, intellectuality, scientific, historic, interest, familiarity or strangeness, exercise, exploration. People appreciate surroundings in which they enjoy themselves. To simplify, a gatekeeper remarked, 'When our visitors leave, they look much happier than when they came in'. Such value can hardly be overstated. Those who destroy riverscape value would say they do it for human welfare (living, working, communications, shopping). Happiness is also part of welfare: and should be part of social policy, and given to all. It also diminishes crimes of boredom, and crimes to get money for the 'happiness drugs' of alcohol and cannabis or cocaine.

Table 1.1 *Lower riverscape values (modified from Haslam, 2003)*

Hydrological and physical

1. *Water supply (for mains).* Aquifers, bogs, flood plains, rivers, brooks. Use is too often overuse and leads to drying.
2. *Water supply for irrigation.* Rivers, brooks, etc. Wetter habitats can be used, but again this leads to drying unless only the collected natural run-out is used.
3. *Storage, dispersal and regulation of flood flows.* Flood water, dispersed on to a flood plain, and released slowly as the waters go down, reduces storm damage downstream (compared to a constricted river channel carrying the whole flow). Bog, fen, marsh and reedswamp outside larger flood plains may trap storm rainwater, and release it much more slowly. Little (and dry) flood plains, allowed to flood, may have a cumulative or local importance. (As with anything ecological, there are exceptions: wetlands that increase flash flooding.)
4. *Long-term water storage* on and in flood plains at various levels, which contribute to stream flow in drier periods (just as regulation, reservoirs, etc., mediate flows).
5. *Lessening erosion and stabilising river banks.* By lessening the force of storm flows and the amount of sediment and detritus carried, damage is reduced when the flood plain is flooded (see 3 above).
6. *Aquifer recharge or discharge.* Aquifers require to be refilled with water (particularly when used or overused for supply), and maximum water soaks in from surfaces above the aquiferous rock that are both porous and continuously wet. Alluvial deposit wetlands are the most porous, but fens and other marshes may also be good sinks. Groundwater-fed rivers and wetlands are, of course, where water discharges up from the ground. The same river or wetland, however, can have water entering by springs and also leaving by soaking down. Although it is obvious that aquifers need to be refilled, the fact is often forgotten: and folk wonder why the water supply is running short when not only is abstraction excessive, but its catchment has been built on or so converted to intensive agriculture that most rainwater runs off to the stream rather than soaking into the ground.
7. *Trapping and deposition of sediments.* When flood waters spill on to a flood plain, the sediment they carry is largely deposited. In modern terms this part-cleans the water though part-pollutes the plain. In traditional terms this made flood plain grassland the most fertile and valuable farm crop. Sediment within the river causes blockages and so dredging.

Landscape

1. *Water economy.* Because of the functions above, landscapes with wetlands have evolved, with those wetlands playing a crucial, perhaps the most crucial, part in the water economy of the region. Upsetting the balance may cause major difficulties and shortages, floods, or both.
2. *Vulnerability.* Wetlands are easily damaged or destroyed by simple land management techniques such as draining, which may have hydrological consequences distant from the treatment in both time and space.
3. *Landscape diversity.* Flood plains, variable in size and type, contribute substantially to landscape diversity, so to biotic, geomorphic and other habitat diversity.
4. *Areas of building soils*, whether bog peat, fen peat or by sedimentation.

Table 1.1 (cont.)

5. *Maintaining topographical variation* due to stream meandering, building soils, altering water level and hence terracing, etc.
6. *Trees and shrubs* form lines of pollards, other trees, wet or dry woodlands along streams, and woodlands and hedges beyond, contributing greatly to landscape character. They can also abate noise in urban areas.

Chemical and biochemical

1. *Clean water passing through soil.*
2. *Nutrient source and sink.*
3. *Immobilising contaminants*, e.g. heavy metals, pesticides.
4. *Provide buffer zones* to maintain water quality, and give habitats for wild flora and fauna.
5. *Constructed wetlands for pollution purification.* The chemical transformations are vitally important.
6. *Air quality improvement*, particularly by trees (which have the largest leaf area) but also by shorter vegetation, filtering particles, and degrading contaminants lifted from agricultural and urban areas (also see 1–4).
7. *Accumulating organic matter*, and so providing a sink for atmospheric carbon dioxide. The total carbon store in peat is enormous. Drainage and those other impacts affecting organic-rich soils may alter the balance of carbon cycling. Release of sufficient quantities of carbon as carbon dioxide aids global warming (carbon dioxide is a 'greenhouse gas').
8. *Storing history.* Accumulating soil also stores and preserves the history of the time, such as artefacts showing human presence and activities, pollen showing vegetation of the time, plant remains showing the vegetation of the site, animal remains, etc..

Plant and animal

1. *Accumulating organic matter* (see above).
2. *Habitat for* endangered as well as common *plant and animal species*, as refuges for species from elsewhere, and, where relevant, as corridors for animal (and plant) movement.
3. *Gene pools* for species present.
4. *Higher primary productivity* than surrounding drier lands (unless drained dry!).
5. Until overexploited, have *high secondary productivity* supporting fowl, fur, leather, feather, fish and other meat.
6. *Produce organic matter* for aquatic and floodplain food chains.
7. *Export organic matter* to downstream ecosystems.
8. *Food chain support.*
9. *Maintenance of biological integrity.* Integrity is defined as having no part or element wanting, a material wholeness, an unimpaired or uncorrupted state. Such a biological integrity of wetland is of ethical and biological – and water resources, etc. – value. It is shown by the diversity, abundance, representativeness, naturalness and rarity of the plants and animals present.
10. *Medicinal plants and leeches*, to disinfect, prevent infection and inflammation and reduce pain and tumour (Neori et al., 2000).

Table 1.1 (cont.)

11 *Crafts*, including thatching (reeds sedges, heather, other small shrubs, tall grasses, rushes), baskets, matting, woven goods with innumerable uses especially from *Salix alba, S. purpurea, S. triandra, S. viminalis*. There are numerous local varieties for different purposes, e.g. *S. alba caerulaea* for cricket bats. Clogs (e.g. alder). Construction (large plants, soils). Stuffing (feathers, fruits, e.g. *Typha*, reed). Candle wicks (rush dips). Bedding, insulation, strewing floors. Timber, etc.

12 *Food and drink*, e.g. watercress, berries, reeds, *Typha* in uncultivated parts, flower-rich meadow and other grassland and, if drained enough, grain and vegetables.

13 *Fuel*. Peat, charcoal, wood.

14 *Timber and withies*.

Economic crops

1 *Plant crops from traditional habitats*, e.g. reeds, cranberries, rushes, withies.

2 *Animal crops from traditional habitats*, e.g. deer, otter, fish, beaver, waterfowl.

3 *Peat, for energy production*, traditionally from both bog and fen. For the quantities needed for power stations, mostly bog, both raised and blanket bogs. Gas production is also from both fen and bog. Quick-growing willows and other species (incorrectly termed 'biomass') are now also used.

4 *Peat, for horticulture*. For the large quantities needed, mostly from bog.

5 *Sand and gravel*, for construction, from alluvial deposits; and for their other constituents, where relevant, e.g. alluvial tin, Dartmoor; gold, Wales.

6 *Cleaning of water*, see above.

7 *Grazing and hay* from converted wetland, marsh hay (tall species) being perhaps the wettest type. Production increases with increasing drainage and intensity of management. As diversity decreases with these and re-sowing, diet may become less balanced, so less valuable.

8 *Arable*, from conversion to drained, tilled ground. Fen peat and silt wetlands are usually particularly fertile, with high yields.

9 *Forestry*, usually conifers on bog and hill peatlands, and poplar and willow on more fertile lowland areas. These are now grown primarily for timber and paper, but – especially willow – also for electricity generation, craft and general farm and country uses. Wood for electricity generation is currently and incorrectly known as 'biomass' production. (Biomass is the total mass of the plant, under as well as over ground. 'Biomass' shoots are cut near ground level, so the stump and root remain to reshoot, while the wood is burnt.) Forestry of native species on naturally wooded wetlands is a valuable sustainable use. These include drier bogs, fens and marshes, and allow mature stands supporting a high and appropriate diversity of woodland plants and animals. Exotic tree species that usually support a poor fauna and flora, and forests frequently harvested the same year over large areas, are not satisfactory, and neither is draining or fertilising wetland so that it will bear trees.

10 *Turf*. The old and traditional meaning of 'turf' was peat, hence the many Turf Fens. However, turf in the modern sense (grass and the top soil it is growing in) can be grown in a grassland habitat, and sold for gardens, parks, etc.

Table 1.1 (*cont.*)

Societal
1   *Important natural heritage*, particularly when scarce.
2   *Representative of personal intangible values.* Wetlands, for an increasing number of people, have a charm, an attraction of their own, one that differs with the wetland type; the vast expanse of brownish bog; the reedbed where visibility is 2–3 m and the sense of isolation is profound; the grassland by the river bank, with the green and diverse land; the flowing water of the river, winding through the valley or cascading down a mountain; and the panorama of the heavens above. These much benefit those who experience them.
3   *Aesthetic values* in a more abstract way, sensory experience.
4   *Education, research and teaching.*
5   *Art and literature.*
6   *Heritage*, natural and cultural (see above).
7   *Recreation and relaxation*, other than the above: active forms of leisure such as walking, birdwatching, sports; quiet ones such as picnicking, visitor centres, car parks.
8   *Sites for impoundments* for water supply, flood relief, recreation, etc.

Values

To sum up, Table 1.1 lists the primary values of the riverscape. The consumptive value of water, and clean water at that, is pre-eminent, but food, fur, feather, timber are important. The non-consumptive ones are easy to pay lip-service to: philosophy, learning, spiritual dimensions and humanitarian concerns (Patten 1994), but they are also easy to ignore, to suppose degradation is really enhancement, or a tenth of the area is as valuable as the whole. In Malta, there was a series of ancient slab bridges over the rivers around Mdina, the capital and main garrison centre up until the sixteenth century. Of five in being in the 1980s, two have been left to rot and fall, one was removed for its stones by a local farmer, one (beside a newer bridge) was removed by the highways authority to show off a brand-new bridge, and the last is likely to go the same way when the existing main bridge is replaced. But Progress is Great!

A thing is right when it tends to preserve the integrity, stability and beauty of the biotic community. It is wrong when it tends otherwise.

2

The natural river and its destruction

Force not the course of the river

Eccl. 4, 26

The threshold to change is lowered by impact

(Evans, 1993)

The concept of naturalness

A straightforward definition of natural is 'untouched by Man'. By this definition, no rivers on earth are now natural: even the polar caps suffer from air pollution, climate change, and more people. Human impact, however, varies from being trivial to catchments totally built over with grossly polluted near-sterile rivers.

River systems are (excluding glaciation) as old as the land on which they flow. Precipitation falls, gathers into streams through gravity. Some evaporates, while the filter of the ground surface, the characters of that surface, and the underground storage all determine the channel flow. Its base flow depends on climate, season (and, regrettably, abstraction). Added to this is short-term storm flow (Petts & Foster, 1985). Older continental land masses, earth movements and climates also influence drainage patterns and how far a river travels. Separating Britain from the continent after the last Ice Age much disrupted river patterns! Sinking Malta, some people consider, has left 20 km streams where these were once the heads of large rivers

River systems are in a constant state of change; change in erosion, in deposition, in patterns horizontally, in patterns vertically, in temperature and precipitation, and in biota. The Icelandic river in the northern tundra (Fig. 2.1), is perhaps as close as can now be found to a natural river: but it has had some

Fig. 2.1. Iceland. Tundra, snow on mountains in summer. River pristine, not far from natural, with meanders, gentle wide banks with numerous niches, steep backs, spurs, variations in depth and flow. The harsh climate precludes the fringes of tall plants found further south. Light grazing (picture from some Icelandic organisation in the 1960s).

human impact for over a millennium, and undergone climate change from warmer than now to colder, during this time (Table 2.1). Climate change alters plant and animal life (and, less, river features).

Two concepts can, though, be used where 'natural' is untrue. In much of North America, and a little of Europe (e.g. parts of central Corsica, Iceland, Sardinia) impact has been light, and Americans term this 'pristine'. Strictly, this means ancient or primitive, but its use here is acceptable. The second concept that can be used is that of a 'traditional river', which, of course, is a concept rather difficult to define. Traditional of what? Change is continual, and has been happening at different rates at different times. For many rivers it is difficult to find documentary evidence of conditions in 1950, let alone in more distant times. We know the period *c.* 1850–1950 was moderately stable, coming after the first round of river and riverside drainage, and before the second round and the coming of extreme traffic and agrochemical pollution, abstraction and channelisation (deepening, steepening, straightening and rendering uniform). At any point in time, though, some rivers are severely impacted and others are not. It is possible, even now, to find European rivers in a traditional state or near enough, e.g. R. Scorse, Normandy, Friedbergerau, Germany, R. Ribe, Denmark, and upper R Clyde, Scotland, among very many (e.g. Haslam, 1982, 1987, Haury & Gouesse Aidara, 1999, Kohler, 1978, Kohler & Janauer, 1995, 2000).

The traditional vegetation of rivers was remarkable for its diversity of niches and species. With little drainage, river level was near ground level, and flooded. The bank edges were irregular (shelter, exposure, different depths), and spits, bars, islands and braided channels, common. Fallen trees added niches (shelter

Table 2.1 *Climate and geomorphic changes of the post-glacial era in Britain (from Gilman, 1994; Godwin, 1978; Higham, 1986; Rieley & Page, 1990)*

(a) General

AD	1900	Warmer	
	1600	Maximum cold, climatic upturn	
	1400	Broads peat pits flooding	
	1200	Cooler, moister	
	1000	Warm	
	500	Wetter	Anglo-Saxon
BC	55	Drier, warmer, hospitable climate	Roman
	500	SUB-ATLANTIC, wetter, warmer. Much peat development	Iron Age
	2500	Climate much as now. *Sphagnum* covering sub-boreal bogs	Bronze Age
	3000	SUB-BOREAL, cooler, drier, c. 2 °C warmer than now, more continental. Settled agriculture. Peat decline, pine spreading over bog	Neolithic
	5500	ATLANTIC, warm (2–4 °C above present), wet blanket bog spreading over hills, replacing pine and birch Raised bog growing in lowlands	Mesolithic
	7000	BOREAL, cool, dry. Pine forest spreading over peat bog Sea level rise, Britain an island.	
	9000	PRE-BOREAL, bogs spread (e.g. Teesdale)	
	10,000	Post-glacial. Cold	Upper Palaeolithic

(b) One area, the Fenland of eastern England

1900	Becoming dry and intensely cultivated.
1650	The Drainage of the Fens (more intermittent than would appear from the simple literature).
Mediaeval, Early Modern	Some drainage, particularly in drier eras.
Anglo-Saxon	Huge fens
Roman	Man-made watercourses, drainage
Iron Age	Build-up of silt, giving the present division of Silt and Peat Fens
1000 BC to AD 0	Sea incursion, extensive waterlogging, open sedge fen
To c. 2000 BC	Sea level drop, freshwater fen spread, and fen passing via carr to wood. Peat increase, trees invaded from the margin. Raised bog developing where alkaline flooding least (Middle Fens, and fen edge)
c. 2500–2000 BC	A vast brackish lagoon, 1–2 m deep, coastal silt deposited, followed by *Phragmites* then inland sedge and woods far inland
c. 2500 BC	Rapid peat development, sedge fen, recent black peat. Sedge fen leading to carr then woods
c. 3000 BC	Sea incursion, waterlogged, freshwater ponded inland. Black peat developed in this
4000–3000 BC	Dry acid peat, south fens remained alkaline, middle, to raised bog (only marginally affected by fen clay)

altered flow patterns) and organic carbon. Woods added variations in shade and the full light of glades. Flow, depth, substrate texture (and so nutrients) all varied. So plants doing well in silt or gravel, shallow or deep water, slow or rapid flow, disturbed and undisturbed, and so on, could all inhabit the river. Species richness was high. Even some nutrient variability was included, since most nutrients are found in silt, least in washed coarse particles. With little impact near the river, damage from flash floods and excess erosion was very much less: the river was adjusted to the incident rainfall.

Human impact

The movement from natural to traditional rivers began in Europe with the significant human intervention of the Romans, who altered rivers by draining land, making canals (e.g. Foss Dyke, England) and by building bridges. They also used ferries and long-distance boats (which cause disturbance, and need wharves). They introduced watermills, which impact the river both through construction and subsequent pollution when used for fulling, tanning and the like. Fisheries, often associated with mills, bring weirs, ponds, channels, disturbance. Flood banks, to protect towns, and navigation banks, to keep flow in specified channels are recorded from, e.g. Rome itself, and over the centuries these spread (twelfth-century records in France, etc.). As cities developed, quantities of concentrated human wastes developed also, so city rivers downstream became polluted.

While populations were still low, and when technology was poor (Roman standards were not maintained) direct interference with rivers was local.

Agriculture became more intensive over the centuries, at different speeds and setbacks, and with river pollution, settlements, industry and communications increasing; altering river position, size and shape; removing water increased, and rivers deteriorated.

Since people were present in Europe early, and followed the retreating ice in the north from 10 000 BC, there was impact (though still local) on the rivers, more from agriculture than from other influences. Felling forests increases flash floods, erosion and sedimentation, through failing to halt and slow precipitation movements. Cultivation has a similar effect and brings increased nutrients with eroded silt and when the land is sufficiently fertilised.

Impacts decrease variability and diversity. A flood bank by the river gives a uniform and steep bank. City pollution gives water in which no, or a few tolerant plant species, can grow.

Human impacts typically reduce available niches, with a consequent loss of species. *Oenanthe fluviatilis* was a species common in the deeper and siltier areas of English chalk streams only 70 years ago (Butcher, 1927, 1933), but is now

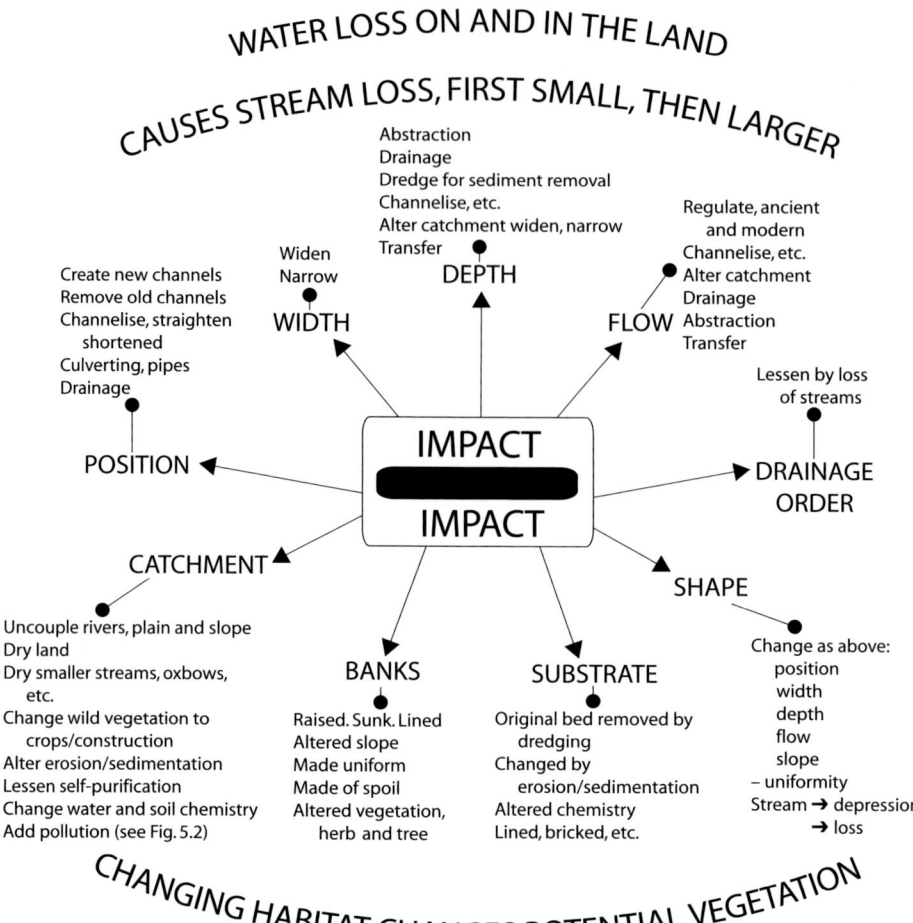

Fig. 2.2. Human impacts: effects on river size, shape and position. (Representative, not including all types and variations.)

rare: because abstraction and drainage have caused shallowing of the rivers and suitable habitats are now rare. When streams in the lower Cairngorms (Scotland) were dredged, *Juncus articulatus* communities, found on gentle, gravelly edges, vanished because the edges became steep, earthen and nutrient-rich because of the disturbed soil. When R. Lark (England) was deep dredged, *Ranunculus fluitans*, able to tolerate the moderate pollution because it could anchor in the hard gravel bed (twining its roots around firm particles), disappeared because there was no hard bed. Impacts decrease niches, so decrease species.

The rate of change has become ever greater since 1950, even given the great impacts of the previous century. There have been near-blanketing impacts of hard surface and agricultural run-off, intensive agriculture, expanding settlements, abstraction and drainage, channelling and effluents (Figs. 2.2, 2.3).

The natural river and its destruction

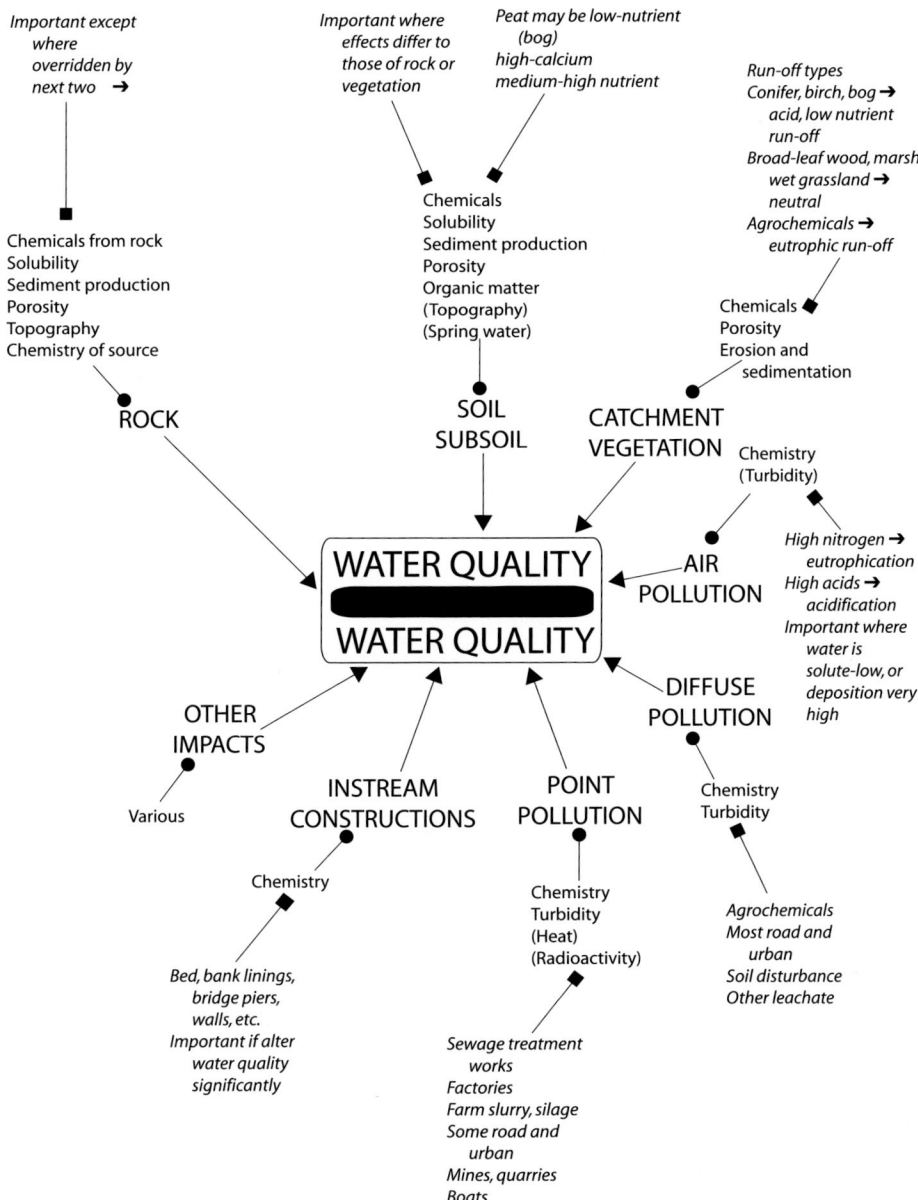

Fig. 2.3. Water quality: principal determining factors. (Representative, not including all factors and variations.)

Traditional vegetation still exists, but is hard to find, and is disappearing fast. For instance, pre-1980 the R. Yare (Norfolk) resembled rivers described by Butcher (1933). Then there was deep dredging and niches, depth and species richness diminished. Before, 20 river plant species in a 25 m stream length was normal. This richness now is very unusual, and has gone from R. Yare. Twenty species usually means a traditional (and non-mountainous) stream. It also occurs in a site with more impact but with two chemical influences, both providing nutrient niches (e.g. clay rock below with chalk water and silt, or brackish and freshwater influence).

River vegetation

River vegetation, being part of the natural heritage of creation, is of ethical and intrinsic conservation value. It helps make the habitat for river animals. It is an important component of the carbon and nitrogen cycles, and the geochemical pattern and processes of the river. River vegetation cleans and purifies water and soil, this is the most important way freshwaters are cleaned naturally. Larger numbers of micro-organisms live on the plant surface than in water, and it is these micro-organisms which are the main chemical factory (e.g. Haslam, 1987, 1990, 1997, 2003, 2006, Seidel 1967, 1968). River plants provide stability, protecting bank and bed to some extent from erosion. They have many uses for people (Chapters 4, 8–10, 14).

For both ethics and ecology, the vegetation should be as close as possible to the traditional or pristine (Fig. 2.4). And at least when new schemes are planned, the planning should aim towards this, not assume (as happens too often) that either any plants will do, or that the planner's favourite species should be planted!

River habitat is complex, an integrated entity of many different features.

Water plants may be entirely under the water, on the water surface, or grow through the water column and emerge above the water. Often those supported by the water may show two or all habits, such as floating leaves on stalks growing up from the soil (e.g. *Nuphar* spp.), or having submerged, floating and emerged leaves (e.g. *Sagittaria sagittifolia*). Many water-supported species have aerial flowers.

Nevertheless, habit does differ with habitat. Emerged species, photosynthesising mainly in the air, are in shallow water, at river edges, or in shallow streams. Water-supported species need space under (or on) water, so are usually in stream centres (Table 2.1, Figs. 2.5, 2.6, 2.7).

Alpine and steep mountainous streams have rapid and whitewater flow over boulders and rock, and river vegetation is either non-existent or limited to mosses on rock and emergents in sheltered edge niches. Vegetation is limited by water force, by flow. Water force depends firstly on topography (from Alps to alluvial plains) but also (a) on precipitation (as slopes steepen, increased rainfall greatly increases water force), (b) on how much of the run-off sinks to become groundwater or evaporates, and (c) whether water from underground springs – which stabilises – is a major source. The German mountains, for instance, mostly

The natural river and its destruction 23

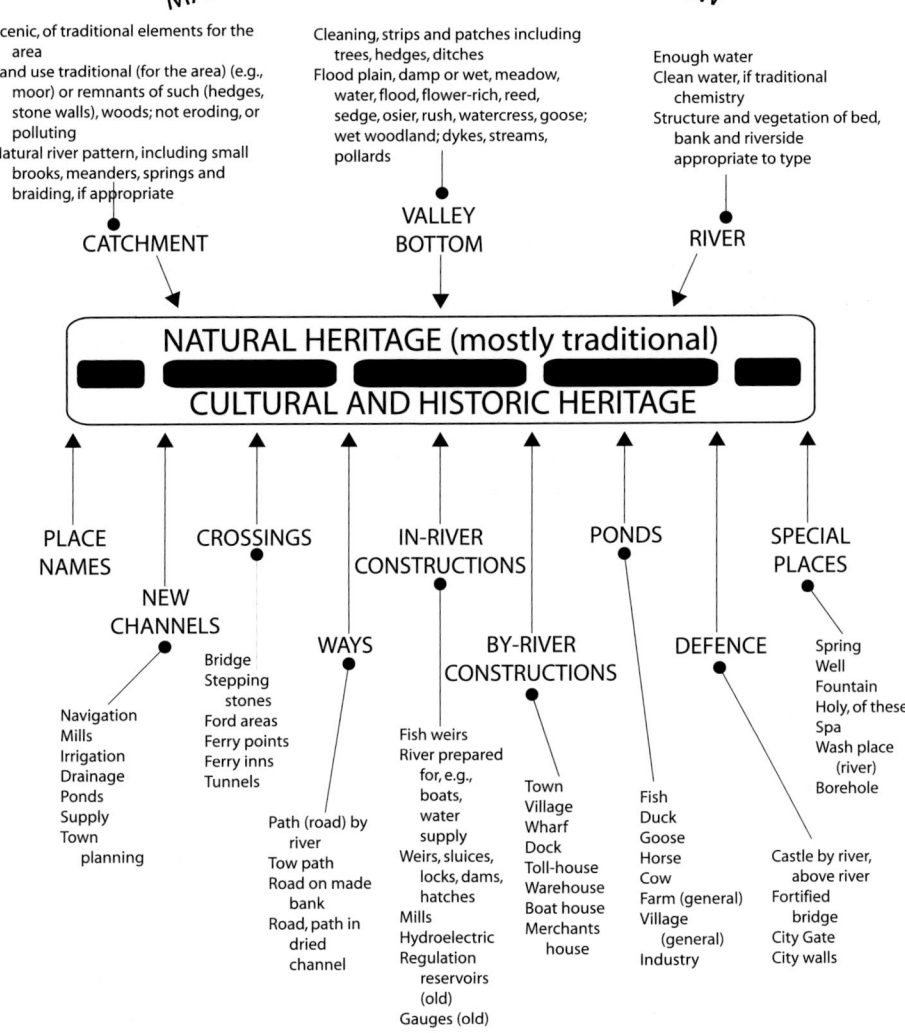

(See Haslam, 1987, 1990, 1991, 1997, 2003, 2006)

Fig. 2.4. Conservation: features of natural and historic heritage. (Some characteristic features only: incomplete.)

have high-force rivers: but not in the limestone Swabian Alps, where the river is spring-stabilised 'lowland limestone'. Water force is therefore a primary character determining river vegetation.

Anyone familiar with chalk or other lowland limestone streams knows they (if traditional, or nearly so) are full of plants, a pleasing pattern of shape,

24 The riverscape and the river

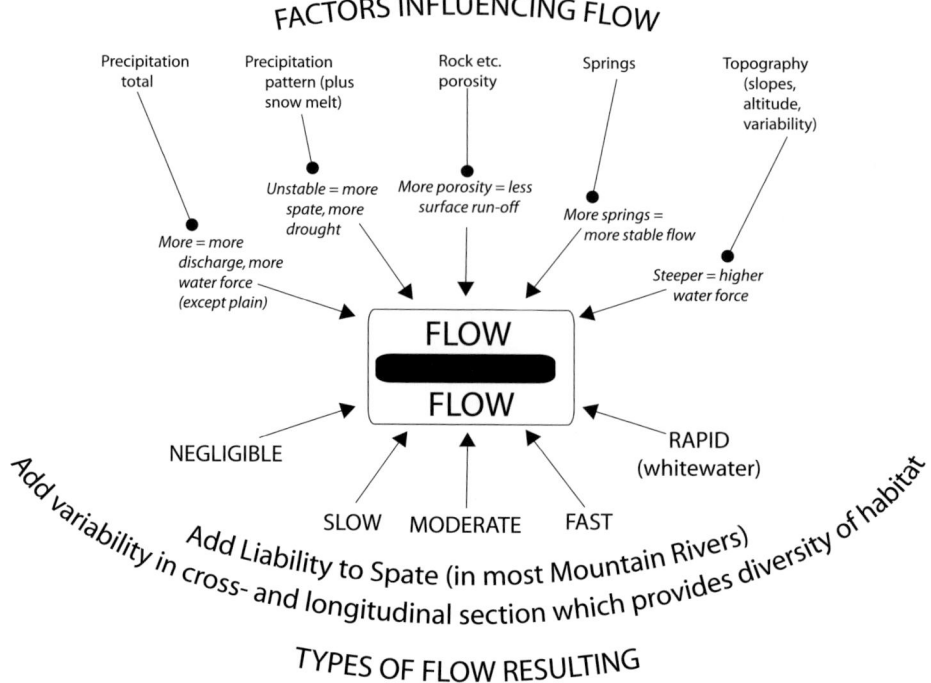

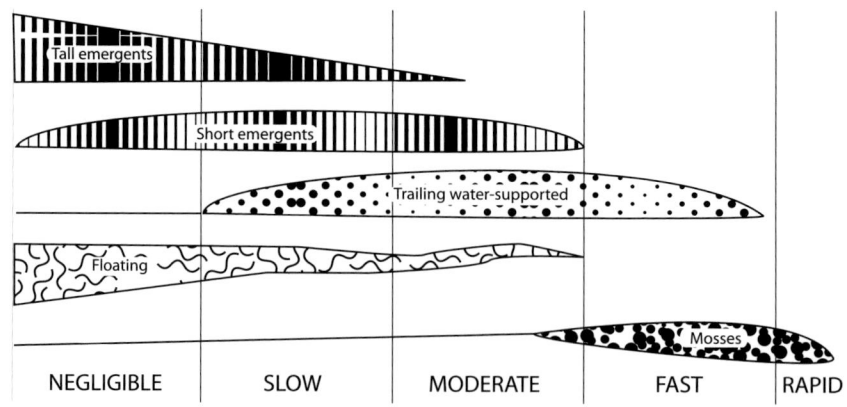

Fig. 2.5. Flow: determining factors and vegetation. (Representative, not including all types and variations.)

texture and colour, the main species having finely divided leaves (*Ranunculus* spp.). Other streams, though, may have water lilies and bulrushes, or little rosette plants under brown water. This is primarily dependent on rock type (Figs. 2.7, 2.8, 2.9 Haslam, 1987). There are many different kinds of rock type, all

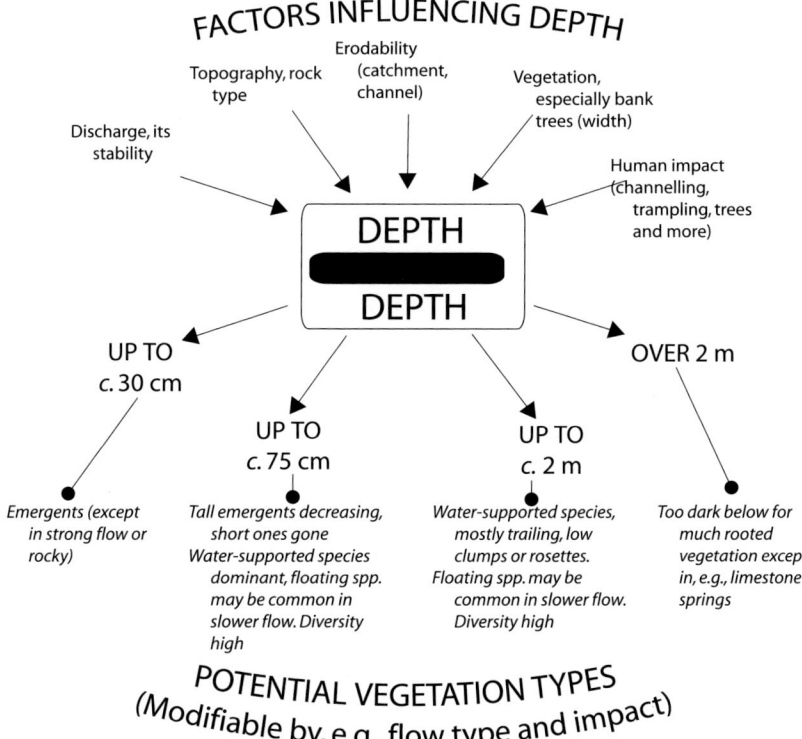

Fig. 2.6. (a) Depth and (b) width determining factors and vegetation types. (Representative, not including all types and variations.)

influencing their vegetation differently. Fortunately they may be summarised into a few major groups: limestone (high calcium, low other nutrients), sandstone (higher nutrients, more silt produced), clay (high nutrients, high silt) and resistant rock (low nutrients). River chemistry is due to these, plus the surface layers (such as subsoil, soil, peat, concrete, plants, if chemically different) (Table 2.2).

Another natural factor distinguishing river types is longitudinal, or upstream–downstream variation. Little rills 15 cm wide and 5 cm deep always differ in vegetation to deep rivers 200 m wide. For one thing, submerged plants cannot grow in a tiny rill! Going downstream, rivers generally become larger (width and depth), water force decreases if passing from steeper to gentler slopes, so substrate becomes finer, and the area of catchment increases. This results in an increase of nutrient status (more nutrient-rich silt in run-off), made much greater if farming becomes more intensive downstream and if other nutrient sources (e.g. sewage works effluents, farm slurry) also enter. *Pollution from hard surfaces increases with the area of used hard surfaces.* Even without the impact, in

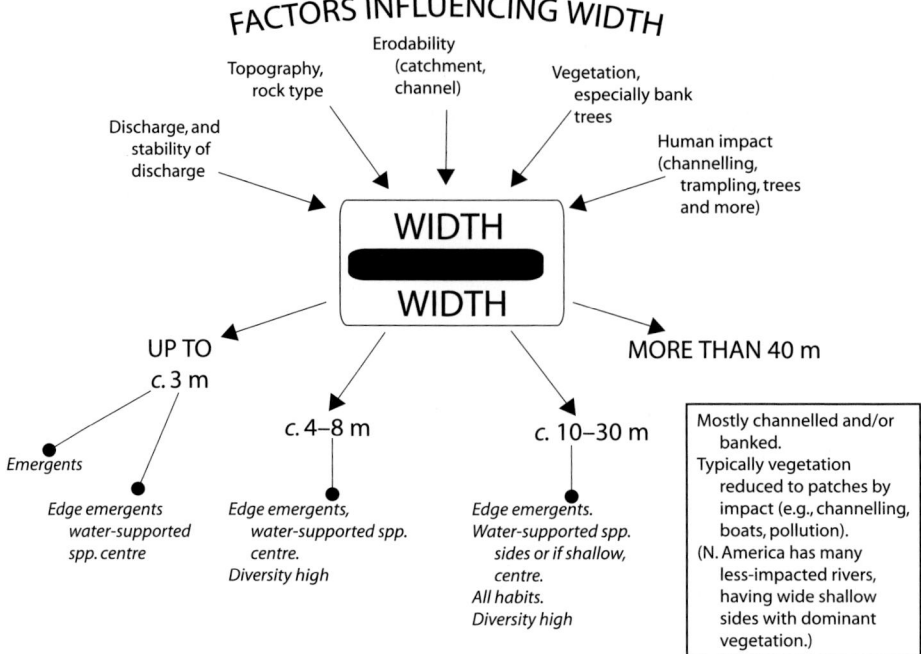

Fig. 2.6. (cont.)

most of Europe it is easy to recognise divisions in vegetation along the length. Since, generally, the vegetation is continuous, changing only slowly, where these separations lie is a matter of opinion. One working well with some 27 000 sites, is:

- Up to 3 m wide, no water-supported species (usually smaller and/or dried brooks);
- Up to 3 m wide, with water-supported species (usually wetter or cleaner, better lit, less disturbed brooks);
- 4–8 m wide, medium streams. Vegetation usually all across in lowlands;
- 10–30 m wide, large rivers. Vegetation avoiding deep or rapid water, etc.;
- 50+ m wide, the primary rivers of Europe, the Danube, Rhine, Rhône and some parts of smaller rivers, e.g. R. Thames (vegetation avoiding deep or rapid water).

Fig. 2.7. River types in relation to landscape and rock type.

However, in the Mediterranean xeric regions of Europe (the parts very dry in summer), and in parts of North America, once the stream is large enough for a good supply of water-supported species, there is little further downstream change. Instead of vegetation covering the bed, it becomes restricted to the sides because the centre becomes too deep or too swift, but the species and community hardly alter. Such rivers, of course, do largely or wholly dry out during the Mediterranean summer (e.g. southern Italy, Sicily, Malta, south-west French coast). North America, instead of having a millennium or more of intense human impact, only has a century or so. And downstream variation in vegetation from 2 m (deeper) brooks to large rivers, is little (excluding that due to deep or rapid water), at least from the mid-West of Canada and US to the east and south to Florida. The plant species themselves vary greatly from north to south, even more than in Europe, but unlike Europe, not along the river. North America has another difference to Europe: chemistry. In both, limestone streams are distinctive, their vegetation differing from the rest. But in North America (area as above) the glaciation and alluvium, prevent the mosaic of vegetation types on the different rock and soil types found in Europe. However, in North America, low-nutrient resistant rocks of, e.g. the Baltic Shield, are as distinctive as the equivalent in Europe (e.g. Galloway, Scotland, traditional streams). Also, in both continents, the top layer may be vital. Peat, organic soil formed with continuous water, may be (a) acid and low nutrient, as Blanket bog with short vegetation, (b) fairly acid and variable nutrients, as in the tree swamps of North America, and (c) fen peat formed underwater with typically high calcium, as in the English Fenland, Broadland, Somerset levels. Alluvial plains also have, of course, alluvium, fine sediment brought down from whatever rock type (soil and subsoil) occur higher in the catchment. Even blanketing glacial drift can contain only material the glaciers have picked up further up the glaciation. The possibilities of patterns and mosaics of chemical types affecting river vegetation, are therefore great.

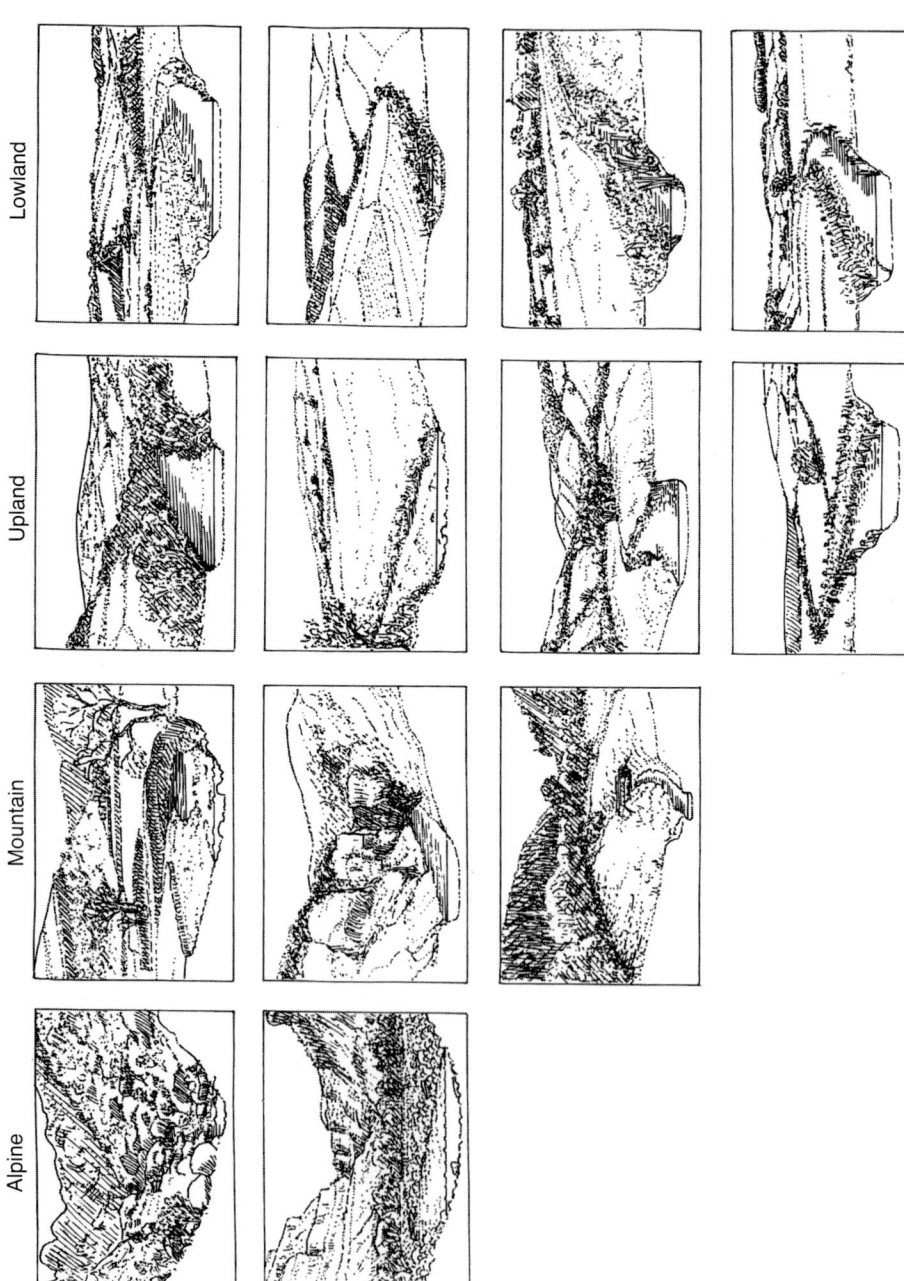

Fig. 2.7. (cont.) Differences are shown in channel position, outline, bank, water, substrate and emerged vegetation. In hills, streams are traditional in lowlands, more managed. Britain. A plateau stream is shown separately, with the lowland stream above (left), the steep slope, and the lowland river on the bottom (P. A. Wolseley in Haslam, 1987).

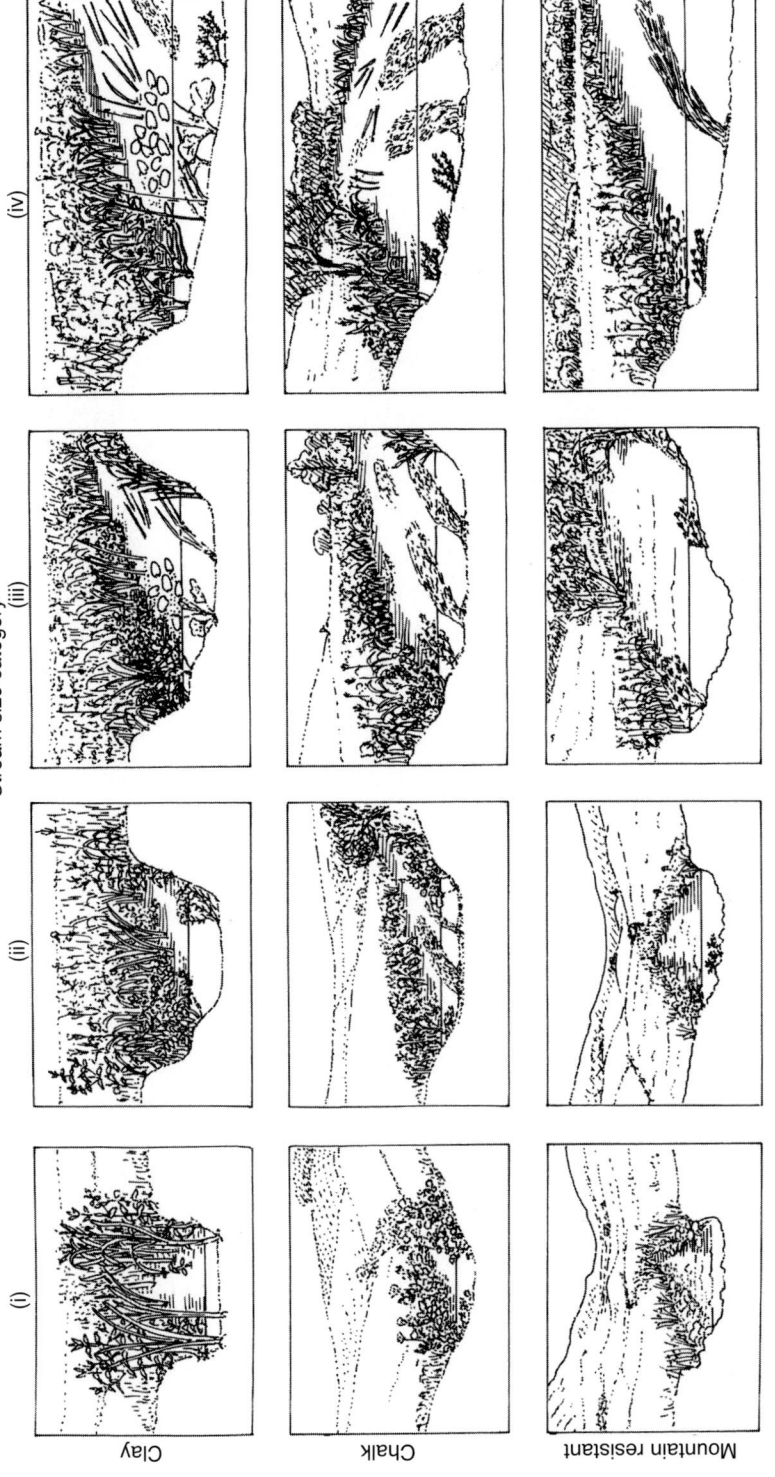

Fig. 2.8. River type in relation to stream size and rock type. Differences are shown in channel outline, bank, water depth and flow, and in the vegetation type, diversity, building block and cover. Streams are traditional. Britain (P. A. Wolseley in Haslam, 1987).

Fig. 2.9. Mosaic in river vegetation with patches of *Alisma plantago-aquatica* and *Ranunculus trichophyllus*. *A. plantago-aquatica* grows only in very shallow water, overlapping with *R. trichophyllus*, which also grows in deeper water. Severe storm flows in winter wash away *A. plantago-aquatica* that is not firmly anchored, so it cannot dominate over *R. trichophyllus* (R. Ghasel, Malta).

So, excluding much impact, river vegetation depends on:

- *Water force*
- *Rock (subsoil, soil) type*
- *Longitudinal, upstream-downstream patterning*

with the first always important, the second less so in North America – for rock type reasons – and the third of most importance in temperate Europe.

Figs. 2.9 and 2.10 show a few vegetation communities, showing the variations with these factors. These are representative. The total number of species is small, so it is their combinations and frequency which is important.

Looking at present traditional streams (e.g. Haslam, 1987; Haury *et al.*, 1998, 2002; Haury & Muller, 1991; Kohler *et al.*, 1996, 2000a, b, c; Sipos & Björk, 2000; Trémolières *et al.*, 1991, 1994; Veit & Kohler, 2003; Veit *et al.*, 1997) with their greater niches and species richness, the number and range of species present in one site is greater (e.g. Table 2.2). This applies to streams in non-extreme conditions. (With extreme features of, e.g. water force or low nutrients, flora is reduced and restricted by these.)

Table 2.2 *Significant river species of west and central Europe, with their habits (Haslam, 1987). Common and diagnostic species, from which most communities can be identified*

(a) Significant watercourse species

The following is an arbitrary selection of common and diagnostic species. Most communities can be identified by reference to these species.

Agrostis stolonifera
Alisma plantago-aquatica
Apium nodiflorum
Arundo donax
Berula erecta
Bidens cernua
Butomus umbellatus
Callitriche hamulata
Callitriche spp.
Caltha palustris
Carex acutiformis agg.
Carex rostrata
Ceratophyllum demersum
Cyperus badius
Eleocharis acicularis
Eleocharis palustris
Eleogiton fluitans
Elodea canadensis
Elodea nuttallii
Epilobium hirsutum
Equisetum spp.
Glyceria fluitans, long leaves
Glyceria maxima
Glyceria spp., short leaves
Hydrocharis morsus-ranae
Iris pseudacorus
Juncus articulatus
Juncus bulbosus
Juncus effusus
Lemna minor agg.
Lemna trisulca
Luzula sylvatica
Mentha aquatica
Menyanthes trifoliata
Mimulus guttatus
Myosotis scorpioides
Myriophyllum alterniflorum
Myriophyllum spicatum

(cont.)

Table 2.2 (cont.)

Nuphar lutea
Nymphoides peltata
Oenanthe crocata
Osmunda regalis
Petasites hybridus
Phalaris arundinacea
Phragmites australis
Polygonum amphibium
Polygonum hydropiper agg.
Potamogeton coloratus
Potamogeton crispus
Potamogeton gramineus
Potamogeton natans
Potamogeton pectinatus
Potamogeton polygonifolius
Ranunculus spp. (leaf length varying ecologically and taxonomically)
Ranunculus flammula
Rorippa amphibia/austriaca agg.
Rorippa nasturtium-aquaticum agg.
Rumex hydrolapathum
Sagittaria sagittifolia
Scirpus lacustris
Scirpus maritimus
Sparganium emersum
Sparganium erectum
Sphagnum spp.
Spirodela polyrhiza
Typha latifolia
Veronica anagallis-aquatic agg.
Veronica beccabunga
Zannichellia palustris
Mosses
Enteromorpha sp.
Blanket weed

(b) Species arranged by habit and habitat

The species have been placed in six groups. The first five are in order of the nutrient regimes in which the species most frequently occur and the last group contains species it is less easy to classify in this way. Species vary in the nutrient regimes in which they occur. Within each group, the species have been subdivided by habit. Species may have more than one habit (e.g. *Butomus umbellatus, Polygonum amphibium, Ranunculus flammula*), but each species is listed only once, under the more ecologically significant or the more frequent habitats. (Some habit groups have none of these selected species.)

Table 2.2 (cont.)

Water-supported species	Fringing herbs and other short emergents	Tall monocotyledons	Tall herbs and similar
1a Species characteristic of nutrient poor habitats			
Glyceria fluitans, long leaves	(Sphagnum spp.)	Carex rostrata	
Juncus bulbosus		Juncus articulatus	
Myriophyllum alterniflorum		Luzula sylvatica	
Potamogeton polygonifolius			
Ranunculus flammula			
Scirpus fluitans			
1b Species characteristic of calcium-rich, other nutrient-poor habitat			
Chara hispida	Berula erecta	Juncus subnodulosus	
Lemna trisulca	Mentha aquatica	Phalaris arundinacea	
Potamogeton coloratus			
2 Species characteristic of less nutrient-poor habitats			
Potamogeton gramineus	Bidens cernua		
Mosses	Caltha palustris		
	Eleocharis palustris		
	Equisetum fluviatilis		
	Equisetum palustre		
	Oenanthe crocata		
	Petasites hybridus		
3 Species characteristic of nutrient medium habitats			
Callitriche spp. (Callitriche cophocarpa, C. obtusangula, C. platycarpa and C. stagnalis)	Apium nodiflorum	Iris pseudacorus	
	Berula erecta	Sparganium erectum	
	Mentha aquatica		
	Mimulus guttatus		
	Myosotis scorpioides		
Hydrocharis morsus-ranae	Rorippa nasturtium aquaticum agg.		
Lemna polyrhiza	(R. nasturtium aquaticum		
Lemna trisulca			
Nymphoides peltata			
Potamogeton natans	R. microphylla and hybrid		
Ranunculus spp., comprising the Batrachian Ranunculus spp.	Veronica anagallis-aquatica agg.		
Spirodela polyrhiza	(V. anagallis-aquatica and V. catenata)		
	Veronica beccabunga		

(cont.)

Table 2.2 (cont.)

4 Species characteristic of more nearly eutrophic habitats

Ceratophyllum demersum	*Alisma plantago-aquatica*	*Carex acutiformis* agg. (*C. acutiformis* and *C. riparia*)	*Epilobium hirsutum*
Elodea canadensis	*Polygonum hydropiper* agg. (*P. hydropiper* and *P. persicaria*)		
Myriophyllum spicatum			
Polygonum amphibium		*Glyceria maxima*	
Zannichellia palustris		*Phragmites communis*	
Blanket weed		*Typha latifolia*	

5 Species characteristic of nutrient rich habitats

Nuphar lutea	*Rorippa amphibia*	*Butomus umbellatus*	*Rumex hydrolapathum*
Potamogeton crispus		*Schoenoplectus lacustris*	
Potamogeton pectinatus			
Sagittaria sagittifolia			
Sparganium emersum			
Enteromorpha sp.			

6 Species not placed in the preceding groups

Lemna minor agg. (*L. minor* and *L. gibba*, particularly when the thalli of the latter are not strongly gibbous)	*Agrostis stolonifera*	*Arundo donax*	*Osmunda regalis*
	Glyceria spp., short leaves (*G. fluitans* with short leaves, *G. plicata* and some *G. declinata*)	*Cyperus badius*	
		Juncus effusus	
		Scirpus maritimus	
		Phalaris arundinacea	

When human impact strikes, niches are reduced, since impact tends to uniformity. So species are lost or diminished. And these species are those able to do well only in the niches: in silt or shelter in swifter water, in clean water, in a firm bed in dredged channels, in lower nutrients (where disturbance raises them) or higher ones (where silt or gentle banks are removed), and so on. Traditional plant communities are thus converted to modern ones by impact. Unfortunately, with the ongoing deterioration, further restriction of communities is to be expected, leaving only species tolerating moderate pollution and the basic uniform river features.

Stream types vary in sensitivity to impact. The most sensitive are mostly those with very low nutrients, bog and calcium-dominant (other nutrients suppressed) particularly. Only a little chemical addition (effluent, run-off, etc.) is enough to quite alter the vegetation (e.g. Haslam, 1987, 1990, 2006; Haslam & Borg, 1998). At the other extreme are the downstream clay streams of England, very nutrient-rich, and able to absorb some (not very toxic) pollution without alteration of the

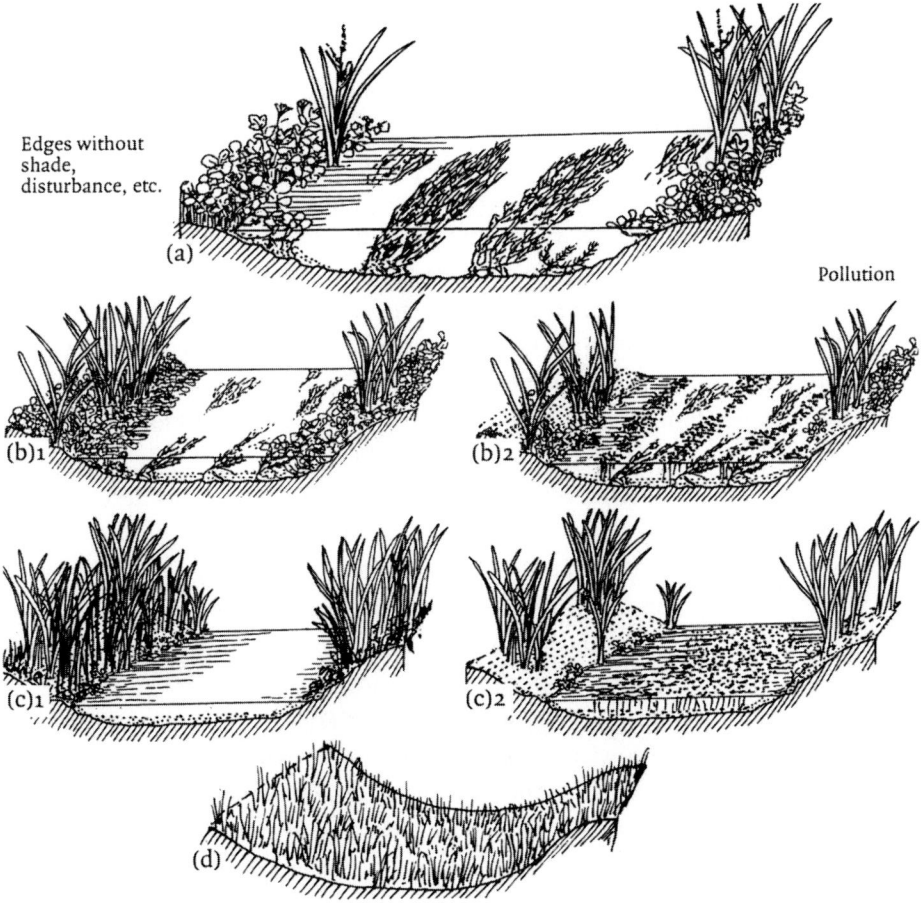

Fig. 2.10. Shallow sequence. The vegetation reacts the same way whether this is due to drainage, abstraction or drought.
(a) Original, traditional stream, (b) and (c) increasingly drying, (d) dried (permanently or temporarily).
On the left, (1) shows a near-clean sequence, (2) a polluted one. (b)1 has the original vegetation even more depleted than (a)1, but also has Blanket weed and a little *Potamogeton pectinatus*.
(b)2 shows the same factors but abundant Blanket weed (P. A. Wolseley and Y. Bower in Haslam, 1997a).

vegetation. Even excess grazing by livestock, felling trees (banks liable to erosion, full light) or the grazing by many swans can skew vegetation.

On a different scale, banks and substrate both vary in sensitivity to erosion, sedimentation, etc., and different species do, also. If sediment smothers a *Berula erecta* carpet, it will decline, while one of *Sparganium emersum* probably will not. This depends on the shape, size and behaviour of the plants. A loose sand bank is very unstable compared with one of resistant rock or even hard clay.

Most non-traditional and even many traditional streams are short of natural organic carbon. Over many lowlands there were, once, forests, and even a line of bank trees drop litter into the river. Fallen trees provide a year-round source as themselves, and by trapping debris. The chemical processes are only now being investigated: but it is already clear that organic carbon and its nutrients are important for energy, purification, storage, bioavailability of nutrients, as well as food for animals. Riparian food enters the rivers (insects, leaves, etc.), and in so doing feeds the energy of the river. (The amount depends on vegetation type and human impact, e.g. Paetzold & Tockner, 2006). Removing debris alters the erosion–deposition pattern, allowing too much erosion. Therefore, this influences vegetation.

Natural flooding is another source of debris; each of the frequent floods brings some to the river.

Vegetation is constantly changing. Plants become established, grow, mature and are washed out, eaten or diseased (death from old age, of plant rather than shoot, is rare or absent except for tall woody plants, e.g. *Taxodium distichum* in south US swamps, *Salix* spp. in south Mediterranean rivers.

In stable conditions there is 'changeless change' (Table 2.3), species and plants come and go, but remain within the same assemblage. R. Don, Aberdeen, Scotland, has three common tall monocotyledons. *Phalaris arundinacea* extends up into the hills, where it is regularly washed away and regrows. Downstream it is up the bank and rarely eroded. *Glyceria maxima* and *Sparganium erectum* are mostly downstream. They, especially *S. erectum*, grow into the river: until washed off by spates. That leaves bare bank, quickly colonised by fringing and other small herbs, until the tall monocots return. The cycle takes *c.* 1–5 years, depending on spates. Haslam (1997, 2006) describes cycles on the bed with, e.g. *Ranunculus* sp., *Berula erecta*, *Zannichellia palustris*, which again depend on anchorage, and washout. But while tall monocotyledons grow away from firm bank anchorage into poor anchorage in the flow, the water-supported species lose firm anchorage in places as silt accumulates there, as well as when expanding.

If, though, the habitat alters, these normal cyclic alterations give the opportunity for change in species assemblage, in community. Bare bed or bank are colonised by different species, those better adapted to the new habitat (more tolerant of, say, pollution, shallow water or shade). The existing species remain until they are lost in the normal course of events, so the changeover is slow. Unless, of course, the change is drastic, such as deep dredging, when vegetation has to colonise anew, or new species may arrive and establish (Table 2.4).

Table 2.3 *Changeless change (Changes of species entering and leaving, with the species assemblage stable, Haslam, 1987)*

(a) Causes of change in selected lowland river sites monitored regularly
About 30 lowland British river sites were recorded about 120 times between 1970 and 1980. The rock types were mainly chalk, clay and mixed chalk-clay.

(1) Badly anchored or non-anchored plants were washed out during storm flows, etc., and incoming fragments became anchored in stable places. Species are usually anchored best in the habitats in which they are commonest. However, bands of floating fragments of Fringing herbs, *Callitriche*, etc., sheltered by uneven banks, tall monocotyledons or others, can be stable for months or even years (stable as a community, though individual fragments are washed in and out) before wash-out occurs, after which there may be re-establishment.

(2) Silt and other banks accumulate and erode, and these often have cycles of vegetation. In parts, silt banks can accumulate and become dry and part of the bank (usually filling in irregularities), and here aquatics are replaced by land plants.
Similarly, plant clumps accumulate silt, and may erode with the loss of the plants, or assist in the development of dry land.

(3) Habitats opened after disturbance, and closed later, and vice versa. Ephemeral species may enter after, e.g. trampling, flow diversions and be subsequently lost.

(4) Plants with rhizomes, stolons, etc. spread horizontally to new places, and older parts die, which may change plant positions.

(5) Dormant plant parts may be consistently present, but due to, e.g. variations in cutting, shading, shoots may be present, or obvious, in some years only.

(6) Shading alters vegetation, and changes occur in the tree canopy, in shading bank plants, and (with the aid of, e.g. cutting) in tall channel plants that shade water-supported species, etc.

(7) Cutting and grazing patterns change both bank and channel vegetation. From year to year the timing, frequency and intensity of the cut/graze can vary, and so can the position of boundaries (e.g. fences) marking the borders of affected places, with consequent differences in vegetation.

(8) Herbicides, by decreasing some plants, cause increases in others as well.

(9) Trampling by cattle (and anglers) may alter bank shape, and, e.g. cattle, anglers, children, sheep, can also alter bank vegetation, and alter channel vegetation either directly, or indirectly, through the effects on the bank.

(10) Dredging (and the passage of other heavy machinery) has short-term effects except when the habitat is altered. This may occur from, e.g. destabilising substrates (effects can last 10+ years), deepening channels, making flow swifter by altering configuration, straightening, removing or making ledges at sides (which provide habitats for a variety of edge species).

(11) Flow type can be altered by weather, regulation (and bridges, gauges, etc.), transfers, dredging, local silting and vegetation patterns. Depositing and eroding, slower and faster flows lead to different communities. Slow flows increase, e.g. *Lemna* spp., storm flows cause washout.

(cont.)

Table 2.3 (*cont.*)

(12) Pollution causes minor or major changes in vegetation. It, and vegetation, may alter gradually (for better or for worse) over several decades, or more sharply over a year or two, and there may be temporary gross pollutions causing short-term damage.

Depth can be altered by similar factors, and deepening, shallowing (and drying) all change vegetation.

Substrate can be altered by the above factors and more. This leads to vegetation changes.

(13) Boat damage can vary from year to year, with consequent variable vegetation changes.
(14) Temperature variations in summer may alter communities (e.g. warm weather increasing *Lemna gibba* cover, hot weather killing some dyke species).

(b) Relative stability of river species over 4- to 9-year periods

Stability (species staying in the same 25 m reach)

Most	Fair	Medium	Low	Least
Lowland chalk (and chalk mix) streams				
Berula erecta	*Apium*	*Glyceria*	*Carex*	*Elodea*
Callitriche spp.	*nodiflorum*	*maxima*	*acutiformis*	*canadensis*
Ranunculus spp.	*Mimulus*	*Mentha*	agg.	*Groenlandia*
Rorippa	*guttatus*	*aquatica*	*Epilobium*	*densa*
nasturtium-	*Potamogeton*	*Scirpus*	*hirsutum*	*Lemna minor*
aquaticum	*lucens*	*lacustris*	Small grasses	agg.
agg.				
	Potamogeton	*Veronica*		*Oenanthe*
	pectinatus	*anagallis-*		*fluviatilis*
	Sparganium	*aquatica* agg.		*Phalaris*
	erectum	Mosses		*arundinacea*
		Blanket weed		*Sparganium*
				emersum
				Veronica
				beccabunga
Lowland sandstone (and sandstone-mix) streams				
Callitriche spp.	*Apium*	*Lemna minor* agg.		*Elodea*
Glyceria maxima	*nodiflorum*	*Myosotis scorpioides*		*canadensis*
Ranunculus spp.	*Sparganium*	*Potamogeton perfoliatus*		*Epilobium*
Sparganium	*emersum*	*Rorippa nasturtium-aquaticum* agg.		*hirsutum*
erectum	Small grasses			*Mimulus*
	Blanket weed			*guttatus*
				Myriophyllum
				spicatum
				Phalaris
				arundinacea
				Potamogeton
				pectinatus

Table 2.3 (cont.)

				Rorippa amphibia
				Veronica anagallis-aquatica agg.
				Veronica beccabunga
				Mosses

Lowland clay (and clay-mix) streams

Nuphar lutea	*(Ranunculus* spp.)	*Apium nodiflorum*	*Alisma plantago*	*Carex acutiformis* agg.
Sparganium erectum	*Rorippa amphibia*	*Callitriche* spp.	*Potamogeton* spp.	*Epilobium hirsutum*
	Sagittaria sagittifolia	*Elodea canadensis*	*Rorippa nasturtium-aquaticum* agg.	*Myosotis scorpioides*
	Scirpus lacustris	*Lemna minor* agg.	*Veronica beccabunga*	*Polygonum amphibium*
	Sparganium emersum	*Phalaris arundinacea*	Small grasses	*Potamogeton crispus*
	(Typha spp.)		Blanket weed	*Potamogeton perfoliatus*
				Enteromorpha sp.

Hill resistant rock streams

Ranunculus sp.	*Phalaris arundinacea*	*Agrostis stolonifera*	*Callitriche* spp.	*Elodea canadensis*
Mosses	*Sparganium erectum*	Blanket weed	*(Carex* spp.)	*Petasites hybridus*
			Myosites scorpioides	*Rorippa amphibia*
			Potamogeton natans	
			Veronica beccabunga	

Lowland resistant rock streams, N.E. Scotland

Ranunculus spp.	*Callitriche* spp.	*Rorippa nasturtium-aquaticum* agg.	*Glyceria maxima*	*Phalaris arundinacea*
	(Potamogeton crispus)	Mosses	*Myriophyllum alterniflorum*	*Mimulus guttatus*
	Small grasses	(Blanket weed)	*Sparganium erectum*	*Myosotis scorpioides*
				(Sparganium emersum)

Table 2.4 *Species particularly tolerant to different types of damage. Blanket weed is long trailing algae, most often* Cladophora glomerata. *Selected types of damage, and of species*

1 General domestic and industrial pollution
(a) Britain:
 Potamogeton crispus
 Potamogeton pectinatus *
 Schoenoplectus lacustris
 Sparganium emersum
 Sparganium erectum
 Enteromorpha intestinalis
 Blanket weed*
 *favoured by (up to fairly severe) pollution
(b) Germany:
 Agrostis stolonifera
 Phalaris arundinacea
 Potamogeton pectinatus*
 Sparganium emersum
 Sparganium erectum
 Blanket weed
 Geographic variation is shown

2 Ochre pollution, Denmark
 Agrostis stolonifera
 Glyceria fluitans
 Juncus bulbosus
 Scirpus lacustris
 Sparganium emersum (higher pH)
 Sparganium erectum
 (partly from Sand-Jensen & Rasmussen (1978), Sønderjyllands Amstkommune (1982).

3 Rice paddy run-off, Italy
 Carex spp. (tall)
 Phragmites communis

4 Wash house pollution, Brittany (France)
 Callitriche sp.
 Berula erecta (less tolerant)

5 Water turbidity (Britain)
 Ceratophyllum demersum
 Lemna minor agg. (floating, not affected)
 Nuphar lutea (half-floating)
 Sagittaria sagittifolia (part floating)
 Schoenoplectus lacustris (most emerged)

6 Shading (from above) (Britain)
 Sparganium emersum
 Sparganium erectum

Table 2.4 (*cont.*)

---

7 Dredging (Britain)
    Species recovering or invading quickly: (some)
    Agrostis stolonifera
    Apium nodiflorum
    Callitriche spp.
    Glyceria maxima
    Lemna minor agg.
    Ranunculus spp.

8 Grazing (French sandstone)
    Callitriche spp.
    Glyceria maxima
    Iris pseudacorus
    Ranunculus spp.

9 Navigation (Britain, The Netherlands)
    Glyceria maxima
    Phalaris arundinacea
    Phragmites australis
    Rumex hydrolapathum
    Sparganium erectum
    (all tough emergents firmly rooted)

River animals

River structure for river animals is the inorganic banks and bed, plus the living vegetation. (The architecture in which the vegetation lives is, of course, just that of the inorganic structure.) Dredging, channelisation, disturbance, boat transport, shallowing, gullying, flood defence, pollution, lining, culverting and more decrease niches, and there are few rivers with none of these niche-destroying impacts. So, too often, there are too few habitats for the great variety of river animals (e.g. no shallow edge means no heron, no fish spawning grounds mean no such fish). Like plants, animals can also use any ponds, pools or small channels available: but most of those that were available in, say, 1700 have now gone (see Everard, 2005).

Because so many are mobile, animals can use temporary habitats, and search for new ones, in a way plants do not.

Vegetation is used by animals for substrate (many invertebrates live on plant surfaces), for shelter (both predator and prey can hide in plant beds), for reproduction (including allowing dragonfly and mayfly larvae, to climb up into the air and pupate) and, of course, for food. Rivers harbour a diverse variety of herbivores including invertebrates, fish, amphibians, birds and mammals and an equally diverse variety of carnivores and omnivores. Animals may even need different food at different stages (e.g. tadpoles and frogs, and the various ducklings that eat chironomids, while the adults have larger food). Swans are currently the most destructive animals, except for large numbers of say gadwall or carp, or livestock. Some animals are restricted to one or a few plants, e.g. reedbug to *Phragmites australis*.

Plant structure is also important. For example, the invertebrate fauna of water-supported species flattened in flow differs from that of the emergents upright at the fringes. Animals also alter the structure. Little ones like caddis fly alter the detail of the sediment, and larger ones like manatee and carp cause major changes. Architectural changes, particularly if sediment is disturbed, alter nutrient fluxes and other chemical processes, and so alter ecology too. Channelling, and other removing of most of the tall monocot fringe habitat, can remove duck habitat, up to three-quarters of the duck population.

Looking at the English R. Itchen, Drake (1995) found poached (trampled) edges had good diverse fauna, but the trampling removed the beetle habitat. There is no one perfect habitat! Diversity is important, giving habitats for all the animals proper to the river type. Water voles need soft and vegetation-concealed banks, waders need shallow edges, but also steeper edges up which they can scramble. Birds and some invertebrates can fly to new places. *Gammarus*, water shrimps, can only be washed downstream.

Vegetation is eaten by animals, and in large quantities. Livestock and deer graze shallow water. Beaver, where present, remove much. Birds, particularly swans, remove large quantities, and so do herbivorous fish. The quantity of animals was, formerly, huge (e.g. Defoe, 1724–7; George, 1992; Norden, 1583). So the quantity of vegetation to support these must also have been great: a huge biomass, *and* a rapid regrowth of vegetation. For most of the twentieth century *Ranunculus* has been, for flood defence, almost a pest species – and cutting it makes it grow faster: one of the better species for supporting large fauna, presumably?

Connections and mosaics

This section moves to look at small-scale variation, that which is known in landscape ecology as mosaics and connectivity.

River systems, the main river and all connecting tributaries, flow downstream. Beside each, there may be a partial or continuous 'green corridor' (riverside without buildings, railways and other blocks). These can support much movement, in both directions, by animals. In the water, some can move upstream as well as downstream, and plants and invertebrates can be swept downstream, and lodge and, if conditions are suitable, establish new populations. Species like *Callitriche* spp. and fringing herbs establish well: many other species, given enough time, can do so and spread by seed. However, Dawson (1980) studying *Ranunculus* in an upper chalk stream, found different ecotypes at different distances from the source, so in general there was no movement.

Winterbournes, chalk streams drying most summers, have ecotypes of *Ranunculus peltatus* that tolerate this drying. Other upstream brooks, once with perennial flow but now dry in summer, lose their *Ranunculus*, because it cannot recover from repeated drying. The winterbournes have had millennia to develop ecotypes, the others have failed to do so in a few decades. This shows that the movement of fragments and seeds, and their ability (when watched, or in laboratories) to become established, does not mean such species can remain long-term or, in just decades, transfer between rivers. Within the river, plants can grow a little upstream, and they and invertebrates can be moved from stream to stream by animals, including people (shoes, fishing equipment, cutting machines, etc., and also deliberate transfers, by anglers or planners).

Even where the flow in a river is year-round, it is not necessarily the case that water is continuous. Weirs without bypasses or fish ladders may prevent animals passing upstream. The apparent continuity has discontinuities. Then, in extreme cases, such as Malta and lowland Majorca, the effect of abstraction and drainage is so great that the only continuous water is during exceptionally heavy storms. At other times there may be surface flow in wet weather, but where fissures occur, surface water disappears and the occasional pools are all that remain (Haslam, 2006; Haslam *et al.*, 2004). Not even a real mosaic of habitats remains, as most of the pools are badly polluted.

In an ordinary river, there are patterns, patterns of edge emergents, of centre submergents. These are longitudinal. But within, there are often mosaics, e.g. of *Sparganium emersum*, *Scirpus lacustris*, *Sagittaria sagittifolia* and *Elodea canadensis* (Fig. 2.11). When plotted, there is a mosaic, but with longitudinal shapes. Riffles and pools have different communities – of invertebrates, and (depending on habitat) maybe of plants also (Haslam, 2006). These mosaics can even occur in uniform conditions, when different plants become established and each develops a different microhabitat (rooting, sedimentation, erosion, flow: and associated fauna). More often the river bed varies in substrate, depth, flow, etc., and the species best adapted grow in each, provided the differences are enough. For instance, in mountain rivers *Ranunculus aquatilis* dominates in the smaller river upstream, and *R. fluitans* downstream. But in the transition region, *R. fluitans* occurs in deeper water, *R. aquatilis* in shallower. Where the mosaic is of

44 The riverscape and the river

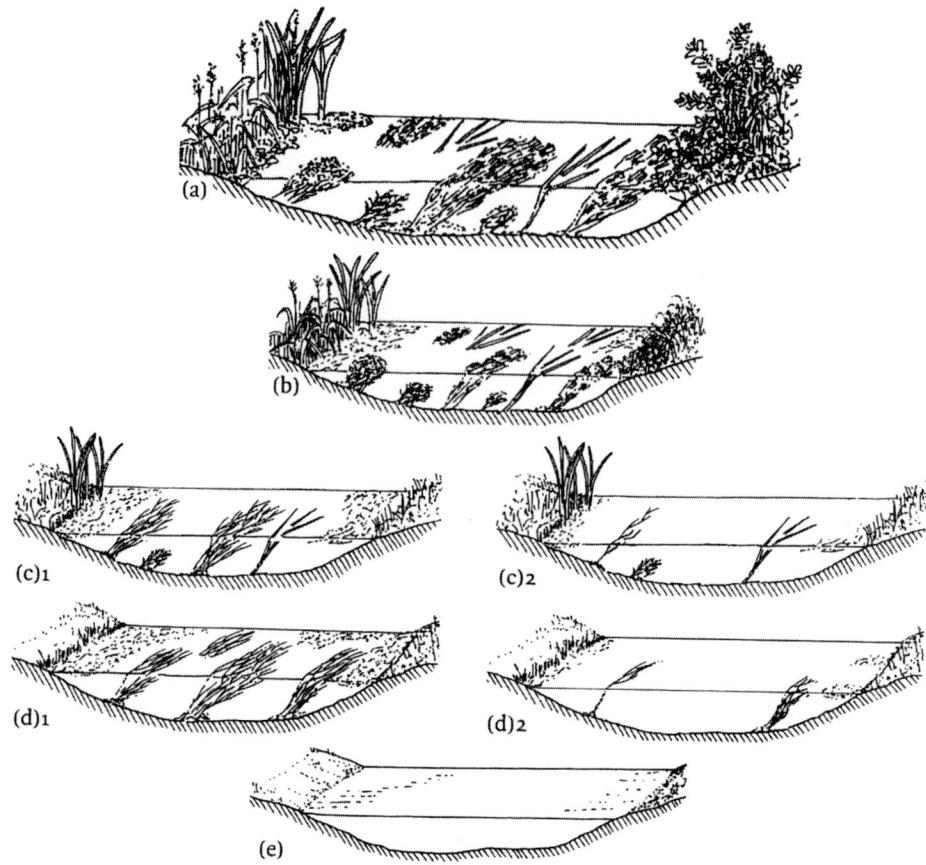

Fig. 2.11. Pollution sequence. A typical effect on traditional vegetation of increasing pollution from near-clean (a), to gross (e). Species present: (a) *Ranunculus* sp., abundant, *Apium nodiflorum, Callitriche* sp., *Myosotis scorpioides, Phalaris arundinacea, Potamogeton crispus, Rorippa nasturtium-aquaticum, Sparganium emersum, S. erectum, Veronica beccabunga*; (b) *Ranunculus* sparse, *Callitriche* sp., *M. scorpioides, P. arundinacea, P. crispus, S. emersum, S. erectum*, Blanket weed. Cover much reduced, *Ranunculus* much reduced, 3 out of 8, instead of 6 out of 10 species pollution-sensitive, (c) (no *Ranunculus*), *P. crispus, P. pectinatus, S. emersum, S. erectum*, Blanket weed. *P. pectinatus* and Blanket weed are pollution-favoured; (d)1 *P. pectinatus* abundant, Blanket weed. (c)2 and (d)1 *P. pectinatus* abundant, Blanket weed. (c)2 and (d)2 follow a different route, different pollution. Both lead to (e) no macrophytes (P. A. Wolseley and Y. Bower in Haslam, 1997a).

substrates, one species can dominate (e.g. *Sparganium emersum*), or each texture can have its own species (e.g. *Potamogeton crispus* and *Oenanthe fluviatilis* where roots could be twined round gravel, *Sp. emersum* and *Sagittaria sagittifolia* in mixed substrates where roots could grow down well, but be protected by small stones.

All these have perennial rhizomes. *Potamogeton pectinatus* survives the winter as turions, which must stay in uneroded but soft soil, and grow up accordingly in spring).

Downstream variation forms mosaics. This is mostly that, e.g. upstream communities are patches separated by the land in-between the streams. Also, a change of habitat downstream can revert stream and community to an upstream form, e.g. when a river is braided (has several parallel, often anastomising channels), and one channel is small, shallow with flow maintaining a gravel substrate more like those of upstream (river size, and substrate silting increasing nutrient status are two of the characteristic downstream changes). Patches of more upstream or downstream vegetation can also come with small-scale topographic change and the equivalent impact of, e.g. weirs. These have shallow, fast habitats downstream and deep, slow ones upstream. The community patches certainly vary with these. They will also vary chemically if the silt of the slower habitat alters the nutrient status sufficiently: which is usually in a downstream or pollution transition zone, when just a little more silt in the substrate moves the community to a more nutrient-rich one. Patches from these (and many other causes) form mosaics within the general longitudinal pattern.

Then there is a network of the whole river system, where – in a uniform catchment – upstream brooks resemble each other, and so do medium stretches, and indeed streams of one catchment can resemble one another. This therefore gives a type of mosaic or network. Of course, in practice pollution and channelling affect some more than others.

Mosaics and patterns of river vegetation occur from:

- changeless change in stable conditions;
- changing change in (slowly) changing conditions;
- habitat patterns within the river;
- ecotypes; different genetic strains growing in (even slightly) different habitats;
- external factors, such as grazing, growing or felling trees, disturbances like building or dredging;
- geographic variations in species.

This last in a way demonstrates the others. Any river species has a centre of distribution, where it is most frequent and where it, in fact, grows in a wider habitat range and occurs more frequently than in the periphery. There, conditions are more difficult, climate is not optimum, and something (e.g. pollution, depth) tolerable in the centre makes occurrence impossible where the plant is already under extra stress (Table 2.5).

Table 2.5 *Geographic distributions of European river plants. A selection of common species from the west and the centre*

Species	Centre of distribution	Main wider distribution (if restricted)
Fringing herbs		
Apium nodiflorum	NW France, England, Ireland	west and south
Berula aquatica	NW France to Denmark	temperate
Mentha aquatica		west and south
Myosotis scorpioides	S. England, W. France	west and temperate
Veronica anagallis-aquatica		south and south-temperate
Veronica beccabunga	Britain	
Rorippa nasturtium-aquaticum agg.		
Tall monocotyledons		
Carex acutiformis agg.		
Glyceria maxima	The Netherlands to Denmark	England to Sardinia
Iris pseudacorus	France	
Phalaris arundinacea	Germany, W. France	decreasing south
Phragmites communis	Far east	SE England to Malta
Sparganium erectum	Ireland, S. England, W. France	
Typha spp.		
Spoon-shaped short monocotyledons		
Alisma plantago-aquatica		
Strap-leaved water-supported		
Sparganium emersum	Brittany to Denmark, S. England	decreasing south
Floating rooted		
Nuphar lutea		decreasing north and south
Oval-tailed fine-leaved water-supported		
Callitriche cophocarpa, C. obtusangula, C. platycarpa, C. stagnalis agg.	France to Denmark	decreasing south
Potamogeton pectinatus		scattered, south
Ranunculus, Batrachian spp.		wide
Submerged 'fillers'		
Elodea canadensis	Belgium to Denmark	

Care, though, must be used! In Germany in *c.* 1980 the major rivers were polluted with turbid water, so vegetation was sparse. Just looking at the distributions would indicate species could not tolerate the deep water they grew well in, e.g. France or Britain. The regional difference was not plant behaviour, it was the man-made pattern of pollution. (At that time the French badly polluted small streams, the Germans, large rivers: and the British – but of course! – had no principles and polluted both equally. The overall pollution of the three was similar.) Again, surveys before 1980 in Ireland showed vegetation – and rivers – of unusually good quality and diversity. The subsequent drainage, of course, destroyed that: it was not climatic or spatial variation.

Various aliens, brought in intentionally or accidentally by people, are becoming part of the European (and North American, etc.) scene. Signal crayfish (which carries a virus) is driving out the native. This happens too often when the checks applied to population in one region (disease, pests, predators, harvesting) do not occur in another with an equally suitable habitat. Zebra mussel is also spreading in deeper rivers. Among plants, *Elodea canadensis* (North American), a pest when first introduced in the mid-nineteenth century, is now non-explosive, and fits like a native species through most of Europe. Its pair, *E. nuttallii*, which regrettably can both be made from *E. canadensis* by pollution (Eaton & Freeman, 1982; Haslam, 1987, 1990) and be considered an independent species, is following suit, overlapping generally in more polluted places. Some new introductions, particularly *Crassula helmsii*, are driving out native vegetation; pests, but so far only locally (e.g. Dawson, 1994). Such patterns are also mosaics: of a kind.

Skewing and loss of vegetation from human impact

Loss of vegetation ultimately means loss of fauna. Species immediately dependent on living plants, particularly specific ones, are lost with those plants. However, many animals, including some coarse fish, invertebrates and others, can live well without macrophytic vegetation, surviving on debris, incoming organic matter from effluents and such-like, and the detritovores that eat these. Trout and salmon anglers demand good vegetation. Those of coarse fish are indifferent (though do not want lines impeded).

The ways vegetation is skewed and diminished have been mentioned above, but will be discussed, here. Diminishing is being less of: instead of 80% cover, there is 40% or 10%, though the species and their proportions are unchanged. This happens when the appropriate habitat is reduced. The habitat type and factors remain similar, but there is less of it. Skewing is when some of the original species cannot do as well in the new habitat, and decrease and disappear (too shallow: often; too deep: infrequent; too fast, too slow, too shaded, too polluted, too disturbed, etc.), so the species assemblage has changed, it is without the proper proportion of tall monocots or fringing herbs or calcium-dominated species or deep water species, etc. (see Fig. 7.1 for the proportions for a few river types). New species tolerant to the new conditions may enter, also.

Pseudo-geographic variations can be unexpected, too. On resistant rock, fringing herbs do not anchor as well as on limestone or sandstone (in equivalent rivers). They are therefore more easily washed off by spate flows in hills (Haslam, 1987, 2006), but grow better in lowland resistant streams. In part of central France, however, this is more exaggerated, and the plants much sparser. Presumably rock type, not ecotype! Again, some sandstones, from rock type or intensive agriculture, lead to much river sedimentation with sand (e.g. parts of France and Eastern England). Loose sand gives poor anchorage (unstable and heavy moving) and (if silt is washed out) even worse nutrients: so, very poor vegetation. The mosaics of such unpredictably unsatisfactory rock types are not due to pollution!

Pollution is now ubiquitous, even from the air. In cultivated and populated places pollutants come from numerous sources (Fig. 2.3). There are many different chemicals (tens of thousands) so there are many different plant responses (Table 2.3). Pollution is marked by loss, skewing and total loss. Obviously, a site without vegetation cannot use river plants for diagnosis! Total loss may indeed be due to pollution, but it could also be due to, e.g. heavy shade, many boats, dredging, paddling. Other signs must be looked for to ascertain the reason for the loss.

Shallowing comes from drainage and abstraction., All aquifers in densely populated regions are abstracted from, and so are many rivers. (Water can even be transferred from one river to another, bringing its pollutants with it, e.g. R. Cam water was transferred some 40 km from an agrochemical factory, and killed tomatoes irrigated from R. Stour, Williams, et al., 1977.)

Abstraction has led to drying and loss of many streams on lowland limestone: those up to 2 m or even 4 m wide, formerly with good vegetation. Land drainage, field drainage has destroyed most smaller tributaries, those which used to flow in so many ditches surrounding the then-small fields. With larger (3–8 m) streams shallowing rapidly in England – where, even in the 1970s, water had been lowered more than on the continent – the threat to rivers is the gross loss found in Malta (Chapter 4). In parts of, e.g. France, the threat is equal. Even mountains are drained!

For sheer destruction of river length, water loss is the greatest killer.

When people want water in their taps but not in their streams or even dampening their land, restoring river water will not happen, except in the occasional few kilometres done for conservation (e.g. R. Cam, R. Piddle, England).

Not all is this bad. Denmark and Sweden are two of the countries where legislation actually *likes* their streams, and the Netherlands has more water than most (not all the River Rhine can be drained away, particularly below sea level).

Pollution, as said above, is ubiquitous. The only free way of cleaning rivers is to allow them to self-purify. This needs sun and much oxygen, as in cascading mountain rivers, or, as is more available and efficient, river vegetation (via its micro-organisms, see Haslam, 2003). Too many planners like to allow much pollution into rivers, and then make sure vegetation is inadequate to clean it (like a sewage treatment works, vegetation can be overloaded).

Although the European Union tries to prevent it, from the 1970s to the 1990s, river pollution increased in, e.g. Britain because, although treatment works improved, hard surface run-off became much worse, and in much of west France (M. P. Everitt, personal communication) rivers with reasonable vegetation became too polluted for vegetation, and in Ireland drainage and channelisation, coupled with increasing wealth, led to deterioration.

Lesser sources of damage are also shown in Fig. 2.2. Most can eliminate vegetation locally.

Usually, there is more than one damage factor present, and vegetation is lowered more by these multiple impacts. If pollution hinders plant establishment, recovery from, say, disturbance will take longer. If the water is almost too shallow, water-supported plants will be small, and trampling will be more damaging.

The south German rivers recorded over three decades (1970s–2000s) by Professor Kohler (Kohler *et al.*, 2003) have shown only minor long-term changes. Denmark has improved (see below), Malta has deteriorated shockingly. Britain has continued the depressing deterioration recorded between *c.* 1930 (Butcher, 1927, 1933) and *c.* 1980 (Haslam, 1982, 1987). When deterioration is assessed, there has to be a baseline and a measure. The earliest ecological surveys seem to be those of Butcher (1927, 1933), and the earliest widespread surveys using one method are the *c.* 34,000 European sites of Haslam (commissioned by CEC) (more details available in Haslam, 1982, 1987, and personal communication, if requested). While survey method and measure are usually related, this is not necessary. Many measures are now available, e.g. River Habitat Survey 1996 – Part I 6002–6728 Environment Agency, Bristol; Part II 6730–7523; Mean Trophic Rank Macrophytic Survey: An assessment of the Bristol Trophic Status of Rivers using macrophytes. Environment Agency. Haslam, 1987, 1990, 1997; Holmes, 1983 a, b; Haury *et al.*, 2002; Kohler & Veit, 2003a, b; European-Union-wide methods will come. However, it is very important to realise an index is only for show. What the plants interpret for the researcher is both more accurate and more illuminating (see, e.g. Kohler *et al.*, 2003; Januer & Exler, 2004; Carbiener *et al.*, 1990; Haslam 2006, 1987; Trémolières *et al.*, 1994).

Restoration and rehabilitation

To restore is to return to what was there before, as dictionaries agree. To rehabilitate means the same, though recent medical usage is 'to restore as far as possible' (someone may remain, e.g. paralysed, after rehabilitation). Both terms are used in river schemes, even when both are incorrect because the planner has no wish to discover what was there before, but merely wants something thought pretty. (A restored site may have an improbable meander; drained steep banks; over-shallow water controlled by groynes; pollution; and some non-native strains of species not proper to that river type anyway.) A restorer may say the aim is to restore normal ecosystem functioning. But how long has the restorer spent studying ecosystem function in a near by 'normal' (traditional?) river? Most probably, little or none, certainly not years. Functioning may happen, but is it 'restored'?

Although over a decade has passed, the following is still too often true: '. . . *In 1994, an agency biologist was asked if his agency had evaluated the success of the many projects he had described., He explained that the need for . . . fish habitat enhancement projects was so urgent . . . that he was obliged to spend all his time building projects, and he had no time to evaluate them.*

This attitude is probably widespread: assume you are doing God's work, do it with great abandon, and don't even admit the possibility that the project might be ineffective or even harmful.

After all, the projects were defined and conceived as 'restoration' or 'enhancement' projects, so they must be restoring or enhancing.' (Kondolf, 1998)

Only if a scheme is effective after at least a decade is it proven successful. At Restoration conferences, the restorers are, very properly, excited about their projects. Unfortunately, too many schemes are barely 3 km long – and what is the length of river further dried, polluted or otherwise harmed in that region, that year?!

Restoration is a useful, growing and developing field, and there are centres of information and expertise, such as in Silkeborg, Denmark, and Silsoe, England. The valuable literature is now considerable, and includes Madsen, 1995; Lachat 1994; Petts & Calow, 1992; Giles & Summer, 1996; and the always up-to-date information available from the centres.

Countries such as Denmark (e.g. Madsen, 1995) like and value rivers, and legally protect them (general restoration 1985 with meanders, banks, biota, etc.;

2 m buffer strip along each and every stream, 1992). They have much to teach others, both in attitude and in having so many restored lengths for enough time to assess techniques.

Countries such as Britain, however, have little money for pure restoration. Up to 5% of the cost of major schemes may be spent on enhancement. The former attitude is that Government considers proper rivers to be straight, uniform, deepened, steep-sided rivers taking water as quickly as possible to the sea, with biota irrelevant (except where anglers pay for fish). But, in deference to those thinking differently, 5% of scheme money can be used (see Chapter 4, EU Water Framework Directive).

As mentioned above, it is of the first importance to try to *restore* the traditional river of that type, not to *design* a pretty or 'ecological' river. This means actually going to look, on the ground, at other rivers of the same type, to discover, as far as possible, the features of the traditional rivers. Figure 2.4 can be used for a first impression. It gives the principal, but by no means all, characteristics to look for. It is divided into, first, natural features and heritage, to be checked and, when poor, improved, and restored, when not interfering with essential flood protection, etc. Second, Fig. 2.4 shows the principal (again far from all) cultural and historic features of conservation value. These should be kept, and if necessary maintained or restored. It is far too easy for a planner to plan a nice meander, obviously of high conservation value, and remove a village earthen wharf because it was unrecognised or thought less valuable than *Berula erecta*. But a wharf a millennium old cannot be replaced! A new meander and *B. erecta*, can. The two sides of heritage should always be considered together.

Figures 2.3 and 2.4 illustrate the type of thought that leads to good practice in lessening pollution coming to rivers. Details vary, but 'lateral thinking' remains priceless.

Money can become available to develop a recreation site, including a river. As with river schemes, it is too easy to plant it all, and then add a little ecology for, e.g. Wildlife Trust members. By integrating good river and riverside ecology from the beginning, really valuable nature reserves, and tourist ecology demonstrations, can be created. When people are going to be somewhere anyway, why not demonstrate the heritage and interest of the river? The more who understand these, the more pressure there will be for good-quality rivers!

To conclude, the primary requirement for traditional rivers is water: water of sufficient quantity, and of suitable quality, and suitable varieties of quality for the catchment. Round that water, the river channel, bank and bankside should be of traditional pattern, shape, texture, diversity, etc. There should be as many niches as possible within the planning constraints. This then permits the traditional biota to occur and develop communities of changeless change, of both plants and animals. There are now numerous river types, though they can be aggregated into categories of rock type, water force (topography) and upstream–downstream variation. When restoring, though, effort should be put into discovering, from other rivers, the closest to the traditional habitat for a particular river. The true traditional river, as shown above, has a wider species assemblage, and less difference between community types. If the habitat for this wide assemblage can be re-created, well and very good. But this fact is no excuse for planting or encouraging other species outside the narrower assemblage, still less for importing strains not native to the locality or, worse still, aliens.

3

The natural riverscape and its modification

Every landscape settled by Man becomes a blend of the natural and the human. It is a fabric made by man.

(Williams, 1970)

Neither war nor earthquake are as destructive of history and culture as too much money

(Rackham, 1986)

Landscape is the basis of human environment . . . the place of many processes influencing life.

(Vink, 1983)

Introduction

Chapter 2 discussed the natural river and its destruction. Many streams have been totally destroyed in the past c.150 years (dried and gone) and more have been destroyed ecologically, having an inadequate, or almost gone, biota. Since the riverscape is needed for people to live on and grow their food on, it is seldom destroyed (by, e.g. quarrying it away), but is instead modified. While water is the medium of the river, the riverscape is mostly in the mediums of air and soil, with water a small, though essential component. However, it is the river (or glacier) that has made the riverscape! And it is the river which makes (or made) its pattern, with its network flowing downstream.

In the long term, the river moves the riverscape to the sea, but this time-scale need not be considered here. The river does, though, move water, energy, sediment, nutrients, debris, pollutants and biota. All move downstream, except for animals with independent mobility, and plants moved by animals or wind.

A riverscape, being so much larger than a river, has even more complex influences. These act at different scales, from the forest, to the footpath and the microhabitats in the pollard willow. The land is organised, by nature (topography – mostly – and the potential biota present) and by impact at a major scale (fields) and minor (beetle banks). Environmental gradients include the following:

- Water
- Its potential energy
- Solutes, nutrients and pollutants
- Sediment particles, with their nutrients and pollutants
- Plant particles, fragments, debris, vegetative propagules (e.g. Bill et al., 1999, found over 9000 drifting seeds per metre stream width per day in an Alpine flood plain)
- Plant and animal particles, considered as organic carbon and energy
- Fish, migrant (also upstream) and, to a lesser extent, non-migrant moving
- Bottom (benthic) invertebrates
- Various other animals, which also move upstream and, birds, particularly move between rivers, and further.
- Floods; water on riverside land during high flows, usually from the river, but also due to rising groundwater or flooding incoming tributaries. These are generally on intermittent narrow plains upstream, and wider more continuous plains downstream. Surface-water floods bring and deposit particles and solutes – including water – carried in the floods.
- Climate: there is most change in long, mountain-rising rivers. These change downstream in temperature (day, night, frost, integrated); wind (exposure and shelter), precipitation (rain and snow), humidity, insolation (aspect and slope). Locally, microclimates may be important (e.g. north and south-facing slopes, and differences from the top to the bottom of a slope).

There is an overlay, or rather, many overlays of human impact. Even features like the tree line (on mountains and towards the Arctic) are determined not just by climate, but by impact. The more the grazing, the lower the tree-line: young trees are eaten and, around the tree-line, re-colonisation is slow (e.g. Bell, 1997, Sporrong et al., 1995).

The layers of the riverscape

The bedrock or glacial drift is the lowest layer. At times they are exposed, though more often they are covered by soil. The soil may be derived directly from the bedrock, as in many non-glaciated regions, or from the glacial drift, alluvial deposits, peat or desert deposits like loess. The nutrients and other chemical content depend on the origin. Above this 'skin' of soil, the riverscape is (or was) clothed with vegetation (except where the bones stick through, and lichens, bryophytes and algae can survive on rock). The vegetation, rooted in the soil, reflects the chemistry and climate. The basic pattern is tundra to the north, which is short, due to the small inflow of energy, next, in the (damp) temperate zones, there are tall forests and grazing. Then, in the south, the Mediterranean summer drought leads again to shorter vegetation, small trees (maquis) and the tundra-like garigue. In (east) North America there is similar tundra in the north, then forest and grazing, but in the south the climate is wet, without a summer drought, and there are forests, such as the Everglades, which are the most productive on the continent because of ample water as well as the greater incoming energy. In both continents, production in the north is limited by lack of incoming energy, in Europe, that in the south is limited by lack of incoming rainfall.

History

People (Neanderthal) reached the west of what is now Europe in the previous interglacial, some 800,000 years ago. Further waves followed, which also had little impact on the riverscape. The Danubian people moved east along main river valleys, reaching the Netherlands by *c.* 4500 BC, but their cultivation was generally simple. In the south there was good though local, cultivation moving wider and north in the Neolithic era. And the discovery of iron (Iron Age) allowed easier forest clearance and agriculture.

The Roman Empire brought high standards of cultivation, north and east to near Hadrian's Wall (built in the second century AD), the Rhine and the Danube. Since then, there have been changes due to technological advance and retreat. On the large scale, these occurred similarly in all Europe (Dark Ages, expansion in the climatic optimum, the Canal Age and such-like). Different countries had different short-term patterns, e.g. importing German farmers to Russia, with their advanced farming ways, under Catherine the Great, and having, in eastern Europe under twentieth century Communism, very large and state-run collective farms.

In England the major changes started with the surprisingly frequent fields of the Neolithic. This pattern was improved and spread by the Romans (early centuries AD). The climate was warm (Table 2.1). The Anglo Saxons cultivated more land, including heavier ground, and often made larger and different fields, which may be the basis of the pattern seen today. Furthermore, changes in sea level have greatly altered low-lying and, particularly, wetland areas, e.g. the Fenland has been drier from natural causes during several periods between c. 4000 BC and now, from climatic and sea level changes, as well as with drainage, between Roman and modern times. The Enclosure Acts of the eighteenth century later allowed open fields, held by the village, to be enclosed for the major landholders. These made major changes, as did the four-course crop rotation of the early nineteenth century, and the land and field drainage from c. 1850. Those have culminated in the return in the late twentieth century of large fields, and the loss of hedges, small tributaries and ditches and the addition of large quantities of agrochemicals.

Then settlements, buildings and other constructions have spread and influenced the riverscape (see Chapters 10, 12–14). Settlements have gone as well as come – not just farmhouse sites but even towns of earlier date may be hidden except to archaeologists. The Black Death of the 1340s, killing up to half the population, was important in the loss of settlement. But so were changes in trade and customs.

The present riverscapes are therefore the result of many overlays of human impact, all more complex than in the summary above, and all acting on the extremely variable topography, geology, geomorphology and hydrology of the original vegetation plus all layers of change.

Because this is so complex, this chapter presents case studies of a few rivers which, between them, exhibit much variability.

Case studies

1   *Waccasassa River, Florida, USA (Fig. 3.1)*

This is one of the least impacted lowland rivers seen by the author: but nevertheless has had light impact for maybe 10 000 years, and increasingly heavier for maybe 150 years.

The relief of this catchment, these riverscapes, is low, barely reaching 50 m, and with only very gentle slopes. The riverscape, the land 'rising' up from the river is (1990) mainly still forested, the floodable – and frequently and regularly flooded – land bears sub-tropical swamp forest, dominated by *Taxodium* spp. (deciduous cypress) and *Nyssa* spp., with extremely rich understoreys and herb layers. The climate leads to more productive vegetation than anywhere further north, as can be simply seen by the size of the largest carnivore, the alligator, and herbivore (though not in this river) the manatee. The forest has clearances for minor farming and very minor settlements and transport. The rainfall is c. 130 cm (cm not mm!) of which c. 10% sinks through the black forest peat into the very porous sand, which overlies aquiferous limestone. The rest goes to

The natural riverscape and its modification 57

(a)

(b)

Fig. 3.1. Waccasassa River, Florida, USA. (a) Pristine, showing uneven channel, many habitat niches, much vegetation (including the spoon-shaped short emergent building block) in an open glade, and swamp forest shading the rest. A wider photograph, showing more of the riverscape, would just show more forest. (b) River still pristine (just), but one bank opened.

evapotranspiration (which is high in the hot climate) and run-off. The run-off is extreme, storms frequently reaching 20–25 cm rain per day.

The soil is very dark, high-organic, and humus-rich. In consequence, the run-off also is very dark, near-black if there has been a long residence time in the soil. This is known locally as 'Blackwater' (cf. the brown rivers flowing from peat bogs in Europe). Most mid-Florida rivers are Blackwater, which is acid (pH up to 7.5, Suwannee, 1985), though where limestone springs rise to the surface, the water is clear, and calcium-rich.

Because the land is so flat, base flow is slow. But, because of the heavy storms, there is sheet flow on land and swirling eroding flow several metres above base flow, in spates. The river features reflect both. Tributaries rise as small rills, slight depressions in the forest ground, even only 10–20 cm wide, overhung by aquatic trees and shrubs. The catchment is $c.$ 50 km long, with large numbers of these tiny tributaries, which gather size as they flow down to the main river or one of its two principal tributaries. Here as elsewhere, when the forest is felled, small tributaries become sparse, because drainage is applied. The peaty soil, being dried and oxidised, disappears. Most riverscapes are just the river and the forest behind because of the low land and tall forest.

Driving forces
- Heat and sun, high and stormy rainfall, on near-flat topography, the two leading to (1) overland sheet flow and high and unstable river flows and (2) black, peaty soil, which colours the water.
- Very productive land while forested, less so when felled and drained (the crops cultivated are ones typical of lower productivity climates, e.g. grass for horses. Rice would be more trouble but more productive).
- Impact leading to some increased and polluting run-off.
- No wish of the inhabitants to develop, for crops or buildings, except locally. This is vital. The whole catchment would change if this wish changed.

2   R. Cam, Cambridgeshire, England (Fig. 3.2)

R. Cam, a 'dull' lowland stream, with no dramatic scenery and a downstream part in the flat Fenland plain, is typical, in its lowland part, of many English rivers.

Until about 10 000 years ago the catchment area of the Cam was glaciated. The modern-day river originates in areas of mixed geological origins, a feature characteristic of many lowland European rivers. The land rises to $c.$ 130 m (more around 65 m), which means some water force in the hillier parts, but less below, where the gradient in the Fens is negligible (down to 1:40 000).

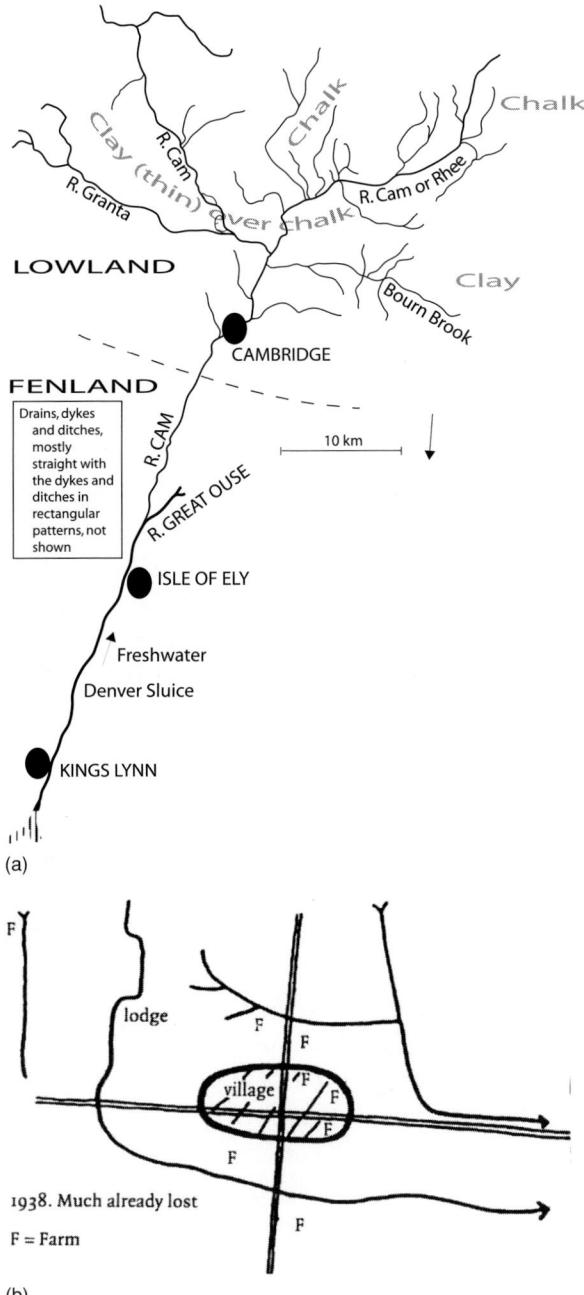

Fig. 3.2. River Cam, England. (a) River map, showing main riverscape types. (b) Watering of the village of Comberton, tributaries in c. 1930. The smaller channels, leading to each farm and various houses, were already lost but the larger diverted channels were still present. (c) Tributary crossing (unmanaged) rather damp meadow to join R. Cam (left). Lowland, land rising beyond. (d) Former river merchants' village (Burwell (on lode, Roman canal.) (e) Ely town wharf. (f) Black peat of the Fenland. Ditches and trees both few.

(c)

(d)

Fig. 3.2. (cont.)

The natural riverscape and its modification 61

(e)

(f)

Fig. 3.2. (cont.)

Quite unlike the Waccasassee River, the R. Cam and its land have been intensively used and managed by people and by different peoples, for at least 5000 years. Recent impact in the Waccasassee catchment is effectively layered over a natural riverscape.

The county town, and mediaeval University town of Cambridge is sited where the lowland 'hills' are merely elevated ground, and divides the upper from the lower river. The University dates to possibly the twelfth, certainly the thirteenth century. Romans, Saxons and Vikings all had settlements here.

There are four main rivers in the upper catchment, to the north R. Bourn, on clay, then passing south and east, R. Rhee rising on small-scale chalk downs, and R. Cam and R. Granta, both on mixed rocks, with an obvious chalk influence.

Drying in the last century, even more in the last half century, has been extreme. Even in the 1970s, the upper and middle Rhee catchment was covered in small chalk streams, running over riverside grass, e.g. near Melbourn and the Mordens. These were perhaps former water meadows. Abstraction for mains supply has removed most of these. R. Bourn, being on heavy clay over chalk, was deeply drained, and lost its good clay-flora streams. Figure 3.2(b) shows, in the early twentieth century, small streams diverted to serve just one farm. A reminder that the 'water on the land is bad' theory is new, such water being essential for farm and house until very recently. This also shows the loss of small tributaries. It illustrates the extreme loss of river length and aquatic habitat.

R. Granta (also drained) had good flood meadows and other wetlands, and some of these remain and are conserved (flood meadows are wetlands flooded from the river, usable as pasture. Water meadows are penned water systems, with channels all over, and a regulated water level). They are not, though, traditionally managed, and the vegetation is in between meadow (mown as well as grazed grass) and reed or sedge wetland. While there is a good deal of grass near the larger streams, the catchment is mostly intensively farmed. Riverscapes are typically European in hill and crop, typically English in shape of tree and shape and presence of hedges. Shapes of the same species do vary across Europe (both genotypes and climate), so the knowledgeable can place any riverscape. (This applies back to the beginnings of portrayal, in the sixteenth century.)

Since people and livestock need water, the old villages are sited on or by a source of water, as shown in Fig. 3.2. The story of one of these streams, that watering Foxton, is told by Parker (1975). The Brook belonged to the community and was necessary for its existence. In four parishes, no village house was over 80 yards (c. 73 m) from the brook until after 1800. This gave easy access for supply, etc. Water use was strictly regulated. In the fourteenth century fines were payable in Foxton for (a) making ponds for watering; (b) widening the brook or diverting it by at least 6 in (15 cm); and (c) for letting the bank fall in, or allowing it to be widened by neglect by at least 2 ft (c. 60 cm). This was before made roads or concrete and if these sins had been allowed, parts of the High Street would have fallen in. Also, the downstream end of the village would have had its water reduced. In the fifteenth and sixteenth centuries offences included: allowing dunghills to drain into the Brook; allowing waterfowl or pigs in it within the village; failing to clean and scour the part by one's own frontage (effectively keeping vegetation as well as silting down); diverting water; and, before 8pm, washing clothes or letting gutters or cesspits drain in. The eighteenth century brought less individual care, ditching being done by someone paid by the parish. Late in the century controls were abandoned, and farmers dug ponds up to a size for eight horses to drink together. The brook was dirtier. As people no longer brewed their own beer (which was a sterilised drink), other drinking-supplies were desirable. Wells were sunk in gardens. As supply decreased, with abstraction and drainage lowering groundwater levels, farm boreholes were dug 1830–70, and two large boreholes for village supply followed in 1873, water-carts bringing the water to houses. As the brook became too dirty for supply, its sole village use became waste disposal. The stream gradually dried up and in about 1960 was put in pipes underground: the final indignity!

In this village, therefore, the history of the brook is known. It illustrates many points:

(a) Regulations are needed to keep a settlement stream in good order.
(b) The parishes were skilled in physical stream management, but not in the control of chemical management – waste put in at the allowed time of 3.30am will not leave the stream clean for drinking at 4am. Many pollutants, including disease micro-organisms, are not visible in poisonous concentrations!
(c) Supply went from brook to wells to boreholes (with water-carts) to mains.
(d) Waterfowl were kept, but the stream was too small (contrast, e.g, Figs 9.10i, 10.13c) for the birds to be on it in the village (they would have caused damage).
(e) That which is needed by man is maintained; that which is not may easily be lost.

The larger streams were also used as fisheries, for mills (e.g. Shepreth, Barrington, Fig. 3.2a) and, of course, for transport. Vikings invaded (at least up the Rhee). Streams barely 2 m wide could take barges, which were common in the region into the twentieth century. Larger and more boats went up R. Cam proper (no doubt stopping on the way), carrying freight for the market town of Saffron Walden, where the main (and stoned) wharf area is upstream of the centre. Villages had just earthen wharfs, too often destroyed by later dredging.

Cambridge was the major port town of the shire. In the early seventeenth century, its Recorder said to King James I: 'This river Cam is current through the heart of the shire, with navigation to the sea, and is the life of traffic to the town and countrie' (Porter, 1969).

The Romans made the Car Dyke as a catchwater drain, collecting water flowing into the Fenland from higher ground, and to take (particularly grain) boats to the sea via the River Trent. Later peoples used the more direct route to the coast (Fig. 3.2). The centre of Cambridge, including the main wharf, was taken out in the fifteenth century by King Henry VI (to build King's College): and was not re-built, there were merely small wharfs above and below.

Downstream of Cambridge, the river flows through the once-wetland, The Fenland. This wetland gives its name to other fens and to fen peat (peat formed under water, with water nutrients). The Fen vegetation was mostly herbaceous, tall monocotyledons (sedges, *Phragmites*, bulrushes, etc.), with many pools and wandering watercourses. Alder and sallow carr occurred on drier areas. Bog was mainly to the west. There was no sub-tropical tree swamp, though in drier places and periods even oakwood could grow (later becoming bog oaks underneath in the peat). Enormous amounts of peat were shaved off (not dug in pits, as in the Norfolk Broads) probably mostly in the mediaeval dry climatic optimum.

The Fenland used to support a solitary population living on wetland products such as fish, fowl, peat, roofing and fencing materials. Eels were a major crop (hence 'Ely'), used for export and rent as well as local consumption. The people moved by boat, by ice (in cold periods), and crossing dykes by poles where bridges were absent. Along the higher perimeter, and on 'islands' were villages, whose people used the near, summer dry, land for grazing, as well as the further land as wetland.

The Romans converted some incoming streams to the R. Cam into access canals called 'lodes'. This meant boat access from the North Sea to, e.g. Wicken (now tiny), Burwell (where former docks for merchant ships were only destroyed in the past decade) and Reach. Reach had an annual Fair with goods from the Hanseatic League, Rhine, and the East. It was chartered in the twelfth century.

Since the seventeenth-century draining, the fertile cultivated peat has been gradually oxidised and lost, and the ground level is now several metres below sea level, and, e.g. *c.* 4 m below the Cam at Upware. So the navigable river is now well-banked above ground level. R. Cam joins R. Great Ouse before Ely. Ely was the principal Isle since Queen Etheldreda, later St Etheldreda, built an abbey there in the seventh century, which became rich, and following a disaster, there is now a great twelfth-century cathedral. Ely had, and has, wharfs: one for the abbey and one for the city. It was a main port, because of the abbey. Beyond Ely, the river has a small port at Littleport, on its way to the sea at King's Lynn, also a major former port. Before a great storm altering its course in 1198, the Great Ouse had a more northerly outfall, passing through the port of Wisbech. King's Lynn therefore suddenly became important, and quickly developed. Like some other river towns, particularly on R. Rhine, e.g. Mainz, instead of growing round the original wharf and market place and church, King's Lynn built more of these along the stream. First upstream is St Saviour's Church with a short wharf. Built soon after is St Margaret's with a major wharf area, including an (ex) navigable tributary into the town. Then a still-old square without a church. Finally, downstream there is the twentieth-century industry: but land- not river-based, using road and rail communications.

Until the main drainage of the seventeenth century, boats passed freely to Cambridge, Reach, etc. But afterwards, to prevent the sea flooding into the fens, Denver Sluice was built and frequently re-built, the latest time early this century. This meant boat freight had to be unloaded and carried round, boats being unable to pass. As road and rail communications developed, boat transport declined.

The final twist is that, barely over 300 years later, the fertile peat is running out. Where once was wetland, then fields divided by dykes, there is now dry peat or even exposed clay, and fields sometimes with hedges. It is also expensive to keep land drained, particularly when below sea level. Large areas to the west and the south are now planned to revert to wetland, giving big nature reserves which will require less maintenance, though give no food. One is intended to reach from the first-ever nature reserve, Wicken Fen (formerly villager strips) to the south perimeter of the Fenland (see Haslam, 2003). Another may be from the (c. 1900) Woodwalton Fen Reserve via the bog peat Holme Fen, to the north west perimeter.

In the Fenland, the man-made or man-channelled dykes and rivers are largely straight lines. In the lowlands, straightening, being less easy, is rather less in the main streams. The man-made diversions, whether to supply mills, farms, gardens, colleges or villages, are nearer straight.

The driving forces governing the Cam catchment (apart from the flows already described) are the following:

- Food production. The lowlands had agriculture intensive for the population, technology and their importance at the time. (Some chalk hills just outside the catchment were cultivated only in the stress of the Napoleonic Wars, some less steep, also in the Second World War.) In the Fenland, pre-drainage, output was low: the population was sparse but independent and near self-sufficient. Converting these people to dependent but healthier farm workers without the leisure for much opium and alcohol, with the land growing vastly more food, was considered (as always) good. The loss of wetlands and biodiversity was substantial.

Drainage of the riverside land in the nineteenth century much improved public health along the main river, as well as agriculture. Later field and stream drainage led to damage as it destroyed rivers, flower-rich meadows and songbird populations. It gave higher crop yields without improvement in public health (see Haslam, 2003).

This has led to widespread pollution only since the mid twentieth century, when agrochemicals and unnecessary silt started pouring off the land.

- Export of fuel, eels, and other fowl and fish from the Fenland, earlier. Peat was transported by water, primarily. The more costly crops were also moved by road.
- Communications. The ancient University and town of Cambridge, could only exist with good communications for both people and goods. The lesser settlements did so too. These were provided by river (see above) and by road, particularly by the Great Cambridge Road to London. (Rail, motorway and, minor, air travel followed later.) The town led to varying but often gross pollution since at least the time of King John, when a new town watercourse was dug, carrying slaughterhouse waste. River pollution perhaps peaked in the nineteenth century when sewage pollution became ghastly.

Ely formed a separate abbey network (seventh century to Reformation), with its Bishopric much influencing the Fenland and its perimeter lowlands from Suffolk to Huntingdonshire, into the twentieth century. Water communications were pre-eminent, given its position. Damage, channelling and pollution of the rivers, as described in Chapters 2 and 4, occur everywhere, though to varying degrees.

- Water demand (as opposed to getting rid of the nasty stuff) is for mains supply and irrigation, and was only co-ordinated in the twentieth century. Cambridge, the major population centre, took water first from springs and streams, then from the aquifer below (first springs, then boreholes) and as this became exhausted and inadequate in the later twentieth century is now reaching further, into Norfolk. Other aquifers are also tapped. Irrigation is primarily from the rivers (– drain the land too dry, by removing river water, then remove even more to wet it again. Not a particularly sustainable use).

No pristine riverscapes occur in the Cam catchment, and traditional ones are only local. Settlement and communications routes still increase. Fields get larger, hedges fewer, agriculture more intensive, and new crops (such as oil-seed rape) appear. In nooks and corners, near some old villages and streams, there are some traditional-sized fields with hedges, but biodiversity is sadly down from even 1950, let alone 1900. Typical English lowland riverscapes are common: in the lowlands, the streams winding (unless straightened) along the valley, the occasional farm by small ones, the occasional mill by the larger one, and villages scattered, sheltering, with the streams, green fields, trees and hedges (but far too little ancient woodland).

3   *River Kbir, Malta (Fig. 3.3)*

Malta is a small (under 250 sq. km) island south of Italy in the Mediterranean, with the usual south Mediterranean winter growing season and summer drought. Being almost entirely limestone, Malta used to be as full of water as a wet sponge, the drips being the many springs welling water. There were 300 km of watercourse, 100 km of main rivers. Now that most rivers are dry most of the time (see Chapter 4), probably half or more of even dry channels have gone. R. Kbir, the Great River, is the largest river system. This size is merely a trivial part of the rivers described above. R. Kbir is a miniature, highly diverse whole river and its riverscape.

The slopes are terraced. This means making flat fields by digging out rock at the back, building a wall at the front, putting stones, etc., on the ground (drainage) and filling the field up with soil, which is thicker in the front than in the back. Terracing is common in the old civilisations of the Orient, and in parts of Europe (Maltese terraces were made between Punic times and now), mostly in the south (though see Chapter 13). It provides flat rather than sloping ground for fields. It is the greatest man-made alteration to the shape of (vegetated) riverscapes. Recently, though, some terraces on moderate slopes have had their walls removed to make larger fields. In contrast to R. Cam, these fields may be *c.* 20 m × 5 m, *c.* 50 m × 10 m or, on the flat, even *c.* 100 m × 100 m rarely, instead of several hundred metres square. Instead of being divided by hedges or fences, these fields have the dry stone walls, free-standing or terrace, made of the local limestone. The general colour is yellow, from the stone and the dry soil in the summer, rather than the forest green of Waccasassee River and the grass green of R. Cam.

The Great Plateau of Malta is hard Coralline limestone, craggy and cliffy at the edges. Six main tributaries, each rising in a ravine, flow off the plateau, coalescing, together with a lowland-rising tributary, to the single watercourse downstream. Above the tip of the ravines are depressions in the plateau, roughly

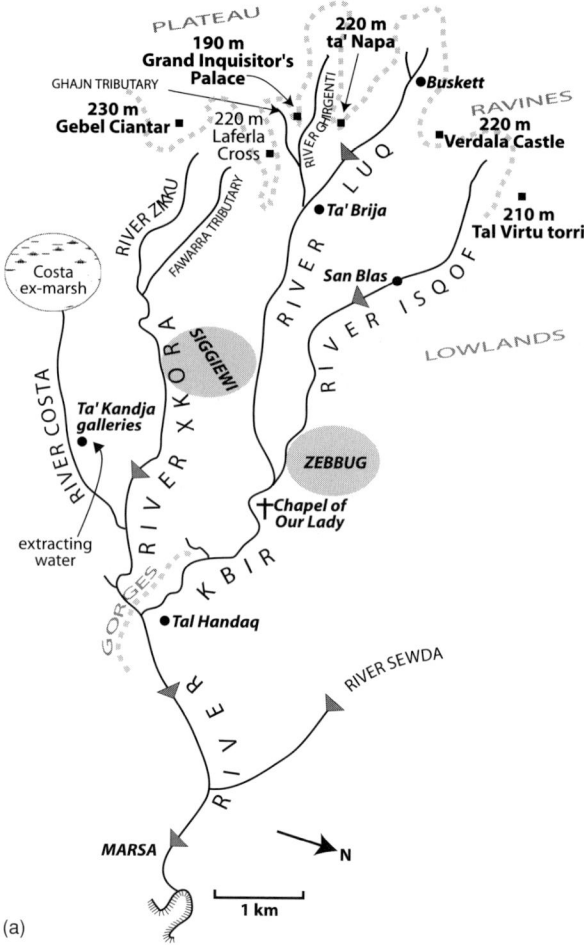

(a)

Fig. 3.3. River Kbir, Malta. (a) River map, showing main riverscape types. (b) Upper ravine of R. Isqof, showing Upper Coralline rock with plateau above (behind viewer with ex-marsh depression), then cliffy with patches of maquis, and springs particularly on its junction with the impervious blue clay layer below. Terracing is concentric (cwm), the soil is fertile and where irrigated can grow good quality fruit, as in (b), another head, with citrus (wetter parts only), also peach, nectarine, medlar. All also grow vegetables and grain. (c) Lower ravine, plateau far left, opening to *Globigerina* lowlands below. (d) Main lowland stretch, with the (dried) river sunk in a small gorge. Arable fields, drystone walls. The fields are not irrigated (no springs or river water), so there are no late-summer crops or fruit. There used to be large springs in the river to the right, allowing a small hamlet to develop, (with defensive-style houses). (e) Former Lake Costa, a sink-hole lake drained after the 1830s (public health) legislation. old buildings are all on the rim. (f) River farm, built by and to use the river. (g) Water level much lowered by dredging. Fertile valley, liable to raiding, so farmer's rooms are 2-storey so in the past people could take refuge upstairs, having pulled up the ladder. (h) River formerly as moat under the high defensive walls of Zebbug. (i) Lower river well sunk in gorge, rocky sides. Formerly grazed by herds of sheep and goats (now rare).

The natural riverscape and its modification 69

(b)

(c)

Fig. 3.3. (*cont.*)

(d)

(e)

Fig. 3.3. (*cont.*)

The natural riverscape and its modification 71

(f)

(g)

Fig. 3.3. (*cont.*)

(h)

(i)

Fig. 3.3. (*cont.*)

delta-shaped, the point tipping over into the stream head in the ravine. These depressions were once marsh, trapping winter water (plus having springs), and they helped to stabilise the flow in the rivers below. The ravines have spring-filled Coralline limestone above, then steep slopes of fertile clay with (softer) limestone below, which extends over the lowlands. A short distance below the ravines (from near 100 m to near 1 km) the rivers are sunk in shallow gorges 5–15 m deep, which cannot be seen from a distance: the rivers are invisible. Downstream the gorges sink deeper, 30–40 m and eventually within hard (but Lower) Coralline limestone again. These Great Gorges have rounded, not cliffy tops, and fewer springs than the ravines. One of the component tributaries is outside this pattern. R. Costa rose in a (now-dried) sink-hole lake in the lowlands, then flowed at ground level until sinking into a Great Gorge. Near the mouth, the gorge diminishes to a small one, then the river passes over the alluvial flats to the sea at the head of Grand Harbour.

The Great Plateau is partly cultivated, partly (to the south) garigue, the tundra-like Mediterranean vegetation with short woody plants and herbaceous winter ones. It also occurs on shallow soil in the Great Gorges. Maquis, the Mediterranean sclerophyll short woodland (with many deciduous shrubs too) is mostly in the sheltered undercliffs of the ravines, places too awkward to terrace, but with, including cracks, enough soil for trees. Towards exposed promontories both maquis and biodiversity lessen. Maquis also occurs in suitable places in the Great Gorges. Deciduous woodland occurs in, particularly one, ravine valley, and evergreen (pine-dominated) wood dominates other slopes. The largest is mostly a seventeenth-century planted wood-garden (for hunting and hawking), though there is a small ancient pinewood to the side. As the knights of St John named the ancient wood The Wood (the "bosc") and the planted wood The Little Wood (Boschetto; now Buskett) it can be assumed the main wood used to be much bigger. Copses also occur in Great Gorges.

Herbaceous communities are mainly ruderal or field, in gorge valley bottoms, waste places, etc. Cultivation is on part of the Great Plateau, on the terraced slopes of the ravines, of course, on the lowlands, and also on the steep but not cliffy slopes, and wider bottoms, of the great gorges. Some of the latter fields are terraces barely 2 m wide and over 3 m high: cultivated only in extremes, or from sentiment! Farming is now mostly by part-timers, leading to intensive cultivation or near-abandoned fields. There is no time to maintain walls, so terraces are at risk and the European Union is helping with repair. Orchards are mostly in the more sheltered and damper ravines, with citrus, the most water demanding, near the heads where are the most springs. Olive is on the driest of the cultivated slopes.

In the 1830s the Government ordered drainage of the freshwater marshes, for public health (fevers, probably including malaria). The 1853 Flora (Grech Delicata, 1853) lists only half the number of species found later (c. 1600), but it includes a good (no doubt truncated) list of water and wetland limestone species, few of which now survive (Table 3.1). There were rivers, marshes and still waters with good biodiversity in the 1940s. The drainage continued, and indeed for small areas still continues, so that even small (e.g. 5 m × 5 m) wetlands (away from rivers and the dredged bird reserves) are indeed rare. In the 1890s, abstraction for drinking water and mains started: and has increased practically every year since, in spite of adding Reverse Osmosis supply in the 1980s. Springs from the plateaux have had what should be their water removed by boreholes, and most remaining water is taken lower, also for irrigation. In about 1890 rivers still flowed down their main length (Haslam & Borg, 1998) certainly for enough of the year for their usual level to be incised on the rock beside (see also Chapter 4). Since then, probably every decade has shown a substantial drying. The once spring-filled ravine streams have winter trickles or only storm flow, the lowland and gorge streams have only severe storm flows: and perennial pools from the few remaining springs in the river bed. The side tributaries, the greater length in the earlier twentieth century, have gone or act as storm-flow channels only.

River vegetation from being good has become sparse and – reflecting the input – pollution-tolerant. What a depressing loss of biodiversity! And in all Malta. The largest coastal alluvial plain was drained in 1861–3 (which much improved public health) and gradually became built, and re-built. It is now a busy, vibrant commercial and industrial area, with, of course, no old centre. There are two towns on the lowland plain, Zebbug and Siggiewi (apart from Qormi, which is now encroaching on the river). These were farming centres, in good fertile land. There were also scattered farms and hamlets on the ravines above. Those are remote, seeming tens of miles from urban Marsa. All old settlements must have a water source: springs, stream or collected rainfall enough for people and preferably for livestock as well. Most remote farms are on springs in the ravines, and on the river beds in the lowlands. The towns presumably had hill springs. Zebbug, at least, had river bed springs, and both had rivers mostly flowing.

Communications were unlikely to be by boat, but were along by the rivers because these were rights of way, giving access to farmland and dwellings. (The government or military road network was centred on the capital.) Paths, now lanes, are along most ravine streams and most of the lowland and gorge streams have a path or lane. (Some are now closed, by hunters.) Particularly between Siggiewi and downstream of Zebbug, there is evidence of much former transport, by people and herds.

Table 3.1 *Loss of aquatic species in Malta*

1853 Probably too few, as surveys partial. (Grech Delicata, 1853)	1990s frequent species
Alisma plantago-aquatica	*Alisma plantago-aquatica*
Apium graveolens	
Apium inundatum	
Apium nodiflorum	*Apium nodiflorum*
Colocasia esculenta	
Cyperus badius	
Cyperus longus (margin)	*Cyperus longus*
Elatine macropoda	
Eleocharis palustris	*Eleocharis palustris*
Epilobium tetragonum (edges)	
Glyceria maxima (edges)	
Glyceria plicata	
Lemna minor	*Lemna minor*
Lythrum junceum	
Mentha aquatica	
Oenanthe globulosa	
Ranunculus fluitans	
Ranunculus peltatus (probably not mis-named for *R. trichophyllus* as habitat differs)	*Ranunculus trichophyllus*
Rorippa nasturtium-aquaticum	*Rorippa nasturtium-aquaticum*
Schoenoplectus lacustris	
Scirpus holoschoenus	*Scirpus holoschoenus*
Scirpus maritimus	
Sparganium erectum	
Typha domingensis	*Typha domingensis*
Veronica anagallis-aquatica	*Veronica anagallis-aquatica*
Veronica beccabunga	
	Blanket weed (long, filamentous algae, mainly *Cladophora glomerata*)
Found in 1920s in rainwater pools on hard limestone (mostly clean water). And surely occurring in 1853! (Borg, 1927)	
Callitriche stagnalis	*Isoetes hystrix*
Callitriche truncata	*Juncus bufonius*
Crassula vaillanti	*Ranunculus baudotii*
Damasonium bourgaei	*Ranunculus trichophyllus*
Elatine gussonei	*Zannichellia palustris*
Eleocharis ovata	
In the 1990s this list was contracted	

A few river species occur very rarely, e.g. *Juncus articulatus, Myriophyllum verticillatum, Potamogeton pectinatus*.

More were recorded 1840–1930, but not in 1960s, e.g. *Callitriche brutia, Callitriche palustris, Juncus capitatus, Myosoton aquaticum, Potamogeton crispus, Potamogeton natans*.

Two damp, formerly fringing species, both tolerant to pollution, are now also frequent within damp watercourses: *Arundo donax* and *Rumex conglomeratus*.

Grazing was an important function of land not easily cultivated, with many herds of sheep and goats (now kept indoors), keeping accessible vegetation short up to the c. 1960s (it now reaches normal heights).

Malta was subject to raids from, particularly, the south Mediterranean until about 1800, with invasion threatened up to 1945, so there were both local and national defences in the R. Kbir catchment. The national ones were forts on each of the Great Plateau promontories which, before recent settlement and tree growth, could watch over all the lowlands to the harbours and sea beyond. The present forts date back from British (1802–1964) to Knights of St John (1530–1798) to (out of this catchment) Roman: and no doubt there were earlier ones. There were, of course, roads to the garrison centres. The valleys provided cover, and were the main ways inland for raiders from the east and north east coasts.

Farmhouses and isolated farmers' rooms had thick walls, slit windows, and often no access to the first floor (ladders that could be pulled up). Raiders wanting food rather than slaves and in a hurry might just take the food and run. The towns had narrow alleys with sharp bends to cause delay (and hope for troops from the forts), and defensive houses. Zebbug, the downstream village, also had a huge wall – and moat – on the valley side. Compared with England, with only one war on the land since 1500, and that a civil one, this is a depressing – though fascinating – pattern.

Lake Costa, a now-cultivated sink-hole in the lowland limestone, drained in the nineteenth century, is the only (large) one like this in Malta, and as such, also fascinating.

A final principal feature is the distribution of the cane *Arundo donax*, the great reed, growing in damp places, but not in deep or scouring water, or on gravel or stones (needs some soil). Once found on banks of ravine streams, it now often covers the bed as the water is less. More interestingly, it occurs on springs and seepage areas, and remains even when water level is well below ground. On the plateau deltas, a few cane patches mark ancient springs. Most clumps are under the plateau cliffs which now have some, and formerly much, spring water, but they also occur on gorge walls, by river bed springs, and indeed in the fields (though there they may mark where water is led by underground channel or pipe to a 'well').

The driving forces of the R. Kbir catchment (apart from the flows already described) are:

- food production, which used to occupy every possible square metre, in a far more desperate way than in R. Cam. Farming is now becoming more of a leisure activity (imported food is cheap and easy);
- communications, between villages and fields, and between main garrisons, forts and invaders;

- defence from raiders in the construction of villages and (later) isolated farms, and the placing and abundance of national defences;
- water. The country changed from being wet to dry from excess abstraction and drainage;
- leisure activities, particularly the shooting and trapping of most species of migrant (and indigenous) birds, endangered or otherwise. The 'best' part is on the south of the Great Plateau. Removing birds affects other parts of the ecosystem also, e.g. allowing enormous numbers of snails;
- quite as bad is the planting of Australian Eucalyptus, of which a five-figure number are probably now in the R. Kbir, and a six-figure one in the whole island. No native tree is this shape, so Eucalyptus – particularly on skylines, such as promontories of the Great Plateau – is destroying native views, sense of place, natural and cultural heritage. Eucalyptus also takes more water than any other tree: not helpful when water is so scarce. It has poisonous oils, so decreases biodiversity (including bird food) around it, and takes up much nutrient from the very shallow soil. But it attracts birds for slaughter: the driving force;
- quarrying for stone occurs both on the Great Plateau and, particularly, around the start of the Great Gorges near Siggiewi, where the land consists of pits, altering any remaining water flow as well as, totally, the riverscape. (Over 80% of Malta's waste is rejected stone: not badly polluting, but filling land fills unnecessarily and being dumped around, too.);
- increased wealth has led to over- (and unsuitable) building, not just in villages, but in the open and formerly beautiful places, too. Control is little. Wealth has also led to destruction of natural heritage by roads and traffic, bird slaughter, pollution, etc. Rubbish, and stone from house or quarry, is freely dumped, particularly by roads in valleys.

(Also see Haslam *et al.*, 2004.)

4   R. Golo, Corsica (Fig. 3.4)

R. Golo rises in the extremely steep and jagged forested Alps of central Corsica (reaching nearly 9000 m), falling quickly to the alluvial coastal plain. Rainfall is up to 1800 mm/year, mostly from September to December, but enough in summer to avoid a full drought. Human impact has never been great, though it has been moderate for many millennia, unlike the R. Waccasassa catchment. It has, in fact, decreased in the last century, when, particularly, the inland population was able to move and find a better living in less remote places. The river and riverscape are in a good traditional state.

78 The riverscape and the river

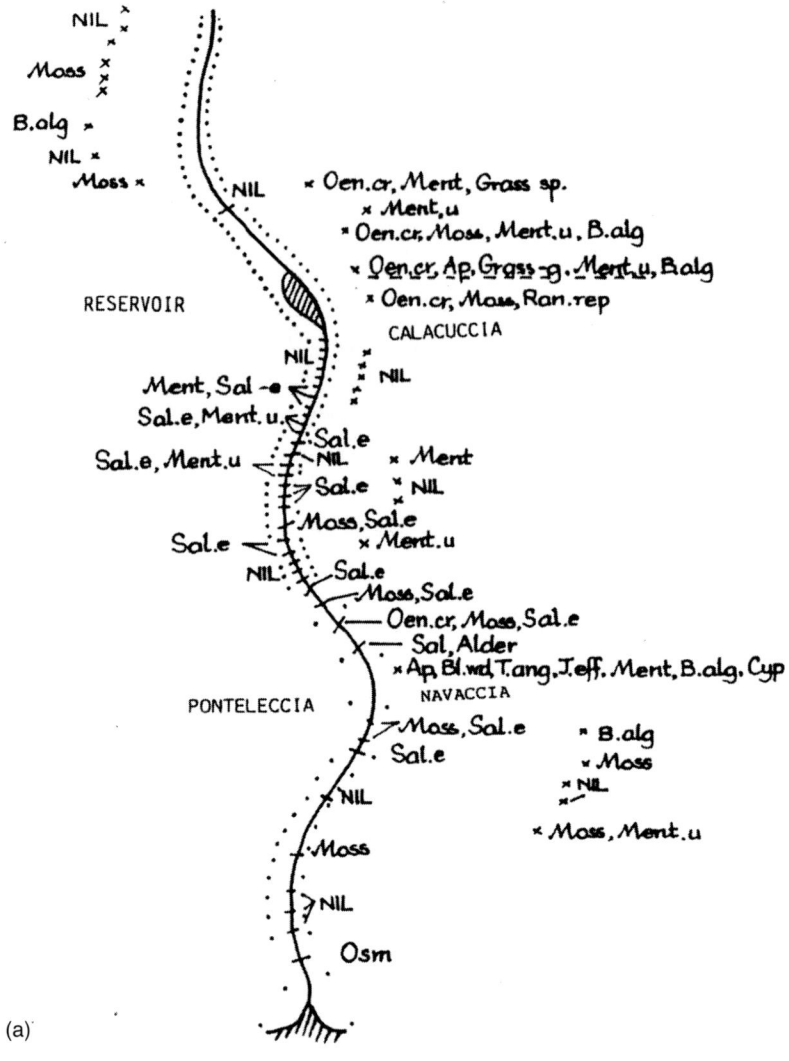

(a)

Fig. 3.4. River Golo, Corsica, France. (a) Vegetation map of main river. Mosses and *Salix* the main species. Very steep valley, and little lowland flow at the base. (b) R. Navaccia tributary, rising on 'garigue-moorland', with more vegetation. (c) Tributaries rising in foothills, much steeper than the R. Navaccia riverscape. See Fig. 13.6 for the upper rivers. (d) Middle river, species include *Osmunda regalis* and Mosses. Species include *Callitriche* spp., *Alisma plantago-aquatica*, *Myriophyllum spicatum*, *Ranunculus* spp., *Cyperus* spp. and *Sparganium erectum*. The whitewater pristine river down the steep mountain has plenty of habitat niches, but few are sheltered enough for macrophytes. The valley is quite steep, and most is forested, suitable open areas (flatter, so falling enables farming) are or were settled.

The natural riverscape and its modification 79

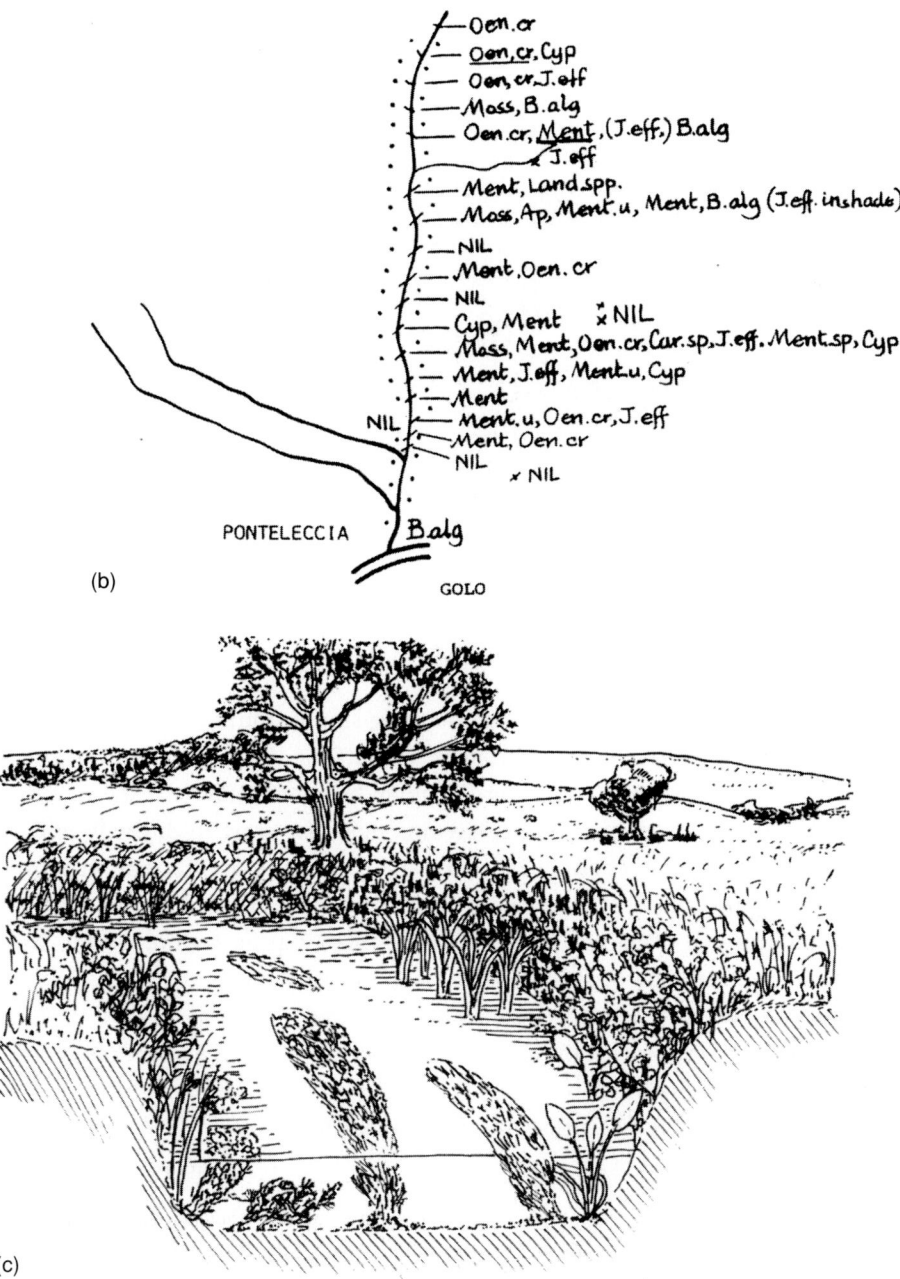

Fig. 3.4. (cont.)

80   The riverscape and the river

(d)

Fig. 3.4. (*cont.*)

With little drainage, there are innumerable small mountain streams, which rise in shallow depressions with gathered run-off, or in steep bouldery valleys. Above the perennial water, the flow line may be marked by bracken or other tall herbs. (In the lower mountains, streams may also start in dry valleys with land plants in the flow channel in summer.) The slopes are garigue in higher and more exposed places, or wooded. Wooded streams are shaded. However, the largest tributary, R. Navaccia, is in a garigue-moor flatter region, with a wide open riverscape, instead of an enclosed, steep, forested one.

Part-way down there is a grassy, open (long-cleared) alp, with an ancient small (and decreasing) settlement. Here, there are also crops irrigated by a network of low-force diverted streams.

The main Golo has exceptionally high water force (as in the Pyrenees) so is rocky, bouldery, and with little vegetation. Water force decreases down in the coastal plain, where the river is embanked to protect the farmland. The cultivated land has been ditched and drained. This is the traditional pattern, before deep drainage and channelling. There are also lowland tributaries flowing to the Golo. Reedswamp species like *Phragmites australis* and *Typha* sp. occur, as does *Arundo* (see above) in places damp rather than wet. There are some lowland tributaries flowing to the Golo.

Terracing has been little: Corsican populations have been low compared to area, unlike Malta, so there was less need for intensive cultivation on slopes.

Driving forces of the R. Golo catchment, apart from the flows already discussed, are:

- food production, traditionally swine in the forests, but also crops on the coast and locally elsewhere. Food is needed only for a small local population (unlike Malta's ever-increasing dependence on imports for life, not just for luxuries);
- exports: cork (and other forest products).

(Water is in ample supply, and the Corsican rock being resistant, there are no large aquifers to exhaust, unlike Malta, so water is not a driving force in the same way.)

5   R. Don (Aberdeen) Scotland (Fig. 3.5)

R. Don rises in the rather rounded Cairngorm (resistant rock) mountains, over 600 m high. It passes down foothills and then through the largest agricultural lowlands in the Highlands before reaching the sea at Aberdeen. The Cairngorms bear heather moor, with bog in wetter places. Upper streams used to gather and wind in the living bog, but peat drainage in the 1980s led to channel straightening, speeding flow and erosion. The brown water became darker while peat was eroding. Further down the mountain, streams were dug out, so replacing nutrient-poor edge vegetation (e.g. *Juncus articulatus*) with that of disturbed-soil banks (e.g. fringing herbs). Nutrient-poor species increased in the rivers, because of the peat. Grassy-grazing increases downhill. The lowlands are cultivated and now that the peat and acid vegetation have gone, and fertility is added, the habitat has changed from nutrient-poor to fairly nutrient-rich. Fields are divided by hedges, while on the mountains boundaries are separated by (Scots) dykes (dry stone walls). The riverscape thus alters from purple moor to (fairly small) fields below.

Tributaries, small and larger, arise throughout the catchment. They are denser in the hills, since rainfall is higher, and drainage and drying have been less. Straightening is incomplete, even downstream, though the land is fairly dry.

Settlement is sparse, crofts with an occasional hamlet in the mountains, increasing to villages and scattered farms in the lowlands. Kintore is a town and, at the mouth, Aberdeen, a city, being the county town, and the main city of the fertile north-east. In contrast to R. Kbir, defences are not extant. Although with a turbulent early history, there has been little unrest since *c.* 1600: the period when the Knights of St John were intensively re-fortifying Malta.

Driving forces of the R. Don catchment, excluding the flows described earlier are:

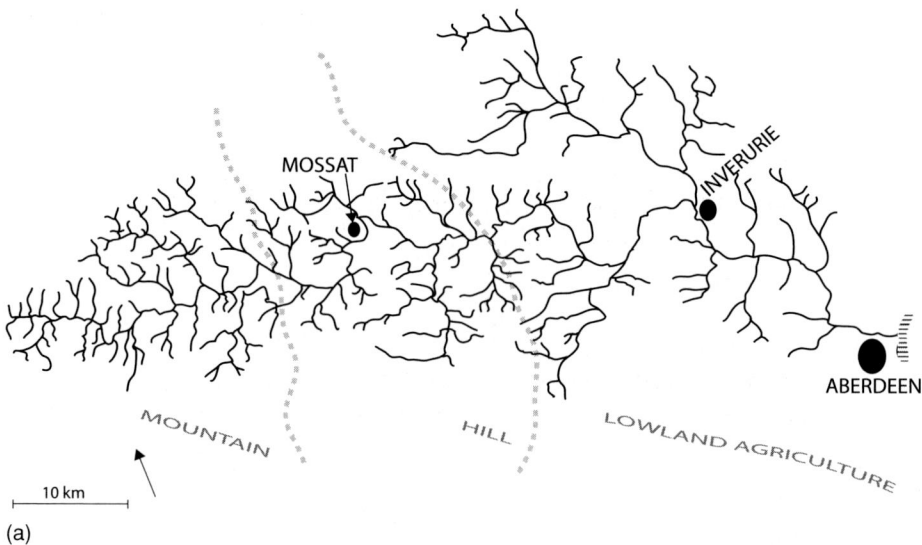

(a)

(b)

Fig. 3.5. River Don (Aberdeen), Scotland. (a) River map, showing main riverscape types. (b) Stream in the Cairngorm mountains, eroding bog peat, moorland, and mountain behind. Run-off, and river water, coloured by the peat. (Contrast Icelandic tundra, Maltese garigue, and Corsican grass-moorland.) (c) Tributary stream in the agricultural foothills, where (ex-) mills are frequent. Fields well managed and productive on nutrient-low resistant rock. (d) Lower river in agricultural lowlands. Features indicate resistant rock, liability to spate from the mountain rains, but generally stable substrate and ample vegetation in various building blocks, particularly tall monocots and oval-tailed fine-leaved. (Contrasted with the very unstable neighbouring R. Dee, with little vegetation and wide gravelly beds.)

The natural riverscape and its modification 83

(c)

(d)

Fig. 3.5. (cont.)

- food production, farming in the lowlands, rough grazing and local small fields brought into cultivation further up;
- sport (red deer, etc.) which has, for a couple of hundred years, prevented intensive efforts to make the mountains more productive, and so has been (until the 1980s) the most important tool for conserving the immensely valuable and unique heather moor;
- fish and oil. The good North Sea fishing provided the main coastal wealth until the oil development of the late twentieth century, which brought previously unheard-of wealth to Aberdeen;
- communications, which, until recently, were primarily by sea for freight, and the better roads were lowland. The nineteenth-century trains opened the formerly (and even now) remote area. An airport followed a century later;
- industry. In the countryside there were many (grain and other) mills in the catchment, and the two large paper mills (and a sugar factory) in recent times;
- drainage (no aquifer, no underground abstraction). Drying was important for the lowlands, but it is less than that of R. Cam and R. Kbir. The 1980s schemes in the mountains were unnecessarily destructive (tourism on such valuable habitat brings in at least as much money);
- general tourism, including winter skiing and summer rambling brings in money, but needs control as the land is easily eroded (Haslam, 1982, 1987, 1990).

6 *R. San Gorg, Malta*

To give a final contrasting catchment, that of the (small, even for Malta: 2 km river) San Gorg can be cited, as totally built up. Since 1950 it has been converted from cultivated terraces to residential and commercial buildings (much of the latter re-built twice). The stream, drying, was put beside the lane, then under the road but with gratings above the stream, then completely hidden except for its mouth. Surprisingly for Malta, it runs all year: but then effluents also run all year, and with polluted water.

Discussion

From the catchments of the R. Waccasassee to that of the R. San Gorg, riverscapes show immense diversity, diversity imposed by nature (rock type, topography, latitude, etc.) and by culture and history. There is no one-size-fits-all pattern, though various strands run through.

Whenever peoples settle, they alter the environment for their own benefit. Food must be produced and there must be ways to travel. The nineteenth-, still more the twentieth- and twenty-first-century impacts, are huge and disastrous, with the increases in population and wealth. To find traditional or pristine riverscapes is a bonus, undeserved because hardly anyone has actively tried to preserve them. Removing water as drainage, abstraction, and flood prevention is leading to unsustainable water deficits, and to the loss of streams and rivers. Those who view, without dismay, the loss of ditches should study Malta and see the later stages!

People can control and 'tame' riverscapes to an extent depending on:

- its nature and location (e.g. lowland, alpine; temperate, arctic; soil type (and what can be done with it); accessibility and potential communications);
- the density, technology and wealth of the population;
- the duration of human impact (early changes may restrict future choices);
- and the water resources.

4

Resources I. Water resources and their loss

> The well-being of the water environment is fundamental to sustainable development.
>
> (J. Gardiner, 1991)
>
> The sustainable development of a country requires wetlands in being.
>
> (W. Mitsch, 1994)

Introduction

Water is the most important component of life on earth. Living organisms are mostly water (e.g. a baby over 70%, lettuce over 90%). All must be able to maintain this content, against the constant pull of evapotranspiration, evaporation and secretion.

The water is replenished, ultimately, from precipitation. Depending on the species, it comes from rain (snow, ice) or dew, and surface, soil or ground water. Where there is life, there is water.

Water therefore passes from rain to river through the riverscape. That which does not, evaporates direct from the rain (varying with climate and surface cover). That which does, may be absorbed above the soil, by plants mostly, or pass above the soil, through it, or through lower levels in the ground (subsoil, aquifer). This last may be little (impermeable rock close to surface) or much (wet peat, alluvium, aquifer).

Sheet flow is usually only in very heavy storms (though these may be frequent, e.g. Chapter 3, R. Waccasassee, or extremely rare). The water may flow to the river or, and more so on steeper land, it may gather into watercourses first. Surface flow, just on or within the soil, is more usual. On slopes, rainsplash and overland flow is discontinuous in space and time, but is a single interacting phenomenon

(Petts & Foster, 1985). Vegetation protects the surface from raindrop erosion, as it intercepts rain above, and its roots bind soil below ground level (Petts & Foster, 1985).

In Malta in the early twentieth century, one-third of the rainfall went down to the aquifers (Borg, 1927), at a time when only about 5% of the island was built up, and terraces and flow patterns were maintained. (Now about a third is built up, and the terraces, etc., not properly maintained.)

The wetness of the land before drainage, in both Europe and North America, is now forgotten, and so assumed non-existent. North America was more recently wet, in inhabited lowlands, so vivid descriptions occur in novels (e.g. Dickens, 1868; Yonge, 1864) In Britain, some well-known descriptions occur in Bunyan (1682) and in Defoe (1724–7). As late as the nineteenth century, doctors would recommend invalids to live on the gravel part of town, as being drier. From Scotland with its blanket bog down south to Malta with its marshes, the land was wet, heavy to till, wet to walk on, very wet and muddy in its roads, wet to an extent now almost unbelievable. Fine ladies were not just being over-refined when they restricted their walking to places which would not ruin their clothes!

As a revulsion from this, it now takes effort to remember that water is the prime resource for the natural world, and for people, their livestock and crops.

The European Union Water Framework Directive

The effects of this Directive will be shown on the land in the next decade or so, and, if carried out correctly, it is the best hope for water protection and conservation for the 27 countries of the EU, from Ireland in the west to Hungary in the east (except for Switzerland) and from Sweden in the north to Malta in the south. In the preamble is: *Water is not a commercial product like any other but, rather, a heritage which must be protected, defended and treated as such.* Its five purposes [Article 1] are:

1. The prevention of further deterioration and the protection and enhancement of the status of aquatic ecosystems. (At present, such a wish is about as realistic as that of seeing Father Christmas in the chimney.)
2. The promotion of sustainable water use. (Anyone can *promote*, who can do it?)
3. The enhanced protection and improvement of the aquatic environment. (Surely a little. But more?)
4. The progressive reduction of pollution of groundwater. (While now it is mostly increasing in populous and cultivated areas?)
5. The mitigation of the effects of floods and droughts. (Where these damage property, something will be done.)

With luck, the bracketed comments will become untrue! The present deterioration is rapid and destructive. It has been greatly under-recorded because it often takes a decade or even more to be sure changes in surface waters are happening and are permanent: and far too often personnel are not in place for that period (official A enjoys a small stream. B sees it dry a couple of times and notices some brown water. C sees a little polluted stream flowing only in winter, not deserving attention. D is surprised to see some water in a ditch in a wet winter. Since A had no reason to expect destruction, no records were made).

The Directive specifies the catchment, the river basin, as the primary unit. A river basin here is the area of land from which all surface run-off flows, through a sequence of streams, rivers and possibly lakes to a particular point, which leads to lake, other river or sea. It is directed that each river basin is to be described in such a way that both impacts and features can be compared from time to time. This, if carried out, will be invaluable. Up to now, various countries (e.g. Britain) have described their rivers by the name of their catchments, but describing the catchment has occurred only when intensive research has been done on a few basins, usually of conservation importance or near a research station. And the project has ended when the grant ended or researcher retired: it has been an individual not a national policy, matter. Under the Directive the loss of the stream mentioned above should be recorded. Provided that both features (from river to flush, arable to wetland, etc.) and impacts (from cultivation to fishing, boreholes to bridges, etc.) are properly identified and assessed, these characterisations will make a huge contribution to the understanding, interpretation and potential improvement of unsustainable and destructive use.

These characterisations are to lead to Programmes of Measures, which in turn should lead to Good Ecological Status. (Basic Measures will be required, Supplementary ones will be either required by codes, guidelines, or be voluntary. High Ecological Status is what would be present in the absence of human impact, theoretically. Since this cannot be found in Europe (Chapter 1), it is Good Ecological Status, close to that referred to in this book as the Traditional, which is to be aimed for. (The difference is that Good Status can be what is imagined in an office, high biodiversity, native patterns, etc., while the Traditional is linked to what used to be, or is still, there, on land or water.)

To try to ensure all freshwaters remain in a good state, or are improving towards it, assessments are required every 3 years, which experience suggests is adequate, provided Environmental Impact Assessments are carried out before waters (including aquifers and small brooks) are altered, and the requirements of the Directive taken into account.

European Union policy should now be based on a combined approach, using control of damage, e.g. of pollution at source (not just at the point of entry of an effluent), through the setting of emission limits and of environmental standards. Since these are mostly non-existent, and nearly all pollutants are never measured (tens of thousands! Most potentially present everywhere on land and sea), there is a possible loophole. It takes much expertise to detect a lowering of biotic quality by 2%, considerable, to detect 20%, though very little for 80%. How much will be done?

Sustainable use means understanding that human impact is integrated with ecosystem functions. Catchment integrity is both the natural flows of water, energy, organisms and sediment, but also that of cultivation, transport, settlements and other economic driving forces. The expertise for this, again, is not yet available.

With these flows downstream, upstream impacts in catchments are likely to influence downstream rivers and maybe catchments. Increasing firm or hard surface upstream increases flash floods downstream, for instance. Overgrazing on hill slopes well above the river can lead to excess erosion above, and excess sedimentation below. Silting up trout spawning areas may destroy a valuable trout fishery.

To consider the catchment as a unit, the impacts as a unit from hill top to sea, should, gradually, alleviate much of this.

The functioning river and riverscape

Over the past 10 000 years (the retreat of the last Ice Age) climate, including rainfall, has varied (Table 2.1). Therefore, its effects have also varied. What is visible now are the integrated past influences, overlaid in most parts by the present extreme impact.

The slope of the riverscape is coupled to the floodplain. It feeds it.

The water pathways of the slope determine many characteristics of landscape, and so of land use, and both affect hydrology. Whether the pattern formed is dendritic or a single pathway depends on rain, rock and topography. Denser streams are ordinarily with impervious rock and more rain. Impact modifies. For instance, a hill to be used for forestry may be drained first, leading to fewer streams, erosion and floods downstream. Later, clear felling may much increase run-off and, again, erosion: with effects downstream. Firm soil may have sheet run-off and stream erosion upstream, floods downstream. A hill stream may be 2–3 m deeper after the hill soil has been rolled compact (see Burt *et al.*, 1993).

Minor streams flow down to meet major streams and they may cross the flood plain with this water, nutrients, other solutes, etc., and biota.

The river of the riverscape is coupled to the flood plain. It feeds it.

The flood plain – traditionally – is the area regularly flooded by the river. More of the sediment, biota and debris it carries may be deposited nearer the river as the water movement slows. The water with its solutes reaches furthest. The plain is fertilised by the flood. Or, of course it may also be polluted. During the flood, there is fresh good habitat – including food – for birds (waders, duck), fish and others. Phytoplankton grow rapidly – and are food. If the flood lasts long, aquatic vegetation can grow, also. When the flood subsides, not just sediment but nutrients, remains of the flood biota, and pollutants, remain. If wetlands border the river, they remain wet as the flood retreats, but augmented. Drier land dries more. The river feeds the plain, and the water stored in the plain later feeds the river. This water stored may be river flood water, it may come from the tributary streams crossing the plain or it may come from underground. Underground water may have flowed laterally from the river or come from the slope above. Not all run-off comes as surface flow. Water moves down in soil and subsoil and reaches the surface in flushes and springs, some beside or in the flood plain (Fig. 4.1). If there is aquiferous rock below, water also sinks into this and, very slowly, moves, leaving as springs in places dictated by rock variations (bedding planes, permeability) and topography. This may include the flood plain or the slope beside. The flood plain, can, therefore, provide water to the river, during lower flows, from a variety of sources and natural base flow may have depended on this.

The network of water movements below ground, though superficial, was great and could be changed by weights (e.g. crowds standing) or stream alterations, etc. Remnants of this still occur. In buffer strips by rivers, when rain flows downslope, it does not flow direct to the river, but wiggles along a flow path. This can be 150 m long in a buffer strip just 15 m wide (Haycock & Pinay, 1993).

This is the coupling of the riverscape and river in the traditional catchment. It is driven by rainfall (precipitation) and gravity, and in one general direction, downstream. All forms one system. Until, that is, impact breaks it into separate parts, so drainage and flood protection separate stream from flood plain, even stream from stream, underground water from underground water (Haslam, 2003), underground from stream and stream channel from water.

This impact loses diversity of habitat, and diversity of water type, as well as total water (Fig. 4.1, Table 4.1). It also compresses habitats: gradients and transitions become a fence or wall, so the variable communities of the transition are lost. Kirby (1992) points out the extreme importance of even tiny wetter habitats, such as footprints in soggy ground, to invertebrate communities. Even the smallest seepage area, muddy patch or transition zone may be vital for the existence of some community.

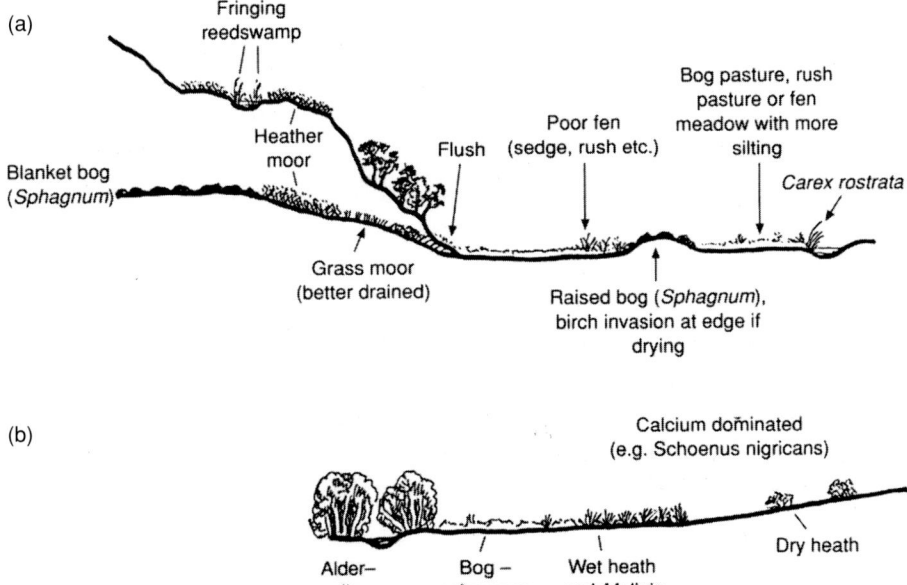

Fig. 4.1. Landscape sections to show representative floodplain habitat. Britain (Y. Bower in Haslam, 2003). (a) Low silting, nutrient-low run-off from bog (gathered run-off from slope as flush), fairly nutrient-low overspill from river. Acid peaty soils accumulate and grow, siltier near the river where most river silt is deposited, peatier away from it. After some drainage and management, this is bearing various types of bog pasture and poor fen. Raised bog may develop in large plains. More drainage, fertiliser, etc., would be needed to develop fertile grassland. (b) Low silting, lowland acid sands, low-nutrient stream. As even low-nutrient silt contains much more nutrients than peat, the silted river banks bear alder-sallow wood. Beyond, lies bog, wet from nutrient-deficient springs from above as well as some river water (non-silty). Up the slope the habitat dries, leading to wet heath (and up-slope, dry heath. (c) Low silting, lowland chalk Downs at side, so run-off water is calcium-dominated (e.g. *Schoenus nigricans*) at the base of the slope, calcium-influenced (e.g. *Cladium mariscus*) further off, where the water is slightly influenced by river flood water. Passing further towards the river, nutrient-rich silt increases. Without drainage, there is fen peat, or peaty silt soils develop. With some drainage tall herb or alderwood (depending on past and present management: assuming marsh hay was abandoned). (d) High-silting. The plain is silt, not peat. There was too much incoming silt for peat to develop. Silt is much more nutrient-rich. The vegetation, when partly drained, is tall herb, woodland and, with some management, pasture. (e), (f) Gravel and sand plains, sediment deposited by the river. These drain well, so are drier, and need little management to grow grass or woodland. Water rises and falls quickly, and no peat can develop. (g)–(j) Water movement in the same habitats, before drainage (i) and (j) are with and without springs. Note water sources. (k) Effect of drainage.

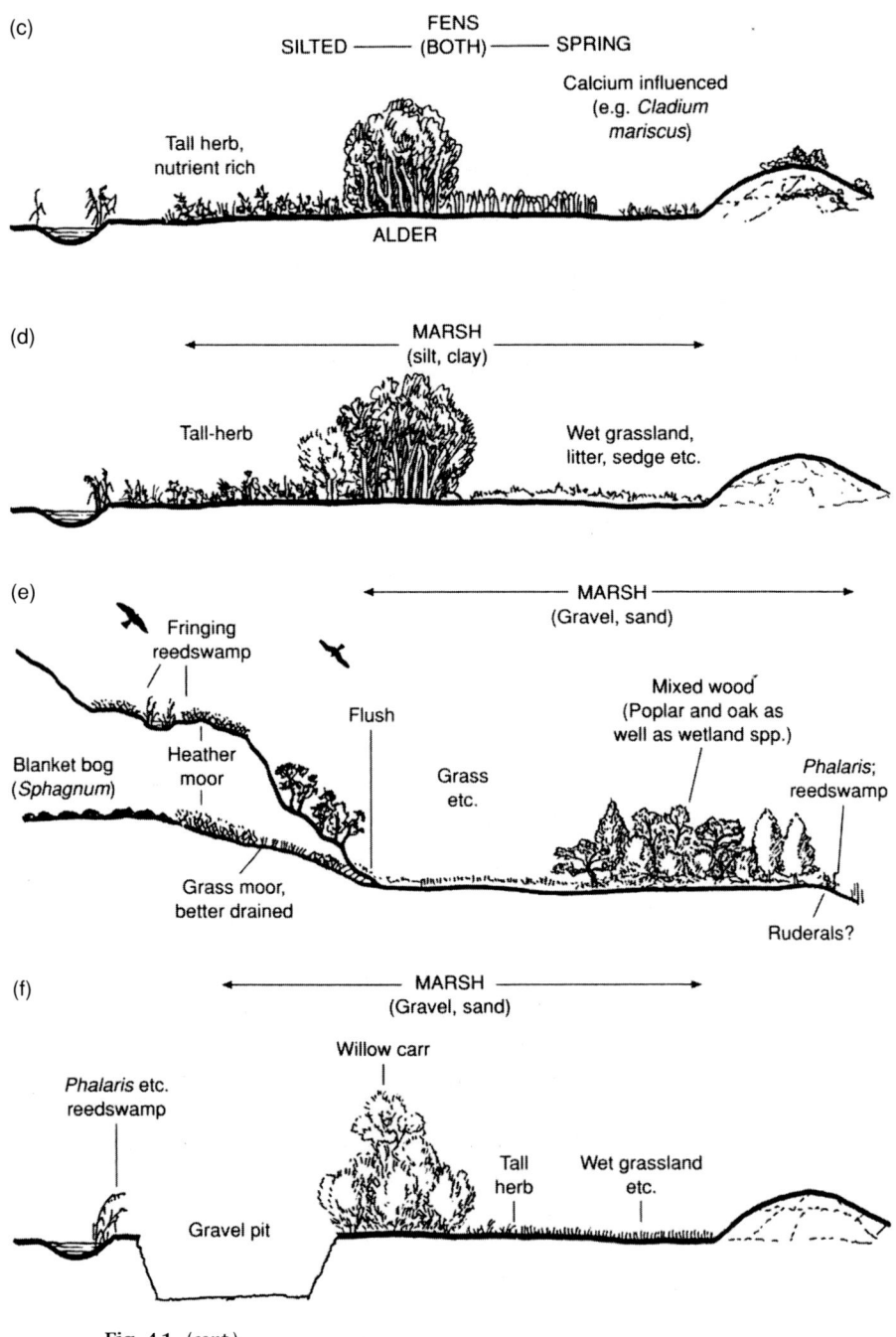

Fig. 4.1. (cont.)

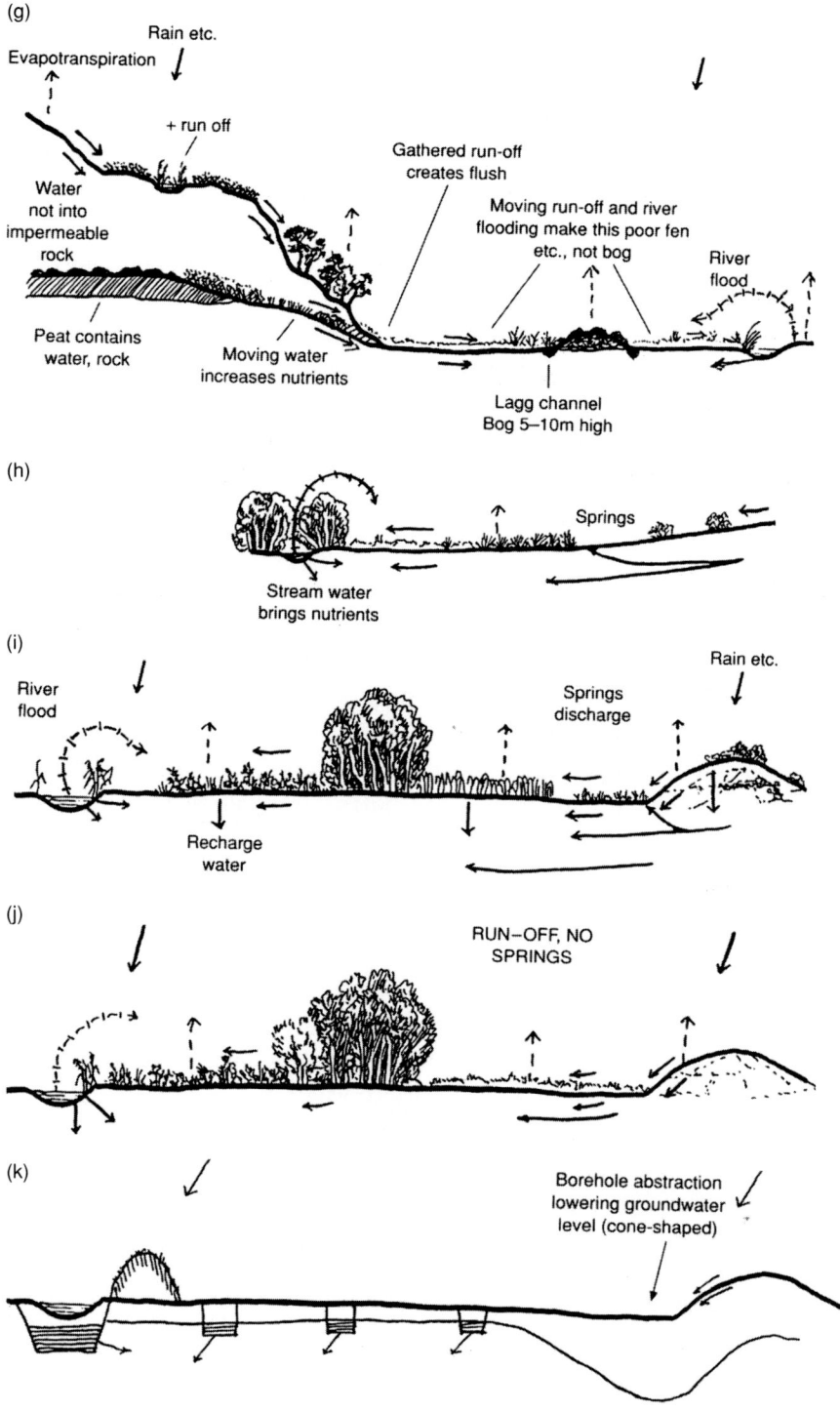

Fig. 4.1. (cont.)

The exact pattern and speed of water movement varies greatly. Van Bouren & Kerkstra (1993) describe an example: a Dutch site with clay hills having sands above and a deep aquifer below. Groundwater flow systems are separated – but exist – and springs feed small brooks. In this system, water sinks down (infiltration zone) rather than up where hill meets low land. The groundwater (from rain and surface water) flows to stream valleys and springs (exfiltration zones). The upper springs are at a nick point in rock type and slope, and are stream sources. The lower ones are where the aquifer becomes thin and incoming groundwater from uphill leads to springs (Fig. 11.3).

Superimposed, there is small-scale topography pattern with its own local flow patterns. This gives dense brooks, between the others. (Note the combined effect of two water patterns.)

This site has arable above, meadows below, with the farms on the slope, where the springs are (springs give perennial water that does not flood). There was much bog and marsh. Drainage then removed wetlands, it intensified agriculture and gave regulated watercourses: decreasing the natural coupling, the hydrochemical gradients, and the groundwater. By this time, heavy rain meant flash floods; agrochemicals and urban run-off fed into shallow groundwater, polluting both it and the streams that fed it. The wetlands were threatened with drought and pollution. The historic riverscape was fragmented for the water cycle and the traditional habitats diminished in biodiversity because groundwater was lost, and polluted. Remedial action was taken for the pollution (this being the Netherlands), urban streams had buffer strips put round them, and agricultural ones were led through marshes.

The example of Malta

This is a sad tale of how a whole – though less than 250 sq km for the largest island – country changed from being wet, with excess water for human use, to dry, with virtually no perennial surface water and human reliance on Reverse Osmosis plants, in less than 200 years.

Malta is mostly limestone, and with around 500 mm rainfall, mostly in winter, the aquifers were filled and provided perennial springs and streams, and winter-wet to perennial marshes. In 1853, Grech Delicata could list ten surface water habitats, including slow-flowing rivers, small rivers, standing waters, and marshes. The species (Table 3.1) were, of course, characteristic of limestone, and included *Schoenus nigricans*, *Glyceria maxima*, *Sparganium erectum* and *Ranunculus fluitans*, all long gone.

Table 4.1 Damage to some East Anglian fens (selected from Wheeler & Shaw, 1992)

Site	Flora	Dehydration	Drains	Abstraction	Dereliction	Tall herb	Scrub	Peat extraction	Reclamation	other
Beeston bog						★	★		Agriculture	Nutrients added?
Beetley and Hoe meadows							★			
Bressingham fen	★★★★		★★★					✓		
Briston common	★★	★★?					★★	✓?		
Brock's watering			★			★				
Buxton Heath	★★	★?		★?			★★	✓	Fires/Sphagnum pulling	
Crostwick marsh	★★	★★	★?	★?						
Ducan's marsh	★	★		★	★★	★★	★★	✓	Agriculture	
East Ruston common	★★★★	★★★	★	★★★	★★★★	★★	★★	✓		Tip
Feltorpe bogs	★★★★	★★★?	★★★?		★★★	★★		✓	Forest	
Forncett meadows	?				★★	★	★			
Lopham fens	★★★	★★★	★★	★★	★★	★	★★	✓		
Cavenham	★★★	★★	★★		★★★	★★	★★	✓		
Poors' fen										
Icklingham	★★★	★★	★★		★★★	★★★	★★	✓		
Poors' fen				?						
Redgrave and Lopham fens	★★★	★★★	★★	★★★	★★	★★	★★	✓		Re-wetted, future?
Fowlmere	★★	★		★?	★★	★★	★	✓?		Watercress

There were five main water sources.

(1) the Upper Limestone springs. This is the top rock layer, lying above clay, and, with a full aquifer, numerous springs welled up at and a little above the impervious clay. These were the principal urban supply, via aqueducts, etc., until the 1890s. Outcrops are scattered, so yield depended on catchment and (the variable) rainfall. Oddly, after mid-August, at the end of the dry summer and before the autumn rains, spring flow increased (Borg, 1927). A few of the principal (human) source areas were Buskett, Fiddien, Isqof, Lunziata and Mgarr (Gozo). These were fruitful areas for wells and boreholes. Indeed, they still are, but the water is now too polluted with agrochemicals, and hard surface run-off for human consumption. Originally, the clean, lime-rich water was very low in other nutrients (kept down by the lime, e.g. Haslam, 2003). Consequently, the stream flora and fauna resembled those of chalkstreams elsewhere in Europe (corrected for latitude). Because of the enormous abstraction and the nutrient-rich pollution, such water has gone, though occasional lime-rich spring areas survive, with a flora depleted through both water loss and pollution. On the hard Coralline, rainwater pools may last for months or be perennial (depending on rainfall) and these bear the closest to traditional vegetation, though not the same.

(2) The deep level springs low on the soft *Globigerina* limestone, which forms most of lowland Malta and at the top of the hard Lower Coralline below it. Rain falling on the lowlands pushes the sea water down below sea level, giving a freshwater lens under the island. A third of rainfall went to this lens (Borg, 1927).

Springs rise in river beds (e.g. Haslam *et al.*, 2004) and earlier perhaps elsewhere. Water supply was uniform all year, though some varied with rainfall.

'Galleries', tunnels through which a short man can walk, were constructed in the Upper Coralline from at least mediaeval times, and from the 1890s in the *Globigerina*, on a national scale. The floors have a central water channel, with walking space at the sides, for channel maintenance. They could be made only 0.5 m above sea level, and be very close to the ground surface above. They tapped the water layers. While the population, and individual water use, was low, these provided ample water, though using care that the low-lying ones did not abstract brackish water that might damage the freshwater lens. Each dwelling was provided with a large roof tank, able to store (minimum) water for a week or two, so the supply could be cut off if the salt level rose. In 1900 the salinity was 200 ppm, in 1947–8, 940 ppm: a clear warning, not taken.

Boreholes with pumps (at first powered by steam) also started in the 1890s for national supply, followed by wind pumps over suitable areas, such as most of the larger Upper Coralline plateaux, for irrigation and local supply. Once pumps are diesel or electric, these last become less noticeable but abstract more water.

Once, irrigated land, summer-wet land, was only within reach of perennial springs, streams or earlier, marshes. Rain, in average wet years, is sufficient for most winter crops. Water was moved by open channel between Roman (pre-Roman?) times and the pipes of the late twentieth century: and indeed some of the stone systems still operate, often with complex patterns, and rules of abstraction (this farm Tuesday and Thursday mornings, etc.).

Farm tanks could be filled from spring or river (and now, from tankers), storing water to be used later, moved by channel or pipe. Bananas were frequently planted by spring or tank. Although it is too cold for the fruits to ripen, they could be cooked.

An elaborate system of field 'wells' brought water sufficient for livestock or short-term irrigation, not for modern, e.g. year-round protected cropping. Few 'wells' tapped underground water. Mostly, they have cisterns below, filled through underground small tunnels (not galleries) or (replacement) pipes.

Drip irrigation is now encouraged, for both summer and winter irrigation, which is over larger areas than before, estimated at c. 1500 ha in 2000/2001. Protected cropping (various) is spreading fast, particularly for luxury or nursery garden crops.

All crops need water, as do the livestock, cattle, sheep, goats, poultry, rabbits, now mainly kept indoors. As in other countries, more water is used for agriculture than for any other purpose. In Malta, 37% (38.6 million m^3) is used for this, only 34% for domestic consumption. Different crops vary in their consumption, e.g. melons high, brassicas low.

(3) Springs and wells in low-lying estuarine plains, which were mainly lost during drainage as they tapped superficial water. The water was brackish and organic-rich, and used for irrigation, e.g. Burmurrad, Mistra, Ghajn Tuffieha.

(4) Marsh and pool water. Drainage was ordered in the 1830s, for public health, to prevent insect- (including mosquito)-borne and water-borne, diseases (Cassar, 1965). There was one sink-hole lake, many marshes in triangular depressions on hard limestone at the source of ravine streams (Chapter 3), ones in low-lying coastal land, and those on low-lying land beside rivers. From the plant life recorded, and indeed the number of eels there once was, these were surprisingly abundant for a 'dry' Mediterranean island. These marshes also fed the limestone streams, with water lime-rich indeed, but also organic-rich. Like springs, marshes stabilise river flow. From Grech Delicata (1853) it is clear many remained in the 1840s, to be lost shortly afterwards.

(5) Direct rainfall, on which all the others depend! The run-off once gathered, flowed to the river, and augmented the stream flow greatly during the wet season. Chemically, it differed. Apart from any solutes and substances brought in, which were likely to be nutrient-rich, the run-off, for a couple of millennia, ran

over cultivated terraces as well as 'wild' land. Water running through and over soil picks up nutrients. Consequently, rainwater diluted the calcium-dominated status of the spring water, and increased the nutrients (partly by making available the bound phosphorus, etc.). So in winter, the start of the growing season (and, for quick-drying places, also its end) run-off water, and the sediment it carried, increased nutrient status.

While spring-fed areas had perennial streams, it is uncertain whether main lengths on *Globigerina* (or other) rock also did so. Certainly, one long river, just above its alluvial plain, had water at a specific level for long enough to wear away rock (Haslam & Borg, 1998). The water in the ground below was nearly up to ground level, intermittently high enough to make a spring, and this helped keep water in the river above when it otherwise would have sunk down in the fissures. (A hard/puddled bed was unnecessary, though possibly present.)

Such was Malta. 300 km of watercourses, marshes and standing waters, boggy ground – fit for geese, for instance (Haslam & Borg, 1998).

And what is Malta? Hardly over 100 km of watercourse, probably. Most dry except after severe storms; only a little with winter flow. Much groundwater in the Upper Coralline abstracted (and too contaminated for human consumption) and nearly all the rest led away from springs, also for human purposes. The trickle of spring-plus-run-off water in the upper streams is chemically altered and too little for good aquatic communities. In the main river channels the underground water has sunk, and whatever hard bed there was has been dredged off, and it has to be a very heavy storm flow that does not sink away in the first few kilometres. Such storm flows are maybe twice a decade (becoming less, each decade!) and, as now unexpected, do damage by moving bed sediment, rubbish and anything else in the way, and flooding.

Many dams are in the dried rivers, built in the 1890s and the earlier twentieth century to collect water for irrigation, or to sink down and replenish the aquifer. Indeed, even in the 1980s it was usual to see pools above, in winter. Most now stand dry, as a mute – and unheard – reminder of the drying since.

Because so many valleys are increasingly built up, even less rain can sink into the ground, and flash floods get worse and worse.

No marshes, no standing waters.

The deep-level springs are a shadow of what they were. Of two, where boys swam (not paddled) all summer within living memory, one has gone, the other is a dirty paddle pool.

One river at least has an underground counterpart (R. Kbir). Surface river water falls into this. This, or these, are not sufficiently known to be a resource – except the known one is used for Reverse Osmosis at its mouth. The water, being brackish, is cheaper to process than sea water.

The Lower or Sea Level water table was over-abstracted in the 1970s, so voters could have all the water they wanted, and in consequence the lens was broken, and the water is too salty for human consumption (let alone too polluted from other sources!), unless diluted by half with Reverse Osmosis water. Even then, in 2005, it was well below EU quality, and many people drink bottled water (much of it imported from cleaner Italy). That option is not open to the natural biota, unfortunately. Since the 1890s, almost every year, more water has been abstracted from the limestone. On the land, this extra drying, loss of water, is noticeable about every 4 years. A unified hydrological system?

Even in the mid 1980s there was very little river pollution. A few areas (pig farms and such-like) were dirty, but most was surprisingly clean. Twenty years on, and badly polluted water is the norm. This has come from increased traffic, roads, settlement, agrochemicals, industry, inadequate sewers, etc. Just two decades to pollute a whole country, and not mind it.

For the past few decades, there has been so little water that most Maltese say 'Malta has no rivers'. Killed.

Without outside assistance such as oil, Maltese would be poisoned by polluted water, and reduced to using little more of that than is needed for drinking. What a waste.

Aquatic flora and fauna are partly, heading for fully, extinct.

And what a warning for other countries! Watching lowland England dry, as in parts of, e.g. lowland France, Germany and Belgium, the small streams have gone, the land is dry, valley bottoms (without larger streams) are mostly dry, medium streams are shrinking – planners are recommended to visit Malta and see the habitat to which they are heading.

Loss of habitat, functioning, forms and processes.

Loss in temperate Europe

Since about 1950, in the more populous and more fertile parts of Europe, fields have generally been enlarged, with a corresponding loss of the small tributaries – later, ditches – which surrounded them. Examining the earlier fields shows when they (or their predecessors) were made, natural winding tributaries on the gentle winding slopes, were diverted to form the field boundaries (Fig. 4.2) Originally, in lowlands, there were numerous small brooks, formed by gathered run-off on rather lower land. Being small, so with low force, and receiving run-off, they meandered down the slope to reach the main stream (and, in ridge-and-furrow cultivation, received water from the furrows). This is inconvenient for field cultivation, so when fields were laid out consistently, these little brooks were diverted to surround fields, both draining, and allowing

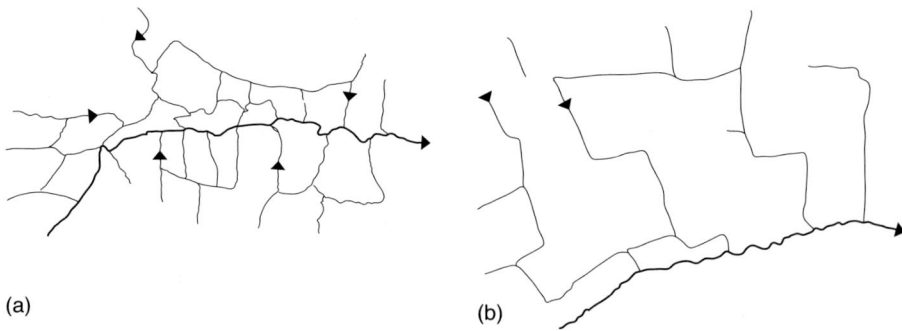

Fig. 4.2. Field tributaries. When lowland or damp land has been turned into fields (from virgin land or ancient fields) rills and small streams are diverted into the drainage ditches enclosing such fields. With the coming of land and, particularly field (under) drainage, and the increase of the latter, these ditches receive ever-less surface water, become drier, smaller, and eventually are lost. (a) Original stream course and later field ditches still present, Mid-Wales. (b) Field ditches becoming lost with modern agriculture, Cambridgeshire.

easier cultivation. When fields were made larger, and water still remained, the ditch-tributaries were diverted again (as also happened with change of culture, e.g. Roman fields superseding Neolithic, then Anglo Saxon, mediaeval, Enlightenment, Victorian, post-Second World War, in England). In that a straight field watercourse does not resemble a natural brook in water habitat, shape, biota, etc., there is a great loss.

Deepening the ditches removed more water.

Straightening the next larger streams much shortened them, decreased the aquatic habitat. So did narrowing them. Deepening them did so yet more.

Field drainage eventually led to an enormous loss of aquatic habitat. Rain landing on fields, instead of running to the nearest furrow, ditch or stream, went down to the under-drains (usually now pipe drains) within and below the fields. This water certainly ran to the main stream in the valley, but was lost to the small ones. The integrated hydrological system is absent.

Early field drainage in England was local, 'bush drainage' (brushwood in underground trenches), and present at least from the seventeenth century, expanding thereafter. Cheap tiles and (at first) earthenware pipes allowed this to spread, vastly in the later nineteenth century, and further technology allowed it to be increased again in efficiency a century later (Cook & Williamson, 1999).

With both land drainage and field drainage, many of the remaining wide-set field ditches receive negligible water, are not maintained, become filled in, and are lost. The job of Hedger-and-Ditcher no longer exists. If, particularly after drying, the soil is made compact and less permeable, heavy rain has nowhere to go, and may become sheet flow with great erosion of field and stream, and flash flood, etc., below. This is usually blamed on that wicked water and climate change. It is not: it is deliberate removal of water resources.

Drainage removes superficial (surface and upper land) water, and therefore those watercourses dependent on these sources, the smaller and non-spring ones. While water is held in the soil and subsoil, it is itself a water resource and emerges and moves only slowly, to reach streams, perhaps via flushes. A drained soil has lost this, and not only has no water stored, but encourages quick run-off and flash floods.

In Britain small streams were mapped in the early twentieth century by the Ordnance Survey, mapped on the same standard on both mountain and lowland. In undrained moor and mountain (where they are still found!) there is a dense network of flowing rills, too small to be marked, but extending a kilometre or two or more upstream of the top of the marked stream. By the 1970s, even more by the 2000s, the lowland pattern was very different. Even excluding abstracted areas and looking just at drained ones, the upper 1–4 km of marked stream could be seen: it was covered in land plants and without the upper network of the hills. Perennial flow started well below the source. This alone illustrates the loss in aquatic habitat.

Drainage may include putting whole streams in pipes underground (e.g. Guernsey; Belgium; formerly Denmark). Streams rise suddenly in non-topographical places: and examination shows they come out of pipes. Or a stream just disappears (and re-appears several kilometres downstream).

Drainage, in a country like Britain, can be of any land, irrespective of heritage loss (which, without the Water Framework Directive, matters to too few) and cost–benefit. Draining blanket and raised bog, for instance, is highly destructive: and does not give, even in lowlands, the most productive crops. But water is 'nasty', and it is a virtue to drain it away (!).

The earlier drainage turned much riverside flood plain, wetlands, flood meadow, etc., into drier but flower-rich meadow. Further drainage turns this to arable or intensive, non-flower-rich grass (e.g. Haslam, 2003), with immense loss to biodiversity and conservation value.

In the Wigan area, between c. 1850 and c. 2006, the number of ponds dropped from 3400 to 1305. Agricultural ponds, the greatest number (85%), have been lost gradually from c. 1700, though in most lowlands the drop was fast after the introduction of tractors. Ponds from deep mining dropped fast after 1880, from open-cast, after 1945; with a further fall after 1970 (Boothby, 2006).

As a pond network turns into pond patches, the system gradually collapses, and by protecting the high-quality ponds and allowing the poor-quality ones to be lost, the high-quality ones become degraded (Boothby, 2006).

In undrained or partly drained land, such as some French wetlands, a river may still be supported in its channel by groundwater below. In more rivers now, it is kept in the channel by the firm, maybe puddled bed. Where there is neither supporting water nor an impervious bed, as in Malta now, rivers dry as water sinks out of them. It is a danger to be watched for elsewhere: that for lack of groundwater; and dredging or otherwise damaging an impervious bed, river water is lost. River water is wanted for, at least, mains supply, irrigation, fishing, boating and waste disposal. The central R. Rhine, on alluvial gravels, leaks laterally. Being in a wet region, this is not great. Suppose, though, that all the Rhine here leaked out and down! No water downstream, and the water table badly polluted!

Water is abstracted as a human resource, one too often considered harmless and sustainable for ever: until it runs out. Removing water from one part of the water system, is sustainable overall only when it is returned to another close by, and even then damage is probable in the abstracted sector. The commonest method of this is to abstract for mains supply and return sewage treatment works effluent to the river, even to put it into the source in place of spring or gathered run-off water. But this is not harmless. Even the best effluent is chemically different to natural, unpolluted water: and effluents do not all remain permanently at the best possible. Then the quantity reflects human use patterns, consistent compared with run-off, though closer to spring. Temperature also differs, though only in the first reaches.

Effluent is not identical to a network of small streams of natural water.

Genuine sustainable abstraction is when a small part of the river water is diverted to a, say, *c.* 200 m long channel, during which diversion it turns a mill wheel, and after which it returns unchanged to the river.

Depending on era, place and type of settlement, water may be abstracted from the surface, whether from spring, river, still water (including reservoirs made for the purpose) or wetland, or it may be taken from below ground, from well (usually a drying spring, or high level water table, the channel bricked or stoned) or, for large-scale use, boreholes from aquifers (or galleries, see above). Abstracted water may be for use a few metres away, or be taken hundreds of kilometres away by aqueducts or pipes (now, mostly pipes, but both old and new aqueducts are also used, e.g. Haslam, 1991).

Abstraction from streams along diversionary channels has been done since early times, and is now found only locally or for specific, new, purposes: such as a fish ladder or bypass. There were various uses, so types of channel:

- for watering a farm or house, as already described. This may be through earthen channels (ditches) dug in the ground or, in the Mediterranean, constructed stone channels (which water could not sink out of);
- larger channels for mains supply;

- for water mills. All the water of a (usually small) stream could turn the wheel. Or, in a large river, the mill could be on a short channel beside the river. Again, particularly in lowlands, the stream's water force could be inadequate to turn the wheel, and a new channel could be built along the contour, until there was a sufficient head above the river on the valley bottom, and a mill was constructed;
- for irrigation. A typical European pattern is for a sequence of small channels to be built on the slope above the stream, running from the stream nearly flat along the contour, irrigating fields there. Water meadows, one form of penned water system, peaked in the eighteenth century. They had dense channels watering the fields, and the purpose was to increase grass production, and its earlier production. In the Mediterranean, stone channels may be laid, to decrease water loss. Irrigation here is usually to allow, not increase, cultivation. Pipes, drips and sprays are now the most popular. Sprays are wasteful. Rice paddies are another form, with both irrigation and drainage channels (Haslam, 1991).
- to carry waste from house, farm or larger settlement to the stream.

Abstraction increases with population. It varies with culture, use only for drinking and cooking being tiny compared with use in a modern city including baths, washing-up machines, street cleaning and industry. Use for irrigation also varies with climate, weather and type of crop required. The (main) Po plain uses huge amounts of water for rice paddies, much less for the people, who are sparse. (Fortunately, even larger amounts of water flow in from the Alps.) Because of the cost and the lower requirement for quality, irrigation water is more often taken from local sources than is mains water. It is estimated that 80% of the water for human use is for irrigation (Cook & Williamson, 1999).

It is the amount of water taken relative to the resources, as well as the total amount, which matters. It is the amount taken relative to the resources per river basin that is important. Europe, and indeed other populated parts, is running out of water. This is hardly noticed because surface water is 'nasty water' (except in, e.g. Denmark and pretty lakes) and better technology pursues water ever further away.

Rock abstraction is only from aquifers and non-aquiferous rock cannot be damaged as much. Abstraction can be only from surface and sub-surface sources: a partial safeguard. Streams not dependent on springs cannot be destroyed by their loss. They are dependent on run-off only. Soil may be shallow or deep, pervious or less so (e.g. chalk, clay). Water stored could be abstracted, before it was drained away.

In aquiferous regions, the top of the aquifer sinks, with abstraction. So springs where water used to well out from this level dry and disappear. As the groundwater level is further lowered, downstream and downslope springs increasingly dry, and the streams they fed and supported dry also. In abstracted aquifers (chalk, etc.) therefore, watercourses which used to be winter bournes, spring-fed in winter, dry; and further down, that which used to be perennial flow becomes winterbourne, and so on, until there are wide valleys with no sign of a stream. Alternatively, on less pervious rock, the upper winter-flowing streams may be rain-fed instead of spring-fed.

Since there has been little change in rainfall over the past couple of centuries, water input to the land remains constant. Therefore, if abstraction stops, water levels can rise again. This has been shown well in London, whose huge water demand is now met from outside the capital, since its groundwater is too polluted. Lo and behold, the water table is rising, and springs starting to flow again!

River regulation is when controls (weirs, reservoirs, sluices, etc.) operate to decrease fluctuations in discharge. A more even flow is easier for planners and water authorities. Severe floods may be diverted to 'washes' (old) or valley bottom fields or ponds. Regulation is a side effect of the many hydropower stations on, say, R. Rhône, and in the past (not under this name) occurred in equivalent dense areas of watermills, where the water held up by one mill tailed back to the next.

The effects of regulation vary. It is beneficial if regulation merely removes what would otherwise be human-induced floods. It is also beneficial when it replaces the held-up water which has formed the habitat for the last millennium. At the other extreme, it is destructive when a swift river of good structure (both bed and vegetation) is replaced by a straight, V-sided deep uniform channel. The resource may be improved or diminished.

The earliest major river works were for flood protection. Rivers were embanked, that is, dug earth, etc. was laid and raised into banks beside the river. This was needed only in towns (and then not at the wharfs). In the country the valley could flood.

This system is still used, as in the Thames embankments in London, the Danube and Rhône embankments where, because of the river size, other means are impractical, and – more unusually – for rivers above ground level where shrinking peat has lowered the ground to below sea level, so the river levels depend on the higher ground upstream, and need to get the water to the sea at the mouth (e.g. the Netherlands, the English Fenland). Embankments now also mean dredging, to keep the water flowing, so a poor aquatic habitat. However, there are often, out of the towns, associated channels given less maintenance and their habitats may be much better. This type of flood protection may include openings to washlands, where flood water can be stored and released slowly later.

Modern flood protection is drainage, used as much for fields as for towns. it is less guiding water at its natural level as lowering it to be well below ground level, so even heavy storm flows rarely rise to reach ground level. Washes are still needed, in some places. Of course, all the changes that have led to flash floods mean water levels rise much more than before. Impact deliberately increased hard and compacted surfaces so that rain runs off near-totally and rapidly, and, on soils, takes sediment with it. Impact deliberately increased speed of flow – so flood – by straightening channels and making them uniform and smooth. Then floods are blamed on climate change. (What will happen if future climate change does substantially increase floods also?) In some places there does seem to be increasing fluctuations in rainfall, though, given records are often of less than 100 years, and rarely over 200 years, time is needed to distinguish cycles from trends.

Discussion

Human impact has therefore much altered and, in general, much decreased water resources, decreased them by lessening the amount of the water resource, and in parts by lessening its quality, so the water available as a resource is much less than the total available. This lowering of quality might, near sea level, mean sea water was, by poor management, allowed into an aquifer from below; or, anywhere, be due to adding pollution to underground water from the land above. All these were deliberate, in that they were done without proper thought for the consequences. These consequences were easily predictable, and were not given proper decade-long (or, for e.g. agrochemicals, several decades-long) trials. This, of course, does not apply to all countries, or all parts of most countries.

So, now, the Water Framework Directive. Management had been moving towards Whole Catchment Planning but EU countries are now required to do so, and do so throughout the country. This is a great opportunity to mitigate the destruction. Fully implemented, it will not restore the old resources, but would much help to limit further destruction and give some improvement. One point unfortunately outside the scope of the Directive is directing plant breeding to produce crop varieties more tolerant to waterlogging. If waterlogging did not decrease yield, field-scale drainage (both as field and as stream drainage) could be much decreased, and water again be stored in the land: so also decreasing the demand for irrigation (which difficulty, also, the plant breeders might address).

Planning water has the disadvantage in that water is essential to life, essential for people, their crops, livestock, industry and other concerns, yet it is also a menace, decreasing crop yield, damaging other property, even killing livestock and, to a very limited extent (in Europe), people. A balance has to be struck. At present, the pendulum has swung too far towards coping with the menace, not seeing the picture as a whole and considering the future water demands of the population (with a few honourable exceptions).

Where resources have been allowed to increase, for instance in fulfilling the demands of the EU Habitats Directive and allowing some drained wetland to revert to wetland, or stopping costly and awkward development of riverside land, again allowing wetland restoration, these have been local, and for reasons other than increasing river basin water resources.

To work with Nature, to re-couple the water links within the riverscape and the river, so that the whole functions, once more, as an integrated unit, that is the aim of the Water Framework Directive, and, it is to be hoped, of other countries also, to give as high ecological status as possible, as well as using water wisely.

In the above discussion, ecological status, natural heritage, the original and traditional vegetation and animal populations, have not been mentioned. Ethically, as well as practically, they have a right to exist, and people have a duty to ensure it. That omission was because so little attention has been paid to it by Governments (even, say, Denmark, not until 1985; Madsen, 1995). (There could, though, as in Britain, be an active legal requirement to preserve fish, which needs a moderate habitat.) The demands of the Water Framework Directive are intended to see to this. That also means water quality (given equal pollution) should improve, seeing that microbes on vegetation, and good-quality soils are the best free water purification there is. (With the lessened pollution envisaged in the Directive, water quality should doubly improve.)

This chapter has discussed how the water, from arriving on the land to leaving it to the sea, forms a complex and consistent whole, driven, by gravity and precipitation, downstream. The impacts of, particularly, drainage and abstraction, fragment this, separating sections, and removing sections by removing the water. The water resources of most of Europe have been both influenced and greatly reduced, reduced so much that, at extremes, there is already a country which cannot survive without reverse osmosis water, since the indigenous water has been made unfit for human consumption. And whose aquatic heritage has largely vanished in about 150 years.

5
Development and variation of rivers

Hill slope water pathways determine many landscape characters
(Burt et al., 1993).

Humans enhance, accelerate and retard natural processes
(Calow, 1998).

The river system is a physical system with a history
(Petts & Foster, 1985)

Upstream–downstream

River and riverscape form a unit. This chapter describes that part of this unit where water flows downstream and forms rivers: rivers of many types.

In general, as streams flow downstream:

Downstream changes in rivers

Characters	With exceptions such as:
Discharge increases	when water sinks underground
Potential energy decreases	downstream gorges
Hill-rising, lowland below	on plateaux
Slope steepest upstream	different topography
Speed of flow lessens	downstream gorges
Gathers tributaries, increasing its size	topography or drying leads to a single narrow stream
Water may be intermittent at source, perennial at mouth	source has high rainfall, at mouth, water sinks underground
Particle size decreases	change in rock type
Nutrients increase	downstream raised bogs
Pollutants increase	town effluents at source, little downstream
Communities change with longitudinal habitat	too polluted, put underground

Table 5.1 Riverscape elements in the Maltese Islands

Topography	Ravine	Gorge	Valley	Lowland	Mesas
	(near source, widening)	(away from source, parallel-sided)	(slope)	(the most abundant)	mostly Gozo. Rivers rise between Upper Coralline tips
Rock	Mostly (not all) Upper Coralline limestone above Clay	Mostly Lower Coralline, Secondly Globigerina	Any	Mostly Globigerina, also plateaux, alluvial plains	
Water supply					
Springs (contaminated)	Many remain. Most lost	A few remain	Very few remain	Very few, but may be 'large'	Some on slopes. Many lost
Rivers (contaminated)	Still flow a little in really wet weather	Storm flow after very heavy rain			Flow in winter storm weather
Marsh	On plateaux above, frequent, now dried. In flat valley bottoms, also now dried	On wider valley bottoms, now dried	Alluvial estuarine plains (now dried)	Local (now dried)	–
Aquifer	Above, level sinking, contaminated by land use and settlements	Level sinking	Level dangerously low, sea level having invaded freshwater lens. Contaminated		–
Terracing	Mostly	Considerable	Mostly	Some to nil	Considerable
Exposure	Lowest. Humid	Low, moderate humidity	Low to high	Fairly low (except plateaux)	

Settlement	Isolated farms by springs. Usually defensive	Fewer farms (less spring water), may be old 'rooms'	Most towns and villages. Now overspilling to valleys	Centre of most Gozitan villages and capital on mesas
Fortifications	Forts above	'Defensive' farms and rooms in old-settled areas (raiding stopped c. 1800, such building continued later)	Old centres 'defensive'	Citadel
Farming	Citrus, other fruit and (mostly) irrigated field crops in wet bottoms, olive, carob etc., on dry slopes above	Some field crops, also olive, carob and much suitable land for goat grazing	Mostly field crops	–
Eucalyptus increasing (remaining) (carob now planted)	Considerable	Less	Increasing	–
'Wild' vegetation	Maquis, carob; garigue above	Sparse maquis, carob; garigue on cliffs	Pockets, mostly on steep slopes	–
Communications				
Roads	Poor (steep)	Poor (steep)	Good	Good
Radio towers		Tops, mostly spread where there are good radio linkages		
Mobile phone towers				
Paths	Good through most of islands, but many now shut by owners			

Characteristic, not sole features given.

The simple vertical, longitudinal pattern envisaged by the left-hand column does indeed occur and occur often enough to justify it. However, it is an unusual river which follows all of these characters. And, within these, there are huge variations, from the River Rhône to the saltmarsh creek, from the Alpine river to the flat lowland stream, and from Iceland to Crete. In addition, there are the many differences found when these characters do not occur. The right-hand column lists but a few of the variations found, and in the study of ecology, variations compose many different river types.

Scale differs greatly. In the central lowland sandstone of Germany, or the lowland clay of English midlands, mile after mile shows a repeating pattern of small streams rising, medium streams winding through vales. Although the tall alps are much more distinctive in shape, looking at just the streams again shows repeating patterns over large distances. The countries do, indeed, show different river types, but the scale of similar topography and rock type is large.

In contrast are the riverscapes where rock type, topography, glaciation or variant impacts give riverscapes in miniature, such as the Maltese Islands, where near every corner shows a different view. To a lesser extent, areas such as the Channel Islands, parts of Wales, Brittany are similar.

The Maltese miniatures are described in Table 5.1. All these types (and more) can be found elsewhere, on a larger scale, but it is useful to see all together from one tiny archipelago. Here are found changes in rock type, from more to less erodable, from calcium-dominated nutrient status to clay, sand and alluvium. Topography, basically determined by rock type and geological history, presence of faults, etc. gives extreme variations. (There is not, though, the more northern variation of glaciated and non-glaciated areas.)

When a vertical profile is looked at in more detail, there are lesser variations, such as the pool-and-riffle pattern, or springs at nick-points on the profile. These too are ecologically important.

Figures 5.1 and 6.2 illustrates some representative horizontal and vertical patterns. Slope varies from near-flat to cliff, longitudinal profile from fairly smooth to step to just varying. Horizontal pattern varies from dendritic and single line to the commonest type of tributaries entering where rock type, flow and weathering have produced the non-uniform valley.

Meanders alter slopes, so do artificial channels. Nick points where rock type, topography or springs break the profile are common. So are the lesser pool and riffle systems, with flatter and steeper reaches.

Rain is uneven, it varies in any one place, when there are dry or wet days or seasons. It varies between places, so a mountain top may have 1200 mm per year, its foothill, under 600 mm, and it varies in intensity: 75 mm in one day may be not unusual, or be so rare as to set a record.

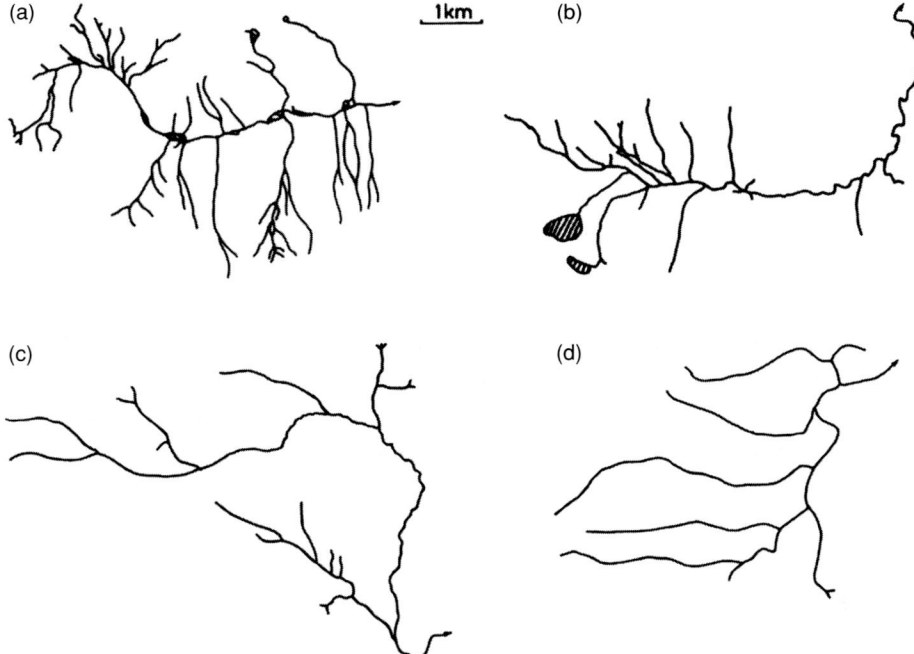

Fig. 5.1. Horizontal patterns of riverscapes. Thanks to the painstaking efforts of the (British) Ordnance Survey, and later bodies, horizontal river patterns are well known and accurate. The river is (unless altered) at the base of the valley, so the river pattern is also that of the riverscape. Vertical patterns are not, quantitatively, well known or accurate, and are without a standard classification.
Horizontal patterns (Y. Bower in Haslam, 1987). (a) Alpine, dendritic pattern, France. (b) Mountain, resistant, Ireland. (c) Dissected plateau stream, resistant rock. The outline is smooth on the plateau above, irregular where it runs down, Germany. (d) Hill stream, hard clay, with smooth lines as the hills are smooth, Italy. (e) Lowland clay-mix, streams natural, their straightness, due to channelling. (f) Lowland chalk (limestone) stream, with few tributaries partly because so much water sinks into the aquifer, partly because abstraction has lowered groundwater and so spring level, Britain. (g) Drained wetland, ancient and irregular pattern, Belgium. (h) Drained wetland, 1970s regular pattern, The Netherlands.

Where there is winter snow for months, the snow melts in spring, from the lower to the upper slopes (other characters being equal), so the sources of the snow melt streams gradually move up the mountains. Of course, large glaciers may have snow-melt rivers under the glacier, so the rivers come to the surface as large and cold, rather than as run-off and warming like the little ones.

Climate change alters snowmelt. In Britain, for instance, at present there is some snowmelt flood of varying but not great strength and duration, in the most

112 The riverscape and the river

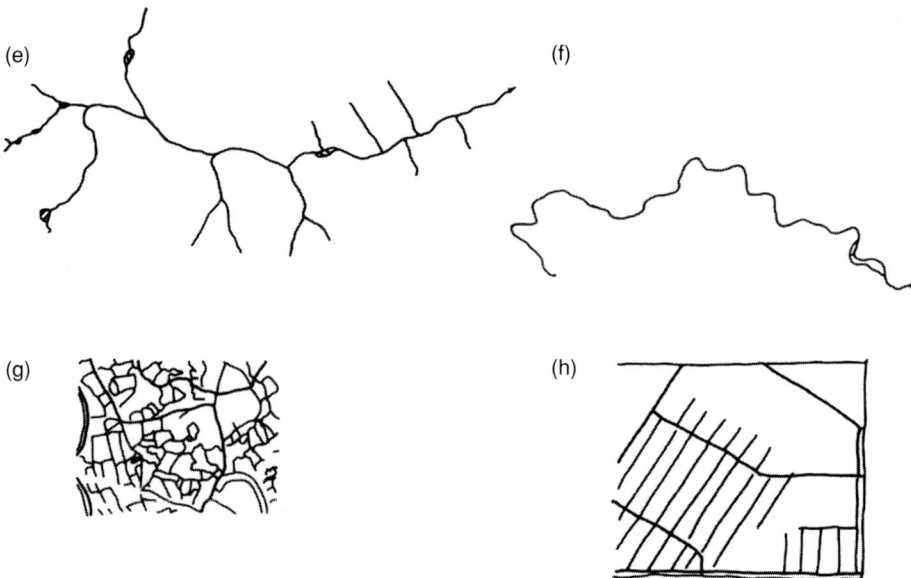

Fig. 5.1. (cont.)

mountainous and northen parts. Two and a half centuries before, and in the very south of England (Hampshire), snow frequently lay for 2–3 months (White, 1788), so giving a substantial snowmelt flood, clearing streams as is now usually not done until autumn. Northern streams would have had much more. A fairly small change in temperature led to a substantial change in ecology.

A single main river channel is what is now considered normal: but a traditional, let alone a natural, river is typically braided in lowland and flood plain areas. The channels anastomose. These are usually unacceptable to people as they take up space. A severe storm, and the stream marking the boundary of a property has moved to give a km less of the valuable flood meadow. It may move unpleasantly near. It may shoal up the navigation channel. It is much tidier and more convenient having a single channel, or, in places where braiding has been left, to use one channel for, say, navigation, one for a watermill, and one for water supply (e.g. R. Itchen below Winchester may be three; R. Loing in Montargis, France, where five channels lead to different wharfs, a moat and a probable mill).

One interesting effect of (abandoned) braiding is that the main channel(s) are the same size as that coming from upstream, and have a continuing downstream progression of biotic communities. However, a small chalk channel which nearly reproduces an upstream one in depth, width, flow and substrate may bear a similar community to that of the upstream one. In the shallow gravelly reach *Berula erecta* forms a carpet, with short-leaved *Ranunculus* dominant, while in the main channel, deeper siltier, long-leaved *Ranunculus, Sparganium erectum, Elodea canadensis* and *Schoenoplus lacustris* flourish. Since Dawson (1980) showed different ecotypes of *Ranunculus* occur within small distances in upstream reaches, and other winterbourne ecotypes, e.g. *Callitriche* spp., differ sharply from downstream ones, what ecotypes are there in the downstream braid channel? Ecologically, their water and sediment are the same as in the nutrient-richer main channel. But they have rippling water, less silt and clean gravel.

When a braided channel is like the main one in depth and substrate, it is so in biota also.

The major European rivers like the Rhine and Danube, formerly braided and anastomosing, were mostly channellised in the later nineteenth and earlier twentieth centuries. These large rivers required relatively high technology. (Channellisation started in Roman times.)

Impacts often increase downstream (Fig. 5.2), merely because, if impacts occur at, say, three a mile, the longer the river, the more the miles and so the more the impacts at a given point. Secondly, in more hilly and mountainous regions, population tends to be denser in downstream lowland parts, so there are also more towns, industry and intensive agriculture, and hence impact on rivers.

Water flowing down has energy, has force. The force is exerted in the bank and bed, and itself increases with the potential energy of the head. This water force constantly acts, constantly pushes and pulls, so it constantly tends to alter bed, bank and flood plain. To carry out river schemes, as in Malta, on the assumption that water will never have force leads to results amusing to the ecologist; except for the waste of money which could have been used to actually enhance rivers.

Pristine, and even traditional, rivers rising where there is low ground (whether lowlands, or small patches in hills) usually rise in damp places, where run-off gathers, or where flush water exudes. Gathering more run-off, the water flows downstream, with gravity, and a river is born. Springs may likewise form wet areas, added to by run-off, or they may be large enough for water to well over and flow down.

So there can be a hierarchy of size, as well as a variation in scale. Small streams may resemble each other within the same habitat. They become larger, in continuous contact with their upstream reaches. There is a continuity along the whole system. Downstream, small streams get larger, they join, and many may join into one.

The river is the result of all processes in the catchment, so there are fluvial processes, and in addition there is a history. The river is a physical system with a

114   The riverscape and the river

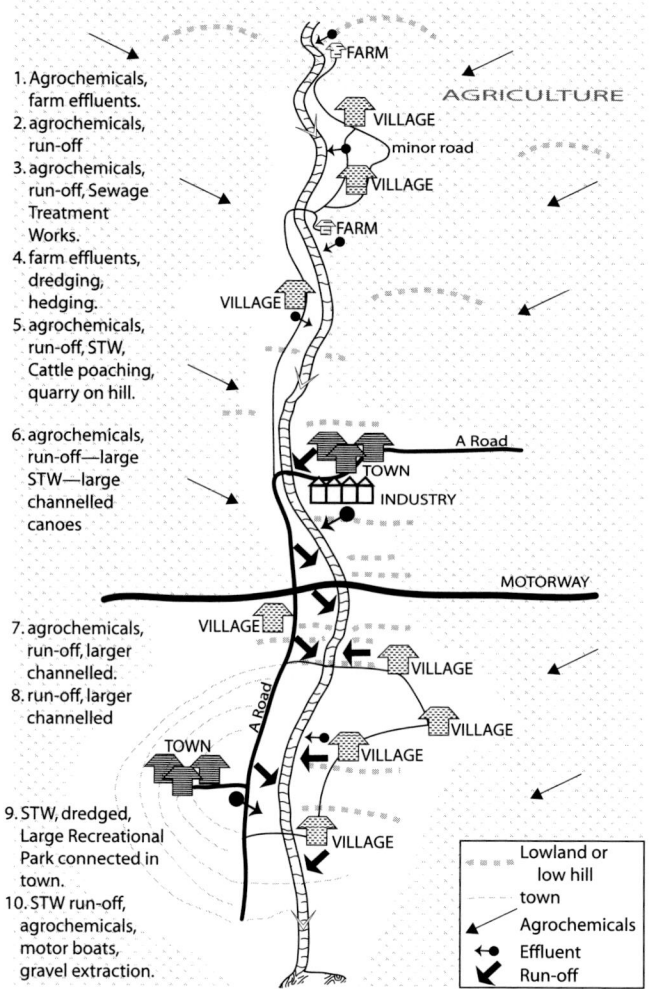

Fig. 5.2. Impacts accumulating downstream on a river (representative). Normally lower reaches are more impacted, including being more engineered, than upper reaches, though this is not invariable. Representational. The further downstream, the more the pollution entering the river: in general. Some, e.g. at Market Harborough, England, 'rise' with the effluent from the local sewage treatment works: not natural water! Downstream there are more effluents (from sewage to silage liquor). The longer the length in agricultural land, the more the total agrochemicals. The more the dirty hard surfaces, the more the dirty run-off and similarly for the other impacts. As against this, self-purification does occur within the river. However, heavily impacted rivers like that depicted are overloaded, as older Sewage Treatment Works are, and purification does not keep up with impact.

history: a history of ages of land use, erosion, sedimentation, flood hazard, water supply. Rainfall, precipitation, forms the flow (directly or as springs and flushes). The run-off depends on climate (or two or more. Within a small area rain shadows can be surprisingly great), geology, topography, soil and vegetation characters. Land management has been vital for a millennium and more in most of Europe. Run-off from precipitation is determined by the filtering ground surface (bare limestone absorbs more than concrete), the type of surface and of sub-surface texture and its storage capacity. Flow into a traditional (non-spring) stream comes in part from the water stored from the previous rains. In rain, water storage reaches the surface, and flows out (Petts & Foster, 1985). Add drainage, and this stored water is lost. The crops become drier round their roots, as intended, but as not intended, the unified water system is gradually lost. The upper streams are also lost – and the upper catchment is dry. Water flow starts well downstream.

In one sense the river is continuous, but in another sense, it may not be. Lakes or sink holes interrupt flow. A gorge inserts swift stony habitat. An alluvial plain in the hills does the reverse. Human impact increases this. A sluice can halt much animal movement, as do drainage and abstraction. These and more factors make discontinuous habitats, both for the river and for its flora and fauna.

Sensitivity

River types differ in their *sensitivity* to both natural and human pressures upon them. In general, a river is less sensitive if it is large and nutrient-rich: large, because, in e.g. 2 m depth a 10% variation in depth will still leave the centre too deep for vegetation (2 m v. 2.2 m), and in nutrient status, in that altering nitrate levels by 10% in either direction leaves substantial nitrates.

Sensitivity can be defined as the amount of reaction of the river system (or part thereof) to a given habitat change. Such habitat change may be physical, chemical or biotic, in the river or in the riverscape; and the ability of the river to recover from such change, in a given period of years.

More complex definitions occur, e.g. Downs & Gregory (1993), but these are usually developed for a single type of change, e.g. farm, effluent, or channelisation, and should be applied accordingly.

Sensitive river types include:

1. those with very low nutrients (e.g. bog, upstream pure limestone), which are easily overwhelmed by added solutes, whether nutrients or pollutants;
2. those with many habitat niches, allowing a wide biodiversity, but where niches are easily removed by, e.g. channelling.

3. those whose biota (or indeed physical factors) are in a near-state of collapse already, e.g. those almost too polluted for their traditional communities to survive; those almost too shallow, those with almost too many canoes. In such a river, an unforeseeable event may push the habitat into a state unsuitable for the community, e.g. an accidental temporary pollution, a flock of herons, a 1-in-25-year drought.

The dimension of time

Horizontal and vertical dimensions are easy to grasp as they can be seen. The dimension of time is more difficult. Except for geniuses, this author considers that no ecologist under 30 should be doing field-scale research or management, because it is necessary to actually watch the effects of time before it is understood. The young student expects what has been stable over one or two summers to remain stable (in terms of decades, and excluding drastic events such as new roads).

The river takes sediment from the riverscape and takes it to the sea. Therefore, the riverscape, over geographic time, is removed to the sea. However, there are intermediate changes. Land and sea level change (e.g. Table 2.1). Sea floods in, depositing sediment. Sea level drops leaving a flat terrace where that sediment lay, and a new one within it is eroded and adjusted to present sea level. Meanders wind slowly on a terrace. Similar effects can come from changes in precipitation, in glaciation, and, of course, with the immense technological change of recent decades and centuries. Water force makes changes in, e.g. rain, land level, regulation, and the meanders deepen with changes in water force, and the habitat alters. Upland sediments, like water, move, and can be stored in flood plains, but can move again.

An unexpected factor is a long time-span from cause to effect recorded in the USA, where the landscape quality of the 1950s was a better predictor of the 2000's quality than were the improvements of the 1990s (Davies *et al.*, 2006). With so much harsh management in so much of Europe, deterioration is necessarily simultaneous. But the slow response of rivers to some improvements could be (partly) due to such a time lag. Best Management Practices tend to arise when the relevant habitat is already much degraded, and they became moderately frequent only in the 1990s (e.g. Dennis, *et al.*, 2006). BMPs much improved riparian biota, and quite rapidly.

Horizontally, a river forms an axis, round which the tributaries or curves of a river are placed, symmetrically or asymmetrically. Within this axis may be secondary axes. Horizontal patterns of small streams vary (Figs. 4.2, 5.1, 5.3) with precipitation, rock type, land form and human impact. These are factors of regional, rather than local or country scale. On steeper slopes, more

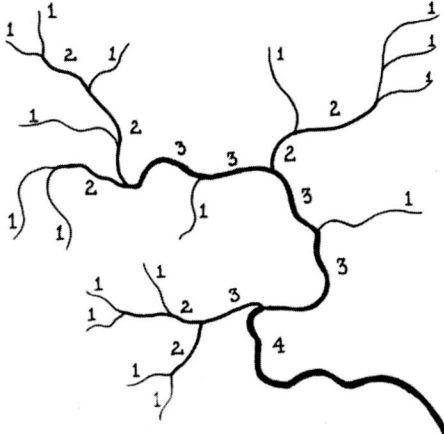

Fig. 5.3. Drainage Order (P. A. Wolseley in Haslam, 1978). This measure of river size is simple, where two streams of the same Order join, the Order is increased. The snags are: what size is a DO1 (in Britain, scientists usually use those showing on a 1:250 000 map)? Why can a DO3 be constructed of two small DO2s or of 40 large DO2s (all joining separately)?

of the precipitation usually reaches the rivers than on more drained slopes. The water force, potential energy, is greater on steeper slopes. Depending largely on land form and rock type, various equal-sized streams may rise and later join, as in, e.g. R. Vyrnwy, Wales, or, at the other extreme, as in the main Moselle gorge, where the huge river winds along the base, with tiny tributaries flowing down the valley sides, making a negligible contribution to the water of the river.

River slope depends on land form (plus impact). River width depends also on water force, rock type and (now, greatly) on impact. However, the two, the width:slope pattern, gives a useful prediction of the vegetation expected (Haslam, 2006, Table 5.2). Correlations are useful, but must be checked to be ecologically valid before they are applied.

> The Dorset R. Avon (Fig. 5.4) is a large lowland river (c.75 km long, excluding tributaries). It is predominantly chalk but with influence from other rock types. The chalk streams are often braided, e.g. the R. Avon and the R. Ebble. The flow is usually moderate. Most of the R. Wylye and the main R. Avon are over 8 m wide, and well over 30 cm deep, the lower R. Avon being over 75 cm deep. The smaller streams are narrower, and except for the R. Nadder, which is on clay, are shallower.
>
> The (main) R. Avon rises on fertile sandstone. The east branch is a typical sandstone stream, with fringing herbs and dominant *Callitriche*. Downstream,

species richness and *Callitriche* both increase. Pewsey sewage led to abundant Blanket weed and *Apium nodiflorum*. The latter, though pollution-intolerant in rivers, is one of the more pollution-tolerant brook species, as it can anchor well in the substratum of shallow brooks. The west branch had been dredged and so damaged. Unusually rapid eutrophication, with abundant *Scirpus lacustris*, occurred towards the confluence, suggesting more pollution or unusually great silting. The confluence is just on the chalk, and there is not enough chalk to influence the flora. The river at this point contains a higher proportion of semi-eutrophic species than would be found on chalk, and a lower proportion of *Ranunculus* and fringing herbs. This is due to the influence of sandstone and its tendency to silting.

The floral attributes of a chalk stream increase downstream as the proportion of chalk in the catchment increases. The transition zone is lengthy as no chalk tributaries enter. Lower down, the chalk influence shows in the abundant *Ranunculus penicillatus* ssp. *pseudofluitans* and fringing herbs, though the eutrophic *Sparganium emersum* also occurs. Pollution then enters, and there is downstream eutrophication and the vegetation is more eutrophic.

The R. Wylye (just) rises on fertile sandstone, but is mostly on chalk, and its tributaries are solely on chalk. It therefore has more chalk influence than the upper R. Avon. The upper river is shallowed by abstraction, so is over-silted and, with minor pollution, also with Blanket weed. *Ranunculus* dominates as expected, except when fish farm effluents add enough (non-calcium) nutrients to allow dominant *Callitriche*. Warminster sewage leads to a polluted community with abundant *Potamogeton pectinatus*. The landscape there is hillier, giving swifter flow and more scour. Therefore, less downstream eutrophication is expected. On the other hand, Warminster sewage was worse than Pewsey sewage. Consequently, the more eutrophic and pollution-tolerant species (e.g. *Sparganium emersum*), and the lower diversities which occur throughout, are probably due more to this pollution than to downstream changes. Wylye town pollution leads to *Potamogeton pectinatus*.

The R. Ebble, R. Till and R. Bourne all flow solely on chalk. R. Ebble is a 'standard' chalk stream. It rises as a winterbourne with silty stretches. These, in summer, retain water longer than gravel, and bear *Mentha aquatica* and *Rorippa nasturtium-aquaticum*. The gravelly stretches bear *Apium nodiflorum*. The top site with perennial flow is polluted by effluent from a cress bed (phosphate fertiliser). *Zannichellia palustris* and *Groenlandia densa* at this site were the only semi-eutrophic species recorded. The stream becomes braided downstream with *Ranunculus c.f. peltatus* and short-leaved *Glyceria* spp. common on the edges with the fringing herbs. Even in the lower reaches, the channels are shallow and barely exceed 5 m wide. R. Till is similar to the Ebble. R. Bourne has perennial flow only in the lower quarter of its length, where the vegetation is typical of a chalk stream. Upstream, the summer-dry channel bears land plants.

The upper chalk streams of this river have a short-leaved *Ranunculus* sp. (probably *R. peltatus*), which variety is able to tolerate very shallow water and temporary drought. The lower reaches have a longer-leaved species. This pattern is typical of chalk streams. However, with abstraction, the length of perennial flow is decreasing.

The R. Nadder is the only stream mainly on clay, so has many semi-eutrophic species, and a more eutrophic *Ranunculus* sp. In 1974, the flow was more turbulent and the bed less silty, so *Ranunculus* had increased and the silt-species and fringing herbs had decreased. These anchor badly in clay. Abundant *Sparganium erectum* in a nearby brook was also indicative of the clay substrate.

Several smaller streams flow into the lower Avon. The upstream ones are typical chalk streams, the downstream have clay influence. The presence of *Alisma plantago-aquatica* is again indicative of clay influence.

The clay influence of R. Nadder extends below its confluence with R. Wylye and R. Avon, seven of its ten species being atypical of chalk. After the further chalk influence of the confluence with R. Bourne and R. Ebble, the chalk influence predominates in R. Avon. Diversity remains high, though there is, throughout, a more eutrophic influence than could come from downstream eutrophication alone, and is attributable to R. Nadder. *Nuphar lutea*, for instance, is very rare on pure chalk. A narrow intermittent band of *Glyceria maxima* is characteristic of a large chalk river. Where the river flows off the chalk downstream, fringing herbs decrease but otherwise there is little change, the river being large enough to retain its chalky character over a relatively short basal length on sands and clay.

The R. Avon demonstrates, in its braided channels, the usual variation and flora with varying physical characteristics. At Ringwood, the slower channel has more *Elodea canadensis* and the faster channel more *Ranunculus*. At Downton the faster channel has less silt and more *Berula erecta, Ranunculus* sp. and mosses. Downstream, eutrophication occurs more in larger siltier channels. In R. Ebble the larger channel (at Nunton) has more *Ranunculus* sp., and *Sparganium erectum*, and the smaller channel more fringing herbs.

(Between 1972 and 1977, most sites showed the minor changes termed 'changeless change', since the species assemblages do not alter (from Haslam, 1982). (1972 details unless otherwise stated.)

When vegetation catches much water, as in various conifer forests, it may either evaporate or be slow reaching the ground. When run-off sinks into the ground through pores, sponge-like structures (peat) or fissures, it is removed from the run-off (see Chapter 4). Conversely, more flash floods come when water runs straight off unabsorbent surfaces.

Table 5.2 *Species distribution in relation to stream width and slope (Haslam, 1978)*

Selected common species, Britain

Main distributions (species occur, though less frequently, in a wider range).
1 Narrower, shallower and, for lowlands, steeper streams.
   Apium nodiflorum
   Berula erecta
   Callitriche spp.
   Rorippa nasturtium-aquaticum
2 Steeper streams, wide-ranging.
   Ranunculus fluitans
   Ranunculus pseudofluitans
3 Central pattern, avoiding slower and rather narrow streams, with unstable accumulating silt.
   Myriophyllum spicatum
   Polygonum amphibium
   Potamogeton crispus
   Potamogeton natans
   Ranunculus spp. short-leaved, some medium-leaved
4 Wide pattern, narrow streams, usually hilly.
   Elodea canadensis
   Phalaris arundinacea
   (*Ranunculus peltatus*)
   Sparganium erectum
   (Blanket weed)
5 Similar to 4, but more restricted and avoiding steeper streams. Includes most of the tall monocotyledons, requiring shallow water, fine soil and little scour, at least at sides.
   Carex acutiformis
   Glyceria maxima
   Phragmites australis
   Oenanthe fluviatilis?
   Potamogeton perfoliatus
   Typha spp.
6 Flatter, usually wider streams. Species primarily of slow flows.
   Nuphar lutea
   Potamogeton pectinatus
   Sagittaria sagittifolia
   Schoenoplectus lacustris
   Sparganium emersum
7 The flattest streams (slopes of less than 1:1000)
   Ceratophyllum demersum

Development and variation of rivers   121

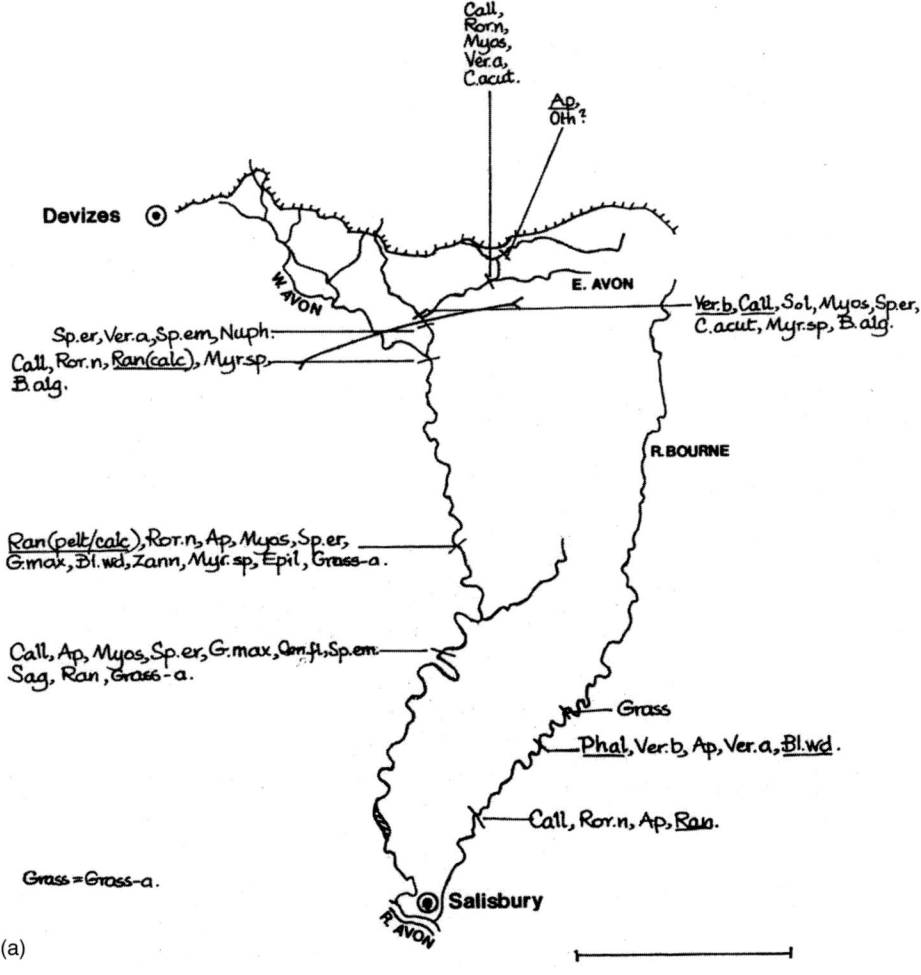

Fig. 5.4. R. Avon, Dorset, England. (Haslam, 1982) see Box. Scale bar = 10 km
a) upper river b) lower river

Right from the source of a river, there are innumerable permutations leading to difference.

The concept of Drainage Order (DO) (Fig. 5.3) is frequently used to explain river development. Superficially it is clear and simple but, like so much to do with rivers, there is too much which does not work. Whenever two DO1 streams flow into each other, the resulting stream is DO2. If another – or ten other – DO1 streams flow into this, it remains DO2. DO2 = DO1 + DO1, or DO2 + DO1. When two DO2 streams join, they make a DO3 stream. This, as before, stays DO3 however many DO1 or DO2 streams flow into it, and only changes to a DO4 when

122 The riverscape and the river

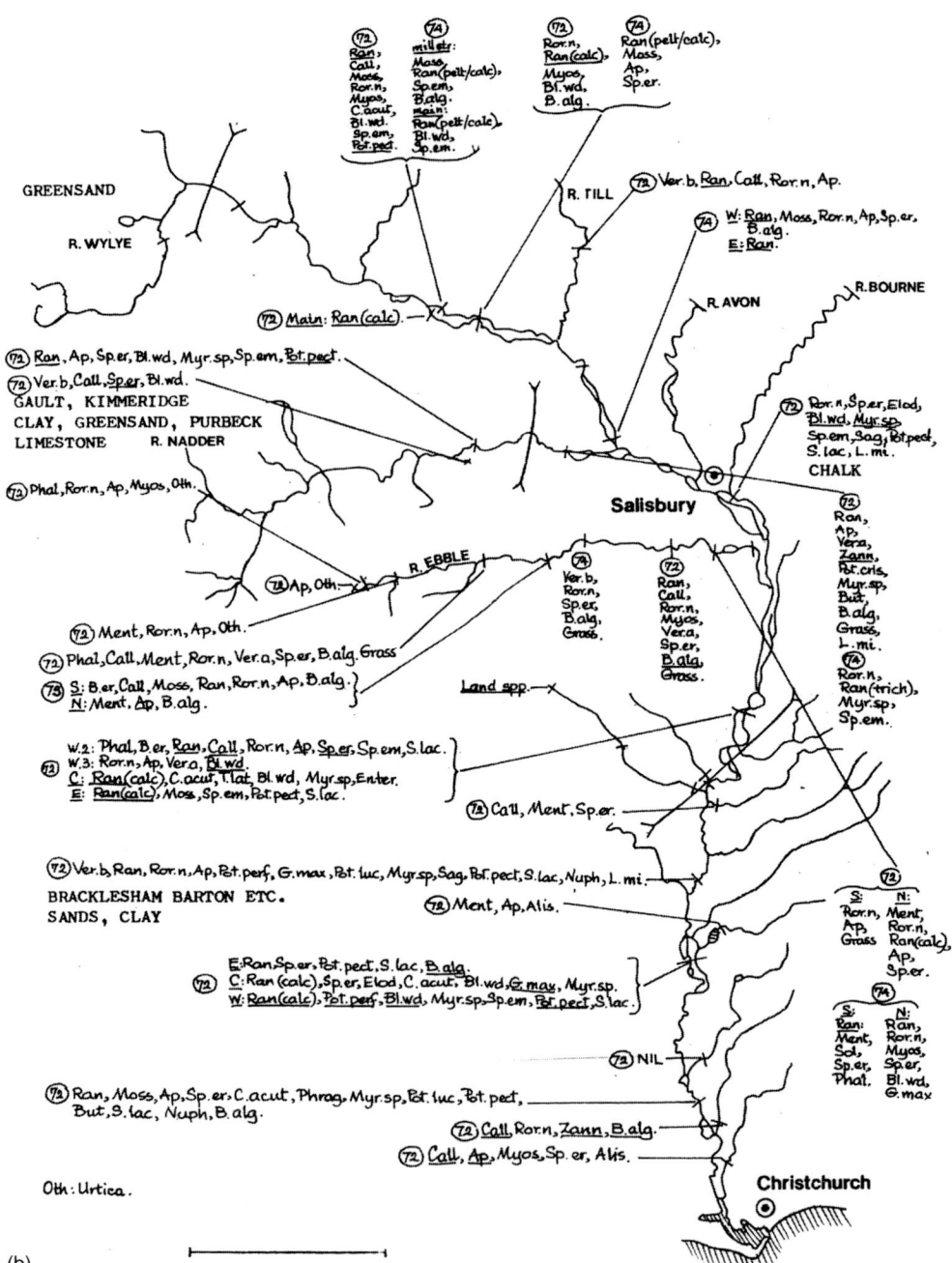

(b)

Fig. 5.4. (cont.)

there is a confluence with another DO3. It is hard to find higher than a DO4 in Britain, though the largest continental rivers reach DO5. Simple.

But, the difficulties? What size stream is called a DO1? 0.5 m, 2 m, 4 m, perennial? In Britain, with standardised OS maps, it can be the smallest on the 1″ maps, or the 0.25″ ones, or the 6″ ones, or the new km near-equivalents, but which should it be? And not all countries have such standardised maps. Moreover, with no recent surveying to assess recent drying, how can there be consistency, when one marked stream is dry, another, perennial? Then there is the logical difficulty. If there are, say, eight streams all 4 m wide with similar discharge, if they flow together one by one, the final stream is DO2. If, though, they flow in a dendritic pattern, it is DO4, with different connotations.

The various tributaries may be near-equal in size and horizontal pattern. They flow together, but each is (at its relevant size) similar. Topography in a repeating pattern (say of rolling Downs) leads to tributaries in a repeating and symmetric pattern. Another repeating and symmetric pattern is where a large stream runs down the bottom of a steep valley (whether in the Belgian Moselle or the English Peaks), and tiny tributaries rise in this steep valley, feeding into the river though bringing very little water. (Here, the valley may be alluvium, the slopes, bedrock.) Asymmetric patterns tend to come from asymmetric topography. This may be due to varying rock type, or to varying glacial history, or to varying sea level history: that is, where another factor becomes important.

The central river axis is the maker, the creator. When, though, impact has changed the channel or the water, etc., the stream is caged, and loses its importance in the valley. Perception is altered: that man is the maker and creator.

Even among the streams placed traditionally, patterns are too numerous to show (Fig. 5.1, 3.3b). The heads found in Malta (Fig. 3.3b), the seepages of Iceland, the torrents of the Pyrenees, the plateau of the Massif Central, all alter the upper streams. Lower down, the streams may be less variable. True, the torrents and the creeks, the moor streams and the chalk ones are still there, but, subject to topography and impact, the shapes and pattern (not, the chemistry and biota!) are more similar. Further downstream again the wide flood plains, the wide meanders, are all more similar again (even when caged, the cages may resemble one another).

Channelling rivers makes them tidy, and putting them underground makes them even tidier. Both show a basic human wish of getting rid of the curves, and, preferably, the water too.

Wet slopes were increasingly pipe/tile-drained or field-drained, mostly in the nineteenth century (perhaps increased in the late twentieth century), draining run-off water underground away from the potential storage in the earth and leading it to the valley below. These are not (usually) natural underground streams.

Looking at maps, aerial photographs and sites, it is easy to see that there were many small tributaries on ordinary grass slopes throughout the country. When fields for cultivation were constructed, whether Neolithic, Roman or Anglo-Saxon – centuries before field drainage – these streams were diverted to go around the fields or through large furrows (Fig. 4.2). Ditches were dug – as tributary channels, not for occasional heavy storms – and hedges, so valuable for sticks, timbers, berries, predator and prey habitat, were also planted. These ditches led in a connected pattern down to the valley bottom and the larger stream there. With field and other drainage, and abstraction from aquifers, the tributary system dried, the ditches no longer needed so much maintenance. In the drier areas they may have become filled in as redundant, and with increasing field size they may be only seen from above or by excavation.

The length of ditch around the fields of a small stream is obviously many times the length of that valley stream. Hence the enormous loss of length of the river as it was, compared to the river as it is. To this can be added the length of (in Britain) lowland streams marked on the 1:2500 000 OS map but lost. In the early twentieth century, the marked streams were not only perennial, but had perennial water extending further than the marked length. These have not been re-mapped, and most have some length, often several miles, of marked stream before the present water becomes perennial.

Lowland country can have apparently miles of (particularly chalk) valley, with no stream at all. This may be abstraction, but may also be piping. The loss of aquatic habitat has been enormous. Biodiversity has vanished. In 1610, Norden listed six water and wetland fowl expected on any lowland manor, and a food resource for that manor. That means they were abundant on the smaller streams, now gone. Where fowl abound, so do their food, and the structures creating their habitat. (See George, 1998, Haslam, 1997, 2006, for a selection of evidence.) Later anecdotes include the number of small boys fishing for minnows in the local brook, the amount of water cress available for food, the number of poachers taking fish: there was aquatic habitat, and in abundance.

> The 'Afon' (Welsh for 'river') Vyrnwy (Fig. 5.5) is a major tributary (c. 15 km) of R. Severn, and is a (resistant rock) mountain stream, in terms of landscape and vegetation. The A. Vyrnwy rises in hills about 600 m high. The upper parts of A. Tanat tributary have 250–300 m falls from hill to river, often entirely in the first mile, while A. Vyrnwy has less steep slopes, so less water force. The water force in A. Vyrnwy is further reduced by a reservoir blocking spate flows from

the source, though its mountain tributaries bring in water of high force. The rivers then flow into a more gentle upland landscape, and the downstream section of the main river which is on soft rock, meanders in a flood plain to its confluence with R. Severn. There is one downstream tributary mainly on soft sandstone.

The small upper streams are mainly 2–3 m wide, and 30 cm deep, with moderate to fast flow and mostly gravel-stony substrates. The water is clear except in the upper catchment, where there is brown-stained water coming from some peat-capped hills. Bog peat is acid and nutrient-poor. The stream banks are fairly low and there is some shading. The channels of the main A. Tanat and A. Vyrnwy above the confluence reach 6–10 m wide and are up to 0.5 m deep. Below the confluence, the channels reach 10–20 m wide, and they are substrate. When the flow decreases in the flood plain, the substrate also becomes finer.

The small tributaries characteristically bear moss and benthic algae, with *Phalaris arundinacea* and *Veronica beccabunga* where there is less water force. Species per site are usually few, but are sufficiently similar to show a consistent species assemblage. An upland tributary, much further downstream, bears tall land species. This is lowland enough and small enough to have negligible scour. When the streams become medium sized, *Phalaris arundinacea* becomes frequent (as is common in hills). As the rivers become larger, *Ranunculus* enters. As usual, this is at first the short-leaved *Ranunculus aquatilis*, and then *R. fluitans* in the larger river of the flood plain.

Just before the flood plain there is a standard mountain flora. It is diverse, with downstream eutrophication indicated by *Ranunculus* spp., *Phalaris arundinacea, Callitriche* sp., Moss, *Elodea canadensis, Sparganium emersum* and *Rorippa nasturtium-aquaticum* agg. Depth fluctuates in the flood plain where substrates are unstable during spates. Most species, except *Ranunculus*, decrease.

The sandstone Maes Brook tributary has some highland influence upstream but suffers both Oswestry effluent and dredging. However, it bears a satisfactory sandstone vegetation towards the mouth.

About 30 sites were replicated in 1973 and 1977. *Ranunculus* spp. declined in the flood plain, presumably due to the drying, and so shallowing of the 1976 drought, as commonly happened. In 1980, the *Ranunculus* was recovering. The more eutrophic species also declined in 1977, but (as in other rivers) this is ascribed to the chance effect of the drought rather than to a trophic change. There is little overall change between the surveys, the two records showing the usual pattern of site variation and community stability (from Haslam, 1982).

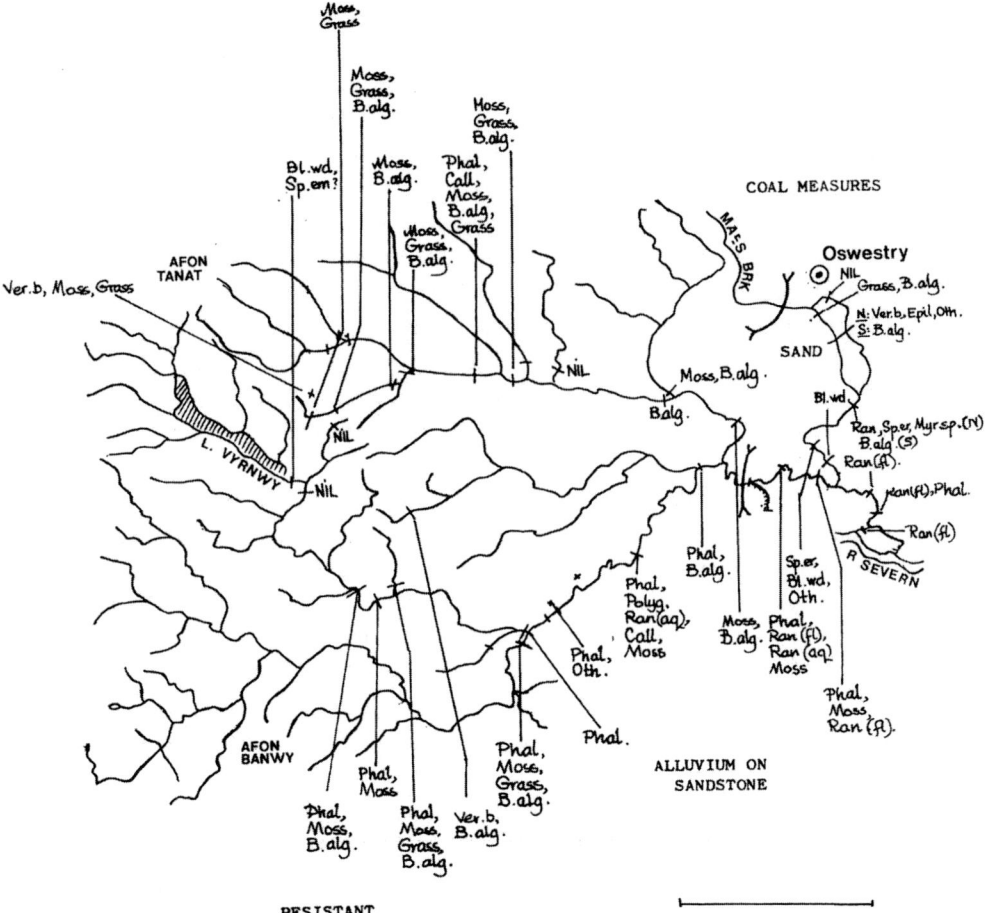

Fig. 5.5. Afon Vyrnwy, Britain, 1973. (Haslam. 1982) also see Box. For fig, scale bar = 10 km.

> The English (Cumbrian) Eden rises on Resistant rock but mostly flows on sandstone. The R. Eamont is a mainly Resistant rock stream, and the R. Lyvenet and the R. Lowther, are both mainly limestone streams. The R. Eden rises in hills over 650 m high and the upper part has steep slopes of 200 m in a mile. By Kirkby Stephen, the valley widens, and though the northern hills are still high and steep, the river is more influenced by the vale and upland hills. The tributaries from the mountains are few and small, with little influence on the main river (Fig. 5.6).
>
> The R. Eamont rises in hills over 800 m high, which have very steep slopes of 360 m in a mile. Its lower tributaries may be either upland or lowland. The effect of Ullswater on the river is to remove much of the spate effect of the

mountains. The R. Eamont has little and infertile vegetation in the steep upper streams (e.g. *Ranunculus flammula* in bog sources; *Myriophyllum alterniflorum* near the lake). The low-lying tributaries also have little vegetation. Below Ullswater, the R. Eamont bears *Ranunculus* in a species-rich community. Vegetation increases downstream, and *Elodea canadensis* enters. In a slow silty millstream, *Elodea canadensis* is a dominant species.

The Cumbrian R. Eden has little vegetation above, but *Petasites hybridus* is occasionally present. The wide, shallow gravelly channel is particularly suitable for this species. Downstream, fringing herbs increase, and then *Ranunculus* enters. Most of the *Ranunculus* is *R. fluitans*. Because of the mountain influence above, the vegetation is a mixed mountain type, rather than typically sandstone.

When the 1973 and 1977 surveys are compared, there is little overall change in diversity in the upper river, but substantial increases in diversity in the lower river. There may also have been an increase in *Ranunculus* abundance. The river here is deep and steep enough for a lessening of flow to produce conditions more favourable for *Ranunculus*. That is, that *Ranunculus* growth may have been hindered by excessive water force. (The river flows to the sea top left of the river map.)

This pattern was described for England, but the principles apply elsewhere.

Downstream variation in vegetation

Typical patterns

This follows typical patterns, reflecting the traditional communities and the impact imposed on them. Characteristic communities of different river types are shown in Figs. 5.5 and 5.6.

There is a clear downstream shift in communities, which is due to the 'natural' features of increasing stream size, nutrient inflow from the land, decreasing flow type, and, e.g. particle size, and to the imposed factors of pollution, land use, etc. (see above).

The downstream variation in community is standard in Europe except for the xerotic regions of the south. From Ireland to Hungary, there is the same basic pattern.

However, it is not ubiquitous. Xerotic Europe, south of a line between Sardinia and Corsica to Naples (and lesser, semi-xerotic, north to S. France and the Po Valley) do not show the downstream pattern (Haslam, 1987). Nor does a good deal of North America (Haslam, 1978 and later surveys of Florida), except for topographical patterning. In the Mediterranean, rivers narrow, shallow or

128 The riverscape and the river

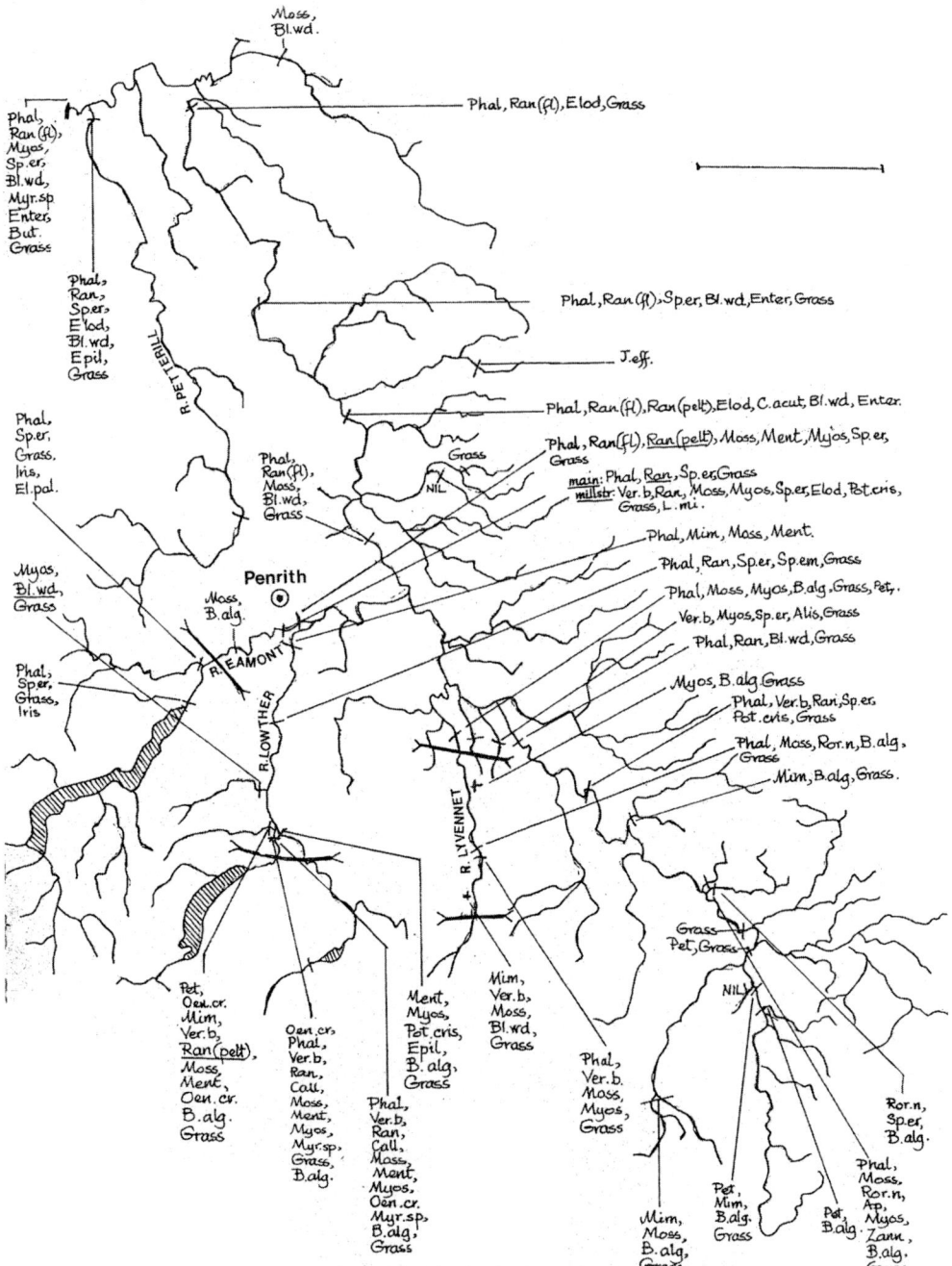

Fig. 5.6.

even dry in summer, so, for instance, the spring fringe of tall monocotyledons becomes a band isolated from the river in summer. Florida has the opposite extreme, conditions are moderately similar all year. There are, of course, great differences in vegetation pattern between the 3 m and the 30 m river, but little in biodiversity.

A second group of rivers has low downstream variation: those with high biodiversity and many niches. As explained in Chapter 2, many niches allow species to grow in rivers which, if all were gone, they could not (e.g. if all shelter is removed, only species of flow can occur).

There are variations with different patterns of slope. As habitat changes (see above), so does plant community. Each species (and hence community) grows in a range of habitat, so habitat change leads to community change. For instance, in the centre of a species' chemical (nutrient) regime, it can grow both in pool (siltier, more nutrients) and in riffle (less nutrients), while near the end of its flow range, it may grow only in the one and avoid the other (the pool being too nutrient-rich, or too slow-flowing, or the riffle, the reverse).

The drained shape of the existing tributaries may or may not lessen the water, but it lowers the water table, so the storage capacity for water in the land. The (usually) steep high bank is a poor habitat for aquatics! So, even when watercourses with water are still present, far too often good quality aquatic habitat is not.

Storm flows are part of downstream variation. Their pattern is due to factors both natural (rain, snow melt, slope and rock type) and imposed (drainage, abstraction, dredging, altering size, shape and pattern). If a river is left alone, both geomorphology and flora (and, consequently, fauna) adjust to the incident storms. There is (1) the pattern of 'changeless change', the way plants are constantly being washed out and re-growing; (2) the pattern of cyclic change when much vegetation (and perhaps bank and bed) are washed away, but very similar patterns redevelop in a few years; (3) alterations, which can be slow, in that species of one habitat gradually replace those of another. Or they can be rapid, as when a major storm removes communities not sufficiently adapted to the new conditions to re-invade, and a sharply different community results (Tables 2.3 and 2.4).

The total number of common river species in (west and central) temperate Europe is less than 100 (Tables 5.3, 5.4): a number possible to remember, but also one where variations in combinations are subtle. In two nearby rivers, each with 15 species in a 25 m reach, each is likely to have at least 10 in common, maybe even 14 or 15. Differences in habitat will show in different proportions of the same species (e.g. more *Ranunculus* or *Myriophyllum* spp. in fast flow, more *Sagittaria sagittifolia* and *Sparganium emersum* in silty places), or different patterns

Table 5.3 *Interpretation of habitat from species lists (from Haslam, 2002)*

British 30 m site with 75% cover, and:		
Tall monocots, three species in a fringe		
Glyceria maxima	*Phalaris arundinacea*	*Sparganium erectum*
Short emergents, seven species in a mixed-dominance fringe		
Berula erecta	*Glyceria fluitans*	*Mentha aquatica*
Mimulus guttatus	*Myosotis scorpioides*	*Veronica anagallis-aquatica*
Veronica beccabunga		
Water-supported species, six, *Ranunculus* abundant		
Berula erecta	*Callitriche* spp.	*Elodea canadensis*
Potamogeton crispus	*Potamogeton perfoliatus*	*Ranunculus sp.*, medium-leaved

Diagnosis

With this ecology, the site must be a middle reach of a lowland soft limestone river, probably 6–15 m wide; the centre partly under 50 cm deep, partly 75 cm or more; averaging moderate flow, with clear water. The banks are seldom steep, the river edge wide and shallow. The substrate is partly firm gravel, partly softer, and there is some silt at the side. There is no major disturbance, but some shallowing (drying) and perhaps minor grazing. The water is calcium dominated, with little pollution.

Reasoning

The site has 16 spp., very diverse; and the three habit groups are well represented. Only 4 out of 16 spp. are pollution-tolerant. Site reasonably clean.

Short emergents are the most frequent, so there is a wide edge, and tall monocots are prevented from invading (grazing?). With only six water-supported species (and no rarer species like *Groenlandia densa* and *Lemna trisulca*) some drying is likely.

Glyceria maxima is silt-associated and avoids fast flow. It and *Phalaris arundinacea* anchor to the bank, but *Sparganium erectum*, being beside the bank, is less stable in wash-out. Firm banks, penetrable by roots and rhizomes, and little disturbance, is indicated.

Mixed dominance of fringing herbs means low nutrients keeping shoots short. six species indicates limestone and, because of their poor anchorage in mountains, lowlands. With the low nutrient range of *Mimulus guttatus*, the site is middle to upper reaches. With the more nutrient-rich *Myosotis scorpioides*, middle.

The water-supported species include an abundant *Berula erecta* carpet, indicating shallow, moderate and stable flow, and clean and lime-rich water. *Ranunculus* sp. dominates, its roots curl round superficial stable stones and gravel. It grows in flowing, fairly clean and deeper water. *Callitriche obtusangula* + *stagnalis* has less cover, so lime rather than sandstone is indicated. *Callitriche* spp. is usually in shallow water. It has very dense, thin, shallow roots, and spreads rapidly by fragments. Wash-out removes and spreads the species. *Potamogeton perfoliatus* needs space, water 75+ cm deep, so is a middle or downstream species. The substrate must be soft for deeper roots to penetrate, firm to maintain anchorage, the water, usually clear. Therefore the site has variable depth and substrate. *Potamogeton crispus* has deep straight roots, anchoring well in penetrable substrates. It avoids strong calcium dominance, so in a chalk stream occurs where downstream eutrophication or pollution has lessened this.

Table 5.4 *Cover-Diversity, CoDi, values in relation to habitat: various examples of its use*

(1) Along a hill stream (selected 25 m reaches)

Habitat	Species (number)	Cover (%)	CoDi number
Typical	3	<10	3
Whitewater	1	<10	1
Sheltered bar	5	10	6
Above weir	5	20	7
Trampled	2	<10	2

By using CoDi, the observer notices the change in habitat, and its cause.

(2) Along a lowland stream (selected 25 m reaches)

Habitat	Species (number)	Cover (%)	CoDi number
Typical	7	25	9
Concave banks (no emergents)	4	25	5
Wide berm (more short emergents)	10	30	13

By using CoDi, the importance of bank shape is emphasised, and will thereafter be noticed.

(3) Longitudinal variation with size and type (consolidated intermittent 25 m reaches)

Size	Type	Country	CoDi number
0–3 m with water-supported species	Lowland clay	Britain	4 if drying or fast 11 if flooded and low erosion
4–8 m	Lowland clay	Britain	13
10+ m	Lowland clay	Britain	15
0–3 m with water-supported species	alluvium	Denmark	14
4–8 m	alluvium	Denmark	16
10+ m	alluvium	Denmark	17
0–3 m with water-supported species	Upland Sandstone	France	11
4–8 m	Upland Sandstone	France	12
10+ m	Upland Sandstone	France	13 (few sites)
0–3 m with water-supported species	Moorland Resistant	Britain	6
4–8 m			10
10+ m			8

(cont.)

Table 5.4 *(cont.)*

The first three examples show the typical – as expected – pattern that of size, as space for plants increases, so does the CoDi number.

So when the reverse occurs – when many sites have been consolidated – some factor damaging to the vegetation can be deduced. In this instance, moorland tends to be on flatter hills, with the water running off steeper slopes below. Higher water force decreases vegetation. Such patterns may also mean increased downstream pollution, channelisation, lining, or other disturbance, and are an indication other causes should be sought.

(4) Assessing total impact: using paired streams (e.g. size, topography, flow, rock type).

Habitat	CoDi
Good Pasture, Britain	12
Intensive cultivation	8
Mountain Corsica (very low impact)	14
Mountain Britain	1
Frontier river, Denmark (low impact as two-country agreement needed)	18
Other branch of same river, Denmark (rather higher impact)	11
Hilly south Norway (low impact)	13
Hilly Britain	6

A stream may not be seriously polluted, channelling could be mild, land use is not abominable, and so on. Each separate impact is low, but the cumulative and synergistic impact is considerable. (Synergistic, because, e.g. pollution leads to shorter roots, so it is more difficult for the plant to anchor in a dredged channel without its hard bed.)

Pollution is not measured by CoDi until it is enough to decrease diversity or cover. If merely pollution-sensitive species are replaced by pollution-tolerant ones, CoDi does not assess it.

(e.g. fringing herbs abundant on islands, or very sparse along steep edges), or all the nutrient-rich species frequent in one, all the nutrient-poor, in the other. These are patterns. If autecology is known, the interpretation is there. Knowledge is essential, including local knowledge, since different ecotypes and different microclimates encourage autecological differences.

Table 5.5 give some characteristics of these common species, showing how, in very general terms, any combination can give an interpretation. To go further, the more detailed autecology in specific areas must be known, including geographic range. In the south of Europe for instance, it is useless to invent reasons of flow or chemistry for the absence of *Nuphar lutea*, which is climatically excluded. Some of the intra-specific European variations are shown, a few species frequent and useful for interpretation in more extreme conditions (north, south, bog).

Table 5.5 *Change over 40 years with shallowing in River Dove, Peak District, England*

Butcher *c.* 1930 (1933)	*c.* 1980
(daforl scale, modified)	
Upper river	Nine sites recorded in upper hilly part
Apium nodiflorum l	Species in at least five sites –
Berula erecta a	*Phalaris arundinacea* (not a Butcher species)
Groenlandia densa o	*Ranunculus* sp. (medium leaves)
Myosotis scorpioides l	Mosses
Ranunculus fluitans d	Benthic algae (not a Butcher species)
Veronica anagallis-aquatica o	Other significant species
Mosses	*Agrostis stolonifera* (not a Butcher species)
	Callitriche spp.
	Veronica beccabunga
Lower river	five sites recorded in lower part
Callitriche sp. a	Species in at least three sites
Groenlandia densa l	*Ranunculus* sp. (medium-leaved)
Elodea canadensis f	*Sparganium erectum*
Mimulus guttatus o	Benthic algae (not a Butcher species)
Potamogeton crispus r	Other significant species
P. perfoliatus f	*Myriophyllum spicatum*
Ranunculus fluitans a	*Phalaris arundinacea* (not a Butcher species)
Sparganium emersum a	*Sparganium emersum*
	Veronica beccabunga
Dominant can be assumed to be >75% cover, abundant, >50%, frequent >25%	5 out of the 14 sites had 25+% cover

Comparing like with like, the species list was approximately halved between 1930 and 1980, and the cover dropped to about a third. The 1980 species assemblage is depleted, mountain in type. That of 1930 gives a rounded assemblage, with, as is proper, dominant *Ranunculus* but also other species, of fringes, of deep silty places, shallow water, and a variety of nutrient regime.

Lists can be made, of common aquatics. The more restricted the habitats, the greater the interpretation from species presence. Downstream patterning and continuums are usually predictable. In detail, a new impact, topographic feature or rock type may impose different patterns. And where, e.g. climate or pristine conditions preclude downstream variation, that also can be seen.

The examples in Figs. 5.4–5.6 give representative downstream variations. The variations are in the nature of the plant and the nature of the habitat. An emergent cannot live in deep water without air for oxygenation. This is a simple physiological reason, and most of the reasons are this simple. Highly complex communities come from the interaction of a mixture of simple factors.

This makes basic interpretation simple. It is also why so often complex analyses and computer models become naive or liable to error, e.g. the reaction of *Myriophyllum spicatum* to silt banks in hill streams, or that of *Nuphar lutea* to pollution in a formerly clean chalk stream, has been omitted, and the resultant patterns computed are not those found in the field.

While each biotic group should be studied separately, the vegetation is more often the best indicator of the health of all groups, since plants provide structure, cover, food, oxygenation and many other valuable chemical processes for fauna and algae.

Cover-Diversity number

When assessing vegetation, and when circumstances are not favourable to using lengthy methods, the CoDi (Cover-Diversity) number, and Tables 5.2, 2.4 can be used. These look at species quality: species of fast and slow flow, low and high nutrients, and requires plant identification (see, e.g. Haslam, 1987).

The CoDi number looks at biodiversity and quantity only. In a 25 m length, the number of macrophytes within the wetted perimeters of the river are the Diversity part of the number. Then One is added for each 10% cover of vegetation (excluding, unless there is a special reason, duckweeds, Lemnaceae, because they blow about), and giving a maximum of 7 (since ecologically there is little difference between 70% and 100%). The Cover and Diversity numbers, added, then give a useful, very simple, value. When walking downstream, in a typical European stream (Table 5.4) the numbers will, overall, increase. But there will be plenty of variations: very steep banks, number down; tree trunk lodged, number up; effluent entry, number down; irregular bank, number up. Because this is so simple, it can be used by untrained observers and for obtaining large numbers of records, to detect habitat variations which affect vegetation in a way not feasible when each analysis takes 15 minutes or more. Unexplained changes in the CoDi number should be noted for future study.

If species can be identified and Table 5.6 be used also, changes in chemical quality can be detected, whether in nutrients or in pollutants. Pollutions act immediately on vegetation: a flow line occurs across the stream where the pollution enters. The affected community becomes reduced, skewed to pollution-tolerant species or both (Table 2.4, Fig. 2.11).

Drying is the other most common cause of loss (Fig. 2.10, Table 5.5). Here first the balance changes, water supported species decreasing in number and cover, and edge ones (if the habitat is satisfactory) increasing. Then the water-supported species are lost, and finally the edge emergents are also lost, leaving just land species.

Habitat variations

All rivers have substrates and beds. But the amount and texture of sediment, consolidated and unconsolidated, vary. Therefore, the plant patterns vary also, irrespective of nutrient regime (except insofar as more inorganic silt means more nutrients). Too much unconsolidated sediment (from erodable rock type or inadequate cultivation) means an unstable substrate, frequently washed away, and a poor rooting habitat. Too little fine sediment means poor anchorage and nutrients. Once more, the principles are simple, but the permutations endless. The community alters with the amount of suitable habitat for each of the species of the community assemblage.

Sediments vary in nutrient status which comes partly from bedrock, drift, subsoil, soil and vegetation, each of which varies, and partly by variations imposed by the type and intensity of human impact. Each solute varies in concentration and in processes. Because the science of sediment and water analysis is not advanced, prediction and interpretation of vegetation relations are still at an elementary stage. It is easy (see above) to use vegetation to detect an, e.g. nutrient-poor habitat, but not to give the ppm in it of, for example, magnesium in its different forms, in water and different types of sediment, at different times of year, in different types of weather and with different types of vegetation and impact.

The status of vegetation types is usually a better guide to the status of other biota, than vice versa. Vegetation forms more of the structure, shelter and substrate for, e.g. food, egg-laying. There are, unfortunately, many reasons why vegetation fails, from whitewater flow to recent dredging. There are more. This is why it does not reach its potential maximum, in both quality and quantity. Reduced vegetation is reduced for a reason. Consequently, with autecological knowledge, the environmental reason can be deduced (or vice versa).

However, from the R. Itchen (below), it is shown that an even doubtful climate change, when a river is already greatly suffering from impact, may add to and collectively make a habitat change. These combined impacts may well increase over the next decades, unless the Water Framework Directive is fully implemented.

Climate, of course, changes continually even when impact does not. There has been a significant warming, in the south of England, in the past two centuries. In the late eighteenth century there were between 3 months and 3 weeks of snow or hard frost each winter (White, 1788). Now three weeks is exceptional, a few days is usual. What has been the change in rivers? Unfortunately, no records help! The eighteenth-century records the improvement in navigation (with tow paths, removal of shoals and weed bands and making bypass channels around weirs), and in flood defence. All these would have had a major effect on the biota, indeed, probably more than the warming! Planners for human resources rightly concentrate on upcoming climate changes. Ecologists should probably be more concerned with the man-made loss of water, of traditional channel shape and pattern, and increase of pollution including that from hard surfaces.

Species interact with each other, and their habitat, among others light, turbidity, flow, pollards, swans, carp, boats, and fisheries. When slope changes downstream, habitat and biota change, though at different distances. When a lowland river falls over a cliff, it becomes a cascade immediately. When a mountain river flows into a plain, its water force and change to lowland vegetation happen slowly. The difference between immediate and delayed responses can be important in interpretation. When rock type changes, or a tributary from a different type, or a pollution enters, there is a change of chemistry, which again may be immediate or delayed. A similar though repeating pattern occurs in a pool-and-riffle system where the chemistry is such that more silt (solutes in sediment, pool) gives a different community to that of less silt (riffle).

Incoming sediment is chemically stronger than water, since it contains so much more solute. Being heavier, it also takes longer to cross the nutrient boundary. The more the particles carried, the more the effect. The more the discharge from one rock type, the more its effect. The stronger the incoming solute compared with the existing one, the more the effect. So, higher solute concentrations increase effect, whether of rock type, land use or contamination.

R. Wylye, England (vegetation)

The upper R. Wylye in the 1970s was a good example of the inter-relation of pollution (both genuine and perceived) and drying, on general deterioration. The river rose in Chalk Downs, was drying from abstraction and being sedimented from loss of flow and unsuitable cultivation. The river vegetation was, as expected, *Ranunculus*-based, with subsidiary *Callitriche*, fringing herbs, etc., and algae on silt shoals. A fish farm released a richer effluent, with enough nutrients to reduce the calcium dominance (Haslam 2003), allow other nutrients to be prominent, and *Callitriche* to be dominant. *Ranunculus* was only sparse, the opposite relationship to that of the chalk brook and like that of a sandstone brook. It was perceived that *Ranunculus* effluent streams from a watercress farm were polluting the Wylye. However, even the much worse fish farm brooks were not affecting the (larger) stream. A little further downstream, the cess pits of the village, pouring into the river, fully accounted for the pollution. The pollution had been correctly seen, but wrongly attributed. Invertebrates, responding primarily to oxygen, show the maximum damage from organic pollution 1–2 km downstream of its entry, when oxygen is least. Plants respond to the toxins instantly, so in this instance plants easily distinguished the various waters, where invertebrates were insufficiently sensitive. Therefore, the chemical patterns were:

- flowing chalk streams, *Ranunculus*-based, low silt;
- chalk streams shoaled up (see above), where much sediment (nutrient) led to short blanket weed on shoals, but did not otherwise disturb the calcium dominance;
- fish farm effluent streams, also on chalk, with sufficient non-calcium nutrients to swing the vegetation to that of sandstone (*Callitriche* sp. predominating over *Ranunculus* sp.) but not enough to change the main river status;
- chalk stream (larger) with sewage effluent reducing and skewing the vegetation;
- chalk stream with little vegetation because it was a play-site for dogs;
- chalk stream with little vegetation because of sewage;
- chalk stream with self-purification allowing some vegetation.

Long-term changes

Climate change, global warming, are long term. Considering the extreme change in drainage, channelling and surface absorption over Europe, no small climate change effects can be detected. Possible increases in heavy rainfall, leading to more flash floods, are almost subsumed into their increase from increased hard and firm surfaces. Felling forests, turning hardly touched grassland into firm soil or intensive arable, creating hard surface, turning slow, water-storing rivers and wetlands into deep, straight, swift channels: the effect of these is only just becoming known. A less stark change awaits study (this is excluding changes in sea and land levels). Figure 2.2 sums up some of the large-scale changes.

R. Itchen, England (invertebrates)

There have been some studies of rivers over time, e.g. Haslam, 1987, 1990, and particularly Kohler (see Bibliography), but, for invertebrates, the fullest examination is by Holloway (2003) on the chalk stream R. Itchen (see Butcher, 1927; Haslam, 1978, 1982) for 34 years. This is enough time to separate short-term fluctuations (drought, major cutting) from long-term trends. The Itchen is a famous trout river, so though it has suffered from water loss, it has been kept as free as possible from other impacts. Anglers pay much money to keep rivers in good condition. Trout need invertebrates (food).

Invertebrates have declined, a few species becoming extinct. Spawning grounds are, of course, essential for good trout populations. Spawning is best in the last 2 weeks of December and the first of January. Heavy rains before this, which cause high water levels, faster flow, water coloured by run-off, later prolonged frosts and low water temperatures, lead to healthier trout fry and better spring invertebrates.

Invertebrate populations were the best in cleared, non-compacted gravel, and in at least 30 cm of water. Because of the water loss, these formerly natural conditions are difficult to find, and rakes and water jets are used to remove silt stuck in the gravel. If the silting is left, it calcifies, which alters the invertebrates.

The habitat changes are:

- decreased flow;
- warmer water – partly because of less spring water (which is stable at about 10 °C when it emerges), and partly because of milder winter temperatures;
- increased contamination, from hard surface and agricultural run-off. In the 1920s (Butcher, 1927) the vegetation indicated domestic sewage discharging from villages. Now, the pollution is more diffuse and more widespread;
- increased fine sediment deposition (from agricultural erosion and hard surface run-off);
- a probable long-term change in rainfall. While the totals are unchanged, falls have been shorter and more intense. This means more intake and deposition of silt;
- loss of water meadows and their stabilising effect, and the silt deposited on them.

Therefore, the changes, small though they are individually, have collectively altered the habitat to be less suitable for trout. When a habitat is close to its limit for certain features (here silting, water, winter temperature), small changes, too small to be noticed by most observers, can change suitability for species. (For loss of snowmelt since the eighteenth century, see above.)

Only one of these factors can be attributed to global warming, and even there, without the loss of springs and water meadows, it might not be enough to make an ecological difference. The traditional buffers of the R. Itchen have been removed, and changes occur.

Brief case studies

In Malta, for the past over 40 years, a certain roundabout has flooded during winter storms. Decades on, the roundabout is a raised circus with culverts and channels: but the amount of flooding and damage has hardly changed. Upstream, the terraced valley with a small village has slowly become a completely built-up valley, and each time the roundabout has been upgraded, the new hard surface has upgraded the flash floods.

A 30-year study in the Sussex Weald (Howarth & Manning, 2006) showed increased arable and, in the river, increased flash floods and decreased (chemical) water quality (though not invertebrates).

The changes on R. Dove, English Peak District, in less than 50 years, have been great (Butcher, 1933; Haslam, 1982). (This period was, of course, before climate change was considered important.) The change (Table 5.5) is attributable to the impact of water loss. Instead of a well-vegetated (carboniferous) limestone hill stream, the river had a shallow eroding flow, with little anchoring substrate, and little water deep enough for the species characteristic of the former depth. The water loss may have been accentuated by removal of weirs retaining water, for drainage.

The vegetation was ruined, and by impact.

Connectivity and mosaics

River valleys are connected, on the large scale, though they may be obstructed and divided on the small scale. Up by the sources, the watershed of one catchment is, ordinarily, that of another, or other, catchments. Therefore, hydrologically there may well be connections between upper streams; as when there is a single channel, at one point flowing west, at another just beside, east, or when there are numerous small tributaries winding through a boggy area, and it seems random (or the last storm), what determines which flows to which catchment. Larger fish and downstream plants cannot be connected in this way. It is just the water and the small organisms it contains that are connected.

Mosaics are both between and within channels. The same community may occur in a similar habitat in one river and also in that habitat in many different streams in, or indeed out of, that river basin. There are repeating patterns, and patterns on different scales, from tiny (as those made by small streams), medium (as in a pool-riffle system), or large (those occurring in a plain by its mouth to the sea). Habitats are patches, small patches are niches, e.g. deep, soft soil forms a niche, in which deep-rooted species can form a patch.

The size of a patch for a particular species to survive indefinitely varies greatly. A metapopulation of small invertebrates may not need much. Salmon need more, particularly as they return (when possible) to their river of origin for breeding. Habitat patches which are continuous, i.e. along much of the length of a river, tend to support species for longer periods than separated ones, where, for instance, a storm can remove not just a larger proportion of the population, but much of the population itself.

A river can be considered a corridor with mosaics of patches (Downs & Gregory, 1993).

6

Development and variation of riverscapes

The real voyage of discovery consists not in seeking new landscapes but in having new eyes

(M. Proust, 1871–1922)

Landscape analysis traces much of landscape evolution, long-term history, health of ecosystems

(Lewan, 2001)

The importance of Sense of Place

Introduction

The catchment, the river basin, contains all the natural capital of the land. The natural capital is what can be used and should remain. The sunlight and the precipitation (plus the other contents of the air and rain) reach the land. Land forms are made from rock. On them are subsoil, soil, alluvium, peat, water, glacial deposits and in, and above again, the biota. This is the capital of the land. There is a constant cascade of this natural capital downhill from source to sea (sediment, water, nutrients, carbon, nitrogen and other chemicals). Development is by the natural processes of the outside events acting on, and interacting with, the land form and what it bears. Impact alters this pattern, decreasing the productivity of the natural biota: by removing it. It may increase the productivity of people-chosen biota (e.g. wheat), or just increase the constructions of man (e.g. houses and streets).

Historically, serious impact begins when grazing domestic animals are sufficient to substantially alter vegetation, when crops are cultivated and the land is divided up, when settlement and communications are sufficient to disrupt

Table 6.1 Riverscape elements in the Eger catchment, Hungary

	Mountain	Foothills	Upper plain	Lower plain
Topography	To 950 m, with, fairly steep, not jagged, relatively even slopes and shapes	Smooth and convex	Flat lowland	Flat plain drained below river level
Rivers	Valley tributaries full with snowmelt, upper ones may dry in summer except after storms. Tributaries well spaced, by the smooth and convex hills	Tributaries perennial, flash floods common after heavy rain in mountains, some straightening	Flow becomes slow into the plain. Straightened tributaries common	Drains and dykes. River embanked (higher level), straightening
Water supply	Run-off, snowmelt, flushes (springs)	More steady than higher up. Large springs (including thermal) frequent	Run-off, rivers from above. Some drainage	Much drainage, ex-wetland
Land use	Forested	Forest higher, vines and other crops lower	Agricultural	Agricultural
	With small flower-rich meadows in valleys	Valley bottoms and flood plains with much meadow above, and cultivation increasing below	Willow-bands often by rivers	

Settlement	Sparse farms and villages in valleys, some now for recreation	The ancient City of Eger, in a 'bowl' in the hills. Other villages	Villages on higher ground	Mostly new, but still mostly on higher ground (or, e.g. church on high point of village)
Defence	A little	Eger guarded the route from N. to S., and, in part, that from E. to W. along the edge of the plain. Ancient castle	No	No
Communications	Poor, now good roads. One train line	River (to Tisza and Danube) Road, later rail	River, roads now good. Rail along edge of plain	

The catchment size is c. 75 × 25 km. The whole of Malta (Table 5.1) is 14 × 9 km.
While the Eger catchment has more variation than can be summarised here, per square kilometre there is negligible variation compared with Malta, and far fewer striking or unique features.

vegetation patterns, and when rivers and other watercourses are changed enough to alter natural water regimes. At present, there are no satisfactory classifications of riverscapes. Many are being developed, but they suffer from being over-general (mountain, plain, e.g. Table 10.2) or so detailed for one region that they are inapplicable elsewhere (see below) (see Chapter 1). Riverscapes are the results of cumulative impact over millennia, of a natural base. The cumulative impact may be that of a single culture, as Iceland (though for hardly more than one millennium), or of many, as England, such as Neolithic, Roman, Anglo Saxon, Viking, Norman, various English, then added to these, the changes in each of these cultures, developed by technology (e.g. farming improvements since *c*. 1800) or by an outside event such as varying sea level (e.g. Broads and Fenland). Both may be drastic or gentle changes (Table 2.1).

Time is a vital element of interpreting a riverscape. Time Past, Time Present (and indeed Time to Come) as an old sundial motto goes.

The miniature archipelago of the Maltese Islands, less than 250 km^2 in area, shows so much variation in river form without significant variation in climate. This helps to illuminate other, larger, riverscape shapes. There is variation in how the valley rises, and how it develops (Figs. 3.3 and 8.5; Table 5.1). Unusual features include the nesting sections caused by the alternation of hard and soft rock beds (Fig. 3.3b), and the terraced slopes. Ordinary riverscapes have flow in channels set by gravity or altered by impact (Chapter 5) but still on the same general slope. Terraced slopes are designed so that flow will cause minimum erosion, with stones in each level for easy drainage and patterning set for water movement (up to ordinary storms). It is almost possible to classify riverscape elements. What is brought out less, is what lies around, above and below the land surfaces.

Table 6.1 and Figs. 6.1, 8.2 demonstrate some different patterns in Hungary. The first difference is scale! The whole of the Maltese Archipelago can fit into a uniform piece of plain or mountain. The hills are higher, the valleys are smooth, the tributaries are well spaced out. Drying is less, and there is no summer drought. Even down on the plain, the area is so large that there are complete catchments within it.

The plain rivers are mostly channelled and straightened, so the visual element is low, the land forms are simple. Arranging the landscape elements is therefore simple, and not easy to reconcile with those of Malta!

Sense of place

Every riverscape is, in detail, unique, but the scale of variations differ. The English Peak District shows much diversity, while the Netherlands wetlands

Development and variation of riverscapes 145

(a)

(b)

Fig. 6.1. Willow, mostly *Salix alba* and reed *(Phragmites australis)* bands along streams. (a) Hungary, lop-sided. (b) England, symmetrical.

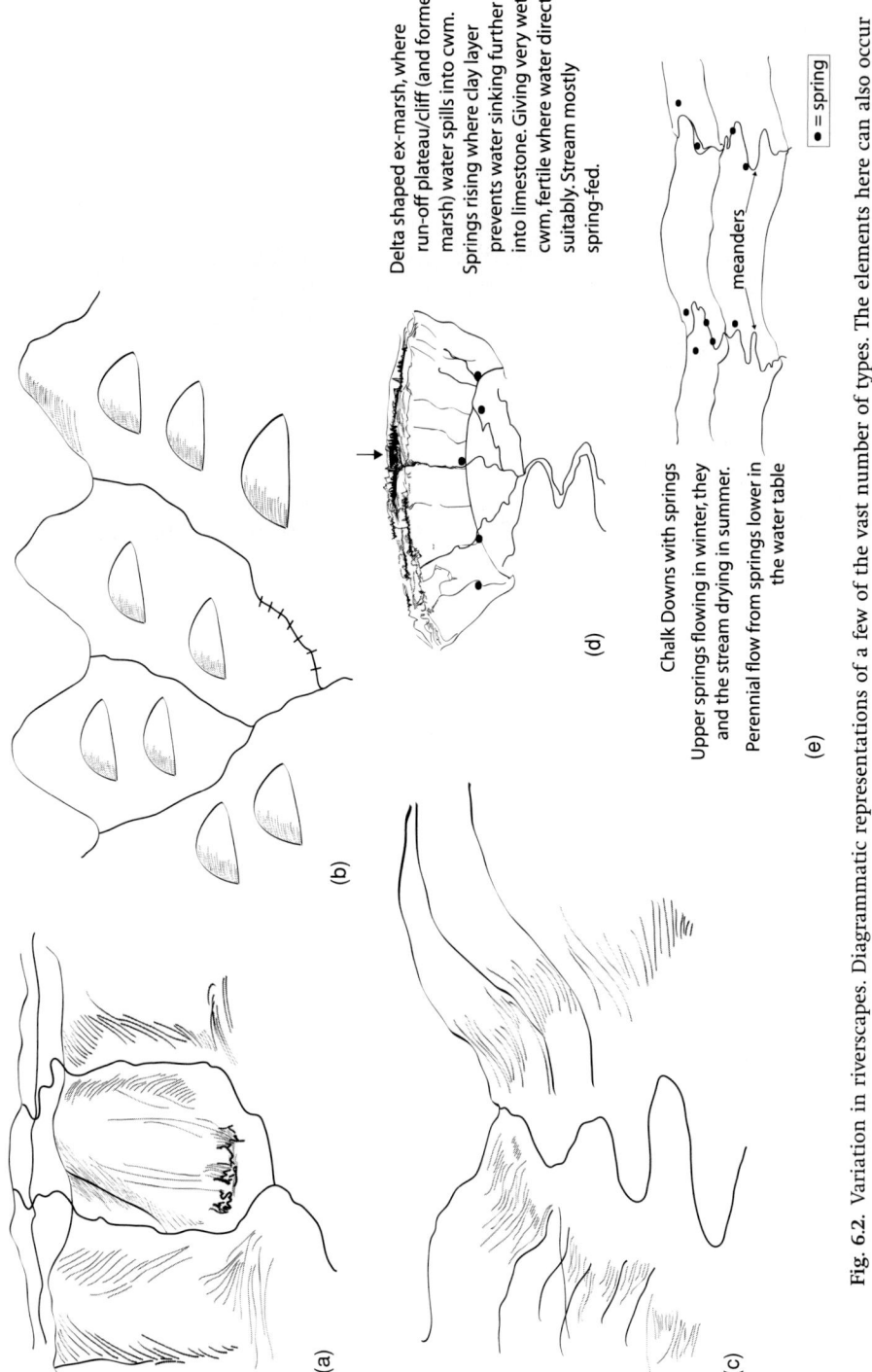

Fig. 6.2. Variation in riverscapes. Diagrammatic representations of a few of the vast number of types. The elements here can also occur separately, e.g. the dissected plateau of (a) can be under 100 m, and so rivers drop gently into lowlands. Hill and mountain riverscapes are the more dramatic, and 'dull' lowland ones (e) much the commonest in Europe.

Fig. 6.3. Mosaics within riverscapes, Peak District, England. This shows patches of wood, grass, arable, homesteads and hamlets, streams, rising lowlands. These patches are joined to form a mosaic.

and the Norwegian tundra have less diversity. Countrywide, Malta has perhaps the most variability for the least area, but Britain has far more than, say, France (which is much bigger) or Italy. All show repeating landscape too (e.g. Scottish blanket bog, French Massif Central plateau). Different riverscapes have a different Sense of Place. Sense of Place (*genius loci*) may apply to a huge valley surrounded by mountains, or to that part of the brook that can be seen from a picnic rug. It is indeed a natural resource. If planners could only be encouraged to look for Sense of Place, and understand that the uniqueness of place, heritage and beauty are irreplaceable, and should not be bulldozed, planted with aliens, built over or otherwise changed!

Patterns (Figs. 6.2, 6.3)

The human eye seeks pattern, it seeks to make random shapes into squares, spirals (which may need much imagination), or mosaics of patches, corridors, connecting one place to another. Connections may be genuine (e.g. ponds with streams, villages with roads), or imaginary (e.g. trees marching over the skyline seen from one particular place).

What makes a mosaic, patch, corridor, etc. is not just the human eye. It is the riverscape purpose of the pattern. For travellers wishing to get from A to B, the road is an obvious corridor. For a dragonfly, the warm but sheltered stream and the bushes beside is a patch, a patch that can hold a population, but may be only tenuously connected with others. Heron may share the stream with the dragonfly, and their fly path to their roosts may be close to the road: but the patterns and connections are independent.

When looking at, and for, patterns therefore, it is important to decide on the purpose: trout? reeds? flood plains? flushes? battlefields of long ago? And to concentrate on that before moving to another purpose. Eventually, it may be possible to link many, but they should start separate. A pattern of beauty is as much a valid pattern as one of grayling! And the beauty, the charm, the sheer pleasure given by riverscapes is not to be ignored in a world where little weight is placed on civilising influences.

Beneath each pattern lies the processes which created them. The processes, though many, are limited (excluding chemical), and therefore interrelations, interdependency, between processes (e.g. run-off) lead to interdependency of community, species and therefore pattern (Bell, 1999). Fields are created where there are farmers, and cultivable land, and most now have boundaries, at least hedges prevent erosion, and give shelter, and ditches drain and irrigate. That is the process. The result is diversity and the growing of crops.

A pattern created by one process may become a starting point for another. Water mills were built where there was suitable water, of course, but also where the local culture dictated (Chapter 12; Haslam, 1991). In England, this was often just outside and downstream of the village (pollution away from villagers). Usually, mills had land (for storage, drying, etc.). In the twentieth century, where was the obvious place to build a village industrial estate? The many 'Watermill' (or 'Mill') Estates give the answer!

A part of each pattern consists of the patch, the mosaic and the corridor, but another part is the boundary, the border of these, where one habitat meets another (see Chapter 11). This, however, adds to all patterns. Visually, aesthetically, there is a difference between a straight-line border, such as a building or a concreted vertical edge, and a fuzzy edge, such as a hedge, a band of tall monocotyledons by the river and a diffuse edge, such as the gradual change from poor fen to mixed grassland, from conifer wood rising to heather moor. This may influence what is noticed, and what is not noticed is unlikely to be studied. Borders may have a great influence on the biota. The edge of the water is the edge of the fish habitat. A wall forms a boundary very different to fish ecology than a reed fringe suited for shelter, cover, food or prey, and with little tributaries or pools behind, which are also habitat.

Edges can be active and vital parts of an ecosystem, and edges of watery places in riverscapes are typically so. As Kirby (1992) points out, even a pool lasting a few days can have a typical invertebrate (short-lived) population, and so can an equally small seepage population. Damp edges are not only biodiverse, they harbour communities not found elsewhere. Also, they are at risk. It is so easy to drain, neglect or destroy little places, and to increase the size of bank or field or road by removing untidy damp places and making nice straight (preferably firm and sharp) lines.

Riverscape construction (Tables 6.1 and 6.2)

Riverscapes and their patterns are connected through both space and time. A series of streams of one river are connected in space, but if they were all there a decade ago, a century or more ago, then there is a continuous connection for that time. The connection is of water, though not the same water, and of biota, though not necessarily even the same species of biota, let alone the same individuals, and thirdly, of impact and management (probably varying). The river continuum is of time as well as space, as is that of the riverscape, changed, slowly or dramatically, over the years. The land form continues, the rest changes.

Within the bedrock there may be space for water storage (sands) or not (gneiss). In the past, aquiferous rock was good for cultivable riverscapes, providing much irrigation and drainage. Now, a wild, traditional or even intensively cultivated riverscape is in a bad way if abstraction has removed most of the water (see Chapter 4), or even if the groundwater is polluted (with pollutants sinking down with the water). If so, even if abstraction stops, and springs rise again, the water rising will not be pure, but contaminated.

Above rock, the riverscape may have:

- alluvium from river or sea;
- glacial till, moraine, etc.;
- peat;
- subsoil;
- soil: inorganic particles from mud to boulder, and humus (dead plant remains). (Peat and alluvium are also classed as soil.).

All these are living systems too, containing millions of micro-organisms and invertebrates, photosynthetic algae on surfaces, etc. Also, there are the populations of macrophytes, and animals from earthworms to badgers. Soil (see Haslam, 2003) is a chemical powerhouse, carrying out a vast number of chemical processes. Many of these take place in or with water. When the land is dried, or otherwise altered, these processes necessarily change, and these changes may

Table 6.2 *Characteristics that give rise to landscape organisation (after Forman and Godron 1986)*

Type	Examples
1. Patches	Disturbance patches
	Patch edge or edge effect
	Remnant patches
	Regenerated patches
	Planted patches
2. Corridors	Disturbance, remnant, environmental resource, planted, regenerated corridors
	Line, strip, and stream corridors
	Shelterbelts
	Width effect
3. Matrix and network	Relative area of matrix
	Spreading and relict elements
	Matrix connectivity
	Homogeneity
	Concave and convex boundaries
4. Overall structure	Levels of scale
	Low and high contrast
	Regular, aggregated, linear, and parallel configurations
	Unusual landscape features
5. Natural processes in development	Geomorphology, landforms
	Openness
	Plant and animal establishment
	Increase in vegetation stature
	River systems
6. Human role in development	Cultivated landscapes – open-field and enclosure methods, villages, traditional agriculture, modern agriculture, geometrisation
	Built-up landscapes, cities, sacred monuments, politics
7. Flows between adjacent elements	Soil porosity
	Vectors – wind, water, flying animals, ground animals, people
	Forces – diffusion, mass flow, locomotion
	Flows of particulates and dissolved substances, surface and subsurface flows, land-to-stream flows
	Boundary function
	Sources, sinks
	Hedgerow effects on fields, matrix effects on hedgerows
	Sound movement

Table 6.2 (cont.)

Type	Examples
8. Animal and plant movement	Continuous and occasional movements
	Boundary crossing frequency
	Remoteness
	Long and short distance plant and animal dispersal
	Latitudinal and vertical migration
9. Landscape functioning	Corridor as habitat, conduit, barrier, and source of effects on matrix
	Functions of breaks, break area, fence effect
	Resistance to movement
	Hospitableness
10. Landscape change	Stability, instability, equilibrium, metastability, general tendency
	Persistence, resistance, recovery
	Physical system stability, recovery stability, resistance stability
	Linkages among landscapes
	Species coexistence
11. Heterogeneity	Isolated and non-isolated systems
	Animal use of cluster of ecosystems
	Heterogeneity-producing mechanisms

not be for the benefit of either the traditional biota (no wet habitat) or people (less cleaning of contaminants).

This 'soil' layer covers all or most of the slope, and in and on it live the outer layer, the vegetation and animals.

Most of temperate, lowland Europe is agricultural landscape, land under crops, most herbaceous, annual, and eatable. Land may belong in large (e.g. steppe or prairie) or small parcels (e.g. 5 m × 1 m Madeiran fields). They may have dividers on a small scale (e.g. some Irish hedged fields) or no dividers on large fields. The dividers may be trees, shrubs (hedges), ditches, streams, watersheds, fences: and the traditional unmarked lines of the field.

This pattern is complex in space and time (see above). The matrix, on which the rest is patterned, can be considered the fields, with corridors, patches and mosaics of the different crops and of small copses and 'wild' corners. The corridors are the field dividers, and, more importantly, the water system, from, e.g. storm flow channel to wide alluvial plain and river. This both controls and is controlled by the field pattern, as described above. The corridors of dividers

Table 6.3 *Effects of heterogeneity on landscapes (Malanson, 1993)*

- Landscapes differ structurally in the distribution of species, energy and materials, and therefore differ functionally in the flows of species, energy, and materials among the elements.
- Landscape heterogeneity decreases interiors, increases edges, and enhances species richness.
- The changes in the distributions of species are controlled by landscape heterogeneity, which is in part defined by these distributions.
- Nutrient flows in the landscape increase with disturbance.
- Flow of energy and biomass across boundaries increases with heterogeneity as well as with species diversity.
- The intermediate disturbance hypothesis applies to landscape heterogeneity as well as to species diversity.
- Landscapes will develop either physical system stability, resilience, or resistance to disturbance.

allow both habitat and movement. Hedges, copses, dry ditches, flooded ditches, bands of tall grass, these and more have their own biota.

Some of this biota is aquatic and wetland. And more of it affects the water regime: the downwards flow of water, of sediment, of organic matter, of nutrients, of agrochemicals. These are influenced by slope, soil depth and type, agrochemicals, crop (months of cover, direction of furrow, species of crop), type of soil, soil firming, maintenance of flow channels, absorption of water. Dividers, particularly if with variation in level (ditches, banks, old walls, raised tree roots), change and alter soil and water movement patterns. Dividers are the main sites of native traditional biota, with field weeds and animals in the fields themselves. Old dykes and hedges though, usually have some remnants of the traditional flora and fauna, as well as species of more disturbed, or more specialised ground. The usefulness of corridors as connections varies greatly with both corridor and species. A 2 m wide grass beetle bank is not likely to help a woodland bird.

Nothing stays the same. In agricultural landscapes, even those not really liable to volcanoes, earthquakes and such-like, quarries and motorways are made, land slips, forests are felled, hedges are removed, ditches are dried, fields alter in size and shape, crop type changes. These all influence riverscape processes. They alter the patches of the riverscape and their connectivity, forming new corridors, making new habitats, removing old ones. Some such changes are cyclic (e.g. woods), others occur erratically (e.g. fire, landslip).

Land was widely cultivated before populations exploded, so superimposed on the agricultural landscape is the constructed pattern, settlements and roads.

In pleasant and populous riverscapes, settlements may develop in a variety of places, given proper water resources. One place may have better river banks, or a more fordable river, or an easier road: but there was choice. In difficult, harsher riverscapes the choice is less, e.g. by the only cultivable land, the only dry land, the only non-raided land, or the only place with suitable water. Constructions form corridors for people, often barriers for animals and plants. They make patches and mosaics, and add to diversity, which may well be good, and to fragmentation, which more often degrades habitat.

Connectivity in a riverscape varies with purpose and beholder, as mentioned above. For a population to survive, it must be breeding, have sufficient genetic diversity, and be of sufficient number to withstand the occasional disaster. The population may be spread over various localities all connected to each other for that species, that is, a metapopulation. An invertebrate confined to shallow transient pools, able to withstand several months drought in a resting stage, needs a constant supply of such transient pools, and, conditions being stable, may remain in one place for millennia. To spread and become successful in time, however, either the species must have a trail of pools, or a means of being carried (mammal, bird, etc.) to distant places, some of which may have such pools and form good habitat. Here, connectivity is small pools in a small area, plus the means of spreading out.

Superimposed again is the surface water network, the main rivers, tributaries, ponds, pools and lakes. While the use purposed is extant (mill lode, navigation), flow remains in both (or all) channels. As and when water dries, all but one channel may dry or vanish, and whether that one is original, or the new depends on circumstances. Gravity favours the lowest channel. A well-made puddled bed and bank, though, may keep water when a straggling winding valley bed course dries. Changing impact may mean a channel erodes deep and remains flowing, or that it vanishes, depending on the new impact. A simple river system may pass, over a millennium or more, over a variety of beds in the same places (see Chapter 3).

Valleys with large plains and rivers form a separate habitat. The riverside land was, or is flooded, actually covered with water, and for long enough each year to severely affect biota (for good or ill, depending on the species). Thus wet land in poorly populated places (e.g. much of Scotland) is just left to flood, while with more intensive agriculture it becomes summer-grazing, leading to grass, and well-drained arable. In land form and river, though, these differ. Small flood plains (too often drained) may be common along rivers. These form mosaics of land form, connected by the river. If there is no flooding they are not effectively connected for the biota. (Plants and animals also reach these from the landwards side.)

Riverside trees are common throughout Europe:

- Wet woodland, e.g. *Salix, Populus, Alnus*;
- Dry woodland (higher or drained land), various dominants;
- Pollards, usually now by medium-sized streams where the dredger has not removed them, present for maybe a millennium, most often *Salix*, but also, e.g. *Fraxinus, Populus*. When riverside grass was wet and grazed, a second crop could be raised from pollards, which are cut above the grazing level, and provide sticks for craft, farm and household uses. Those left now are mostly riverside, kept, fortunately, for heritage reasons;
- Hedges marking field boundaries (higher land, not plain, usually);
- Lines of trees along the banks, may be close, may be well spaced, and, depending on the habitat, of wetland species such as *Alnus, Salix*, or a wide range of dryland species, e.g. *Quercus, Fraxinus, Betula*;
- Tree lines or bands surrounding smaller streams (wetter or drier).

More interesting is the way the shapes of the riverside trees vary, *Salix alba* in England, France and Hungary (Fig. 6.3), for instance, are distinctive. Put down anywhere in Europe – until the present mixing of genotypes becomes countrywide, and possibly even then, since wind and weather also affect shape – the observer can detect locality.

A typical country picture to most Europeans would include a stream, trees by the stream, and grass. Too often, this is now folk memory (wire and arable having replaced tree and grass), but there is enough, both actually and on TV, to keep the country picture alive.

Pattern follows process. The processes of the riverscape have water as a fundamental element, for itself, for what it carries, for where and when it is, and for the processes it facilitates or hinders. Figures 6.2, 6.3, 11.2 show some part of both these, and the variation seen when riverscapes are examined for different purposes. Variation occurs between riverscapes, due to land form, rock and other material, type, vegetation, outside influences (migrating moose, reindeer, landslip, lightning, flood) and human impact.

The moisture of the riverscape, which depends on precipitation, and land shape and constituents, influences both the native and traditional vegetation and the crops grown. Sunlit and shaded places differ in moisture, so in soil moisture, and flow and tributary patterns.

Figure 6.3 show some of the ways mosaics occur on riverscapes. Trees form mosaics, whether as wood, hedge, maquis, or indeed orchards, which differ from the others in that they are not usually the local woody species. Crops may likewise be imported and new strains developed, e.g. potatoes. Trees are usually good for the water regimes of the riverscape. The exact positioning of riverside trees varies with culture as much as with habitat. In SW France they grow on the banks themselves, within the channel, while this is forbidden by law in Britain.

This also applies, though more regionally, to the maintenance of, particularly, smaller streams. French and German engineers behave differently: so the Rhine Valley and Alsace are quite clearly under both influences. Crossing borders, e.g. within Flemish areas but between France and Belgium, for all the Flemish similarities of the people, the streams are managed and polluted in the way of the countries not of the peoples (Haslam, 1987, 2002). Given equal other factors therefore, different nationalities produce different riverscapes.

Recent floods

Central Europe has had many floods since 1990. This writer has inspected hilltops with lovely concrete-lined 0.5 m streams, passing water rapidly downstream instead of sinking slowly into forest litter. Roads form marvellous water-collectors and routes of speedy flow. Adding torrents to the valley bottom streams means erosion, and flooding further down. Oh the wicked forces of nature! Felling forests, building motorways or resorts, just altering, on a hillside, a perennial woody crop to an annual herbaceous one, cutting down a short line of trees, filling in a cross-ditch which used to trap eroded sediment: these alter flow on and through the soil, so they affect the water regime of the top slope, and last, the city downstream. This has become much worse since *c.* 1930, when removal of soil water became widespread (though worst in Britain), so the buffer of thin water was lost, the buffer which took in and let out water, and 10% extra or less made little difference. Secondly, technology and ideology were able to affect the land so much more easily. These varied from 'Britain must never again become dependent on imported food' in the west, to 'Communist collectives are the only way to manage the land' to the east. And now 'In our supermarket, out of season fruit is sold all year'. Europe has been bedevilled by concerns quite other than maintaining and sustaining the heritage of the region, growing crops suited to the valley and the local inhabitants. Floods and consequent insurance claims happen. It is high time that riverscapes were returned to their traditional way of managing their rainfall. A once in 100-year flood may well be considered acceptable. But why should this be turned into 1 in 20 through bad upstream management?

There is, though, possibly also a climate change. Micro-changes in weather occur all the time, and these lead to small changes in habitat and biota, as described elsewhere. A possible longer-term increase in storms, projected into the future, would mean more floods (e.g. Nisbet & Thomas, 2006), and should be planned for. Increasing woodland on flood plain – and hill – is an obvious course.

Discussion

Increasingly, riverscape management is imposed by governments, EU directives, local governments. This leads to more uniformity. Even those few directives intended to benefit the environment (e.g. Biodiversity, Habitats, Birds, Water Framework) lead to decrease of differences (preserve this habitat, make it look like that one, rather than restoring it to its traditional state). This requires, to put right, real knowledge. Mosaic theory comes second. The pattern seen, of mosaics of tree patches connected by corridors of tree lines or hedges, look, as a pattern, similar whether or not the trees are indigenous genotypes. The behaviour of both in relation to water and soil movement may also be similar. But the habitat value of the riverscape is very different.

The river, of course, drains the riverscape and removes its land to the sea (if external factors, do not intervene). The framework is land form and water regime. After this human impact affects the riverscape, its vegetation covering and other biota, and the way it is otherwise used by people.

7

Building blocks of river vegetation

The public perception of river corridors and the conservationists' understanding may differ greatly

River architecture

Rivers vary in their structure, their architecture (Fig. 7.1). This structure is, firstly, that which surrounds the water: the bank, bed, rocks, shoals, vegetation and its shade, together with artefacts such as bridge piers, weirs, millwheels and altered banks. The natural structures are due to the factors already discussed: land form, geomorphology, discharge, erosion, sedimentation, rock type (Chapters 3 and 5). These are then modified by engineering, trampling livestock, burrowing animals, boats, anglers, constructions and other activities.

Plants are influenced, often controlled by this inorganic structure. They grow because of, by, in and over it . . . or avoid it, as the case may be. The presence of some plants may also influence the structure of others (Chapter 5).

For fish, the vegetation is as much part of the river architecture as is the gravel in the bed. Some invertebrates live just on plants: plants are their river structure. The same applies to some diatoms and other periphyton.

The identity of 'structure' therefore varies with the organisms using it. Substrate structure is the most important building block in mountain and rocky streams, indeed may be the only sizeable building block in really swift water. But in lowland streams the gentle, earthy substrate is also a vital building block. The type of substrate (soft, gravelly, etc.) and its depth, control which species can grow on it (Chapter 2), the detailed surface pattern influences or controls

(a)

Fig. 7.1. Architecture of vegetation in rivers (P. A. Wolseley in Haslam, 1987). (a) Good band of tall monocots, rather poor oval-tailed. Lowland limestone, France. Species include *Apium nodiflorum, Callitriche* spp., *Sparganium erectum, Phalaris arundinacea* and *Iris pseudacorus*. (b) Intermittent band of fringing herbs, moderate cover of oval-tailed fine-leaved submergents. (Hill limestone, England.) Species include *Ranunculus* sp., *Mentha aquatica, Myosotis scorpioides* and *Rorippa nasturtium-aquaticum*. (c) Narrow band of tall monocots high cover of floating-leaved (near and strap-leaved (far) submergents (Alluvium, Britain). Species include *Nuphar lutea, Ceratophyllum demersum, Lemna minor* agg., *Sparganium emersum, S. erectum* and *Enteromorpha intestinalis*. (d) Low cover of oval-tailed fine-leaved species (Limestone, France). Too swift for much vegetation, spates mean varying depth and scour at the edges. Species include *Ranunculus* spp. and Mosses. (e) Very low cover. Too swift for much vegetation, but usually a stable water level so, once dredged, *Petasites hybridus* (spoon-shaped short emergents) can grow on the banks. (f) Mixture of many building blocks NEAR PRISTINE (Limestone, Ireland). Before first dredging, innumerable habitat niches, and a mixed-habit community, including *Ranunculus* spp., *Alisma plantago-aquatica, Glyceria maxima, Juncus effusus, Iris pseudacorus, Oenanthe crocata, Phalaris arundinacea* and *Sparganium erectum*. (g) Mixture of many building blocks. PRISTINE (Resistant, Sardinia). Unmanaged, with innumerable habitat niches, and a mixed-habit community, including *Alisma plantago-aquatica, Apium nodiflorum, Callitriche* spp., *Cupularia viscosa, Cyperus badius, Cyperus* spp., *Juncus* spp. (several), *Mentha aquatica* and (several), *Potamogeton* spp., *Ranunculus* spp. (several), *Rorippa nasturtium-aquaticum, Scirpus holoschoenus, Sparganium erectum* and Mosses.

Building blocks of river vegetation 159

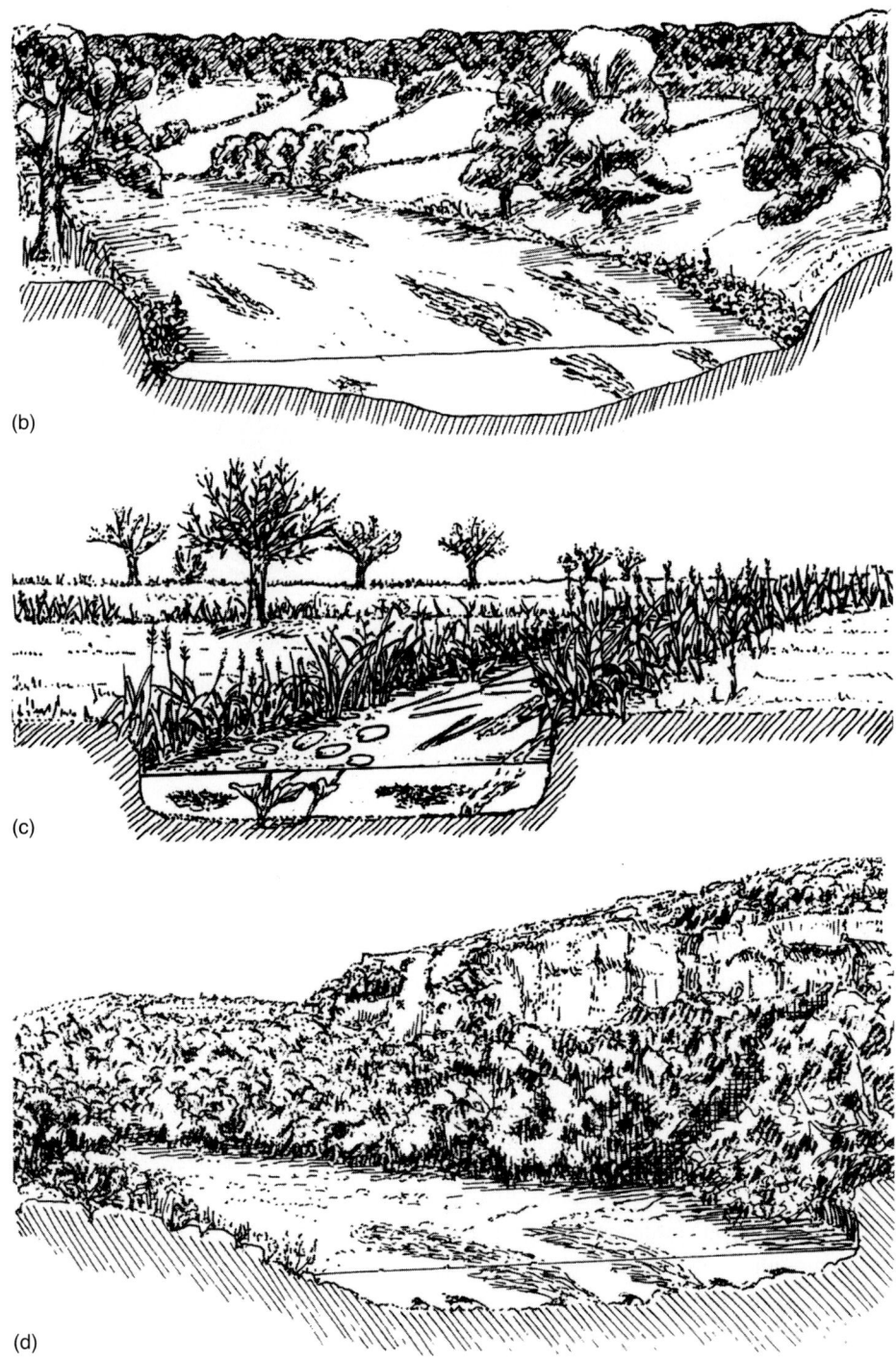

(b)

(c)

(d)

Fig. 7.1. (cont.)

(e)

(f)

Fig. 7.1. (cont.)

not just its invertebrates and periphyton, but how, in detail, plant species can colonise: and hence form their own building blocks as they grow. Different types of substrate also control fish breeding, bird behaviour (can a heron stand there?).

Silt carries most of the solutes (Chapter 2). Therefore, the pool part of a pool-and-riffle system, or the silt shoals at the sides of mountain streams, carry more nutrients. And, if the rest is too nutrient-low, many enable larger or different vegetation – structure – to grow.

Vegetation architecture is not uniform, either within or between rivers. It differs in species and in the habit and distribution of these species. Appearances are different. *Typha latifolia* is not only very like *T. domingensis*, but reasonably like, say, *Sparganium erectum* or *Glyceria maxima*, which also are tall monocotyledons forming bands in shallow water edges (Fig. 7.1, Tables 7.1–7.3).

Tall monocots are therefore a *building block*. Whether they are present, where they grow is a primary part of the character of the river. Secondly, the actual species differ in texture, in colour (type of green) and – often – in their exact

(g)

Fig. 7.1. (*cont.*)

position on the river edge. Each differs in habitat range, though most overlap. Both the presence and pattern of any building block are characteristic of a habitat, its river type, and the impacts on it. Tall monocots may dominate bands over a kilometre wide at the side of a little-engineered part of the Mississippi, while a 0–2 m band in the middle Danube reflects its narrowing and channelling.

The tall monocot building block is absent in cascades with no sheltered places. It is potentially present in most other habitats where the roots, requiring deep soft substrate, and their tall shoots (requiring to remain upright most of the time) can grow.

Habit and habitat are related, and habit means below-ground, as well as above-ground, parts. Within swift water, plant shoots are stream lined, and because of the erosion of fine particles from the bed, the roots can anchor in consolidated gravel or mixed substrates. Roots reaching *c*. 1 m down, however, anchoring by their depth rather than by twisting round stones, and stiff shoots unable to bend in flow are not appropriate to life within swift water with coarse substrates.

Examining architecture

In general, the more complex, diverse and abundant the architecture (whether inorganic or organic), the better the biotic quality. Because niches

Table 7.1 *Building blocks of river vegetation*

A. Emerged species
1. **Tall monocotyledons**, tall species of *Carex, Cladium, Cyperus, Glyceria, Iris, Juncus, Panicum, Phalaris, Phragmites, Scirpus, Sparganium, Typha* and suchlike.
2. **Fringing herbs** (mostly dicots), particularly *Apium nodiflorum, Berula erecta, Mentha* spp., *Mimulus* spp., *Rorippa* spp., and *Veronica* spp.
3. **Spoon-leaved herbs** (mostly monocots), e.g. *Alisma* spp., *Canna* sp., *Damasonium alisma, Rumex* spp. and *Sagittaria* spp.
4. **Rushes and horsetails** (shorter than 1.), e.g. *Eleocharis* spp. *Equisetum* spp., *Juncus* spp., *Rhynchospora* spp. and *Scirpus* spp.
5. **'Fillers'**, small, wide-leaved, may start growth in water, and in Europe are usually aliens, e.g. *Crassula helmsii, Hydrocotyle ranunculoides*.
6. **Polygonums** and **Miscellaneous**.

B. Water-supported species
1. **Oval-tailed, fine-leaved**, species of *Ranunculus*, the main European dominant of faster and limestone rivers, also of *Cabomba, Callitriche* (in faster flow), *Eleocharis, Elodea* (in faster flow), *Juncus, Myriophyllum, Potamogeton* (grass-leaved), *Utricularia* and Blanket weed (in faster flow).
2. **Oval-tailed, wide-leaved**, mostly wide-leaved *Potamogeton* spp.
3. **Strap-leaved**, e.g. species of *Sagittaria, Scirpus, Sparganium, Vallisneria*. Most may also have emerged leaves or shoots.
4. **Floating-leaved** (a) rooted, e.g. species of *Hydrocotyle, Nelumbo, Nuphar, Nymphaea*. (b) free-floating, e.g. species of *Azolla, Hydrocharis, Lemna, Riccia* and *Trapa*.
5. **'Fillers'**, as above, but also including solely water-supported species, e.g. *Callitriche* (part), *Egeria* and *Elodea*.
6. **Rosettes**, e.g. *Littorella, Lobelia*.
7. **Mosses**.
8. **Miscellaneous**.

multiply, so do diversity and richness, of both plant and animal life (excluding pollution and disturbance).

1. Which building blocks (see below) are present?
2. Where is each, in the reach, and what proportion of the relevant habitat does it cover?
3. What is the inorganic structure, flow, width, depth, substrate, texture, chemistry? How variable?
4. What is the bank type, height, slope, vegetation, management? How much diversity of habitat? Of vegetation?
5. What land use and other impacts are influencing the vegetation and habitat?

Table 7.2 Habitat of emergent building blocks

	Height (approx) m	Shading potential	Rooting depth m (approx)	Anchoring potential	Root toxins[4]	Nutrient status	Flow tolerance	Depth tolerance	Spreading potential	Competition potential	Bank slope tolerance
Tall monocots	0.75–3	+++	0.5–3	+++	++	Any	++	+	+++	+++	++
Fringing herbs	0.10–1	++	0.1–0.50	+		++	+	+	++	+	+
Wide-leaved herbs	0.5–1	+[5]	0.50–1?	+++++	–(?)	+++++	++	+	+++	++	+
Small sedge/rush	0.05–0.25	++	0.1–0.50?	++	+?	+++	+	+	+++	+	++
Small grasses	0.05–0.40	++	up to 0.50	+ (plus more)	++	All	+(++)	+	++	+++	++

1. Maximum usual potential is stated. The ranges given are commonly exceeded downwards, less frequently upwards.
2. Each group differs in appearance. Tall monocots, in particular, can be distinguished at a distance, as being upright thin shoots, usually in fringes or patches, typically marking the river's edge.
3. Each species has its own and distinctive habitat within that for the group, see Table 7.3. Species ranges often overlap, but are not identical, e.g. one tall monocot extending further into mountains and less far south (*Phalaris arundinacea*), another more frequent on silt (*Glyceria maxima*) or salt (*Phragmites australis*). Different colours make building blocks different, e.g. the yellow-green of *Glyceria maxima*, the full green of *Sparganium erectum* and the glaucous *Phalaris arundinacea*. Different texture (size and position of leaves, of fruiting bodies) also alter appearance. But all the tall monocots very obviously belong to this group, visually.
4. Toxic exudates are most effective where not washed away by flow.
5. Low because usually sparse.

Table 7.3 Habitat preferences within the one building block of tall monocotyledons. (Selected species)

	Deep[1]	Hardly[2] flooded	N. or S. Europe	W. or E. Europe	Colour (Y: yellowish; B: blueish; G: mid-green)	Leaves[3]	Spreading potential (max.)	Competition potential (max.)	Nutrient status[4]
Acorus calamus				E	Y	L	++	++	
Butomus umbellatus	+		N		B	L	+	+	H
Carex acutiformis/riparia		+	N		G	L,B	++	++	
Cyperus longus		+	S		G (dark)	L,B	++	++	
Glyceria maxima			N	W	Y	H	+++	+++	H
Phalaris arundinacea		+	N		B	H	++	++	L
Phragmites australis					B/G	H	+++	+++	L,H
Scirpus lacustris	+				G (dark)	S	++	++	L,H
Scirpus and Juncus short spp.		+			G (mix)	S	+	+ (too short)	L
Sparganium erectum	usually only in water		N		G	L	+++	++	
Typha spp.					B/G	L	++	++	H

[1]Normal, not full habitat ranges. River, not (the wider) still-water ranges. All may develop into marked fringing bands, or be sparse or absent. They are seldom in mixed dominance, but may be in parallel bands (e.g., *Glyceria maxima* above *Sparganium erectum*) or mosaic clumps.
[2]In addition to shallow-flooded
[3]Leaves arise from or below ground level, L. Leaves arise from tall stems, H. Leafless shoots arise from at or below ground, S. Leaves bent over above, giving flatter sward, B.
[4]Can grow in low nutrients, L, in high, H (dystrophic water excluded).

The building blocks and their habitats (Table 7.1)

Nature is infinitely variable, and many species do not fit into categories devised by people. They are intermediate, or vary as they grow, or vary with habitat. Most European species, though, fit into the categories of Table 7.1.

Plant pattern in the river is made up of shape (including size), texture, arrangement and colour. Leaf green is of many shades, pure greens from pale to dark, and mixed greens with blue, yellow, or brown. Texture shows in, for example, the difference between *Cyperus* or *Cladium* spp., sedges whose tips are bent over at the top, and other tall monocots like *Acorus calamus* whose tips are vertical, or, among the fringing herbs, the 'tidy' look of *Veronica beccabunga* compared with the sprawl of *Apium nodiflorum*.

The two main groupings, though, are the water-supported plants (on or under the water), and those which gain most of their growth and oxygen above the water, the emergents.

Emergents (Tables 7.2, 7.3) typically grow in shallow water, so are often at the sides with water-supported species towards the deeper centre, but sometimes throughout the channel if the water is sufficiently shallow and slow. Rivers with this pattern, or with boulders and whitewater, form *foci* for riverscapes throughout Europe and indeed North America.

Flow is the primary factor (Chapter 2). Tall emergents, which are often also wetland species, peak in negligible or slow flow: they may, that is, grow in fast flowing rivers, but only in sheltered places such as edges or islands. Before there was much impact or channelisation, the pattern of the building blocks was more variable (Fig. 7.2).

Figures 7.1–7.3 show tall emergents are in the least flow, in shallow or just dry places. Since competition between river plants – little though it is – is primarily by shading, taller emergents shade and kill shorter ones, and short emergents shade water-supported species (see Chapter 5 for the effect of wash-out). Within the water, shading is more complex. Where plants grow upright, as in canals and dykes, they can shade each other. Also, a blanket of small floating plants like *Lemna* or *Azolla* can remove most light, and few or no macrophytes occur below it. In flow, plants are flattened to a greater or lesser extent, so shading by the taller may be irrelevant. Clumps often have some self-shading, but unless a great deal is shaded, shaded little-photosynthesising parts can be fed from lit ones.

Habitats of the main building blocks are shown in Fig. 7.1 and Table 7.1. Emergents and free floating species grow most in the shallowest water, but the emergents also extend up landwards and the floating may reach into deeper

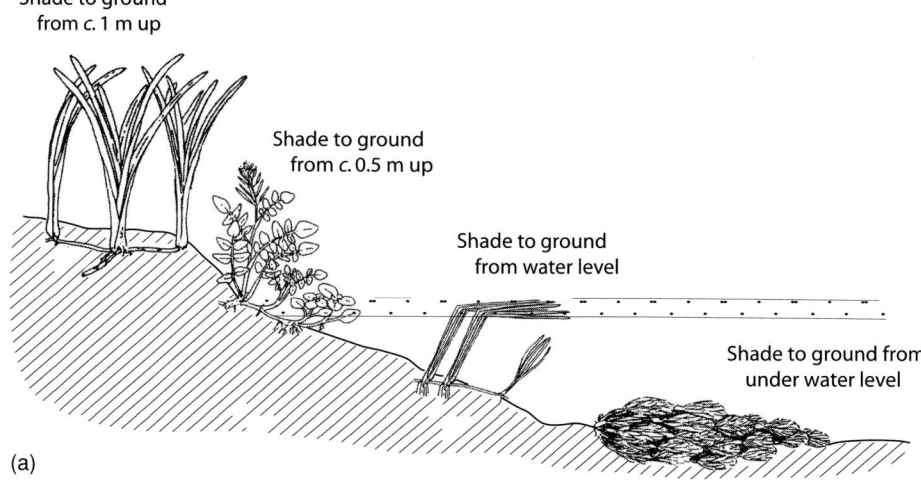

(a)

Fig. 7.2. Vertical relations of communities. Few communities have 100% cover in flowing water. (a) Different layers each shading those below. While all layers can cast 100% cover and kill all beneath, generally tall monocots and fringing herbs are the most likely to, and those in the water are more likely to have gaps between: 75% cover within the channel is at the high end of normal. Competition may be intense, particularly for emergents on the fringes, but it may also be non-existent, and is seldom crucial for community patterns among water-supported species. (b) Large lowland clay stream, Britain (P. A. Wolseley in Haslam, 1987). Channel dredged and channelised but not recently, gentle low underwater bank, unstable silt shoals at side. Species include *Nuphar lutea, Sagittaria sagittifolia, Scirpus lacustris, Sparganium emersum, Elodea canadensis, Lemna minor* agg., *Rorippa amphibia, Sparganium erectum* and Blanket weed. Architecture with (from (a)), layer A dominating and shading against the bank. Layer B is the same but in an indentation, presumably recently made and layer A has not had time to colonise. Layer C has *c.* 75% cover, but because of the way plants move in the water there is only a little space for other plants, though shading is incomplete. (c) Stream flowing off the Ardennes, Belgium (P. A. Wolseley in Haslam, 1987). Lop-sided channel, the natural shape resulting from flow meeting and adding to, concave and convex banks and bends. Species include *Ranunculus fluitans, Phalaris arundinacea, Sparganium emersum* and *Elodea canadensis*. Layer A is reduced by the swift, especially storm, flow and layer B even more so. Channel cover of layers D and E is *c.* 50% with mostly large swinging clumps. The best substrate for these is mostly occupied. Shading is the primary relationship but there are many, if not most habitats in which it does not apply, layers and species do not overlap, because of substrate, water depth, flow, rooting space, clump behaviour and (not shown) disturbance, grazing and many forms of human impact.

(b)

(c)

Fig. 7.2. (*cont.*)

water. Short emergents cannot grow in the heavy shade of taller ones, so they avoid the tall, growing more riverwards, or where the tall are absent. Rooted floating plants can grow in deeper water only if their shoots can grow up to lit parts. (This depth also varies with water clarity.) Submerged plants are usually streamlined, but may avoid flow by staying close to the bottom like the rosettes of *Littorella*. Species like *Lemna* spp. require quiet water for explosive growth, but the occasional frond can be swept along in flow. In engineered rivers, and indeed in many traditional ones, width is roughly proportional to depth. Width in itself has little effect on vegetation, except in determining edge patterns and proportions, but width is generally easier to estimate than depth, so can be used for study (in suitable areas). Bank slope and diversity are usually more important for building blocks and biodiversity.

Patterns in building blocks vary with both depth and flow patterns.

Table 7.4 *Comparison of the importance of some building blocks in Europe and (E. and Central) North America*

	Europe	N. America
Emerged		
Trees	(+)	++
Tall monocots	+++	+++
Fringing herbs	+++	+
Spoon-leaved herbs short	+	+++
Spoon-leaved herbs tall	+	+++
Scramblers		+(+)
Small grasses	++	+
Water-supported		
Oval-tailed, fine-leaved (e.g. *Ranunculus* spp.)	+++	+
Oval-tailed, wide-leaved (mostly *Potamogeton* spp.)	+	+++
Strap-leaved species	++	++
Floating-leaved species	++	+++
Small-leaved 'fillers'	++	++ emerged forms also important

Most native species in each continent are different.

Europe and North America (Tables 7.4, 7.5)

Interestingly, although the same building blocks occur in both continents, the proportions found in rivers differ. In North America trees become truly aquatic (*Nyssa* spp., *Taxodium* spp.) not just like *Alnus* spp. and most *Salix* spp. This means more tree swamps. Tall monocots form the same building blocks, though usually with allied, neither the same nor widely different species. Fringing herbs, in contrast, are sparse, usually lime-restricted: and often alien, in North America. They are replaced by short herbs which are wider-leaved, better rooted, less bushy so less easily washed away. *Alisma plantago-aquatica* is one of the few European equivalents. This, and the fact that the dominant oval-tailed (and gravel-growing) river species in Europe are *Ranunculus* spp., and in North America, *Potamogeton* spp. are, so far, mysteries. There is generally a wider band occupied by floating leaved species like water lilies in North America, but this is explained by less engineering, so more shallow water at the sides.

Tall monocots

Table 7.1 shows tall monocots occupy stable non-rocky edges. Landwards they may fade into wetland, but more usually are excluded sharply by

Table 7.5 *European and North American plant similarities Selected species of temperate latitudes*

1. The same species in both continents. +E indicates alien from Europe, +A, alien from North America.

Alisma plantago aquatica	Myriophyllum spicatum +E
Apium nodiflorum	Phalaris arundinacea
Azolla filiculoides +A	Phragmites australis
Ceratophyllum demersum	Potamogeton crispus +A
Elodea canadensis +A	P. natans
E. nuttallii (part +A)	Ranunculus trichophyllus
Equisetum fluviatile	Rorippa nasturtium-aquaticum
E. palustre	Solanum dulcamara
Hippuris vulgaris	Typha angustifolia
Juncus effusus	T. latifolia
Lemna minor agg.	Veronica anagallis-aquatica
L. minuta +A	V. beccabunga
Mimulus guttatus +A	Zannichellia palustris

2. The same species, but differing in habit or habitat.

Berula erecta	P. pectinatus
Potamogeton gramineus	Utricularia vulgaris

3. Different species, but with similar habits and/or habitats

Europe	North America
Callitriche cophocarpa, C. obtusangula C. platycarpa, C. stagnalis (common)	Callitriche palustris (infrequent)
Carex acutiformis	Carex stricta
Cladium mariscus	C. mariscoides
Eleocharis palustris	E. spp.
Glyceria maxima	G. canadensis, G. grandis
Mentha aquatica	M. piperita
Myriophyllum spicatum	M. exalbessens, M. spp.
Nuphar lutea	N. advena, N. variegatum
Nymphaea alba	N. odorata, N. tuberosa
Ranunculus spp. short-leaved Batrachian, including R. trichophyllus	R. longirostris, R. trichophyllus
Sagittaria sagittifolia	S. americanum, S. eurycarpum, S. cuneata
Scirpus lacustris	S. validus
Sparganium emersum	S. chlorocarpum
S. erectum	S. americanum

competition from land plants, dryness, grazing, cultivation or construction. Riverwards, tall monocots are removed by scour (whether perennial or in floods), engineering, or water deep enough to cover much of the leaves. Roots and rhizomes usually grow deep, anchoring firmly. They are intolerant of trampling. Much grazing usually replaces them by grasses. They also grow sparsely in heavy shade, so when the original native woods were present, tall monocots were presumably sparse in forested rivers.

Within the group, the species have different preferences. *Phalaris arundinacea* usually extends further up hill streams and least far into lowland waters. *Sparganium erectum* grows furthest into the river; *Glyceria maxima* is typically associated with silt. *Phragmites australis* grows further into brackish water. Geographically, *Phalaris arundinacea* cannot tolerate south Europe but *Cyperus* spp. occur there instead.

Fringing herbs

Fringing herbs are most frequent on limestone, but grow everywhere possible in Europe (physical habitat, geographically), except where nutrients are too low. They mostly grow in shallow edges where tall monocots are prevented by, e.g. scour, grazing, soil type, disturbance. Where not in long fringes, they may grow well in sheltered indentations of scouring rivers. If tall monocots can invade, they will, and will then shade out the fringing herbs. Eventually scour, JCB, grazing, or other disturbance, removes them, and the quicker-colonising fringing herbs re-invade.

Most species may occur together, in mixed dominance, where low nutrients (high calcium) prevent large growth. Competition is virtually absent. In nutrient-rich clay, though, clumps grow large, monodominant, over-bushy: and easily washed off. Polluted *Apium nodiflorum* in Malta grows thick and over 1 m high! There is a nutrient range (*Mimulus* spp. and *Veronica beccabunga*, are low-nutrient species, *Apium nodiflorum*, high). Texture also varies. *V. beccabunga* is shiny, *Rorippa* spp. sprawling (when large). Flower colour may be blue, white or yellow, and leaf colour ranges from blue-green to yellow-green. *Apium nodiflorum* and *Myosotis scorpioides* are the two most likely to develop yellow shoots with organic pollution, like *Glyceria maxima* among the tall monocots. *Apium nodiflorum* and *Berula erecta* can grow as submerged carpets in lime-influenced streams.

Wash-out of these bushy, short-rooted plants depends on the flow actually reaching the plants, not in the flow elsewhere in the channel, plus how well the plants are anchored (Chapters 2, 5). Wash-out means fragments, and these can potentially propagate downstream. Growth means extending into areas of scour or other poor habitat, e.g. grazing or shading. Cyclic growth can occur: invasion, spread, loss and renewal of habitat, and invasion again. In suitable habitats tall monocot invasion can interrupt the cycle, shading and killing the fringing herbs. Fringing herbs, particularly *Rorippa nasturtium-aquaticum*, may in turn, overgrow and kill *Ranunculus* and *Callitriche*.

Wide-leaved short herbs

Most are monocots (though *Rumex* spp. are dicots). They hold the same position as the fringing herbs (see above) and are almost as quick to recolonise after washout. In North America they are often on edges drying in late summer. In Europe, such edges are common in Italy, and fringing herbs dominate. The two commonest European plants are *Rumex* spp. (particularly *R. hydrolapathum* in the north, *R. conglomeratus* in the south) and *Alisma plantago-aquatica*. Their ranges overlap, but *Rumex* spp. extend further landwards, *A. plantago-aquatica* waterwards.

As a building block, these are only local in Europe, as in the Po plain and in Malta. They can overlap with, or substitute for, both the tall monocot and the shorter herb bands. They are more frequent as sparse species in other building blocks.

Rushes and horsetails

These also, as building blocks, are of only local importance, and are usually species of *Eleocharis, Equisetum, Juncus* and *Scirpus*. Undredged low-nutrient (e.g. moor) streams may be fringed, on gravel or stone, by *Juncus articulatus*, small near-source, steep-chalk streams, by *Equisetum fluviatilis*. Streams of steeper moors, rush-pasture, and recent dredging may be fringed by *Juncus effusus*.

Short grassy vegetation

This is usually just above rather than just below the water line, and occurs in two main habitats, firstly low-nutrient, moor and heath streams, and secondly ones grazed or regularly cut. The most frequent are *Agrostis stolonifera* on clods fallen in to the river, and often persisting for many months, and small *Glyceria* spp., which are anchored to the bank and flop into the water. *Glyceria fluitans* may cover over dykes or slow streams with shallow banks and medium nutrients. More nutrient-rich and sparse grasses – not building blocks – are moderately frequent anywhere.

Tall herbs

Tall herbs (such as *Epilobium hirsutum, Filipendula ulmaria, Urtica dioica*) are mostly damp land, rather than aquatic species, and are more properly building blocks of the River Corridor (Table 7.6). However, well-developed bands may shade and prevent any aquatic plant growth in small and narrow streams, so

Table 7.6 *Bank vegetation*

1. **In undrained** (pristine, some traditional) **rivers**, banks are usually short, as water level is close to ground level. There is therefore little on-bank vegetation, though there may be valuable bank-top vegetation. Where water level fluctuates or erosion is particularly easy there may be 'cliffs' (or wide, very gently sloping edges, banks).
2. **Bank, or bank-top vegetation** may extend for long lengths, or be in mosaics. If traditional or pristine, either is satisfactory. If under the influence of, e.g. dredging, disturbance, steepening bank slope, all are less satisfactory, and mosaics (which have the potential to bear more species) are better.
3. **Satisfactory bank-top, riverside vegetation includes**: Traditional grassland, moor, bog, wood, wetland, wet woodland, pollard, park grassland, any buffer strip vegetation (for clean water entering streams).
4. If **vegetation** is being **planted** it is ESSENTIAL that the species are (1) native, not aliens, and (2) local strains. Planting alien species or strains is destroying the natural heritage of a locality.
5. **Banks in**, particularly, **drained land** are steep, with disturbed (dredged) substrate, so with raised nutrient status. The commonest, and most dreary – apart from lining – is tall herb vegetation. This is bushy and poorly anchored (e.g. *Epilobium hirsutum, Urtica dioica*) and can be eroded by storm flows. Fortunately most is in smaller streams with few spate flows.
6. **Recommended building blocks for river fringes**. All, in their appropriate habitats!
   Tall monocotyledons. Only a flood hazard when over-abundant. This is preventable by river centres being deep (1+ m). Smooth and well-anchored populations are good for bank stability. Look well.
   Fringing herbs. Look well. Easily washed off so no flood hazard.
   Others. Rarely hazardous. Deep roots or rhizome wefts bind well.

   Woody plants

Corylus avellana	Neutral to alkaline
Crataegus monogyna	Acid, neutral, alkaline
Malus sylvestris	Neutral to alkaline
Populus alba	Neutral to alkaline
Prunus spinosa	Neutral to alkaline
Quercus spp.	Acid, neutral, alkaline
Salix spp.	Acid, neutral, alkaline

7. **Recommended species to plant on banks** (Neobold *et al.*, 1989).
   (a) Grasses
   Agrostis capillaris. Likes poor conditions. Good binding of soil.
   A. castellana. Cheaper. More productive. Good binding.
   Anthoxanthum odoratum. Likes poor conditions, short, tufted, attractive to livestock.
   Cynosurus cristatus. Likes poor conditions, short, tufted.
   Festuca ovina. Drought-resistant, low productivity, tufted.
   F. rubra. Low productivity. Good binding.
   Poa compressa. Stress-tolerant, low productivity.
   Trisetum flavescens. Stress-tolerant, low productivity.

Table 7.6 (cont.)

(b)	Herbs	
	Achillea millefolia. Medium height, nectar source, deep-rooted.	
	Daucus carota. Medium height, neutral to basic soils, deep-rooted.	
	Hypochaeris radicata. Nectar source.	
	Leucanthemum vulgare. Medium height. Neutral to basic soils. Nectar source.	
	Lotus corniculatus. Tufted, little enriching (unlike clovers, which should be avoided). Good food source, several species.	
	Primula veris. Fairly short. Early pollen source. Spreads well.	
	Prunella vulgaris. Short. Pollen and nectar source.	
(c)	Woody plants which bear large numbers of invertebrate species and plant easily.	
	Alnus glutinosa. Neutral to alkaline. (Care! Disease spreading)	
	Betula spp. Acid to alkaline.	
	Fraxinus excelsior. Neutral to alkaline.	
	Quercus. Acid to alkaline.	
	Salix spp. Acid to alkaline.	
	Among bushes of drier land, *Prunus spinosa, Crataegus avellana* and *Malus sylvestris* are particularly rich in invertebrates.	

are included here. As they mostly require nutrient-rich habitats, they are typical of dredged banks in drained land, with high fairly steep slopes which are not grazed, cultivated or shaded. Their only merit is that texture and colouring vary within an otherwise uniform structure (cf. tall monocots).

Three species are recent immigrants, spreading from the east along river banks across Europe. *Heracleum mantegazzianum* (Giant hogweed) is a pest, since it not only takes over the bank but it is the 'wrong' shape and too big, bigger than others in this building block. Worse, it has poisonous (photosensitising) sap. Eradication programmes have not yet been given the resources to be successful. *Impatiens glandulifera*, Indian balsam blends in well with the native species, and if it spread less, would be a welcome addition to an already mostly man-made building block. *Fallopia japonica*, Japanese knotweed, fits in less well, but much better than *Heracleum mantegazzianum*.

Where was vegetation?

Although, before much impact, grasslands and browsing land (grass plus woody) were common, tree swamp, wet woodland and dry woodland were also abundant and shading. Why, therefore, does so much native river vegetation exist?

- Where there are shading woods there are
  - glades where trees have fallen and vegetation is abundant, as in parts of N. America now;

- particularly in unengineered rivers there may be a shallow water habitat out of reach of shade: islands, shoals, braiding, or just shallow water in the centre.
- Where hedges and trees are planted, as these develop, open water is less likely: except where roads and other constructions make breaks (and as above).
- Trees, particularly pollards, may have been planted distantly, unable to shade much water.
- In the south Mediterranean deciduous trees are still frequent along suitable riversides. These trees come into leaf in early summer, as they do further north. Because of the mild winters, though, by this time the river aquatics which started growing in mid-winter, have grown enough, and can die back from shade or drought.
- In the far north, mountain, moor, heath and tundra vegetation is too short to shade streams of any size. The same applies to garigue in the south.
- Floods and herds of grazing animals may prevent woody plants growing around the river.

Animals and structure

Animals – to different extents – alter structure by eating vegetation, epiphytes and invertebrates, and by burrowing, swimming and general disturbance. Animals are *part* of the river! It is easy to look briefly, see the vegetation patterns, and forget the animals. The size of the animal in relation to the vegetation is important. A small animal finds a clump of moss provides as good, or better shelter than a *Ranunculus* clump; a fish does not; and a beaver or swan thinks little of the shelter of *Ranunculus*.

Water voles need banks covered, e.g. by tall monocots, for burrows and movement along streams. It has in fact been said (Benneta *et al.*, in Bailey *et al.*, 1998) that if the riparian fringe is wide enough, water vole are (reasonably) safe from mink, and thrive. In ordinary engineered rivers, mink eat and destroy the water voles. Mink in Europe are aliens from N. America, escaped from fur farms.

Invertebrates can colonise virtually any river habitat, their shapes, sizes, life cycles and habitat preferences being so wide (Kirby, 1992). Open edges, shallow water, tall herbs, trampling, shrubs, river bottoms – all are good habitat. Crayfish burrow into banks, but most smaller invertebrates have only minor direct influence on structure, by biting off bits and such like.

Invertebrates are, of course, necessary to the good functioning of a river. Detritivores and omnivores particularly break down dead organisms, and most are prey to larger animals.

Swans are probably the most destructive European water birds, being widespread, pulling up and eating huge quantities of near-surface vegetation. This decrease in vegetation alters structure, though as so many species can regrow quickly, it seldom alters vegetation type or quite destroys it. Local explosions of herbivorous fish, turtles, duck or other birds can clear most or all vegetation, leading to fresh colonisation when the animals decrease. Excluding these, river architecture provides many different habitats, thick and sparse, tall and short, with varying texture, and leading to faster and slower flows. Different fish, and sizes of fish, can inhabit different parts of this highly complex habitat.

The presence of animals infers the presence of their nutrient fluxes, which usually do not affect architecture, but are important in themselves (however, great flocks of birds can produce nutrients harming plant structure).

Water-supported vegetation

In the typical engineered river, and many traditional ones, emergents fringe the sides, and water-supported plants grow in the centre. This is not invariable. Shallow water in the centre may allow emergents to grow; deep water by a vertical bank, may bring water-supported not emergent species there. Figures 2.7 and 2.8 show the typical pattern, and Fig. 7.1–7.3 shows examples of the varied architecture found within the water. Architecture is different seen from above and horizontally! It depends firstly on flow. In still water (e.g. drains) species can be vertical. In whitewater, any plants present are (near) horizontal, on the substrate. Flow controls what space, vertically and horizontally is available in the habitat. Emergent presence is controlled by flow (among other habitat factors). The water-supported species depend on flow for their shape as well as their occurrence.

Flow generally increases from side to middle, so the habitat changes with this (see Chapter 5 for washout and cyclical and changeless change). The most frequent or dominant species are generally the most stable, least likely to change over time: they are the species most characteristic of the habitat. Sparse and less characteristic species are more likely to come and go (Haslam, 1987).

In shallow water, so usually the smaller streams, water-supported vegetation can grow right across the stream (other factors being suitable). In deeper streams, light may be too little on the ground to allow vegetation. Rivers carry sediment and become turbid. It is rare for vegetation to grow over 1 m deep, but in sediment-free limestone springs it may grow to *c*. 3 m, or in very clean conditions, even 6 m. Usually, though, going downstream, vegetation changes from being across the stream, to being confined to the shallow edges.

Strap-leaved species

The straps may be well underwater, as, usually, *Schoenoplectus lacustris*, or mostly floating in the water, as *Sparganium chlorocarpum* after mid-summer. This building block is common, but is seldom the sole block over any distance of river. Their habitat is restricted: not too deep, not swift flow, nutrient-medium to nutrient rich (with a few exceptions like *Sparganium angustifolium*). Ability to withstand storm flow means here the ability to re-grow from well-anchored rootstocks.

Free-floating

These are independent of depth, but are very dependent on flow (being so easily moved by it). They are also dependent on nutrients (not usually growing well in low status) and, oddly, latitude. The larger species are mostly southern (e.g. *Eichornia*, *Pistia*, *Salvinia*, *Trapa*, though *Hydrocharis morsus ranae* and *Stratiotes aloides* occur further north). Smaller species include *Azolla* and *Lemna* spp. (There are also bottom-floating species like *Ceratophyllum*.) This building block can cover and smother huge areas of suitable habitat, destroying low-growing plants, and, if depleting oxygen sufficiently, fish, and other animals. They may also be patchy or sparse.

Texture varies greatly, from the grainy, tiny and flat *Lemna* spp., to the large, spiky rosette of *Stratiotes*, and, in colour, there is the blue-green of *Pistia*, the red shades of some *Azolla*, and the bright green of *Eichornia*. This is a uniform life form, but not a uniform habit or in Europe, building block.

Rooted floating

On the surface, these may resemble the free-floaters, but water lily pads are often an important part of the building block, and all surface parts are joined to the substrate, so within the water the structure differs.

Oval-tailed fine-leaved

Ranunculus spp. is the most frequent. It is a main building block from Scandinavia to Malta (in, largely, non-clay and well-flowing rivers). *Cabomba caroliniana*, an import, is spreading in Hungary in the same habitat. *Potamogeton pectinatus* in most of Europe is favoured by organic, industrial and brackish pollution, and its dominant clumps are diagnostic for this. There are other species, likewise building blocks when abundant, such as *Callitriche* spp. (common),

Myriophyllum spp. (frequent), *Zannichellia* spp. (occasional). The oval-tailed fine-leaved building block, rare in central North America, is, often with good biodiversity, characteristic of Europe.

Oval-tailed wide-leaved

These are mostly *Potamogeton* spp., and usually in central N. America, where this building block takes the place, in Europe, of *Ranunculus*. There are usually more species present in a reach than there are of *Ranunculus* in Europe. In Europe, this building block is very local; two floating-leaved (*P. natans*, medium nutrients, *P. polygonifolius*, boggy), four fairly frequent species with submerged leaves (*P. coloratus, P. crispus, P. lucens, P. perfoliatus*). Even these are seldom abundant enough to qualify as building blocks, and others to do so are rare. They are usually associate rather than principal species.

Small-leaved fillers

Though often streamline in swifter water, some of these are underwater, e.g. *Elodea, Egeria*; some have surface leaves and are intermediate to oval-tailed, e.g. *Callitriche*; and yet others grow emergent as the summer progresses, e.g. *Micranthemum umbrosum, Crassula helmsii*. This is a miscellaneous group, varying in shape, texture, colour and the position in the water: but, in Europe they are usually accessory rather than main building blocks, except locally.

Mosses

Mosses are usually small, but may be obvious and adding to vegetation patterns especially on boulders and rock.

Miscellaneous

Short rosettes are sparse. Submerged rushes, mainly *Eleocharis, Eleogiton* and *Juncus* are locally important as building blocks (e.g. Galloway, Cornwall). Their shape and texture differ considerably from the oval-tailed fine-leaved group.

Many species, of course, fit into either none or several classes. Those in several classes include *Sagittaria*, strap-leaved (rooted) when young, then floating rooted and finally belonging to the short broad-leaved herb habit. All add to the diversity and value of the river, and, in small reaches, to pattern, texture and colour.

Conclusions

If there is, in a river, a diversity of depth and substrate (and not over-impact) diversity of architecture will follow, and the diversity of fauna associated with these. Normally, there is some diversity of architecture even if depth, flow and substrate are fairly uniform. In general, architecture influences fauna more than vice versa, excluding severe damage from large animals, usually local.

Control of architecture is by natural causes, but, these days, also as much from impact. Losing water loses space for vegetation. Polluting water skews and reduces vegetation, and therefore reduces structure. Channelling greatly alters habitat, therefore vegetation and other biota.

8

Building blocks of flood plain vegetation

People are linked to ecology and landscape.

(McFarlane, 1999)

Space matters, Mosaics control fluxes of energy, matter and information. Structural differences lead to functional differences.

(Malanson, 1993)

Introduction

Rivers that transport, or used to transport, much sediment, create flood plains: subject to their geomorphology. The plains have (or had) one or more river channels with flowing water, and a greater width over which the water spreads in wet periods, and on which the water drops its sediment, or allows fen peat to grow. Active flood plains are intermediates between river, lake, wetland and dryland. Sedimentation, erosion and currents are all parts of the system, which change over time. Water may be running or standing, perennial or periodic. Overall, these are near-flat over the whole. There may be, however, sharp variations of level (terraces) where flows and land levels have changed in the past, and an earlier flood plain has been eroded and lowered, and this may have happened several times. If water level has risen, the old plain has been covered with new (flood) sediment. There may be lakes, some ox-bows (cut-off meanders). River courses change over time, slowly, or drastically with severe storms. Where there is a flood plain, there is, necessarily, room for a river's course to move. Meanders increase, and are cut off as oxbows, braided courses come and go. Tributaries enter the river at different places. Changes of watercourse lead to changes in flood plains.

Flood plains may be very small, a few metres wide and not much longer. In smaller lowland streams they range from this to the common *c.* 20 m wide. The 100–200 m plain is very common, usually further downstream, formerly managed as wet or flower-rich grassland, now usually dry grassland or arable. The largest are plains many kilometres wide downstream on large rivers like the Po and Danube. Even the Thames and the Severn have flood plains several kilometres wide. Near the sea, the plains may differ in creation, an estuary being slowly filled by sediment or peat as rivers slow on nearing the sea. From this came the Fenland and Romney Marsh in England, and much of the Netherlands (from the Rhine and Meuse) and the Camargue from R. Rhône.

Going downstream a river, there are typically repeated flood plains. These occur even in mountains in flat places, though generally plains increase in size downstream (Fig. 8.1). Once rivers are drained, even if they are embanked, the coupling of river and plain is lessened or lost (Chapter 2).

The building blocks (Table 8.1)

The substrate

The substrate is an important building block of floodplains, as it is in rivers: the level (from underwater to dry land scarcely flooded), its physico-chemical composition and its texture. Chemically, it may vary from nutrient-low (e.g. poor fen) via richer marshland to calcium-dominant (low other nutrient) peat and very fertile sediment. These days, highly polluting solutes and sediments may be deposited also, of course. Vegetation depends on substrate chemistry.

Coarse substrates such as gravels allow flood water to sink quickly through them, and may dry too quickly for wetland or aquatic vegetation to grow, even if floods are frequent. Fine substrates hold water more, and puddle more easily, so remain wetter for longer. Fen peat can form under near-perennial water, without incoming sediment, and highly organic silts are intermediate. These differences thus alter chemical and water regime, as well as texture, and so alter communities.

The open waters

Open waters may be:

- main rivers (single or braided);
- tributaries coming in from the side of the flood plain;

Building blocks of flood plain vegetation 181

(a)

(b)

Fig. 8.1. Effect of severe impact on the building blocks and the diversity they bring on wet grassland (Y. Bower in Haslam, 2003). Figure 4.1 illustrates typical building blocks, communities, for a variety of floodplain and other wetland communities. Figure 8.1 shows the loss to over-intensive agriculture, with no heritage, very low biodiversity: but a high yield for people. (a) Near-traditional, species-rich, varied structure, ditches, trees. (b) Re-seeded, uniform short structure, ditches drained, tree line (far) replaced by fence.

Table 8.1 (a) *Habitat features formed by different water sources*

Principal water source	Nutrient status (unpolluted)	Principal wetland types	Soil type formed	Water level when formed
RAIN	Very low	Bog (raised and blanket)	Bog peat	Above main water level. Within or above bog's own water supply from rain. Perched.
RUN-OFF[a]	Low to high, depending on catchment surface	Bog, valley, Poor fen, (Calcium-dominated fen) Rich fen Marsh	Bog peat, Poor fen, peat rich, fen peat, organic-rich silt organic-poor silt	Formed under water. Drying causes loss (oxidation, erosion so for peat to accumulate, dried time must be little or nil
GROUND WATER	Depends on aquifer type, includes calcium-dominated	Calcium-dominated fen (poor fen, marsh)	Calcium-dominated fen peat (nutrient-poor peat, silty)	
RIVER WATER	Fairly low to high, depending on catchment	Poor fen, Rich fen, Marsh	mineral to organic-rich	Deposited under water. May be dried rest of year (i.e. storm flooding only), but is then organic-poor. May be flooded all year, or anything in between

[a]Including sub-surface run-off and shallow groundwater derived from near-catchment.

Table 8.1 (b). *Water regimes of different wetland types*

Principal habitats (wet)	Water sources (main)	Water movement[a,b]	Water fluctuation[a]	Water level (usual)[a]
Bog	rain (run-off)	little	little	at surface (for growth)
Poor fen	(any except solely rain)	varies little to considerably	some	constant flood to constant damp (wet, for growth)
Calcium-dominated fen	Groundwater (or lime-dominated run-off)	some	little with perennial springs, more with run-off	constantly (or seasonally) near or above surface (wet, for growth)
Rich fen	water carrying little or no sediment; now mixed waters	fairly variable	little to considerable	constant flood to (now) constant dry (wet, for growth)
Marsh	River originally. Water carrying sediment. Now mixed waters	fairly to very variable	little to much	constant flood to (now) constant dry; may grow with storm flood alone

[a] Excluding severe drought and flood.
[b] Water moving through, in or over the wetland.

Table 8.1 (c) *The effect of water level fluctuations*

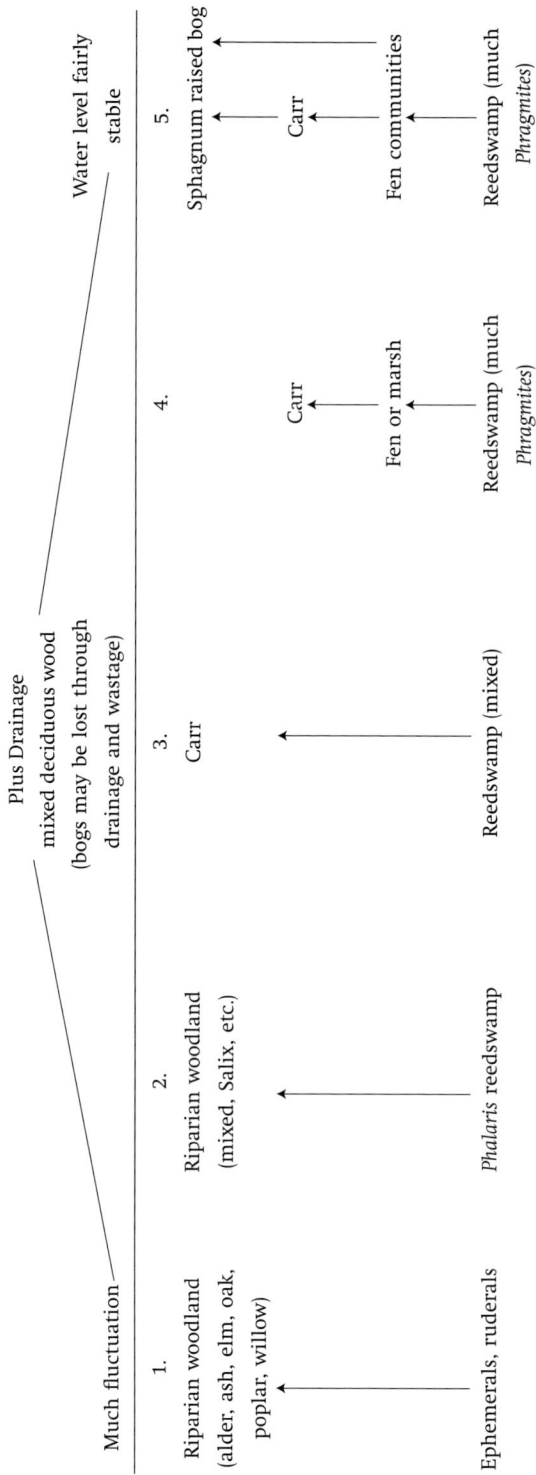

1. Hardly present in Britain now (2000). (Reservoir shores come close.)
2. Often small and fragmented in Britain. No peat. (Some gravel pits.)
3. Frequent. Peat improbable. (Some gravel pits.)
4. Remnants common. Past history of sites is stored in the peat.
5. Remnants common, active succession by bog of carr (when wet enough, rare) of fen vegetation (rare and often incomplete). Past history of sites is stored in the peat.

Table 8.1 (d). *Management for some types of fen and marsh herbaceous vegetation, in similar water regimes*

Phragmites commercial reedbed	Winter, cut, usually annually. (Nutrient-medium to nutrient-rich)
Cladium	Summer-cut every three to four years (calcium-influenced or -dominated). Commercial sedge bed
Tall grass	Summer-cut, once or twice a year (nutrient-rich, wet)
Medium grass-dominated community	Summer-cut, about twice in nutrient-rich habitats, once in poorer ones. Or with light grazing
Wet grassland short grass	Grazed and/or mown more intensively than the two preceding
Rush-pasture	Grazed (less often mown), in nutrient-low places or ones (unintentionally) managed for *Juncus* spp.
Short sedge or rush communities	Summer grazing or mowing. Variation in the patterns of these, together with variation in soil and water, leads to a wide variety of communities. The higher the nutrient status, the more the treatment required to keep vegetation short (but less so than for wet grassland)
Tall-herb community	Develops from any of the others, if abandoned, and if nutrient-poor also dried to release nutrients through mineralisation, etc.

These communities are created by management. This is either prolonging into drier places communities typical of wetter ones, or creating large areas of herbaceous vegetation of types otherwise restricted to local areas of, e.g., shallow soil and disturbance. (Management here includes abandonment.) In the natural succession, these habitats would be covered by carr.

- oxbows, lakes, marshes and forming fens;
- other pools (natural) and ponds (man-made), from old fish ponds, to gravel pits;
- dykes and ditches may have been dug in drained but not dried plains. These are in a criss-cross pattern in large areas, the pattern being straighter and simpler in more recently drained places (Fig. 5.1; Haslam, 1987, demonstrates such patterns);
- a catchwater drain may have been dug on the outside, parallel with and close to the higher ground, which catches and collects, both run-off and the water from incoming tributaries, and diverts it away from flooding the plain;
- a second drain may be parallel to and beside the river, and similarly collect water, letting it into the river (at a lower level) intermittently.

Such a pattern is also found in low-lying, but not flat flood plain, riverside fields.

Open water habitats can be arranged in numerous patterns, and control a large part (or very little), of the architecture of the flood plain. Traditionally, open waters were all connected, whether by open water, by winter floods, or by water movement through the top soil. Drying has separated much.

Where there are beavers, there is much change. Beavers alter structure, by building dams and eating and felling young trees. This creates pools and alters flow and substrate, giving a mosaic of habitat in different stages. The European beaver (now being introduced westwards from its remaining habitats in the east) causes less disturbance than the North American species. This also is spreading from its remote haunts, down some of the rivers it inhabited before Europeans came. Beavers, being part of natural rivers, are part of conservation, and are valuable for other biota, too. As long as there is space for their pools and wetlands, they are useful.

Structure constantly changes, and does so even more with human impact (e.g. Fig. 8.1). The basic building blocks, of water and substrate, control the habitat, until human impact removes the water.

When the river is cut off from the flood plain, the plain loses the incoming solutes, sediment, biota, and fluctuating river water. The plain may still flood, from tributaries, from rising groundwater, or river water seeping laterally. Or, the plain may become too dry for regular flooding.

When the river is cut off from the plain, its pollutants are cut off, also. River pollution in too many parts, from Hungary to Ireland, is serious and would damage the land. Indeed, sometimes for conservation there has been a choice between allowing polluted water onto a wetland, or letting it dry as in Wicken Fen, England. The former was chosen. Within a few years, the effect of this pollution on the nearby traditional communities was serious. Pollution-sensitive water plants restricted to high calcium, vanished, e.g. *Utricularia* spp., and wetland ones changed, e.g. *Phragmites australis*, grew larger, denser, and became significant. The pollution in the Rhine flood plain near Strasbourg is also serious. *Potamogeton coloratus*, *Chara hispida* and *Juncus subnodulosus*, among others, can no longer grow in affected watercourses (Carbienier *et al.*, 1990).

This cutting off of the river, however, is not only recent. It has been done for over a millennium, for navigation and flood defence, so recent impact, though widespread and intensive must not be blamed for all!

When there is no overland river water, the mosaic of open waters is likely to decrease, and the deep winter foods are certainly cut off. The plain therefore becomes more uniform.

The flooding of riverside land with silty water was the principal means of fertilising such land.

Vegetation of the open water

See Chapters 2, 5 for these building blocks.

The block of the land regularly flooded from the river

Such land was, of course, normal, but in agricultural or settled areas is now much restricted. The flooding occurs in Europe in mountainous, and other non-populous areas, and where riverside wetlands are either preserved, or where it is too expensive to drain the land. In a European wetland like the Fenland and the Somerset levels, villages, e.g. Soham, Upware, Glastonbury, Athelney, were on higher land. Around, some land would be drained or higher and be 'winter land', grazeable throughout the year, while wetter land was 'summer land', grazeable only in summer and then the wettest land bore fish, waterfowl, fuel, thatching reed: marsh, not land products. The Danube delta is much flooded. In the low-lying parts of USA, in Florida, Georgia, etc., there is much riverside flooded land, often tree swamps.

In general, deeper floodwater deposits more sediment (nutrients) and lasts longer near the main rivers (see Haslam, 2003 and the vegetation descriptions below). Indeed, until the coming of cheap fertilisers, meadows on flood plain land (water- or flood-meadows) were usually, as at Glastonbury, the most valuable land on a farm or manor.

Removing the annual silt fertiliser decreases nutrient status, since the nutrient inflow left is just that from tributaries, if they exist, and groundwater upflow, if that occurs. Tributary status depends of course on the catchments but (see Chapter 5) is likely to be lower than that of the main river. Any springs at the wetland edge, and groundwater (apart from that polluted) are fairly or very nutrient-low, solutes having been cleaned by passing through the soil or rock (e.g. Haslam, 2003; Haycock & Burt, 1993). (It is, of course, possible to have, e.g. sulphur or salt springs, but these are rare.)

Therefore, over the centuries river-deprived wetlands tend to become of lower nutrient status, especially landwards, where most new water comes in. One English fen had *Phragmites* peat well over 1 m deep, so *Phragmites* had been dominant. However, the medium-nutrient *Carex paniculata* and the even lower-nutrient *C. appropinquata* grew. (Both are peat-formers, but here any such peat had gone.) Nutrient deprivation changed the communities. The Dutch water system is highly complex and connected. Polluted Rhine water is feeding minor watercourses and increasing and skewing chemical status over large areas, moving along watercourses, polluting them and their riversides. Drying the flood plains, of course, changes communities even more (for water quality, see Table 8.2).

Vegetation and habitat types, impacted or planted

These vary greatly! With so many possible building blocks, diversity is high, between and usually within floodplains.

Mosaics of different types are plentiful. In addition to grass fields and reed beds there are small corners of copses or nettles, reeds or rushes. These may be of high biodiversity value. They may also be connected by, e.g. dykes, hedges, streams, roads or may be close enough for interactions to occur.

Not all blocks can be listed, but those not of traditional wetland include:

- arable (dry);
- grassland, improved (dry or fairly so) or unimproved (damp or wet). Unimproved grass, better known as flower-rich meadow, is valuable and threatened (and see below). Improved grass has agrochemicals and may be temporary (ley) in a rotation;
- field dividers – hedges, ditches, fences. Even the last forms a corridor for some biota! Hedges are, surprisingly, not necessarily useful corridors for wood biota between woods (for their function, processes and distribution, see Barr & Petit, 2001);
- riverside trees and hedges. These may be the edge of wet woodland, or separated tree lines fringing wide rivers or heavily shading small streams. Trees are more often old than new-planted, as trees are now too often unwanted in agricultural areas). And there may be that ancient form of use: pollards, harvested above grazing level (once for use, now for heritage);
- constructions by people, including, e.g. farms, villages, towns, wharves, weirs, mills, ponds for duck, salt, or horses.

To put buildings on a flood plain is a foolishness, justified when the plain is fairly narrow or the site the best for a river port or water mill. (Interestingly, regular flooding in a vibrant town is much less unhealthy than when the town is dull or the dwellings squalid.) With recent technology expensive drainage allows housing; and too little cost–benefit data is available. For recent settlements the Dutch, with so much experience of living at and below sea level, have the greatest expertise, and can manage satisfactorily. More recently, a flood plain housing estate in Midland England, was badly flooded. It transpired the good folk of the new estate had complained about an ugly bank blocking their view. The kindly council removed it. The flood protection staff, who were not consulted, were not

Table 8.2 *Outline of CORINE Wetland Classification (from Commission of the European Community, 1992).*

(a) Overall summary		
51	**Raised bogs**	
51.1	Near-natural, often domed, very rare. Communities interrelated, functioning as a unit.	
	51.11	Hummocks, ridges and lawns, higher and drier, e.g. *Sphagnum magellanicum, Oxycoccus, Erica tetralix* (14 subdivisions follow).
	51.12	Hollows, rain-filled, temporary or permanent (2 subdivisions follow).
	51.13	Pools, large, permanent, near the centre of bogs or along tension lines. Characteristically with plankton, often e.g. *Sparganium minimum, Utricularia* spp., *Nymphaea* spp. (2 subdivisions follow).
	51.14	Seeps and soaks, run-off paths to laggs around the bogs (3 subdivisions follow).
	51.15	Lagg rings of water, intermediate mire, acid fen, sometimes e.g. *Eriophorum angustifolium, E. vaginatum, Carex rostrata, C. flava, Parnassia palustris.*
	51.16	Pre-woods. Colonisation by e.g. *Pinus* spp., *Betula* spp.
51.2	Purple moor grass bogs, drying, mowed or burned.	
52	**Blanket bogs**	
52.1	Lowland, west coastal, e.g. *Sphagnum auriculatum, S. magellanicum, S. compactum, S. papillosum, S. nemoreum, S. rubellum, S. tenellum, S. subnitens,* other mosses, *Molinia caerulea, Eriophorum angustifolium, E. vaginatum, Scirpus caespitosus, Rhynchospora alba, Narthecium ossifragum, Erica tetralix, Myrica gale, Drosera rotundifolia, Calluna vulgaris.*	
	52.11	Black bog-rush swards, with *Rhacomitrium lanuginosum.*
	52.12	*Sphagnum*-algal carpets, water logged pool edges, bog surfaces.
	52.13	Deer grass swards.
	52.14	Oblong-leaved sundew (*Drosera intermedia*) communities, slopes with surface water movement.
	52.15	Bulbous rush communities, shallow drainage channels and pools.
	52.16	Flushes, deep hollows and pools, *Potamogeton polygonifolius* etc.
52.2	Hill, Sphagnum abundant, and e.g. *Eriophorum vaginatum, Calluna vulgaris, Erica tetralix, Rubus chamaemorus, Narthecium ossifragum, Scirpus caespitosus, Drosera rotundifolia, Rhacomitrium lanuginosum.*	
	52.21	Cotton grass-heather (ling).
	52.22	Cotton grass (*E. vaginatum*), species-poor.
	52.23	Hill. *Sphagnum* spp. hummocks of the preceding.
	52.24	Dwarf shrub, cotton-grass.
	52.25	Woolly fringe-moss (*Rhacomitrium lanuginosum*).
	52.26	Wet heath.
	52.27	Flushes, deep hollows and pools.
53	**Water fringe vegetation, reed and sedge swamps**	
53.1	Reed beds, usually species-poor, often monodominant, stagnant, slow-flowing or waterlogged.	

(*cont.*)

Table 8.2 (cont.)

	53.11	Common reed beds (*Phragmites australis*) (3 sub-divisions follow).
	53.12	Common clubrush beds (*Scirpus lacustris*), intolerant of drying, tolerant of water movement.
	53.13	Reedmace beds (*Typha* spp.), tolerant of drying and pollution.
	53.14	Medium to tall waterside communities (10 sub-divisions follow).
	53.15	Reed sweetgrass (*Glyceria maxima*), ditches, brooks, grassland, flooded with eutrophic water, rich associated flora.
	53.16	Reed canary grass (*Phalaris arundinacea*), tolerant of drying, pollution, disturbance, land edges, often degraded.
53.2		Large sedges, *Magnocaricetum*, *Carex* or *Cyperus*, damp depressions from oligotrophic mire to rich fen, wet, or partly dry towards land.
	53.21	Large *Carex* beds (18 sub-divisions follow, with different dominants).
	53.22	Tall galingale beds (*Cyperus* spp. except *C. papyrus*) (2 sub-divisions follow).
53.3		Fen sedge beds (*Cladium mariscus*), calcium rich, etc.
	53.31	Fen *Cladium*, species-rich, fairly open.
	53.32	Valencia.
	53.33	Mostly Mediterranean waterside, species-poor.
53.5		Tall rush swamps. Juncus invading grazed and trampled poor fen, marsh, etc.
53.6		Riparian core formations, along permanent or temporary Mediterranean watercourses (2 sub-divisions follow).
54		**Fens, transition mires and springs**
54.2		Rich fens.
	54.21	Black bog-rush fens (*Schoenus nigricans*), low altitude, declining or extinct.
	54.22	Brown bog-rush fens (*S. ferruginosus*) (3 sub-divisions follow).
	54.23	*Davalliana* sedge fens, diverse, often extensive, mostly near or in Alps, refuge of many rare species (2 sub-divisions follow).
	54.24	Pyrennean rich fens.
	54.25	*Carex dioica, C. pulica* or *C. flava* agg. fens (Dioecious, flea, and yellow sedge fens) (6 sub-divisions follow).
	54.26	Black sedge alkaline fens (*Carex nigra*), calciphile spp., brown moss.
	54.27	Russet sedge fens (*Carex saxatilis*), high calcareous mountains.
	54.28	Ice sedge fens (*Carex frigida*), seepages etc. in Alps etc.
	54.29	The same in Britain.
	54.2A	Spike rush fens, *Eleocharis quinqueflora*.
	54.2B	Greek flat sedge (*Blysmus compressus*) fens.
	54.2C	Bottle sedge (*Carex rostrata*) alkaline fens, brown mosses.
	54.2D	Alpine deer grass (*Scirpus hudsonianus*) fens.
	54.2E	Deer grass (*S. caespitosus*) fens.
	54.2F	Middle European flat sedge fens.
	54.2G	Small herb alkaline fens.
	54.2H	Calcareous dune slacks, rush-sedge fens.
	54.2I	Tall herb fens.
54.3		Arcto-alpine riverine swamps, rare glacial relics, neutral to basic, *Carex* spp., *Juncus* spp. diverse.

Table 8.2 (cont.)

	54.31	Riverine swards, *Kobresia simpliciuscula*, etc.
	54.32	*Carex bicolor* etc., swards.
	54.33	*Typha* spp.
	54.34	British mica flushes, *Carex* spp., *Juncus* spp.
54.4	Acidic fens	
	54.41	Alpine cotton-grass (*Eriophorum scheuchzerii*) lake girdles.
	54.42	Star sedges fens *Carex nigra, C. canescens, C. echinata* etc. (10 sub-divisions follow).
	54.43	Apennine acidic fens.
	54.44	*Carex intrisata* Mediterranean etc. fens (3 sub-divisions follow).
	54.45	Deer grass (*Scirpus caespitosus*) acidic fens (5 sub-divisions follow).
	54.46	*Eriophorum angustifolium* mires with a Sphagnum carpet.
	54.47	Dunal sedge acidic fens.
54.5	Transition mires. Mostly small sedge, floating, *Sphagnum* or brown moss. Important refuge of threatened animals and plants.	
	54.51	Floating meadows of slender sedge (*Carex lasiocarpa*), *Sphagnum* or brown mosses, etc. (2 sub-divisions follow).
	54.52	*Carex diandra* quaking mires, open diverse swards.
	54.53	Bottle sedge (*Carex rostrata*) quaking mires (3 sub-divisions follow).
	54.54	Mud sedge (*Carex limosa*) swards (2 subdivisions follow).
	54.55	String sedge (*Carex chordarrhiza*) swards.
	54.56	Peat sedge (*Carex heleonaster*) sedge hollows.
	54.57	Beak sedge (*Rhynchospora alba*) quaking bogs.
	54.58	*Sphagnum* and cotton-grass rafts.
	54.59	Bog bean (*Menyanthes trifoliata*) and marsh cinquefoil (*Potentilla palustris*) rafts.
	54.5A	Bog arum (*Calla palustris*) mires.
	54.5B	Brown moss carpets, diverse, not acid.
	54.5C	Cotton-grass (*Eriophorum vaginatum*) quaking bogs.
	54.5D	Purple moor grass (*Molinia caerulea*) quaking bogs.
	54.5E	Narrow smallreed (*Calamagrostis stricta*) quaking bogs.
	54.5F	Alpine deer grass (*Scirpus hudsoniana*) quaking bogs.
	54.5G	Iberian deer grass (*Scirpus hudsoniana*) quaking bogs.
54.6	White beak sedge (*Rhynchospora alba*) communities, dug peat, flushes, etc.	
37	**Humid grassland and tall herb communities**	
37.1	Meadowsweet (*Filipendula ulmaria*) and related communities, fertile alluvium, bog pasture, often colonised after disuse, with e.g. *Angelica sylvestris, Cirsium palustre, Deschampsia caespitosa, Epilobium hirsutum, Eupatorium cannabinum, Lysimachia vulgaris, Phalaris arundinacea*.	
37.2	Eutrophic humid grassland, nutrient-medium to rich, often winter-flooded, wet or damp, may be fertilised.	
	37.21	High-level humid meadows, very diverse, including *Caltha palustre, Lychnis flos-cuculi, Trollius europeus, Lotus uliginosus* (9 sub-divisions follow).
	37.22	Sharp-flowered rush (*Juncus acutiflorus*) meadows.

(cont.)

Table 8.2 *(cont.)*

	37.23	Sub-continental *Cnidium dubis* meadows, most flooded.
	37.24	Flood swards and related communities, may be intensively grazed (2 sub-divisions follow).
	37.25	Transitional tall herb, abandoned hay meadows.
37.3		Oligohumid grassland
	37.31	Purple moor grass (*Molinia caerulea*) meadows and related communities (2 sub-divisions follow).
	37.32	Heath rush meadows, humid mat-grass swards, peaty, *Nardus stricta*, *Juncus squarrosus*, etc.
37.4		Mediterranean tall humid grasslands.
37.5		Mediterranean short humid grasslands.
37.6		Eastern supra-Mediterranean humid meadows.
	37.61	Greek.
	37.62	Apennine.
37.7		Humid tall herb fringes.
	37.71	Watercourse veils, screens of e.g. *Calystegia sepia*, *Cuscuta europea* and ruderals lining watercourses (5 sub-divisions follow).
44		**Alluvial and very wet forests and brush**
44.1		Riparian willow formation.
	44.11	Pre-alpine willow brush (2 sub-divisions follow).
	44.12	Willow brush (other) (7 sub-divisions, divided on species and location, follow).
	44.13	White willow (*Salix alba*) gallery forests.
	44.14	Mediterranean tall willow galleries (5 sub-divisions follow).
	44.15	Canarian willow (*Salix canariensis*) galleries.
44.2		Grey alder (*Alnus incana*) galleries (2 sub-divisions follow).
44.3		Medio-European stream ash-alder (*Fraxinus* spp., *Alnus* spp.) wood, intolerant of permanent wet, alternately flooded and drained.
	44.31	of brooks and springs (5 sub-divisions follow).
	44.32	of fast-flowing rivers.
	44.33	of slow-flowing rivers (2 sub-divisions follow).
	44.34	N. Iberian alder galleries (4 sub-divisions follow).
44.4		Mixed oak-elm-ash (*Quercus* spp., *Ulmus* spp, *Fraxinus* spp.) of great rivers. Flooded in high floods only. Very diverse in the most diverse European woods, closest in type to Pleistocene ones. Mainly Rhine, Danube and Elbe.
	44.42	Residual mid-European, degraded and species-poor.
	44.43	Balkan (2 sub-divisions follow).
	44.44	Po, relicts but diverse.
44.5		Southern alder-birch (*Alnus* spp., *Betula* spp.) galleries (10 sub-divisions follow).
44.6		Mediterranean poplar-elm-ash (*Populus* spp., *Ulmus* spp., *Fraxinus* spp.) forest, multilayered, alluvial (18 sub-divisions follow).
44.7		Oriental plane (*Platanus orientalis*) and sweet-gum woods (*Liquidamber orientalis*), mostly riparian (5 sub-divisions follow).
44.8		Southern riparian galleries and thickets (6 sub-divisions follow).

Table 8.2 *(cont.)*

44.9		Alder (*Alnus* spp.), willow (*Salix* spp.) and bog myrtle (*Myrica gale*) swamp woods, fens and marshes.
	44.91	Alder swamp woods, usually sallow (*Salix* spp.) below (5 sub-divisions follow).
	44.92	Mire willow (*Salix* spp.) scrub of fens, flood plains, lake edges, etc. (4 sub-divisions follow).
	44.93	Swamp bog myrtle (*Myrica gale*) scrub, drying fens, regenerating bogs.
44.A		Birch (*Betula* spp.) and conifer swamp woods.
	44.A1	*Sphagnum*-birch woods, peaty, acid fen or bog (if bog, little peat building) (3 sub-divisions follow).
	44.A2	Scots pine (*Pinus sylvestris*) bog woods, bogs and transitional mires.
	44.A3	Mountain pine (*Pinus rotundata*) bog woods. Alps, etc.
	44.A4	Sphagnum-spruce (*Picea* spp.) boggy woods (2 sub-divisions follow).

(b) A shortened example

(In: 54 Fens, transition mires and springs)

54.2 Rich fens. Mostly peat- or tufa-producing small sedge and brown moss communities, permanently waterlogged, soligenous or topogenous, with a base-rich nutrient-poor often calcareous water supply, with some peat formation. *Carex davalliana*-type vegetation (nutrient-rich Parvocaricetum). Various sub units. In serious decline, though a few large examples are left, found in pre-Alpine Bavaria, pre-Alps Italy, mountain east France, north east Germany, coastal marshes of north France, south east and north England, Wales, and Ireland.

    54.21 Black-bog-rush (*Schoenus nigricans*) fens, not at high altitude. *Juncus* may be abundant, other species include *Carex lepidophylla, C. hostiana, C. panicea, C. pulicaris, Eriophorum latifolium, Molinia caerulea, Dactylorchis incana, D. praetissina, D. purpurea, D. transiana, D. transvides, Epipactis palustris, Parnassia palustris, Pinguicula vulgaris*, brown mosses. Declining or extinct.

    54.22 Brown bog-rush (*Schoenus ferrigeneus*) fens.

        54.221 Peri-alpine brown bog-rush fens, with grasses, small *Carex* spp., *Eriophorum latifolium, Drosera* spp. *Pinguicula vulgaris, Parnassia palustris* etc.

        54.222 Scottish brown bog-rush fens, base-rich Perthshire flushes.

        54.223 Baltic brown bog-rush fens. North east Jutland, Isles, north east Germany.

    54.23 Davalliana sedge fens, diverse, often extensive, including numerous *Carex* spp., *Juncus articulatus, Scirpus caespitosus, Molinia caerulea, Potentilla erecta, Parnassia palustris, Pinguicula vulgaris* and many more, and the moss layer with *Dropanocladus intermedia, Cratoneuron glauca, Campyllium stellatum*. Most Alpine or peri-Alpine, where they are the refuge of many rare species, elsewhere in decline.

        54.231 Species-rich Davalliana sedge fens.

        54.232 Deer grass (*Scirpus caespitosus*) sedge fens, *S. caespitosus* dominant, species-poor.

    54.24 Pyrennean rich fens, uncommon calcareous fens in the Pyrennees, with small *Carex* spp., *Eriophorum latifolium, Juncus articulatus, Parnassia palustris*, etc.

pleased when they were blamed because the protection bank had gone. Water mills may be floodable typically the family lived upstairs. Otherwise the proper place for settlement is above flood level, the edge of higher land, 'islands' on old higher terraces, even by and in old river beds, where there has been deposition of coarser (e.g. gravel) material. (This drains better, and does not contract.)

Archaeological investigation shows many traces of settlement along river banks, and the use of rivers, with ports, wharves, boats, boatyards, and religious sites. Soil and peat built up in flood plains preserve the artefacts in it, whether small (e.g. waterlogged infilled wells) or large (villages) (G. A. Wait in Haslam, 1997a). The Moselle was canalised and made suitable for shipping in as early as AD 58, though little more was done between Roman and mediaeval times (Haslam, 1987). The Elder Pliny describes water mills in the first century, but their spread was slow, though by the eleventh century they had reached Scandinavia and are described in the Norse Sagas.

Many 'old' existing sites of farms and villages (let alone the thousands of water mills recorded in *Domesday Book*, 1086 (Darby, 1971) are on the site of these earlier ones.

Traditional vegetation types

Floodplain wetlands

(see Haslam, 2003 Fig. 4.1, Tables 8.1 and 8.2).

Rain-dependent

(a) Bogs

Bogs are entirely rain-fed. To occur, rain water must stay on the surface, so *Sphagnum* (or equivalent) can establish. Once underwater fen peat or alluvium have built up to the water surface, bog peat can grow: provided, of course, there is no nutrient-rich or sediment-depositing flooding. Once growing, a *Sphagnum* shoot holds water just below its tips, so covering the surface. Surface loss, evapotranspiration, is reduced because most water is subsurface, downwards and sideways loss is reduced, because of low permeability. *Sphagnum* continues to grow and dome-shaped raised bogs develop, from a kilometre or so to hundreds of kilometres across. Climatically, they occur down to S. France (Moore & Bellamy, 1974). They can be stable for thousands of years.

These bogs are highly acidic, with a short woody (e.g. *Calluna*) or shorter (e.g. *Eriophorum* spp., *Drosera* spp.) vegetation mixed with the *Sphagnum*. Biodiversity is high, and the texture and colour are different to all other flood plain building blocks. Bog can start wherever the water table is sufficiently high and stable. This is now rarer than it used to be, though it still occurs, e.g. the Netherlands, very locally in the English Broads. Raised bog peat has commercial value, formerly as domestic fuel, now for compost, or as in Canada and Ireland, for power stations.

(b) Source marshes

In Malta, above and beside some rivers, there used to be marshes which were primarily rain-fed, and sited above impervious limestone. (Some pools still exist, and stay wet until past mid-summer.) There were also some springs. Since this is too far south for bog, calcareous marsh developed (*Schoenus nigricans*, *Cyperus* spp.).

Run-off dependent marshes

In these, rain is of minor importance compared with run-off (unless the rain is severely polluted). Solutes in the run-off come from the catchment above, so reflect their chemistry (rock type, soil type, land use).

(a) **Valley bogs**, which surround a nutrient-poor stream in a nutrient-poor valley, with a small or negligible flood plain. The riverside receives stream nutrients, and so may bear carr. On the slopes above, bog develops. If this dries, it becomes heath (bog only forms under water, even if the water is that held in wet *Sphagnum*). Texture and colour resemble raised bogs, though valley bog may be greener.

(b) **Poor fen**, which often occurs with nutrient-low run-off on a nutrient-low plain seldom or never flooded by rich river water but kept wet. This type of fen is usually short, e.g. 0.25 to 0.5 m high, fairly diverse, typically with *Carex* spp. and *Juncus* spp. so they have a characteristic texture as well as flora and fauna.

(c) **Other**, more nutrient-rich run-off will lead to more nutrient-rich habitats of the types described below.

Groundwater dependent wetlands

Their water comes from springs, particularly ones at the landwards edge of the plains, but also from on or above them. The vegetation varies with the nutrient status, short or tall, nutrient low or high. Flushes at the edge of plain may form small wetlands (Fig. 4.1). Water may well up in the wetland, particularly in winter, as the groundwater table rises. Spring water is remarkably stable, so the water level in the habitats is also stable, whether of uniform level or in a series of pits, or on levels changing over the plain, such as arise from peat cutting. Wetlands fed from beneath have less stable water levels.

These wetlands do not, now, receive river sediment or pollutants or much run-off: if they do, these overwhelm the spring water and habitat. Otherwise they vary greatly in vegetation. There are calcium-dominated fens, highly restricted by lack of phosphorus and nitrogen, poor fens with low nutrients, reedswamps with more nutrients, tall herb fens with high nutrients, carr and woodland.

If these fens are drained, nutrient status as well as water and so potential vegetation, can change. Nutrients are held in the soil and peat, and drying, and even more, disturbance, releases those nutrients (Grootjans, 1985; Haslam, 2003; Prach, 1993; Prach *et al.*, 1997). All change, but the most spectacular are calcium-dominated communities, with *Schoenus nigricans, Drosera* spp., and *Pinguicula vulgaris*, the most nutrient-poor fen vegetation, turning into tall herb, the most nutrient-rich, all by releasing stored nutrients on drying.

The most studied calcium-dominated peats are in the Netherlands, where the water is derived from calcium-rich sediments. The effect, though, is stronger in England where the water comes from pure chalk or other limestone which is more lime-rich. Most calcium-dominated fens are groundwater fed, but some are run-off ones, the run-off coming from limestone above. To grow peat, though, there must also be perennial water, probably groundwater.

Other groundwater habitats (Table 8.1) have more nutrients. River-fed wetlands are the most common type formed. These are commonly alluvial, created from river-borne sediment. Flood plains may also develop fen peat. Unlike bog, this develops under water. Organic debris builds up, and forms humus which then becomes peat. This depends on perennial flooding, and little or no sedimentation. This means usually the far end of wide flood plains, where the flood water has already dropped its sediment. The main areas have calcium-rich water, in which fen vegetation grows well. If there is much sedimentation, it is alluvium, or organic-rich alluvium which develops. Where peat develops, it usually accumulates up to water level. At water level, it stops, as it can no longer be fed by rich water. If ground level sinks, it can resume. If not, raised bog can develop. If drained, it is fertile for agriculture, or if unmanaged, there can be succession to tall herb (disturbed) or woodland.

Large rivers may have large flood plains, but there are plenty of small ones, too. Around the hilly coasts, say, of Britain, France (Corsica) and Iceland, are innumerable small estuarine flood plains, used for rough grazing if at all, and just left to flood in storms. The same also applies to many small flood plains further upstream. Even in an agricultural area, if a few metres of riverside land floods, and is not cultivated because of the flood, so what? Until sediment fills up the wet area, or there is a land or sea change altering level (so leading to dry land or lake), a river-fed flood plain results.

Conditions governing soil and peat development change, and Tables 8.1 and 2.1 illustrate some changes within the same places: changes in water and sedimentation regimes, leading to changes in substrate, water regimes, type and so

Table 8.3 *Water quality comments (after Haslam, 1994)*

(1) Removal of the quality and quantity of water under which a community developed will, in time, lead to the loss of that community
(2) Water composition depends on water management and weather as well as on water resources
(3) Man's impact on groundwater systems fragments these, so increasing chemical and hydrological separations
(4) For the protection of a drying wetland, more water is needed of the original quality, not just water of any type
(5) Communities are very sensitive to chemical composition, and vary with this. Mosaics and other patterns of vegetation develop with corresponding patterns of water quality
(6) Drying (from drainage or abstraction) leads to irreversible changes in peat chemistry
(7) Many fen wetlands developed with calcareous groundwater, which is being abstracted from the fen supply for domestic use
(8) Polluted groundwater is increasing, and is likely to become unsuitable for sustaining some wetlands
(9) Air pollution, now only locally severe, may increase, and lead to a wider range of influences (e.g. nutrient-rich, acid, heavy metal)
(10) Mild or moderate pollution may take decades or even centuries to develop its full influence on an affected wetland, though severe pollution starts to act quickly
(11) In the (sparse) habitats where it is possible, rainwater filtered through peaty soil elsewhere in the catchment may be similar in composition to clean groundwater, and be substituted for it
(12) Wetland communities, particularly those with large perennial dominants, may maintain themselves for decades in changed water regimes in which they can neither reproduce themselves nor become re-established after disruption
(13) Community viability must be known before changes intended for conservation in chemistry (including pollution) or hydrology are approved

the type of vegetation supported. Human impact alters this natural pattern of course.

It is possible to drain huge wetlands, as seen in the Iraq reed beds in the 1990s, but that was not done for cost–benefit. To drain the Danube delta would not make cultural or commercial sense. To have drained much of the Netherlands, where the life of the nation depends on drained land, is another matter.

Building blocks of river plain vegetation (Table 8.2)

As always, it is impossible to classify vegetation satisfactorily, as so many intermediate and unusual types exist. Here descriptions follow the CORINE 1992

European Commission scheme, which is European and useful for this discussion. (Classifications abound, and rightly so, since different ones are devised for different purposes.)

Community number 53 Reed and sedge swamps, water fringe vegetation

Wetland reedswamp is more diverse in type, and more stable than river fringe communities. Reedswamp communities are often species-poor and monodominant, though diversity may be high in mosaics of communities. The general building block of reedswamp is subdivided by factors including plant habit, water regime, chemical regime (including substrate) natural grazing and human impact. In the natural state the habitat dries, and woody plants invade, as in all wetlands.

Community number 53.2 Sedge swamp

Magnocaricatum is within the last, as containing tall thin Cyperaceae. These communities tend to be in drier, less flooded places, than reedswamp. Taller *Eleocharis* spp. and *Juncus* spp. are also grouped here. Variation is with species as in reedswamp (above).

The large tussock sedges, e.g. *Carex paniculata, C. elata*, spread out their leaves, so usually cast incomplete shade rather than the heavy shade usually found under reedswamp, so subsidiary species – on the ground and on the tussocks – may be abundant. In typical habitats, different trees colonise different tussock species: for instance birch on *Schoenus nigricans* (nutrient-poor), but sallow on *Carex paniculata* (richer), etc.

Community number 54 Fens, transition mires and springs

These are mainly short sedge communities, *Parvocaricatum*, which are generally shorter and richer in species than the *Magnocaricatum*. *Carex* spp, *Juncus* spp., and others of similar habit are prominent. Grazing may reduce sward to semi-sward to non-sward, and, if the grazing is light, diversity can become very high. Tree invasion of course occurs in drier parts.

The more calcium-influenced communities (see above) are usually on lime-rich aquifers, and on headwaters. *Parvocaricatum* may be generally sward, semi-sward or tussocks. They are mostly very diverse. In richer habitats, *Magnocaricetum* and tall herb occur, though the communities are classed elsewhere.

Acidic fens barely occur within flood plains, the nearest being at the head of raised bogs or around nutrient-poor lakes. *Eriophorum scheuchzeria* is typical on the continent.

Transition mires are, naturally, a mixed group, mostly peaty, ranging from quagmire (Dutch, quaking fen) to small 'corner habitats'. There are enough nutrients for those short, but non-bog species which are shaded by taller vegetation and removed by many forms of impact (from drying to extraction). Short *Carex* spp., *Eriophorum vaginatum* and both *Calamagrostis stricta* and *Molinia caerulea* are characteristic. They are not bogs, they have more nutrients than poor fens, and less impact than bog pasture.

Community number 37 Humid (damp) grassland and tall herb communities

These intergrade with each other and many others. A wetland sufficiently dry, at least dry for part of the summer, and grazed, becomes grassland. This is species-rich, and of high conservation value. If neither over-dried, nor given much agrochemicals, it is now called flower-rich damp meadow or grassland. This was the best livestock feed before modern agriculture, and because there was so much of it, conservationists failed to take action when it was disappearing and became rare. EU policy is now to increase the habitat: but how much still has viable original genotypes in its old and decayed seed bank? And if there, will they be swamped by well meaning people planting alien genotypes?

The typical nutrient-rich (sediment-fed) flood plain grassland merges into the low-nutrient bog pasture so common in, say, the valleys of Welsh resistant rock hills.

Trampling lowers nutrient status, holding nutrients in the soil (Verhoeven 1992; Haslam, 2003), so pasture can occur alongside far more nutrient-rich tall herb vegetation (Rodwell 1992, 1995; Haslam, 2003).

Both floodplain grassland and tall herb can be colonised by woody plants, given abandonment and enough time (which may be many decades or just a year or two, depending on habitat).

Tall herb occurs on abandoned nutrient-rich dry wetland, whether over large areas or in neglected corners. In large areas there can be a mosaic of different communities, varying with habitat (e.g. R. Luznice, Czech Republic, Prach, 1992a, b), or history (e.g. Breck Fens, England, Haslam, 1960, 2003).

As far south as Malta, tall herb does not exist. The species are geographically absent, and this may account for *Phragmites australis* growing in much drier places. Tall herb may suppress *Phragmites* in dry habitats.

Community number 44 Alluvial and very wet forest and carr (brush)

CORINE lists ten groups, mostly sub-divided, illustrating the variety. The primary genera are *Salix* and *Alnus*, but many others may occur, e.g. *Populus* (wet), *Fraxinus, Betula* (damp), and *Quercus* (drier). As building blocks, distribution and pattern are the primary elements. The secondary ones are the species involved, giving texture, colour, height and general shape. The diversity of prominent species tends to increase going east in Europe, and also within North America. The species-poor woodlands of west Europe are unusual. The third layer of elements is the shape of the individual trees, which differ over Europe. A band of *Salix alba* with *Phragmites australis*, can occur over small streams from, e.g. England to Hungary (Fig. 6.1). In different regions the trees are of different shape – as indeed they are in other places. On the mini-scale, woody building blocks differ.

Deciduous trees are the common flood plain ones across temperate and southern Europe. Southern maquis, which is evergreen, is usually above flood level. In the north, the woody plants become coniferous (as on high altitudes in central Europe). In the far north, there are no woods, only short woody plants in tundra.

Many small streams have dried (Chapters 2, 5) in recent decades. Often, these remain – at the least as dried ditches – in the wood when they have vanished from the agricultural plain beside. The wood has been drained only passively because of the field drainage. In riverside grassland, it is often possible to trace the line of old (dried) streams by pollards, sallow bushes, etc.

51 raised bogs

As explained above, these may grow on damp (not flooded) fen or mineral soil, and may cover large areas, as in The Netherlands, and, on a smaller scale, the western English Fenland. Bog creates its own landscape and its high, perched, water table.

These wetland building blocks are combined in many different ways. One riverscape may contain one, two or numerous blocks. Generally, short vegetation means low nutrients, difficult temperature, water or harvesting. In Europe, flood plains are influenced by human impact, whether just by light sheep grazing or by arable cultivation. Wherever native species dominate, they are present because allowed by people.

Case studies (Fig. 8.2)

R. Eger, Hungary

This rises in the mountains of NE Hungary, and flows south, via the Tisza flood plain to flow into R. Tisza. The upper catchment is mainly wooded hills, on a fairly small scale, with many valleys. Here there are some flower-rich

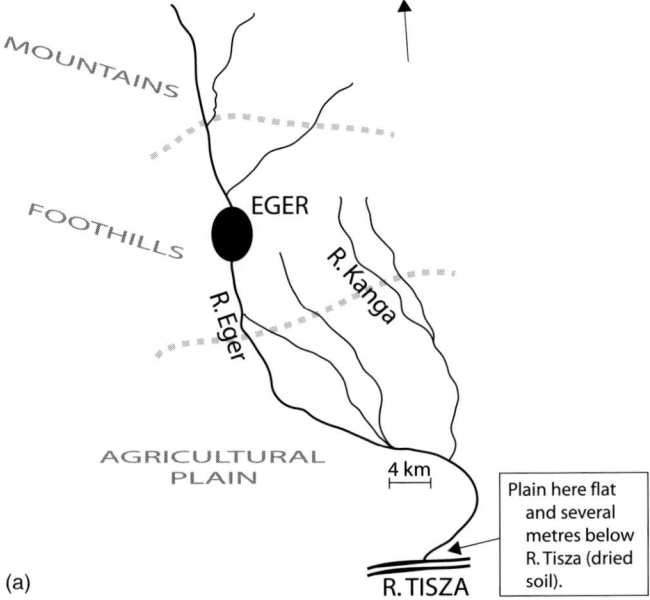

Fig. 8.2. The valley of River Eger, Hungary. (a) Map. (b) In the lower mountains, with their characteristic shape, most slopes are forested, the rest, grass. Low management gives a nutrient-rich, flower-rich meadow. Settlement is mostly at the valley bottom, around the river though (mostly) away from flooding. (c) Foothills with cultivated widening valley. Eger city is strategically placed in a similar but larger bowl at the entrance to the mountains, with an ancient fortress (and mostly baroque, built after the Turkish occupation). Originally accessible by boat. (d) Lowland straightened rivers, with willow fringes, in agricultural lowlands. (e) Flat plain below river level, near with drainage ditches (being lost: over-drained) near confluence of R. Eger and R. Tisza.

meadows on small flood plains. Flowing down, by the town of Eger there is a narrow plain, which downstream becomes wider and more continuous, with low hills beside, until it reaches the main Tisza (afterwards Danube) flood plain. In the hills, the plains still flood. Land use is forestry, and there is no need to drain deeply. On riversides in little valleys with narrow flood plains, *Salix* spp. tree bands, with *Phragmites* beside and beneath, are common. Approaching the foothills there are intermittent larger plains, drained to grassland or arable. Arable increases in the downstream plain, though there are still riverside fringes of willow and perhaps reed.

The river was canalised and made fit for both navigation and flood prevention in the seventeenth century. The river was walled. With drainage and walling, water decreased, and the city fishery was lost.

(b)

(c)

Fig. 8.2. (cont.)

(d)

(e)

Fig. 8.2. (*cont.*)

R. Lark, England (Fig. 8.3)

This lowland river is on (mostly fertile) sand over chalk. It gave access, via the Great Ouse, from the North Sea at the Wash to the great abbey and town of Bury St Edmunds (and the settlements between). The Lark was canalised for easy navigation up to Bury St Edmunds in 1600. Above the city there are intermittent small flood plains, now grass or arable. In the city, the ground

204 The riverscape and the river

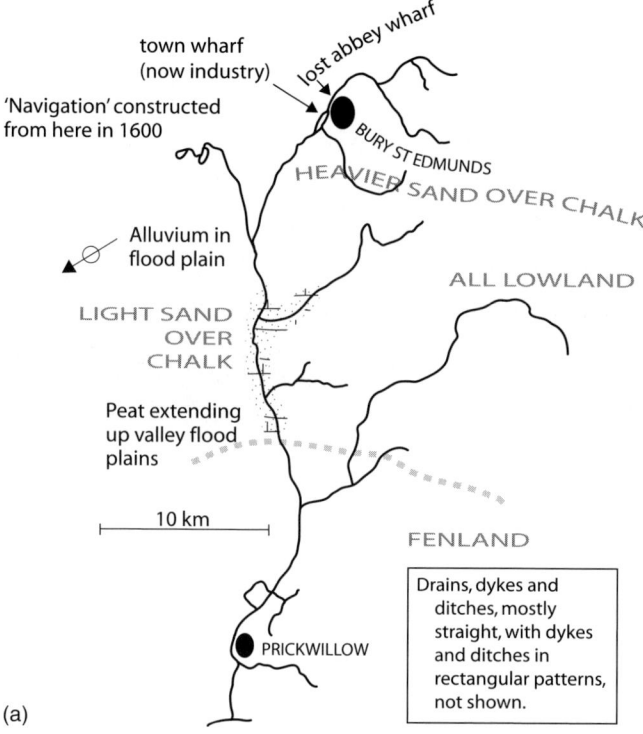

(a)

Fig. 8.3. The valley of River Lark, England. (a) Map. (b) The great water gate of Bury St Edmunds abbey, around which grew the city. (St Edmund was martyred by Danes.) As common, a cathedral city, even if remote, had a well-born population (though less so than Eger). (c) R. Lark was canalised in 1600 (unusually early) to give easy access to Ely, Cambridge, Bedford and the midlands and the continental towns beyond the North Sea. This picture shows a part where the canal was built above the original river (lower ground to right of canal). Smiling agricultural riverscape, grass near river. Downstream there is a flood plain, some wetland (see Icklingham Poors' Fen, Fig. 11.3). Most is pasture or (semi-abandoned), some ex-marsh hay, now tall herb or planted poplar. The Drift in that region is less fertile, some even nutrient-low, much recently wooded. (d) Former mills (these re-built from water mills) at Mildenhall. Down in the Fens, the country is like Fig. 3.2, a flat, drained, agricultural plain.

slopes up from the river, so there is little flooding. As is typical of Abbey towns, there were two sets of wharfs, one for the abbey, the other for the town. The downstream, town wharf area is now an industrial estate (perhaps from a former watermill area, see Chapter 11). Downstream, a fairly narrow (e.g. 100–200 m) but continuous flood plain gradually develops. Most of the plain is grass or cultivated, but there is a little ex-Poors Fen (formerly available to villagers), osier and alder–ash wood, abandoned horse-fodder and other meadow. The central

Building blocks of flood plain vegetation 205

(b)

(c)

Fig. 8.3. (*cont.*)

(d)

Fig. 8.3. (*cont.*)

area formerly bore unique fens, and wet grassland. In the past 30 years it has been drained, abstracted and dried.

First, river flooding developed wetlands. After canalisation, rising groundwater kept grassland wet in winter, and grazing which compacted soil and kept nutrients low (see above) and maintained poor-fen species like *Eriophorum angustifolium*. Osier woods were for craft and timber. *Phalaris–Glyceria* meadows provided good fodder (including for London horses). Thatching, fuel, other craft and minor uses came from the Poors Fens on which villagers had rights. Ditching made fields more suitable as pasture. The first were parallel and across from the higher ground, later in straight patterns. Abstraction and further drainage removed most of the spring water, and the high water table. Neglect is now turning pasture to *Magnocaricetum*, and most wet-requiring, short-lived species have gone. Alternatively, *Phragmites* and tall herb has changed to rough pasture with grazing. Some tributaries had flood plains, also formerly used for fodder. Some of these fields have been planted with poplar (*Populus alba*) in recent decades.

The third and downstream section of the Lark is in the Fenland. It flows through this large peat plain to join the R. Great Ouse. In the early twentieth century the Fenland was more drained and bore more arable than the plains of the middle section, though much less than now. Dykes were then numerous, and hedges and plantations absent. It took the late twentieth century to ruin

Building blocks of flood plain vegetation 207

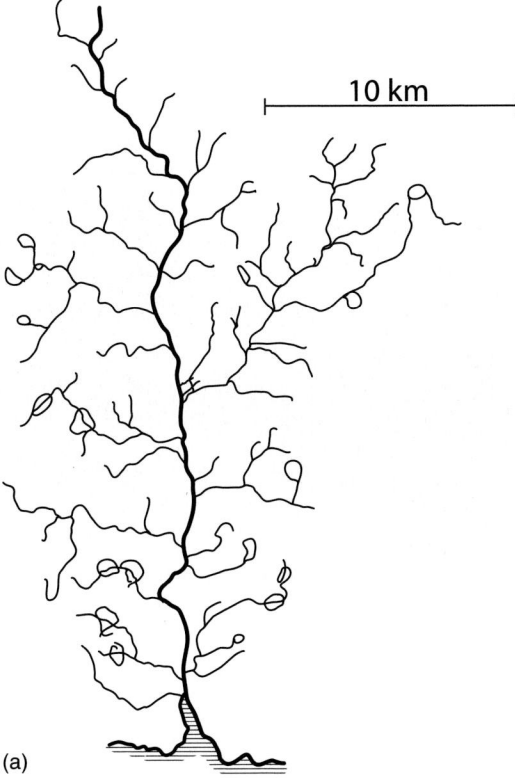

Fig. 8.4. (a) The valley of River Halladale, Scotland. (b) Mountain, moor, bog and drained grass on the coarse sediment beside the swift Highland river. (c) Further down stream, strath (valley) opening out. Unlike the Eger, these mountains are nutrient-low, with acid peaty soil and vegetation. There are a few clumps of birch (on drained soil), but no forests now (see Chapter 13).

the best of the middle sector, in that fen peat was still being made in the wettest parts in the 1960s. This was *Phragmites* peat or (in the past) open water organic mud.

R. Halladale, N. Scotland (Fig. 8.4)

This river gives a further contrast. It is a mountainous, boggy catchment, with human impact. Grazing in the flood plains both makes and keeps pasture: these bright green areas stand out in the general browny moor and boggy riverscape. The river, too, is brown, from carrying bog peat. The main river rises high in the hills, with swift flow and bouldery substrate. Most tributaries do the same, or rise in blanket bog, these starting as brown bog, flowing slowly.

208 The riverscape and the river

(b)

(c)

Fig. 8.4. (cont.)

A little cultivation occurs near the mouth where there is – now – more and better soil.

Small flood plains occur along the main river, which flooded almost naturally, and mostly grazed by Highland cattle and deer (except for the cultivated mouth). There is some bog-pasture.

R. Ghasel, Malta (Fig. 8.5)

R. Ghasel has negligible old flood plain, though a large new one, an estuary, silted up since mediaeval times. Previously, this was a valuable port. The remains of a guard tower were still present in 1400. It was probably still marsh, primarily reedswamp, into the nineteenth century. It is now a cultivated plain. (*Phragmites australis* is still present, in and at the edges of the damper seawards fields.) A wide, straight river channel was constructed, to the sea, which is now dry, infilled and cultivated.

'Weedy grass' is the closest to wetland vegetation. Deep-laid causeways show the former presence of wetland. Dried marsh also occurs occasionally above the present channel sources. Most of the river is now dry for most of the year (see Chapter 4), and even the spring-fed upper part has most water abstracted or dried. The dried, dredged beds vary from stony to earthen. Low riverside land, ex-marsh, is intermittent, and little native deciduous wood remains, though a little is planted. The Ghasel plains have passed from wetland building blocks even to dryness in under 200 years: a depressing loss.

Far from wishing to conserve the remaining archaeological and national heritage, the Government (2006) is planning to put a new 40 m wide fully concreted channel down the plain. An even more depressing loss.

Discussion

Flood plains slope downstream. It may be very very slightly, but, being beside, and created by, a downwards flowing river, they all slope down. Therefore all the flows of river and catchment (see above, and Chapters 2–6) pass through the flood plain.

In other features flood plains differ: they may be sandy and a few metres wide or huge areas of flooded peat wetland. They do not even all form continuous corridors. There may be many kilometres between flood plains, where the river valley is narrow. There may be a bottom just a little wider than the river, bearing and containing small floods. There may be many a long mile of arable or ley between any form of wetland (fen, marsh, flower-rich meadow, or wet woodland) though some of these still do occur.

(a)

Fig. 8.5. The valley of River Ghasel, Malta. (a) Upper river, in wide valley, dredged, in small flood plain, terraced fields above, patches of carob (tree) along cliff-and-spring lines in the hard limestone slopes far. (b) Upper middle, in soft limestone lowland, small gorge, walled up so more of the valley could be terraced. Wall breaches not mended. Olives to left, fruit to right; (abstracted and dried). (c) Stretch formerly converted for water storage and (wrongly) planted with poplars (now spreading) to lessen water loss. The last part of the river to have borne good aquatic vegetation. (d) Lower middle, walled, wide channel, looking to the 1600s St Paul's seafarers' chapel, set to welcome seafarers walking up the river to the old capital, Mdina. (e) The Great Gorge, partly removed by quarrying, arches mark the Victoria lines fortification, built across Malta in the late nineteenth century. Here are St Catherine's Church, and (out of sight) St Paul's cave church and cave ammunition dumps. (f) Floodplain, formerly a main port and silted up in early modern times. Old causeway centre. Good agricultural land.

Given the number of building blocks outlined above (which list is incomplete), the diversity of flood plains is not surprising. Even the arable ones show diversity, of soil, water regime, field dividers (distribution, field size, type, pattern, height), trees (woods, hedges, riverside, pollards) and crops. Each river basin has its own variability and characteristics. Land use has moulded the country,

Building blocks of flood plain vegetation   211

(b)

(c)

Fig. 8.5. (*cont.*)

(d)

(e)

Fig. 8.5. (*cont.*)

(f)

Fig. 8.5. (*cont.*)

and the country then moulds the thinking and the people that live in it (it is unfortunate that, nowadays, too much of the country is moulded by those who have never seen it, but live in far away towns!). Intensive land use may have been (in some sort) for several millennia, or for barely a century. But, from soil to trees, all the riverscape is moulded by human impact.

Traditional or pristine wetlands, formerly covering much of undrained, regularly-flooded plains, are now few. In populous areas they are as controlled by human impact as is the arable. The reed beds of Norfolk exist only because centuries of harvesting and management have developed them, in land now dry enough for carr, but easily accessible for reed cutting. Raised bog is destroyed for gardening or power stations, fen peat is near-destroyed for arable. These are all under human control. Traditional wetland communities (Table 8.2) depend on nutrient (and pollutant) status, water regime, and impact.

While, in general, Europe and agricultural North America are getting drier, and water shortages loom, this is not universal. Individual plains have been kept wet by individuals for various reasons. Conservation organisations have kept a few. There are also larger issues. EU policies sometimes now encourage wet places (meadows, reed beds for bitterns, the Water Framework Directive), less intensive hill use, and less food production. The effect of these on habitat is yet to develop.

Table 8.4 *English Broadland change and deterioration (Parmenter, 1995)*

Selected, representative examples
(1) East Ruston Common – Kings Fen. Borehole 1974, fully working 1985
  1797 rough pasture.
  1810 well-drained (for 1810!), well fenced.
  1832 controlled peat cutting, rush cutting, grazing.
  1840 gravel and sand extraction.
  1885 marsh.
  1909 litter, rushes and mixed fodder (bullocks), peat cutting almost finished. Soft peat and mossy beds, usually with a hard bottom 1 m down, but also dangerous holes. Sphagnum beds usually safe to walk on (note: bog developing above, not inside, fen). Sedges have firmer bottom than reed.
  1919 floating carpets over unknown depths, and 60 cm hidden drops into peat cuttings. Slippery putrid mud.
  1921 drought. Deeper holes remained wet.
  1929 wet marsh with mossy bottom (i.e. drying).
  1958 attractive area of mixed fen.
  1970 abstraction started beneath.
  1975 probably too dry and burnt for *Carex limosa*.
  1984 at least 2 m of water on marsh in June (no longer permanent).
  1985 very wet summer, but abstraction at full extent, and can walk over fens and flushes in ordinary shoes. 60 cm drop in water in two months, up to 30% of former water intercepted.
  1989 *Juncus-Molinia*, invasion of acidophilous and tall herb communities (*Urtica dioica, Rubus fruticosus* agg., *Calamagrostis canescens, Epilobium hirsutum*, sparse *Phragmites australis*). Peat oxidation. Birch invasion. Catastrophic deterioration.
  1992 Sphagnum gone, numerous birch seedlings, *Carex acuta* still present along seepage lines.
  1993 more drastic change. Very dry, severe burns. Gorse (a completely dry land species) invades. Winter pools, though, killed birch seedlings.
(2) Mown Fen, East Ruston. Affected by same borehole
  1797–1920s as last.
  1957 lost: *Anagallis tenella, Drosera anglica, Epipactis palustris, Eriophorum angustifolium, Liparis loeselii, Ophioglossum vulgare, Parnassia palustris, Pinguicula vulgaris, Sphagnum* sp., *Stellaria alsine, Thelypteris thelypteroides, Utricularia intermedia, U. minor*. Calcium-rich, nutrient-low species.
  Still present: *Caltha palustris, Carex rostrata, Hydrocharis morsus-ranae, Menyanthes trifoliata, Osmunda regalis, Peucedanum palustre, Ranunculus flammula, R. lingua*.
  1958 mostly alder (sallow carr, herb fen). No more mowing and grazing.
  1973 a little sedge mowing.
  1983 sedge beds abandoned, scrub invasion.
  1985 rapid scrub invasion, very dry. Narrow band of wet heath above fen: still present: *Eriophorum* sp., *Peucedenaum palustre, Phragmites australis* (a fen or marsh where this species is worth mentioning, is in a bad way!), *Potentilla palustris, Sphagnum* sp.
  1989 too dry to regenerate *Cladium*. Water 75 cm below surface instead of 45 cm above.
  1993 botanical interest (i.e. rare or specialised species) lost.

Table 8.4 (cont.)

(3) Dilham Broad. Representative of many
  Late-nineteenth century: drying (early).
  Mid-twentieth century: drained for agriculture.
  1990s well-drained grazing marsh.

(4) Sutton Broad Fen
  1797 broad (lake).
  1826 broad.
  1840 open water of more regular shape.
  1884 discontinuous swamp.
  1903 harvested *Phragmites, Typha angustifolia* near edge. Still some quaking fen.
  1909 quaking bog and mowing marshes, unreclaimed, usually flooded in winter.
  1962 *Nymphaea* pools gone since 1955. Reed.
  1963 'early' herbaceous fen.
  1970 *Liparis loeselii* all right.
  1980 *L. loeselii* on tussocks of *Carex appropinquata* and *Schoenus nigricans*. Bryophyte carpet. Calcium-rich.
  1990s drying, deteriorating through lack of management. Still one of the most floristically rich areas.

(5) Ranworth Broad Marshes
  Thirteenth, fourteenth and nineteenth centuries, peat cutting.
  1797 fen and wood.
  1838 fen (and wood). Peat cutting.
  1879 with a duck decoy (a pond designed to attract and capture ducks, usually using tame decoy ducks).
  1883 in a dry year can (if walk quickly) cross with water boots.
  1885 open fen.
  1902 dangerous bogs and swamps.
  After 1940s, loss of management and e.g. *Liparis loeselii*.

(6) Decoy Carr, Acle
  Calcium-dominated 'good' fens deteriorated because of greater drainage, drying out principally between 1969 and 1980s. In 1990s, it was quite dry, with too much carr. Dams were put in the dyke network in 1992 putting water level back to around ground level.

(7) Thorpe Marshes
  Circa 1830, Norwich (Whitlingham) sewage treatment works (STW) brought effluent in River Yare flood water. Constructed after a cholera epidemic.
  1955–75 works expansion increased the pollution.
  1990s bypass construction altered the drainage. Gravel extraction both sides of the river. Damaged by STW pollution, construction and extraction.

(8) Reedham Marshes
  1838 grazing marsh, wind-pump drained.
  1855 often flooded.
  1907 semi-improved pasture.
  1960s part flooded from abandoned drainage, developed to good reedbed.
  1990s much reedbed, some sedge beds and others (including *Juncus subnodulosus*), the highest number of fen communities of any Broadland fen.

(9) Ashby Warren
  Acid valley bog lost by abstraction. (A little drying Sphagnum in conifer plantation, etc.)

The abandonment of Communism in Eastern Europe meant the abandonment of some unpopular farming policies, and the Czech Luznice valley was left to flood again and recover its wetlands. Areas of over-polluted groundwater are no longer abstracted, and ground level rises.

Time, like an ever-rolling stream, bears all its sons away. They fly forgotten as a dream, dies at the opening day (I. Watts, 1719). Table 8.4 shows wetland changes in different sites over the past few hundred years. No memory remains of most earlier parts. In consequence, the happenings also have been ignored, like a forgotten dream, when interpreting and planning genuine 'restoration' to an earlier state. And indeed ignoring it, means ignoring certainly an interesting, probably a unique and fascinating heritage, of archaeology, culture, history and natural processes, vegetation and fauna.

It is very difficult for those under 30 and working with time, to understand the workings of time on vegetation. Processes of succession, mosaic formation and destruction, changes of community with cyclic change, invasion (e.g. of trees), and habitat changes, are huge, but slow, and time is needed to see and understand them. A good example is a small spring fen, drained and dried in the 1970s. In the 1950s it had peat at water level, was dominated by *Schoenus nigricans*, with an established cycle dependent on the development of its tussocks, and a high and stable biodiversity. Nearly a century before, peat was cut, with deep pits and some *Schoenus nigricans* but more *Cladium mariscus* (which can better tolerate water level variations). Without historical records, how could either of these be discovered, when no suitable peat or habitat was available for investigation? (See Haslam, 2003 for other examples of such changes.)

9

Resources II. Plants and animals, cleaning and minerals

Land is a resource on which people can draw. Land use superimposed over natural structures and processes produces both natural and cultural heritage.

Introduction

The river and the land are a unity, an entity which would exist even if there were no flora or fauna. They are, however, a vital resource for such biota, including people. All living things are made mostly of water, and none can make all the water they need. The water and the land (together with the sun) provide the materials of life. Some of these resources are of direct benefit to people, for food, shelter, clothes and more, others benefit people more indirectly. All being part of the natural world, deserve (but may not get) protection and preservation.

Resources of rivers and other fresh waters

These include those flora and fauna which are useful to people now or in the historic past, and which are partly or wholly associated with fresh water (Table 9.1).

Grass is the primary resource of wetter, traditional flood plains (as described above and in Chapter 10).

Arable on now-dried flood plains is the commonest present use, on both narrow and wide plains.

Fisheries

Fish used to be the principal crop from the rivers, fish in huge numbers and many species, providing protein for those unable to afford expensive meat,

218   The riverscape and the river

Table 9.1 *Values of riparian ecosystems (from Malanson, 1993)*

Economic
Reduce downstream flooding
Recharge aquifers
Surface water supply in arid regions
Support secondary productivity, e.g. for fisheries
High yields of timber
Transport corridors
Water supply and electricity
Construction materials and waste disposal
Agriculture and livestock
Settlement

Social
Recycle nutrients, tighten spiral and storage
Store heavy metals and toxins
Accumulate organic matter as a sink for CO_2
Intermediate storage for sediments
Natural heritage
Recreation
Aesthetics
Natural laboratories for teaching and research

Biological
Special habitat for some endangered or threatened species
Refugia for upland species
Corridors for species movement

protein which was available locally, required no nurturing and was fresh, and free or cheap, at least in part. In earlier Christian times those abstaining from meat in Lent, on Fridays and eves of Holy Days could eat fish, and indeed beaver (as beaver had tails in water). This was partly a public health measure, as fresh fish (or beaver) is much healthier than rotten beef (killed in October except in the very south, and with poor preservation). (It was also, in coastal Britain, partly a naval measure, seamen being trained.) In the *Domesday Book* (England, 1086) practically every village on a suitable stream is recorded as having one or several 'fisheries' that is, places where fish were caught 'commercially', i.e. for more than a house or two.

Perch ('as fresh as perch of Rhine' was an old saying before the age of pollution), roach, loach, pike, bream, carp, gudgeon, trout, salmon, sea trout, grayling, tench, millers thumb, crayfish (crustacean), were all welcome food, and even small fish, e.g. minnows and fry could be eaten or used as bait and livestock food. Eels were a special case. Quite enormous numbers teemed in the rivers and flooded wetlands. Eels were a staple food, not a delicacy for the rich. In the Fenland they could even be used as currency. Rising 35 000 eels per year were caught at Wisbech in the twelfth century, and were used to pay rent and to buy goods (Darby, 1983).

Now, the water is little, and the fish are even less, since pollution has been added, decreasing habitat suitability. In fact, in the 1950s under Communism, in some industrial parts of East European rivers, e.g. Danube, the remaining fish were toxic. Worse, by the 1980s and over a much larger area, fish exposed to sewage works effluent were becoming deformed, and skewed to femaleness (oestrogen and pesticides in the effluent). Fish need to eat and take in water for oxygen. Pollution harms through their gills, and kills or harms their food organisms, whether invertebrates, small fish, plants, or micro-organisms. These may be unable to grow, or grow fast enough to supply the required food, in depleted and polluted water. Few now eat river fish: except in those parts where low population or care for the rivers has maintained the rivers, such as most of Scandinavia, and much of Scotland, and the Netherlands. Also, there are rivers, such as the English chalk streams, where anglers are prepared to pay huge sums for trout fishing. This money allows rivers to be kept in good condition (e.g. R. Test, R. Avon, Hants).

Fish have been caught in many ways: fish weirs (kiddles), alone or combined with mill weirs, by nets (across the river or in the hand), traps (eel, gudgeon and other), by lines, by hand, by paddle, with dogs hounding them into traps, with spears, with forked sticks, from banks, by wading or by boat. As communications improved in the eighteenth century, vast numbers were exported to capitals (e.g. Defoe, 1724–7), and fish populations started to drop. (To accommodate the previous numbers, fish must have been as dense as now seen on coral reefs.)

In present times, fishing is primarily for sport, with fish eaten in clean parts. The 'game' fish of trout, sea trout and salmon require fairly clean water, and clean gravel spawning grounds. In Britain, anglers pay more for this than for 'coarse' fishing for, e.g. perch, roach, loach. Those species are more tolerant to pollution – and are hardly eaten. ('Perch of Rhine' is less attractive than before.) Commercial (and research) fishing is likely to be by large net, electric fishing, poison (temporary), or spear guns, which further reduce the depleted populations. On the continent, in e.g. Scandinavia and the Netherlands, trout and salmon still occur in the sort of lowland rivers from which they are long banished in England, and the distinction between the two groups of game and coarse fish hardly exist. (It does in N. America, though with different game and other fish species.) Commercial river fishing is more to the east of Europe, and in Communist times could unfortunately be of polluted fish.

Eels are unusual as their trapping and catching has nearly always been for food, not for sport. Although now only local, a little eel trapping is still possible in England, and more, on the continent. The loss of wet grassland with its channels and pools, as well as river water pollution, and over-fishing, has led to their great decrease.

In now-dry Malta, eels have almost or quite disappeared. In the early nineteenth century, the streams and marshes crawled with them: they got into wells, into cisterns, into reservoirs and, even in the mid-twentieth century were, by the more rural people, put in their roof tanks for domestic supply to keep the water clean. They could, then, be caught in estuaries, if absent in rivers. Alas, a trapped eel cannot migrate to breed in the Sargasso Sea, and the population dies out. The last stream eels were probably those in R. Xlendi (Gozo) in the 1980s. They have not been recorded there since.

Crete is an island more fortunate for water than Malta as there are high mountains bringing more rainfall, and less aquifer (aquifer can be abstracted). Nevertheless, it also has lost most of its rivers and some fish. In Venetian times (1210–1650) there were large numbers of tench, pike, eel, trout and bream amongst other fish in the mountains. These provided fresh table fish for inland villages and towns, even closer than sea ones, and variety for coastal settlements (also see Haslam, 1991; Rackham & Moody, 1996).

Fish farms are locally frequent on rivers, and under the name of 'fish ponds' have been around for millennia (see the Prophet Isaiah). They require adequate and fairly clean water. They are usually, though not only, for trout and salmon. They provide sport fishing, fish to re-stock rivers ('put and take') and commercial fishery, recreation fishery (on site) and watercourses. Too much river trout is now from fish farms, and so of non-native genotypes, or too much alien species, such as rainbow trout.

There are also large fish ponds, constructed for commercial fisheries, often carp. These were made across Europe, up to late mediaeval and early modern times in Eastern France (Dombes), and the Czech and Slovak Republics, and as late as Communist times, in Hungary. In Hungary, fish are still a Christmas dish.

River productivity can be roughly judged by the size of the largest animals present: if manatee, hippopotamus and crocodiles are abundant, so is their food, and the habitat is tropical, where growth is quickest. The equivalent in temperate Europe are the carnivorous otters and introduced mink, and the herbivorous beavers and muskrat species. And where are those?!

Birds

Birds can be divided into wildfowl (duck and geese and wild swans in countries without swan laws, and to a small extent, waders); and domestic fowl, (duck, domestic geese and semi-domestic swans).

The natural resource of waterfowl was always available, to be caught by traps, nets, decoys, spears, arrows, line and other means, and later by guns and more sophisticated decoys. In sparsely populated parts, all waterfowl were freely available. In denser areas landowners and tenants might have a right to protect their land from trespassers, though *ferae naturae*, in Common Law countries, were free, whether on common, government or privately owned land. As well as meat, duck provided eggs, bedding (feathers: eider and geese being particularly well thought of), other stuffing and minor uses. In England, in the seventeenth century, a manor was expected to have, for its owner, most or all of mallard, widgeon, teal, bustard and wild geese (Norden, 1610). The eighteenth century saw gross over-exploitation. Defoe (1724–7) records one decoy yielding 6000 duck per week during the season (many waterfowl are migrants, and unavailable in winter). Such numbers were unsustainable. The much smaller present populations are conserved, killing being strictly regulated in most of Europe (though not in, say, Malta), so are now a resource for ethical, aesthetic and habitat maintenance reasons, not for commercial use (Table 9.2).

Mallard and other domesticated ducks were kept on any piece of water (pinioned), on the village pond, the farm pond, the fish pond, the cottage pond (in parts, each cottage had a pond, Mitford, 1829), and any water source. 'Duck Lane' is a common feature of villages. It led from the High Street to the communal, yet individually owned duck area. Indeed, though more now for tradition, ducks and duck-houses can still be found in some, e.g. Czech, French and German villages showing the former pattern. Dense ducks pollute. This is less serious in separated ponds than on the river.

While duck are nearly self-raising, and merely need protection (foxes, thieves), flocks of geese eat huge amounts of vegetation, so needed to be – in unenclosed land – moved from place to place for grazing and water, so as not to turn the habitat into a sea of polluted mud. A few geese could be in cottage ponds, but for flocks there were goose meadows, with tall grass. Their keepers were mostly girls (goose-girls). Geese were much more valuable than ducks, since as well as meat, eggs and feathers, they provided (writing) pens. From at least the early seventh to the early nineteenth century, goose quills were the main pens; quill pens (which were 'mended' by sharpening tips with a pen knife). Like domestic ducks, geese were available all year. They were the standard English Christmas dinner for centuries ('*Christmas is coming and the geese are getting fat, please to put*

Table 9.2 Major habitat requirements for some animals

Species	Shallow water	Submerged plants	Emergent plants	Tall herbs	Trees and shrubs	Sun	Wind shelter	Shorelines	Marsh	Ponds	Lack of disturbance	Other
Dragonflies	★	★	★	★	★	★	★	★				
Fish	★	★										Deep water
Amphibians	★	★	★	★		★		★				
Dabchick	★	★	★							★	★	Fish
Great crested grebe	★	★	★								★	Fish
Grey heron	★	★							★		★	Fish and amphibians
Mute swan	★	★		★			★	★	★		★ (for wild ones)	Grazed grassland
Mallard	★	★		★			★	★	★		(★)	
Other dabbling ducks	★	★					★	★	★	★	★	

Species									Notes
Tufted duck and pochard	★	★	★						
Redshank	★			★	★			★	
Lapwing				★	★	★	★	★	Short grass or bare ground
Ringed and little ringed plover and common tern	★				★		★	★	Bare shingle
Migrant and wintering waders	★				★	★	★	★	
Kingfisher	★		★					★	Nest banks
Sand martin							★	★	Nest banks
Sedge and reed warblers		★	★						
Water vole	★	★	★		★				
Otter	★	★	★		★	★		★	Fish and amphibians

Modified from Andrews & Kinsman (1990).

a penny in the old man's hat.') By the mid-nineteenth century, intensive farming in yards with artificial food and troughs of water were common.

Mute swans in most of Europe had a special status in Roman times, and from at least the seventh to the nineteenth centuries. Indeed, most laws have lapsed rather than being repealed. They were royal in England, and royal, aristocratic or guild elsewhere. The birds were pinioned and kept on the river and other water bodies. They were used as evidence of status: for special banquets, as gifts to VIPs, as the Christmas dinner of the aristocracy. They also yielded swansdown, much sought-after. Their importance declined in the eighteenth century, and populations fell even more drastically with the expansion of leisure angling after the Second World War, when swans died from eating lead weights. Populations have recovered slightly: but the seventeenth-century quote of counting 2000 from the mouth of R. Avon to Salisbury (*c.* 40 km) is not likely to be repeated. The present water loss is quite enough to account for the loss. It means lesser productivity for vegetation, of which swans need a vast amount. *Ranunculus* grows more, and more quickly when cut, so presumably selectively flourished with abundant swans. Added to this are the direct effects of pollution and disturbance.

In England, the value of swans was such that they were most carefully overseen. They could only be taken from the river in late summer, when the new cygnets were marked for their owners. This led to other water bodies like town moats, ponds, and swan pits (which could be found down 'Swan Lanes') being used for keeping birds for eating at other times. (Indeed, anyone could keep swans if they were not on rivers.) A tradition still kept is the swan-upping on the Thames, to check the royal swans: now for conservation, not for Palace banquets (partly from Ticehurst, 1957).

Mammals

Beavers are good eating, and (see above) their naked tails made them classed as fish, eatable during Lent and fast days. Their fur is water repellent, and was used for hats from at least the tenth century to the change of fashion in the mid-nineteenth century when other water-repellent materials became common. By then, however, the European beaver was all but extinct, and the North American one restricted to remote mostly mountain areas. Gerald of Wales, in the twelfth century, observing the (only?) Welsh colony, finds them very different to the (to us, peculiar) tales of beaver in far-away Europe. Scottish ones persisted some time longer.

Trial introductions of beaver are now in progress, and it is much to be hoped this fascinating mammal will again become common: where the pools created by their dams are not harmful to people. The European beaver is less destructive to riverside trees than the North American, luckily. Their pools give water habitat (fish, duck, amphibian, insects, plants), and margin habitat (for waders, wetland, plants, grazing mammals).

Otters, being less useful, kept up their numbers well until the river alterations of the nineteenth century. Their fur was less valuable, their meat used only when better was unavailable. Indeed, otter hunts still produced reasonable numbers until the organochlorine pesticides and major drainage of, in Britain, the 1970s. At this time the huntsmen received much blame for their cruelty, and the far more guilty river authorities and farmers received none. In France and Spain pollution was mainly responsible for their decline. In S. Italy, it was also due to bank disturbance from gravel extraction. In the Netherlands trapping was important. Loss was Europe-wide, from a variety of impacts.

Otters, when in large numbers, are both a sporting resource and a farm pest. They are now wanted for conservation. In literature, the late change from bad to good otter is shown in the difference between *The Water Babies* (C. Kingsley, 1882) and *Ring of Bright Water* (G. Maxwell, 1960).

Mink, from North America, were introduced for fur, and inevitably escaped and are now naturalised through too much of the land. As escapes, they are not a resource, and they compete with otters and (unless habitat is excellent) destroy water voles.

Muskrats, of various species, may be caught or cultivated for their fur. They are more a wetland than a river group, but coypu damage river banks as well as wetlands. Native to Europe, coypu, like mink, were introduced to Britain in fur farms, and escaped. Unlike mink, they caused economic damage (river banks, reed beds) and so much money was devoted to their elimination. Mink, just destroying native fauna, are allowed to increase and multiply.

Other animals

Freshwater pearl mussels, when in sufficient quantity and not all harvested for a quick profit, are a useful but, because of the size of the European river populations, not a very valuable resource. Scottish, like most European river pearls have been over-harvested. Chinese and Japanese rivers produce most of those now on the market.

The use of water for bees was described as far back as Virgil, and what he described is still seen, e.g. in Hungarian grottos. Bees like clear fountains, mossy surfaces, some shade (olives or palms, in Virgil), with rocks or willows so the bees can alight on them and open their wings to the summer sun.

The medicinal leech (*Hirudo medicalis*) was used for bleeding to reduce fevers and remove 'humours'. This use has discontinued. However, leeches have a strong

Table 9.3 *Commercial value of wetlands*

If a wetland is destroyed, its value to mankind is lost. Mitsch & Gosselink (1993) consider the cost of some of the same functions if done outside wetlands:

Hydrological functions	Money-requiring replacement techniques
1. Maintaining water quantity.	Pipe from far away.
2. Maintaining water table.	Wells.
3. Maintaining surface water level	Dams, pumping water, irrigation pipes etc.
4. Regulating floods	Sluices, flood defence works, drainage.
Chemical functions	
1. Maintaining drinking water quality	Purification plants, inspectorates, laboratories, collection of run-off, small effluents, etc.
2. Cleaning effluents, urban run-off, etc.	Sewage Treatment Works.
Biotic functions	
1. Food for people and domestic animals.	Agriculture. Food imports.
2. Thatching, livestock litter, crafts, etc.	Other, partly artificial roofing, bedding, craft materials.
3. Maintaining species and genetic material.	NO replacement possible.
Societal functions	
1. Heritage value	NO replacement possible.
2. Aesthetic and spiritual values	NO replacement possible.
3. Recreation specific to wetlands	NO replacement possible.

(See also Haslam *et al.*, in Westlake *et al.*, 1998.)

anticoagulant and this is a small but increasing use. British needs are supplied from France, the drainage, drying and polluting of lowland English habitats having reduced the populations in the nineteenth and, even more, in the twentieth centuries.

Wetlands (Table 9.3)

Plants

The principal river crop is watercress, grown in shallow, clear, usually limestone, water, spring-fed so the water temperature and level are stable. Cress beds using this water can be made beside or in the stream. When the water was suitable, the village fish ponds, when no longer useful, could be turned into cress beds. Cress, also, is a fading resource now. *Colocasia antiqua* has an edible bulb, formerly grown as salad in the south Mediterranean, e.g. Crete (Rackham & Moody, 1996), and Malta.

Acorus calamus, sweet flag, is of medicinal value, and was introduced by monasteries where it did not occur naturally, and became naturalised, though seldom spreading far, even in the over a millennium available. It is now used in perfumery: a very minor resource.

Scirpus lacustris, the rushes used for chairs, basketwork, and, for centuries, for strewing on floors (often with other species, such as meadowsweet, for scent), grow in *c.* 0.5–2 m of water in lowland nutrient-rich rivers (usually with clay). Now, due to decreased vegetation, much management, and the unpleasantness of harvesting (particularly in polluted water giving rashes, sickness, fever, diarrhoea and headaches), there is little harvesting in Britain. The Dutch, with larger and cleaner water bodies, export rushes.

Hardwick Hall (England) is still kept with Elizabethan-type rush matting on the floors. Brewer (1881) records that Rush-bearing Sunday, held close to the Church's Saint's Day, was when the church floor rushes were renewed.

Flax and hemp are land crops, but were steeped in whatever local water was available. The water of N. Ireland was particularly good for linen production (until cheap cotton imports led to the decline of that industry). Hemp could be grown in very damp land, like the English Fenland. In Malta it was steeped in fountains, and later thought to bring malaria (mosquitoes encouraged in stagnant, organic-rich water?).

Unlike in rivers, plants are a most important wetland resource.

Rice is the staple food for the largest part of the world's population, and it grows in wetlands: flood plains, low land with penned water, terraces with streams directed to flood each paddy as they flow down. In Europe the primary region is the Po plain, which has a complex, near-penned water system of different in-flow and out-flow watercourses. The Rhône flood plain has a simpler system. Further north, it is too cold for rice.

Other than rice, wetland crops, like river ones, are of less value than they need to be. Woods, carrs, scattered trees (park woodland) and individual ones exist. Individual riverside trees, particularly in the west, have been pollards. Pollards, (trees harvested for withies above grazing level) (see Chapters 8, 10) are another resource whose value has diminished over the centuries particularly in the west. Timber, charcoal, food for swine or, with sparser trees, other livestock, furniture, withy-made artefacts and other goods are all sourced. *Salix alba* has many cultivars, developed for different uses, such as tanning, furniture, fences, baby cots, ladders, ropes for fishing boats, and, back to the Iron Age at least, basketwork. Baskets were shaped differently for different purposes (e.g. pigeons, fruit (see Purseglove, 1989). Alder was used for clogs, which were much used by the poor until shoes came down in price. Only in the twentieth century did they come to be regarded as typically Dutch.

Flood plain woods vary from the mostly flooded, to the drained, and species vary accordingly. The number of tree species also increases from the west to continental Europe (Haslam, 2003). All were managed, and their species controlled. Many are now abandoned 'for conservation'.

Trees stabilise banks, and they clean water and soil (see below). Table 9.2 lists some stabilising trees. Rivers may double in width if trees are removed.

Reeds, *Phragmites australis*, are the most abundant European wetland plant, from Ireland to Hungary to Malta. When all possible crops were intensively cultivated, reed beds were carefully managed. Reeds were used for thatching, furniture, pens, inner walls, fencing, litter, insulating, stuffing, and for making drinks. Usually there were dykes for access, and regulating water level. Water needs to be fairly dry in late winter, or iced over, for harvesting; and flooded for at least a few months for reed growth, and to prevent tree invasion.

A recent and still-growing use of (artificial) reed beds is for water purification (see below).

Other reed bed and wetland crops are now little. *Typha* spp. are, in small quantities, included in thatching reed bundles, and also have former uses for stuffing, drinks, etc. In N. America, *Typha* are more abundant than *Phragmites* so are more used for purification. (Purification systems use the toughest and easiest-grown of the effective species.)

Cladium mariscus, growing in high-calcium but rather lower other-nutrient wetlands, is good for thatching, fuel, litter, etc., but is now usually used for decoration and roof ridges on reed- or straw-thatches. Other tall sedges have similar uses, but usually locally only and their beds are small in area.

The drier reed marsh beds overlap in water regime with the wetter grassy ones. Management determines the crop: and recent abandonment increases the loss if resource species are replaced by more useless ones (tall herbs are common in, say drier English former hay beds, and the abandoned Czech wetlands of the R. Luznice flood plain). With proper management, marsh hay (edible wetland grasses, like *Glyceria maxima* and *Phalaris arundinacea*) was valuable fodder, as the grasses grow tall (up to 1.5–2 m) though, unlike shorter grasses, they do not regrow from buds at ground level after grazing. Sheaf or litter is a more mixed, shorter grass/sedge crop, generally tougher than grass, so used more for, e.g. litter, bedding, and insulation. It is generally an intermediate crop: a wetter area harvested too often for taller plants, a drier one semi-abandoned. In East Anglia such fodder beds were often abandoned when cars replaced horses.

Marsh hay meadows grade, with increasing dryness, into wet grassland (often flood meadow, sometimes water meadow). As mentioned above, meadow, mostly damp or wet, was often the most valuable land. Flood meadows are flooded from the river or groundwater for part or all of the winter, with little control apart from dykes (drainage). Water meadows are penned water systems, giving extremely valuable pasture and hay, usually on soft limestone. Spring water is calcium-rich and clean, and forms a substantial part of small river discharge. Controlled flooding from the river warms the soil for early growth, brings fertilising silt, prevents growth slowing from drought, and dries the land for livestock access.

The result is the 'early bite', the earliest grass in late winter, and the most productive grassland devised before powder fertilisers and biocides. 'Water on at a trot, off at a gallop.' River hatches divert water to semi-parallel channels crossing the meadow (at a gradient of 1:400 to 1:800), from which it trickles over the grass downslope until meeting another set of semi-parallel channels which collect it, and run it back to the river downstream, having dropped its nutrient-rich sediment. This 'floated' soil is 3 °C warmer than dry soil. Drainage after irrigation further increases soil aeration and grass growth. Careful control of water is essential: too wet leads to rush-pasture, too dry, to ruderals (weeds). Annual management differed in detail with the area, but examples are:

1600	1999
Winter: irrigate with muddy water.	Irrigate, 7 days a week November and December. January irrigate 5 days a week, February 4, March 3, April 2
March to April: drain, graze sheep or cattle	Cattle graze two weeks at a time
May: irrigate a day	}
June: 1–2 hay cuts	}
Summer: irrigate overnight, cattle graze 2 weeks at a time	} }
Autumn: irrigate with muddy water (only)	Irrigate. Some maintenance work

Water meadows covered around 40 500 ha between the early seventeenth and nineteenth centuries, mostly on the Wessex chalk (in Britain) but also scattered up to central Scotland.

There was, therefore, much diversity of structure, from hatches and sluices to the channels and their patterns. Diversity was relatively low in the grass, that habitat being rather harsh, but very high in the channels. Fish were abundant (e.g. lampreys and eels in ditches, salmon and trout in larger channels), and so were birds, snakes, amphibians, and invertebrates. A good richness of plant species also occurred in the channels (section from Everard, 2005).

With only minor or no flooding, flower-rich meadow is excellent and balanced nutrition. In some countries it is maintained like other wetland crops. It developed under careful and specialised management, and without that it deteriorates. In Britain, since 1930 nearly all (97% by 1988, Purseglove, 1989) has been replaced by monodominant forage grass with agrochemicals. These have unbalanced nutrition, and loss of biodiversity, heritage, Sense of Place, *genius loci*. Without varied architecture and a good seed bank, wildlife is greatly diminished. There are no goose meadows! Where now are the abundant fritillary meadows, needing stable conditions and flooding to instigate growth? Each flower-rich meadow developed under different management, and possibly different water, soil, and is, or too often was, unique. Mitford (1829–32) describes vain efforts to transplant fritillary in Berkshire meadows: even when the Duke of Marlborough transplanted half an acre of meadow, down to two foot (*c.* 60 cm), the fritillary dwindled.

A few dampland plants have specialised uses. These include *Juncus effusus*, soft rush, widespread on river banks and damp rush grassland. Rush lights, rush dips, were the lighting of the poor for centuries. Each burnt for about an hour, and White (1788) reckoned 1200 was the usual winter supply for a cottage. The great reed, *Arundo donax*, a Mediterranean species, is good for pipes (of both kinds) as well as, being larger, firm screens, windbreaks, broom handles, thatch, furniture and general tourist and farm use. A new use is to identify the site of springs and seepage areas, even if recent drying has lowered ground water.

River banks

River banks are usually a valued resource for wildlife and plants, partly as the land–water interface, partly as a greenway for longitudinal movement of animals and plant propagules. When small areas of grazing were still valuable, they could be – and locally are – still used for livestock. The tall herb vegetation found on steep dredged (so higher nutrient) banks is less valuable.

Peat

Peat is a major resource. Fen peat (nutrient-rich) when drained, is very fertile for crops (e.g. the Netherlands, English Fenland). It is also easily dried and oxidised when drained and, cultivated, so it is a finite resource, now becoming deficient in the Fenland, where it is underlain by clay, ever-increasing on the surface. Bog peat is infertile, and nutrient deficient, but can be made to bear crops.

All peat, mixed in with mineral soil in gardens, makes soil good and tillable. It has been known for over 40 years that peat, an exhaustible resource taking thousands of years to create, should not be used for the trivial pursuit of gardening, particularly as alternatives are available. Consumption, unfortunately, increases.

Peat turves are the traditional fuel of small settlements on peat lands, and as such are sustainable. The huge amounts excavated for power stations in Ireland, are not, though Canada and Finland say their fuel excavation is supportable.

The Norfolk Broads and various Dutch lakes were dug out for fuel. The Danes were cutting sizeable amounts in 500 BC, and were doing so in East Anglia from AD 850. The land dried, and more was cut. But in the thirteenth century sea level rose, the pits flooded, and in the fifteenth century fishing rights had replaced turbary rights (George, 1992). The same climate changes affected the Netherlands.

Animals

(For fish in flooded wetlands, see above).

Both waterfowl and land birds live in wetlands, whether open or sheltered, short, grassy or tall sedgy or reedy or carr. Table 9.1 shows some examples. When these were abundant and both harvesting and export were easy, they were over-exploited (e.g. a dozen 12-horse wagons stuffed with fowl were sent twice a week from Peterborough to London, Defoe, 1724–7). Now, in most populous parts of Europe, killing is strictly controlled.

In North America with much later (even just twentieth century) exploitation, shooting was strictly controlled (so many of each kind of duck). Also, steps were taken to increase the populations, including increasing nesting habitat up north. Different birds have different habitat requirements so a diverse habitat structure (height, shape, species, water regime, etc.) and diverse water regimes, is good.

Minerals

Sand and gravel excavation and quarrying.

Such excavation from the river bed and bank is mostly in S Italy and Sicily, but excavating from the flood plain beside, making pits separate from the river, is much more widespread. When exhausted, such pits may be re-filled or turned into lake nature reserves or recreation sites.

Water is, of course, a major resource in wetlands and indeed damplands (Chapter 4).

The further riverscape

Here the resources are for farming, settlement, communications, industry and recreation, and most other human purposes are not further described, as they are discussed in Chapter 10 and in the landscape ecology literature. The value for cleaning is described below.

Table 9.4 *Examples of chemical removal in constructed wetlands (see e.g. Athie & Cerri, 1987; Hammer, 1989; Reddy & Smith, 1987; Rubec & Overend, 1987)*

	% removed
Nitrogen	25–97%
B.O.D.	55–90%
Suspended solids	54–98%
Iron	82–99%
Toluene	99%
Chloroform	32%
Benzene	99%
Tetrachlorethylene	25%
Phosphorus	20–99%
C.O.D.	85–95%
Manganese	9–98%
Pathogens[a]	86–99%
p-Xylene	99%

[a] Faecal streptococci remain the longest, so they, not *Escherichia coli*, should be measured.

Purification, the cleaning of pollution

A wide range of pollutants have been tested and found to be decreased, removed or made less harmful (gone, transformed, adsorbed or absorbed, Tables 9.4 and 9.5) in dry, damp and wet habitats. All unpoisoned land with microbes, plants or oxygen cleans.

Wetlands are particularly effective, and, increasingly, this power is being used in constructed wetlands for effluent purification (Athie & Corri, 1987; Cooper & Findlater, 1990; Gunnison & Barko, 1987; Hammer, 1989; Mitsch, 1994; Moshiri, 1993; Neori *et al.*, 2000; Olsen, 1993; Reddy & Smith, 1987; Vymazal *et al.*, 1998; Vymazal, 2001). They are designed to maximise purification. Their snag is that the area needed is far greater than in a conventional sewage treatment works, so they are not generally relevant for cities. *Phragmites* is the commonest species used in Europe, *Typha*, in N. America, these being tolerant and effective. Towards the tropics floating species (e.g. *Eichornia crassipes*) may be used. Since different species lead to rather different transformations, having a few associate species improves efficiency. ('Wild' wetlands and village ponds have always been used by nearby small settlements. But large towns, e.g. Orlando, Florida, may now use them for effluent, too.) Page & Rieley (1992) describe the use, over-use

Table 9.5 *Selecting best management practices by pollutant: rules of thumb (after Novotny & Olem, 1994)*

Pollutant	Methods of control	Vegetative
Sediment	control erosion on land and stream bank	cover crops and rotations
	use best management practices that capture sediment	buffer strips
	dispose of sediment properly	
Nutrient and miscellaneous effluents and run-offs	minimise sources	crop rotations and management cover crop, buffer strip, change crop or grass species to one that is more nutrient demanding
	take into crop all that is applied to the land or contain and recycle/re-use	
Animal waste pathogens (bacteria, viruses, etc.)	minimise source	buffer strips
	minimise movement so bacteria die	constructed wetland/microbial filter
	treat water	
Metals	control soil sources	crop/plant selection
	control added sources	crop selection
	treat water	constructed wetland/microbial filter
Salts/salinity	limit availability	crop selection, saline wetland buffer, land-use conversion
	control loss	
Pesticides and other toxins	minimise sources	plant variety/crop selection
	minimise movement and discharge	buffer strip, wetland enhancement
	treat discharge water	constructed wetland
Physical habitat alteration	minimise disturbance within 30 m of water	buffer strips
	control erosion on land	wetland enhancement
	maintain or restore natural riparian area vegetation and hydrology	

(over-loading and pollution) and cleaning of a village wetland, Wybunbury Moss, Cheshire.

Chemical transformations are primarily by micro-organisms (Table 9.3), and these tend to be densest on plant roots and soil/water interfaces, though adequate numbers occur on leaves and shoots in both water and air, and soil.

Plants are not just hosts, however. *Phragmites* for instance, is a filter for incoming sediment, collecting and converting it and keeping pathways from the surface to deep soil, with its roots and rhizomes. Roots, in particularly, exude oxygen and chemicals on which microbes can feed. Plant litter adds humus, including cellulose, with all the chemical transformations these bring. *Phragmites* mediates a habitat for mineralisation, nitrification and denitrification (Haslam, 2003; Hofmann, 1991).

Landscape planning for purification is being pioneered in N. America. New or existing (but low-value) wetlands are used to catch poisoned water and sediment (sediment can be removed as needed from such traps and be, if clean enough, returned to fields). Agrochemicals, urban run-off, farm effluents, etc., are funnelled into wet meadows, marshes and ponds, which are regained or enhanced. In the last resort, the river receives all remaining pollution (e.g. Mitsch, 1994). The river is very efficient, but is easily overloaded and becomes chronically polluted.

In contrast, England has been busily removing the purification zones in riverscapes and overloading rivers. Hedges, walls, copses, ditches all hold up water movement, allowing pauses for some cleaning, and the collection of eroded sediment. Even small ridges (ex-field boundaries) in fields can halt sediment and slow water flow.

Study of downslope water movement shows the flow paths for underground and overland flow. Cleaning aids, appropriate to the landscape, can be inserted in these places.

The simpler kind of insertion, 'buffer strips' are now frequent. These are bands of varying width beside watercourses. Two metre bands are required by law in Denmark, and even this narrow width is truly effective (and it also far enhances the stream habitat, for both animals and plants). This is spreading, and has started in, e.g. England and Wales. Fifty metres removes all nitrogen (except in very light soil), so is the ideal, but not often practised.

Buffer strips have been most often placed by medium or large rivers. However, it is the little rills in farmland which need them most. Here discharge is tiny and the agrochemical input is huge. Also, some steadying of pollution inputs is advisable. Road run-off entries can well have buffer strips downstream to help neutralise the pollution. Unpoisoned land beside a river stops run-off pollution. This allows the natural cleaning power of the river to clean this. Just 1 km of clean land can make a significant difference to the pollution in the river. 10 km – not an unreasonable length – can make a great difference, and enable the river to clean some more pollution.

Buffer strips halt up to 90% of nitrogen and sediment, and up to 75% of phosphorus in the short term. The larger and more diverse the vegetation structure, and the more the either permanent water or alternations between aerobic and anaerobic conditions, the better the cleaning. Peat and heavy soil clean the best. Underground flow – in good conditions – is not direct, in a 15 m strip, the flow path can be 150 m: allowing much more cleaning. Residence time, whether in pool or buffer strip, is important (see Boon et al., 1992; Boeye, 1992; Hughes & Heathwaite, 1993; Haycock & Burt, 1993; Haycock & Pinay, 1993; Haycock et al., 1993; Haslam, 2003; Prach & Rauch, 1992; Reddy & Smith, 1987; Mitsch, 1994). Buffer strips stabilise and maintain banks, to a considerable degree.

Some attention should be paid to species. Willow, *Salix*, and poplar, *Populus*, beside rivers are both efficient, with large and varied structure below and above ground. Alder, *Alnus*, the third common by-river genus fixes nitrogen from the air, so is not the first choice for its removal! (Of course not only native species, but native and preferably native local ecotypes (strains) should be used: not what foreign trees the local supplier chooses to grow.)

People have imposed pattern on the riverscape. Recently, high crop yields have been the priority, which lead to high pollution. Traditional farming knowingly or unknowingly gave flow patterns which were more sustainable for clean water, water resources and soil resources. Future planning should take these into consideration: a sustainable riverscape and a clean river. There should be flushes and damp patches, wetlands little and large, buffer strips, beetle banks (like buffer strips, but away from rivers), ditches, tree lines, any breaks in smooth landscape. These lead to a pattern of strategically placed structures for sustainable riverscapes. If true costings are used, proper landscaping can prove economically beneficial. Dirty water, dirty soil, and flash floods all come expensive, once all figures are put in the same budget.

Materials

Where flood plains are composed of reasonably pure sand or gravel, this may be extracted for industrial purposes. Gravel is taken, in particular, (S.) Italian and Sicilian rivers, from the bed itself, which is very polluting. In the Lower Rhône valley much sand is extracted, but from beside the river, so pollution is little. Central English rivers with gravel or sand plains also have extraction beside the river, and exhausted pits are frequently used for recreation and conservation, e.g. Melton Valley Park, Ouse Valley lakes. Dried wet grassland

Table 9.6 *Recreation sites, rivers and wetlands*

To do:		
Angling	Ecology	Riding (cycle, horse)
Art	Education	Rowing
Birdwatching (including from hides)	Paddling	Swimming
Canoeing	Picnicking	Walking
Craft	Power boating	Water skiing
Cultural heritage	Punting	Wild fowling
Driving by	Research, Projects	Wildlife observation
or such as are appropriate to the site		

is thus turned to lake: but without expert management very poor habitat can result. This is needed for banks, water depths, islands (no mammal predators), and such-like, and perhaps for planting (for proper conservation, local strains of local species are needed!).

Recreation

Recreation varies from negligible to being a great money-spinner. It is merely summarised here (Table 9.6). Likewise, it varies from being low impact to being destructive. Planning needs much knowledge and thought, to give visitors an enjoyable and exciting time, and to keep good populations of the traditional vegetation and wildlife. This subject is not covered here, see, e.g. literature supplied from national and international conservation, amenity and recreation organisations (Haslam, 1997; Westlake *et al.*, 1998).

10

Building blocks of the riverscape

Culture is the hidden hand of land use planning. It marks the edges, selects the sacred and useless, and leads to place names, maps, aesthetics and ethics. There are traces of different eras, overlapping layers. The landscape is written with age-old spiritual and symbolic meaning. It is the work of ancestors, including travel, artistic, literary and historic associations.

Neutralising landscapes into building blocks of countryside will lose its symbolism, so lose the understanding that landscapes are important.

(Alümae *et al.*, 2001)

We have no idea what value future generations will place on our traditional rural landscape. But it is up to us to make it possible for our own children to husband the assets we leave behind us and to take proper care of them.

(Sporrong *et al.*, 1995)

Cultural landscapes and biodiversity should be regarded as a primary resource of development, sustainable environment and cultural tourism.

(Wildig, 2000)

Introduction

The riverscape is composed of the river (or ex-river) at the bottom of the valley, the flood plain around it (if present), and the valley leading above. The pattern of the river, horizontally and vertically (Fig. 5.2) may set the pattern of the riverscape (or it may be too insignificant or the rest be too striking). Variations are huge, with topography, rock type, climate (past as well as present) and, overall, the effect of impact. From a distance, important characters include: the horizontal pattern of the river (tributaries, meanders, braiding); water flowing fast (whitewater) or slow; whether there are prominent boulders and rock; whether there is an emerged fringe of plants, and whether this is tall monocots, fringing herbs or other; whether the water has obvious plants, and if so in what pattern, whether clumps, narrow, trailing, submerged or floating, and whether banks are visible at a distance (sand cliffs, on the convex sides of meanders, are particularly showy).

If there is a flood plain, then it is possible to see its size, its relation to the river, and its horizontal pattern. Flood plains are normal, found discontinuously, rarely continuously, from source to mouth. They may be tiny or the size of the Mississippi delta. The narrowing and widening of the plains is accentuated when the land beyond slopes steeply: and generally plains increase in size downstream. Like all such statements, there are exceptions, with plains above and a gorge to the mouth.

The colour and texture of plains vary: wetland greens, forests of, primarily, poplar, willow or alder; and where more managed, grass and arable. This makes a contrast with the uniform greens and yellows of arable fields making a chequer-board patterning. There may be old pollard willows winding along river banks.

There may be open waters in the plains, pools and creeks in the wettest marshes, frequent dykes in the wet by managed plains, less frequent dykes in more drained land, but in fully drained land all drainage features may be lost (except, perhaps, for pumping) and field dividers be fences or hedges (with some dry ditches).

On both river and floodplain, of course, constructions may be present (see Chapter 12), making contributions to the view small or great, ugly and beautiful, heritage or not, and related to river or wetland, or not.

The valley beyond, however (Fig. 10.1), is both much larger and even more variable and complex. The scape may be plain or alpine in topography; Mediterranean to temperate to Arctic in climate; productive for crops to, say, tundra where both soil and cold preclude much cultivation; and in population, sparse or as dense as Malta (with $c.$ 400 000 in $c.$ 250 km^2).

Population and available resources determine the type of land use and exploitation. These include cultivability, industrial resources, river and valley transport, and the proximity of main hubs and capitals. Culture, however, determines how these operate, and which of the resources are considered. A few examples include: surface iron can be used with low technology, back in the Iron Age; deep-sited iron, and cars, have to wait for higher technology. The Black Death in the 1340s killed near-half the population of Europe and technology then flowered to replace manpower. In the eighteenth century town streams were commonly put underground as sewers, throughout Europe. Some, though, were widened to make ornamental waters: both typical of that century.

Building blocks of the riverscape 239

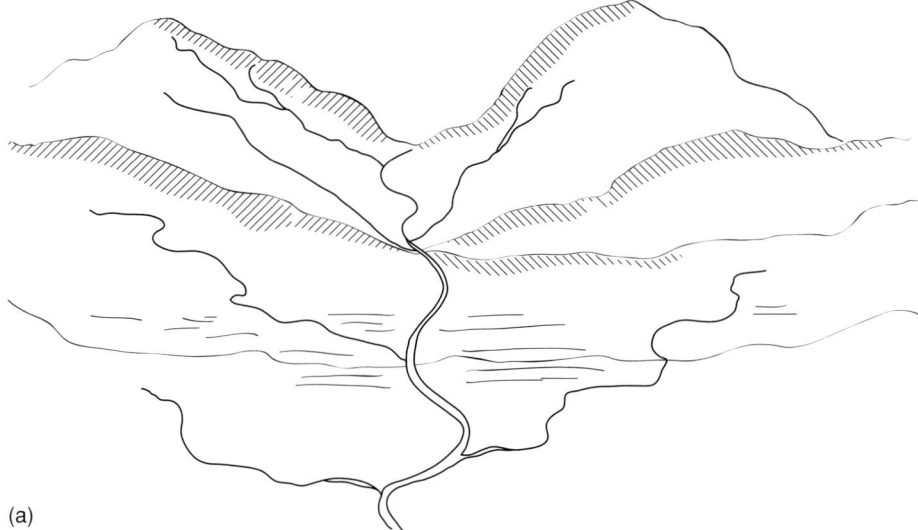

(a)

Fig. 10.1. Generalised plan of riverscape – Riverscape perspectives. (a) A representative (not built-over) riverscape as seen at first glance. It is also what is noticed by an observer studying **topography**. It shows hills and valleys, their slopes and size, and the main rivers. (b) What is seen by an observer studying **water regimes**. In addition to the principal streams and rivers, there are minor brooks, which can be detected on the ground or by the vegetation around them. Some may now be dry, but still show the earlier regime. There are a few ponds, and also flushes (seepages) where run-off or rills have gathered and been held up (usually by a flatter slope), and emerge. Finally, in the agricultural lowlands below, small tributaries have been diverted to go around, not through, fields. These are drained (though less efficiently than the later under-drainage). Some may only have carried storm water. Many may now be dry except after severe storms. (c) What is seen by an observer studying **settlement**. There is a town, two villages, and isolated farms up in the hills. Once, this was a semi-industrial area, since there are the remains of six water mills. The well-built old stone bridge in the town indicates past importance and wealth. And the old wharf shows past river trade. (d) What is seen by an observer studying human **communications**, the main and minor roads and paths, the past navigation, the (in fact) past beacon, the (now recreational) carrier pigeons, the telephone poles (erected to the town as telegraph poles), the electricity pylons, the mobile telephone masts and (some of) the view points that form 'invisible' lines of communication. (e) What is seen by an observer studying **woods, trees and shrubs**. There are two plantations, riverside trees, clumps and copses, and others. With both species and distribution, much can be deduced about the distribution of animal (and plant) distribution: river-side willows bring river-side birds, insects, etc. (old willows usually have more invertebrates than any others, Newbold *et al.*, 1989). (f) What is seen by an observer studying *Ranunculus* or otters.

240 The riverscape and the river

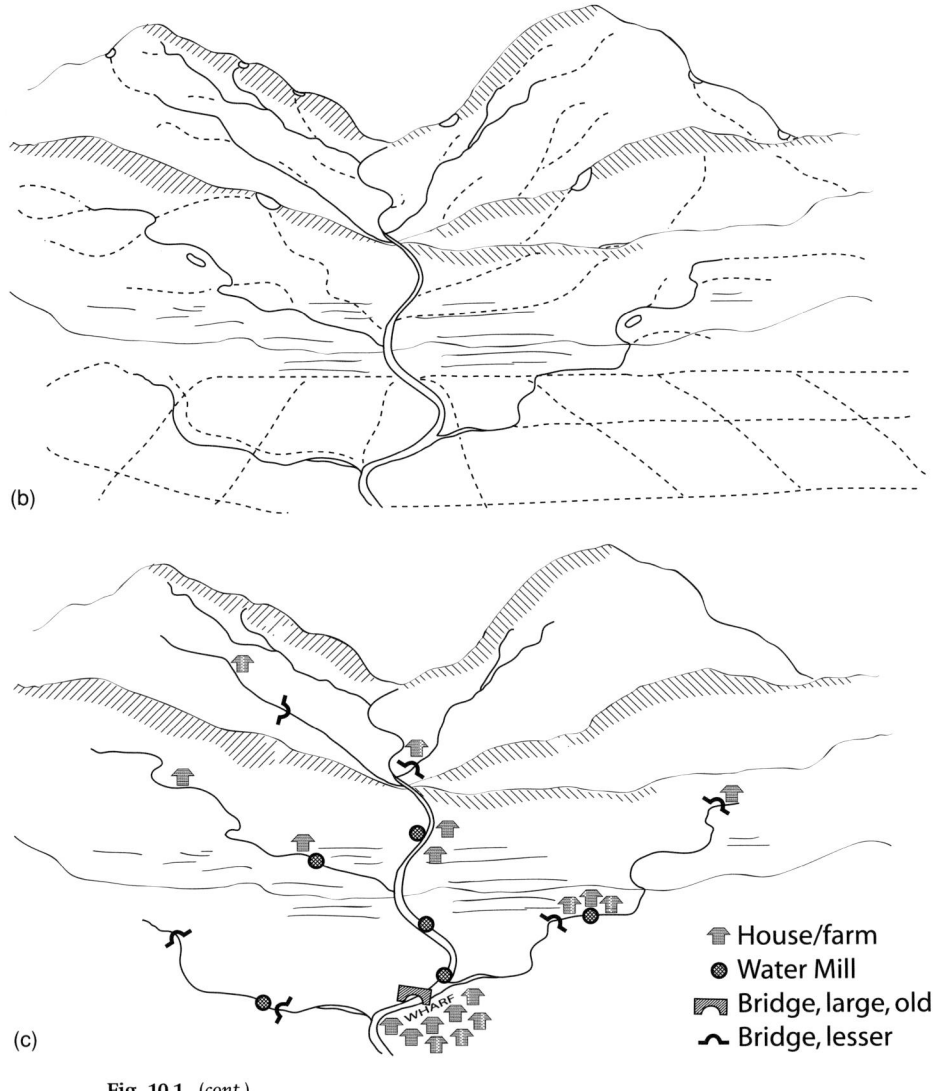

Fig. 10.1. (cont.)

It is possible to identify and classify landscape features, and type and degree of impact, in small regions. No satisfactory method has yet been devised, however, for large areas (apart from the simple hill/lowland, etc.). It is more important to understand the smaller scale and the culture.

Case study: Malta

Table 5.1 separates the elements and building blocks in tiny Malta. The Upper Coralline limestone is the top rock layer, outcropping as semi-flat capping,

Building blocks of the riverscape   241

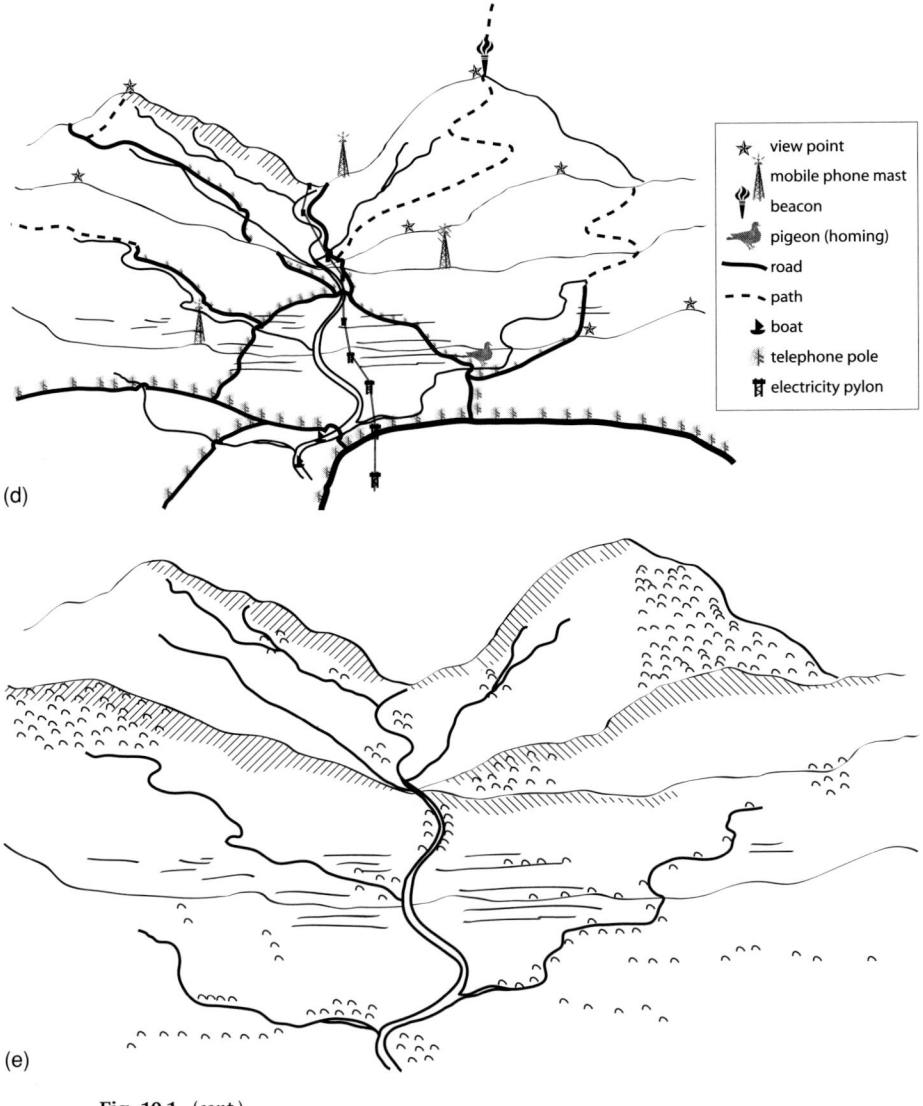

(d)

(e)

Fig. 10.1. (*cont.*)

removed over most of the islands, exposing softer *Globigerina* limestone below. The Upper Coralline is more on plateaux and ridges in Malta, and caps on high small mesas in Gozo. Malta is intersected by ravines eating into the plateaux. In Gozo, rivers rise down the slopes and pass between mesas. This is already a major difference in the riverscape (Fig. 10.2). The gorges sink below lowlands and their previously flooded valley bottoms are now mostly dry. They may have narrow fields in steep(not vertical) gorge walls. Houses are few. Most of both Islands is cultivated, being fertile *Globigerina* limestone lowlands. At the extreme there is

242 The riverscape and the river

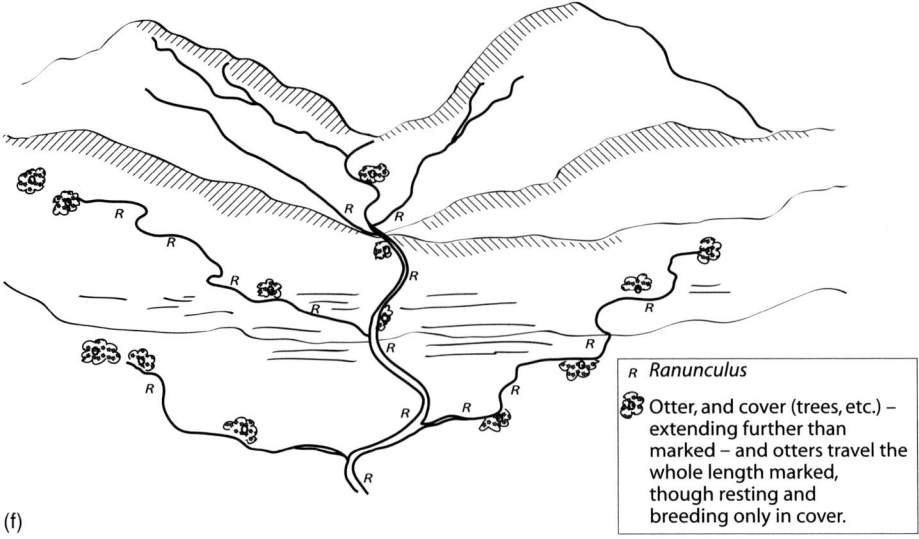

(f)

Fig. 10.1. (*cont.*)

Fig. 10.2. Mesa riverscape of Gozo. (Contrast Malta, Figs. 3.3, 8.5.) The central mesa, on which the Citadel was built. In earlier times people could sleep and live within the protective walls. The capital city of Victoria developed around this. R. Sara crosses in centre. Terraced fields.

no distant riverscape, just a gap, unseen until close, where the (dried) river bed drops below land level. The rolling valley lowland riverscape so characteristic of lowlands from Ireland to Hungary, is missing.

Hills (except for quarrying) stay still. Water changes. In Malta it has been moved, for irrigation and house watering for millennia, in small channels and for centuries in large aqueducts for towns, and pumps have been in use for a century. Pipes have replaced most channels recently. But, a century ago, the rivers flowed, which now they do not (see Chapter 4). Once, the slopes were too steep and with too little soil for high quality farming. They were terraced and crops were productive. Earlier, a small population needed but little food, and when raiders were numerous, it was advisable to sleep in a defended village: indeed in Gozo, for a time (after 1500), most slept in the defended Citadel. There were many fortifications, because of invasions and raiders (Chapter 3). The varied history of the riverscapes is still exhibited, though it is vanishing rapidly (the placing of defensive farmhouses, villages, look-outs and forts, and major garrisons).

The land use depends, of course, on the soil (depth, transported, fertility) and water supply. Water is most in the spring-fed ravines where until recently there was much flow. Now pumps, diesel, electricity and wind extract so much water that the streams are (nearly) dry. In practice, abstraction for irrigation is unlimited. In these windy isles, shelter is important. Citrus in particular requires shelter and water, and so citrus is within the heads of ravines followed by, e.g. peach, nectarine, medlar orchard. Olives, in contrast, grow well in dry exposed fields, particularly where their long roots can grow down several metres to water. They may be grown on the dry slopes of the ravines or gorges.

The appearance, in the last two decades, of a major new building block, Eucalyptus trees, is highly unusual. This alien tree damages water resources, soil nutrients, biodiversity (its oil is toxic), and it is a different shape to any native tree. Malta is not unique, of course, in having plenty of new housing.

Riverscape description

What is missing from this description of Malta is much history, and most social history. Most of what remains can be simply analysed. But trying to fit it to lowland England is just not feasible. There are too many features. Separate displays are needed for each European type. Such is indeed being started.

The English Countryside Commission and English Nature (combining into Natural England) are publishing a series of landscape leaflets, named as Assessment and Conservation of Landscape Character; or Characteristic features of

Nature Conservation Interest; or Characteristic features of Nature Conservation and Landscape Interest. These, like their titles, vary. They may or may not include:

- classification with detail;
- general description of the landscape;
- field details;
- drainage information;
- rivers and floodplain data;
- habitats such as ancient woodland;
- written and artistic history, indicating how people, over time, have reacted to the landscape
  (Countryside Commission, 1991a, b; undated, various).

These, being the first available for England are indeed useful, but the descriptions tend to be more evocative than are the building blocks. A (shortened) excerpt reads: *The broad coastal plain has an isolated atmosphere. Within its predominantly open landscape, variations . . . arising from the long history of piecemeal drainage and reclamation. . . . The more recently drained . . . marsh . . . is characterised by narrow dykes and pools, interspersed by the rich pasture land.* How could this fit into Fig. 10.1? In maybe two decades, surely such syntheses will become available, but at present the reader must rest with either detail or generalities. (For Europe, landscape organisations are preparing a map, of 1 km square detail, of landscape features, and this will provide the basis for much analysis.)

Harper *et al.* (1992) considers a catchment-scale approach, using the hierarchy of river systems. The whole river may be 10^3 m, altering over 10^5–10^6 years. Within this, then may be a segment perhaps 10^2 m with a variation time of 10^3–10^4 years, a reach, 10^1 m and 10–10^3 years, a pool-riffle system, 10^0 m long and altering over 100^{-1} years, and finally a microhabitat, 10^{-1} m and 10^{-1} years. Just because a river ends on reaching the sea, is there a difference in principle between a small tributary and a small independent river? Sizes differ, and the size can be that of the catchment (with tributaries) or just a tributary debouching into river or lake. There are enormous rivers like the mighty Rhine, with tributaries, both tiny and the size of big rivers in their own right. The size studied can also be the size of site studied.

The Living Landscapes Project (Warnock *et al.*, 2001) uses Landscape Description Units usually 5–10 km^2, which are relatively homogenous, and are generally repeated. (Many, but not all, landscapes are repeating.) These records define the elements of landscape. Unfortunately GIS is used more than field study, so an element of distance is introduced. The data are then sorted by TWINSPAN, into:

- river valley (riverscape) and other
- farmed landscape and other.

Then the following are examined:

- land form, geology, soil, tree cover, settlement, farm types (including tenanted, large landowner, small landowner);
- finally, cultural information adds an important dimension.

Rackham (1986) looking at the history of the English lowlands found the following (Table 10.1)

Here, the building blocks are listed and visible. The history of each requires (and received) research, to confirm the field deductions. Yet, even more than the Countryside Commission descriptions, Rackham is looking at one facet. A most important facet providing much of interest: but not including, say, drainage or water resources. This illustrates the present impossibility of combining all facets!

Therefore, to understand building blocks of the riverscape, each must be looked at separately. Each layer (defence, invasion; field pattern and villages; topography, etc.) can be understood independently. Integration is possible in small areas and where a range of expertise is available, but it cannot be expanded to general principles.

There are countries, like Malta, when turning a corner or looking back usually changes the scene. The geomorphology plus land use, ecology and settlements vary in a very small scale. One view always significantly differs from another. This can be contrasted with, say, the sands of Denmark. Here, over much of Jutland for mile on mile, the usual markers remain the same. Views differ in detail: one farm alone here, a group there, one hilltop is rather higher than another. But essentially these are repeating riverscapes, their Sense of Place, their building blocks and their arrangement remain similar. The similarity is physical and biotic, and of the period of the early twenty-first century. Their history can have been more diverse in, say, trade routes, battlefields, marl pits. But the impact of the last century has smothered over, smoothed over, the differences, and the repeating elements are now the more prominent features of, say, mills, Pilgrim's ways, drainage or field dividers.

Building blocks which drive riverscape development

In Malta, water is the limiting and driving factor. Human use was and is controlled by that. Soil terrain and fighting are lesser, though important factors.

In Sweden, however, meadows are or were the driving force of village society (Sporrong *et al.*, 1995). Meadows are on the valley floor and, where suitable, also

Table 10.1 *Ancient and planned countryside (Rackham, 1986)*

Ancient Countryside (Essex)	Planned Countryside (Cambs)	Notes
1. Now		
Hamlets and small towns	Villages	Anglo-Saxon
Ancient isolated farms	18th, 19th-century isolated farms	characters 8th–11th centuries.
Hedges not straight, mixed species	Straight, mainly hawthorn hedges	Can describe trees, e.g. pollard stumps on boundaries, Mixed species hedges
Roads numerous, not straight	Roads few, straight	
Many public footpaths	Few	
Woods many, often small	Woods absent, or few and large	
Pollards, if present, away from habitation	Except riverside willows, pollards absent or in villages	
Many antiquities of all periods	Few, usually prehistoric	
2. Old		
Open fields nil or abolished c. 1700	Early to Enclosure Acts	Enclosure lost strip fields more than hedged fields. A 1598 Essex village for instance has been thinned by loss, but its features stand
Most hedges ancient	Modern	
Much heath	Rare, with little bracken and broom	
Many often small woods	Nil, or few and large	
Many non-woodland trees (e.g. oak, ash, alder, birch)	Few, mainly hawthorn and alder	
Many ponds	Few	

up the slopes above. It is the meadows that provided the energy, the energy to fuel the livestock, and so work the arable fields. Therefore, meadows provide the energy which is transformed into food (and is returned to the meadow as fertiliser). After over a century of artificial fertiliser, it is easy to forget the importance of grass when artificial agrochemicals are absent. Sweden often has:

- wood on hills (fuel, timber, sticks, charcoal, pig feed);
- villages on dry gravel;
- meadows below;
- arable – part of which is now abandoned – in-between.

The tree line depends on use and tillage (below the mountains) (and see Chapter 13). Wide-ranging livestock on poor pasture may be another driving force, one where water is essential for livestock and settlements, but otherwise it, and the riverscape, are of lesser importance (except where this is only the far edge of a settled, farmed riverscape).

Again, navigable rivers of populous districts, and capital cities or craft (industrial) towns may drive the riverscape. Before the coming of railways in the mid-nineteenth century, and good roads and air travel in the mid-twentieth, water transport could be a main reason for siting settlements (e.g. Uppsala, R. Eköln; London, R. Thames; Rome, R. Tiber; Ribe, R. Ribe; for capitals). Water access was a primary requirement for siting the towns, with farming behind to support the town, and other communications to reach out from the town, Villages are dependent on towns, when they are available. There can be linked towns. Bamberg was a major craft river town on R. Main. Upstream, feeding off and supporting the larger town, is the small craft centre of Forcheim. On the Danube, Donauworth was a major trading town, and in the same way little Landsberg is found upstream of the R. Lech. Gunzburg, downstream on the Danube, is the associate of large Ulm. River transport makes places accessible, particularly for freight, but also for people.

Capitals, whether of countries or counties, harbour officials and VIPs, who produce no food but need to be fed and, moreover, have money for quality goods (furniture, stone and timber, silk, coal, spices, china). Typically the land near is cultivated and sends in food, but other goods are brought from far away. The capital drives the land, and river use, around it.

River trading towns like Namur, R. Meuse, and ones with more sea trade, Bruges, R. Boudewijn, Amsterdam, R. Amstel have a similar effect. The area affected depends on the population. A trade route once established can be expanded by new, initially smaller towns. What starts with a rowing-boat full of apples can expand to major shipping. When a new resource is discovered, such as steam power, new towns grow round that resource. These may be river-associated from historical patterns like water mills being converted to steam, much water being needed for drinking, in all times, or a great new canal taking the place of the old. Or the new resources may be sited in new places, with or without direct river use, like a new factory (with water) or mobile telephone masts (without water). The countryside is altered accordingly.

Mass movements of people to new less-impacted areas, like Iceland in the late first millennium, or North America from the seventeenth century on, bring great changes. Cultivation, settlement, craft alter riverscape. Even those living largely on fish, still tend to settle and build as near river mouths as avoids flooding, and use the available riverscape.

The immense increases in population in the past couple of centuries and the more recent immense increase of wealth have led to equally immense riverscape changes. Rivers, except for some main trade routes, are seldom used for freight transport. Recreational transport, though, may be a driving force for local areas and local wealth. However, holiday boat travel encourages the marginalisation of rivers in public opinion (use for holidays is not use in real life). It also means constant taming of the rivers, since holiday traffic demands ease, safety and stability; and incoming road traffic bringing supplies. It rarely much influences local farming. Other recreation brings traffic, perhaps settlement, and whatever goods are required.

Far more destructive has been new settlement, blanketing large areas with settlement, altering everything from water resources and floods to drainage, soil, agriculture (none), light pollution, incoming supplies, communications and other facilities. In addition, farming may be less for the local market, than for the 'global village'. Intensive farming loses wild plants, hedges, woods, aquatic habitats and the associated fauna. Suburban gardens are no substitute! The 'global village' dictates crops, in a way impossible before agrochemicals, good communications and other technology. Local varieties, local self-sufficiency, have almost gone: except on the fringes, in tundra for example. The parts more difficult to cultivate may be abandoned (e.g. near Heraklion, Crete: St Julians, Malta); the farmers being able to get better-paid jobs elsewhere. So, the upshot is more intensive crops where farming is pleasant and abandonment where it is difficult. The changes since 1945 are more destructive of heritage than ever in the past (e.g. Rackham, 1986). The building blocks are driven by wealth and population pressure.

Building blocks that can be alterable by people, will be altered, in the direction pushed by different driving forces, only a few of which are described here.

The effect of land use changes

All changes to the riverscape affect the river directly or indirectly. Changes in precipitation, on the land, e.g. heavier or lighter, more or less rain, date of snowmelt, all these affect run-off, so the discharge pattern of the river, and the movement of water to it. Changes in soil texture affect movement to the river, and so do changes in field size, in the ditch/tributary system around fields, in under-drainage, drainage, or abstraction. Changes in soil chemicals affect river composition. Changes in soil particles reaching water change processes. Changes in crops affect water movement, particularly as to when fields are bare. This also influences whether and what bird food is produced, and nesting sites available. Changes to water passage such as ditches, hedges, the grouping of trees, cattle-drinker ponds, ridges of land, all these influence water movement. The faster the movement, the less the land is properly watered, and the greater the flash floods.

All are altered even more by dense houses, roads and other settlements. Those cover the soil and prevent water intake and direct its surface movement and the pollution it collects.

The stream, with open flowing water, also influences stream structure. So do people, by dredging, channelling, straightening (or the reverse); by the removal, in addition, of weirs, sluices, locks and other obstructions.

Aquifers grade from deep, with a turnover of tens of thousands of years, to gathered run-off merely in soil and subsoil, flushes rather than aquifers. With water comes sediment, solutes and organic carbon. Some is filtered out when the water sinks in, but as run-off gets more polluted, so also does ground water. Hence the importance of unpoisoned surfaces above ground water collecting areas. The aquifer is a building block as it determines spring flows, spring position and groundwater level (though these are lost with over-abstraction).

Not just aquifers, but all the underground water regime is unseen but a major building block. In general, before human impact, the pattern is simple. Large areas of aquifer are spread, giving springs at suitable points (geology, dips in land above). Then, further up slopes are infiltration areas, where water is coming in from rain, filling up the aquifers, driving the water going out. But when abstraction or drainage have happened the aquifer becomes lower or split into various parts, or both. Spring areas decrease and may even reverse, becoming dry infiltration areas. Altering levels and type of water may quite alter vegetation patterns. There may be a long delay for the alteration. Communities formerly flooded with lime water from below may take years for annuals and small plants to change, decades for tussock and long-lived herbs and trees, to change to the community adapted to the new habitat, flooded less and with a different chemistry, e.g. say, acid sands, not lime-rich run-off. On slopes, particularly lower ones, and valley bottoms this makes a reason, but an unseen reason for odd patterns of vegetation (Haslam, 2003).

Field-dividers may be absent. This occurs with open-field cultivation, each farmer knowing his land, or with open range for livestock perhaps at a fixed number per household. Otherwise land is divided. Hedges are particularly English, but are also found in, e.g. Normandy, and parts of Canada. Lines of trees occur more in France. Dykes are normal in wet land, and the other kind of dyke, the wall, in Scottish hills, Malta and elsewhere where stone is easier to find than woody plants.

Trees

Rackham (1986) describes hedgerows with trees from the twelfth century: their species, the general appearance, and the changes from Anglo Saxon times. Hedges gave both use and, from this feature, Sense of Place (timber, fuel, withies, sticks, charcoal, farming, grazing). Trees humanise landscape (Edwards, 1962). Trees are an integrated part of design. Wood naturally falls into streams and rivers, and provides habitat (slowing of water, microhabitats, and, of course, the organic carbon needed for so many river processes). It is gradually being realised that there should be as much wood as is possible without increasing floods. 155 000 km of British hedges have been lost between 1947 and 1985, and more since (Rackham, 1986). Such loss – and others – loses beauty, wildlife, antiquities, meaning, freedom (access and open spaces). Rackham (1986) points out that such destruction is irrelevant to increasing food production. The French have had less urge to destroy than the English. Much landscape and old town centres are still with us, fortunately. France, in 1962, had 20% woodland, Sweden 50% and Britain, just 7% (Edwards, 1962), and probably less now.

Riverscape trees include all land varieties on the slopes above. Those with the streams vary from majestic pollards striding the lowland river, to the mixed dominance flood plain forest of the Danube, to the group of graceful birches beside the highland stream in a cleft, or the southern appearance of tall deciduous trees where all above – and round the small tributaries – is short maquis or shorter garigue.

Over Europe, tree species vary. There are flood plain forests, varying in species, and so texture. Monodominance – from nature and management – is more to the west, in Britain. Riverside trees grow (perhaps planted) where they are allowed. They are deciduous, even in Mediterranean maquis and garigue (unless the riversides are dry enough for evergreens). Tree planting is an admission that conservation has failed. It also erodes the historic landscape and encourages destroying wild trees and planting urban ones (Rackham, 1986). Bad examples are planting Eucalyptus where maquis should be (Malta), conifers where deciduous (Britain), and alien willows or guelder rose where native ecotypes should be (Britain: much encouraged by the Dutch, who supply many).

Salix–Phragmites bands occur from west to east, but in Britain they are in wet, floody areas, while in Hungary the habitat can be drier, wet only with snow melt and storms.

Riparian wood provides shelter, cleaning, biodiversity, decreasing erosion and consequent extra sediment and the benefits listed above. Forest decreases the development of flash floods, provided the amount of water is within the capacity of the forest to hold. Above this, forest does not lessen flood (e.g. Peterken & Hughes, 1995; Harper *et al.*, 1997). Land woods are described by, e.g. Rackham, 1976, 1986, Peterken, 1996; Pieterse, 1975, and Edwards, 1962. It is interesting to realise that pre-human and early human landscapes included much park grassland, which is suited to both grazing and browsing animals.

The more the encouragement to run-off to enter the soil, and the more obstructions there are to water movement, the better, less flood, cleaner water, less gullying, less property, etc. damage.

Rolled soil, bare soil, no obstructions, encourage trouble.

Building blocks for individual species

Bats

Richardson (2001) listed the desirable components of riverscape for bats as:

- **Woodland**, with mixed tree species, mixed habitats (rides, glades, sheltered edges; and young and old trees and fallen timber). These provide food and shelter;
- **Fields**, preferably grassland with cattle or horse grazing (see Haslam, 2003), and wide margins for insects, and flight paths. Muck heaps add to insect life, farm buildings to roosting sites. Mowing should be late enough for insects to have completed their life cycle.
- **Parkland** with grazing, giving trees for roosts and insects, and livestock for these insects;
- **Gardens**, which provide shelter and varied plants, so varied insect swarms, and may have species attracting moths like tobacco plants (*Nicotiana*) and jasmine.
- **Varied buildings accessible to the bats**, such as the belfries of churches, roofs, cellars, walls, for roosts.
- **Water bodies** to attract breeding insects, and with tall edge plants.
- **Heathland**, providing night insects and sheltered edges to trees, hedges, dells (south-facing being best).

This is integrated observation which could lead to habitat for more bats. There are corridors and patches, and even a motorway can pass through without damaging the habitat. A riverscape can be studied for its building blocks for bats.

Otters

Habitat can also be analysed for otters. When numerous, they were, legally, pests (e.g. England, sixteenth century). They were killed for fur, for sport, and as a farm pest (attacking fish ponds, eel traps, grain stores for the vermin living there). Now that they are rare, trouble is taken to preserve them.

Otters are territorial (up to 40 km for adult males, may be only 10 km for family groups). Otters roam riverbanks, the land behind, and the rivers. Their required building blocks are:

- *long lengths of reasonably suitable habitat*. Otters need cover, overhanging trees, good spreading tree roots (like *Fraxinus excelsior*, *Acer pseudoplatanus*), overhanging grass and tall herbs (on ditches and narrower streams);
- they may travel short distances in the open, but need *safe secure places*, for males at least every 5–6 km, and at least 20 of them;
- otters will travel 1 km or more along ditches and small brooks to reach *good habitat, that is, good for hunting, breeding or lying up*. This should give:
- *enough cover* at intervals for holts and other safe places, and have numerous streams or dykes of various smaller sizes. Back from the river, the undisturbed tall vegetation must extend 10–50 m, at intervals. Behind that, on the main land of the riverscape, there can be any activity that does not pollute the water. (The unpoisoned Otter Bands are also Buffer strips, and partly clean incoming water.);
- *enough food*, mainly fish, in the water (land feeding should be extra only as it leads to pest control);
- *the greater the human disturbance, the more the cover needed*: mountains with, as commonly found, low disturbance can form good otter habitat, if there is only 10% of the river, reaching only 10 m back from the river, of thick wood, tall vegetation, peat banks or rocky outcrops;
- finally, otters need *fairly clean water*: not turbid, because they hunt by sight, and not toxic (particularly pesticides) as otters eat fish and small mammals, which have already accumulated, and these poison otters. (A principal reason for their post-1945 decline was pesticides.)

Building blocks for urban dwellers

Suburban dwellers on housing estates, looking at the riverscape around it, generally wish building blocks of:

Near the house

- A nice view, preferably of country, of green fields, river, woods, hedges, trees or hills (a pretty riverscape, in fact);

- there should be, therefore, visual links outwards;
- and rural ones;
- and birdsong;
- then public lanes, paths and open accessible places for recreation (walking, picnicking, musing, study);
- absence of pesticide spray, fierce dogs, scrap metal, ugly fencing, and even, of straight channelled rivers.

Away from the house

- For the rest of life, different things, and sometimes conflicting things are wanted, communications, good roads and transport, cheap food, the pipes, wires and masts of utilities and the construction driving them (the electricity generating plants, the sewage treatment works). Some are below ground and do not impinge.

For those who know no other, monoculture fields, though not pretty, are adequate. The riverscape is there to be ignored or overcome for the main purposes of life, and enjoyed, for recreation. This can be combined with any other conservation demands, with care. (River paths with many people are not compatible with otters at that time or in that side of the river.)

The wishes of the semi-self-sufficient farmer, before mains water reached outlying parts, were different:

- siting of the farm depended on water even more than shelter or whim;
- the farm itself was a building block of the riverscape;
- visual and aural links were needed to keep track of the crops, livestock and workforce and perhaps for neighbours;
- tracks (from roads to paths) were needed to get crops to market, and bring in goods for home and farm. Public footpaths were not for recreation, but to reach, quickly, the village, church, places of work, etc.;
- field size, shape and boundary type were inherited, and would be changed only for good reason: erosion of soil meant loss of fertility, and so storm water movement and erosion were to be slowed;
- the stream provided water, food (fish and duck) so was to be tended;
- crops had to suit the water regime, and fertility, and accessibility (e.g. for ploughing);
- woods and other trees and hedges were needed for direct uses (see above).

Population used to be dense, ploughing, sowing, weeding, milking, looking after livestock. The empty country of the early 2000s where machinery is substituted for man is something quite new in history.

Bitterns

Bitterns require much less complex building blocks, and the EU Bittern Project, by providing these, has increased the population:

- large (several hectares) areas of reedbed, either with plenty of dykes and pools, or deep enough for fish in part of the bed;
- clean enough water for the fish to be non-toxic to the bitterns. This often means the water must be from a source other than the river.

Batrachian Ranunculus

Finally, the building blocks for a species group more dependent on the river itself: Batrachian *Ranunculus*, the group of filamentous-leaved submerged buttercups, are abundant in suitable rivers, and these abundant populations need:

- *flowing water*, but not (usually) whitewater;
- *without high nutrients* (except for calcium which can be dominant);
- *not much polluted*;
- *depth*, from c. 25 cm to 2.5 m, varying with species. The maximum depth is usually determined by water clarity. *Ranunculus* grows deeper in better light. Conversely, some ecotypes of *R. peltatus* can tolerate regular summer drying;
- *no frequent disturbance of soil*;
- *no heavy shade* over the relevant area;
- within its *geographic limits* (decreasing in the far north);
- *firm substrate* so short roots can anchor securely round gravel or stone. This restricts dominant populations to sloping, lime-rich, resistant or sandstone rivers.

Buffer strips and beetle banks

Plant seed and insect populations have been greatly reduced by intensive farming. Buffer strips beside streams clean incoming water (Chapter 4). Beetle banks are placed beside boundaries, like hedgerows, woods, fences and walls, particularly in central Europe, as in Austria and Switzerland. Beetle banks are also made running across large fields.

This is an important building block, partly for the seeds and insects, also for all that eat these, birds and mammals, and, not least, for the effect on water movement (see above).

A riverscape with wide buffer strips around both sides of the streams, including the small field tributaries which receive the most agrochemicals, and plenty of other unpoisoned strips, is cleaner and more valuable for conservation, of both land and water.

However, most high-yield European fields are underdrained. These are efficient, and the frequency often great and unknown. If field pollution runs direct to the river, it is not cleaned by a buffer strip! It must be altered to flow through, e.g. marshes, pools, and these may have good biodiversity (e.g. Stoate *et al.*, 2006), and are new building blocks.

Historical examples

Lincoln

The town (later city) of Lincoln, England, on R. Witham has a direct route (*c.* 60 km) to the sea. The Romans, however, connected it not to the sea, but via a new canal, the Foss dyke (*c.* 16 km) to R. Trent, and from thence to the sea (over 50 km). The lower Witham riverscape is now a perfectly ordinary one of a drained channelled river running between drained farmed wetlands and lowlands.

However, in Anglo Saxon times the land was mostly flooded, and treacherous. Remote abbeys were sited on islands in this near-lake. It was only much later that the river was channelled, and made navigable to the sea.

Vale of Evesham

The Vale of Evesham (*c.* 20 km long), in the English West Midlands, is, as the name suggests, a gently sloping riverscape with R. Avon (over 200 km) at its centre. Part of this slope (excluding the main river) was described in 984, and painted in 1715. The stream then described (when it would have had many small tributaries) is now hardly more than a dug wet ditch. But it is still in the same place, a millennium on, but with drainage and mains water has lost its riverscape importance.

Its Bronze Age fields were small, long and narrow, made after the forests were felled. The Iron Age and Roman roads are still traceable or important (these are out of phase with the present landscape). Roman fields followed the earlier ones, but the grain, pattern of the riverscape was changed by the Anglo Saxons, who gathered the peasants into villages, for protection against the Vikings. The present landscape is an only slightly modified version of the Anglo Saxon. The 1715 picture shows the present basic pattern, and most hedges are still in place. Drainage is the primary difference.

Discussion

Every landscape settled by Man becomes a blend of the natural and the human, is a fabric made by Man, who can attempt to analyse construction and design. The shorter the human use, the easier is it to lose heritage (Williams, 1974).

Ditch banks are an important feature in intensive landscape use and for conservation and their physical structure.

The danger of using building blocks in a simple way is that of neutralising landscape, making it lose its symbolism. Planners fail to understand its importance (Alümnae et al., 2001). If only a single perspective of a feature is used, that is dangerous. It emphasises the importance of considering many facets, when studying the riverscape. Some are inescapable. The valley has a bottom, even though it may be just a twentieth-century housing estate. Others need holistic thought, as the perspective of the swan, of the salmon, of the natural land feature (spring) and the constructed one (church). Sacred features of the riverscape are a unique perspective: the visiting of Derbyshire Wells on Ascension Day with flowers, in the tradition of the time of Cicero.

Table 10.2 gives a small outline of the variety of building blocks, and the complexity of a riverscape inhabited by so many animals and plants, each with their own requirements, and that superposed on the geology, topography and (original) water regime, influenced by its climate. This, for interpretation, is a complex study.

The fourth dimension is time, of riverscape changes, and this is also necessary for interpretation. Some examples have been given above. Others include the rising of the tree line in the Alps, now that young slow-growing trees are not eaten, and in Malta, the woody plants of garigue and short maquis growing taller in half a century after goats have been kept indoors. The difference between inaccessible cliffy habitats and goat-reachable places has gone.

Variation in riverscape leads to variation in the value for flora and fauna. Generally, the more the human impact, the less the ecological value. When most of the riverscape is poor, connections between habitats, creating metapopulations, are very helpful, e.g. ponds, streams, wetlands, woods. It must, though, be habitat for the other biota, not that which is for people. Hedges and woods for many of their species, are different habitats (Barr & Petit, 2001). Dykes in a network in wet grassland are good connectors of habitat. There are also connections just by human sight, which are valuable for the human population, such as to be able to see the next village on the next hilltop. This is a connection, for friendship, trading, mutual defence (and indeed rivalry).

Table 10.2 *Building blocks of riverscapes*

This summary demonstrates (again) how difficult such classifications are (see Chapters 1, 5, 9). Placing major features is simple. Devising a scheme to separate and describe realistically the myriad of unique riverscapes is not yet possible. Within each category the variations are great (contrast Tables 4.1, 6.2 and see Chapters 13–15). Woods, for instance, are coniferous in high latitudes and altitudes, maquis in dry areas in the south, and the deciduous forests in between have fewer abundant species in the west than in the east of Europe, And that is before separating out each type of, say, coniferous forest, its well-being and size, and the controlling factors of, e.g. water, nutrient regimes and exposure. (a) below shows some of such features in a very limited habitat.

(a) Detail

Variables to consider to make a hedgerow classification according to their ecological functions (Baudry & Bunce, 2001).

Hedgerow scale	Variables
Components	Presence of ditch, bank, vegetation layers
Vegetation structure	Height, width at ground and canopy level, cover of the different layers
Type of tree and shrub management and frequency	Pruning, trimming, cutting, laying, replacement
Management of shrubs	Frequency of trimming, use of herbicides
Management of the herb layer	Grazing, mowing, herbicide, fire etc.
History	Ancient, newly planted
Landscape scale	
Network pattern	Connections among hedgerows, with woods, moorland, etc. Density of hedgerows
Land use in adjacent field	Crop succession, presence of cattle
Topographic position	Upslope, along stream corridors
Landscape history	How much did the landscape change in the last decades

(b) General

1. *Geomorphology (topography, geology)*. Mountains, hills, lowlands, plains. Rock types. Shapes, slopes, scale (sizes) dissected, mosaic, network, connectivity.
2. *Altitude, latitude* and the climatic factors associated.
3. *Water regime*. The basic developer of topography, through interacting with (1) (e.g. erodability) and (2) (e.g. hurricane liability). Springs, streams, rivers, pools and lakes. Horizontal and vertical patterns, sizes and longevity. Influences of particularly severe factors, e.g. ice and snow, or summer drought.
4. *Vegetation*, that vegetation commonly referred to (incorrectly) as wild or natural: forests, grasslands, wetlands, aquatic, bogs and smaller types like cliffs and sand dunes; and types found only in a particular climate, e.g. tundra (north), garigue (south).
5. *Animals as, or influencing Building Blocks*. Herds of large grazers and browsers form such blocks, and great flocks of, e.g. wildfowl, may also. Smaller animals act in proportion to smaller scale vegetation. Pests and diseases altering the animal balance may react back

Table 10.2 *(cont.)*

	on the plant communities. So may alterations in the predator-prey balance. (Removing beavers vastly alters river shape and flow and riverside vegetation, for instance.)
6.	*Plant and animal communications.* Corridors, networks and mosaics in water, air and on land. These are building blocks because, if obstructed, extinction may result.
7.	*Agriculture* (horticulture, forestry, aquaculture). This covers most of the land surface of Europe, though with many variations due to climate, water, nutrient and exposure regimes, density of population, and local preferences for foods. A flower-rich meadow is a different building block to ley, lettuces, lemons or lime (*Tilia*) tree woods.
8.	*Settlements* are of all sizes from isolated and remote farms as in Iceland, Norway, to the huge conurbations of, say, London or Rome. All need water, and are placed so (when small and before mains supplies) they obtain it from local sources. The indirect supply from the mains has permitted both new settlements away from water, and the enormous expansion of older ones. The planning (intentional or unintentional) of settlements is governed by the principles in Chapter 12, but the shape and size of houses, the placing of churches and other communal buildings is governed by both local building materials and, even more importantly, culture (compare, say, a Scottish croft and Swiss chalet, a house in central Amsterdam and central London). Recent smothering by blocks and concrete is all too widespread.
9.	*Communications for people.* These include paths, lanes, roads and motorways, with their attendant bridges, tunnels and cuts; railways, with similar attendants; airports and flight paths; above-ground lines for telephones, electricity, water (aqueducts); below-ground lines for electricity, water, sewers and other services; and air paths for TV, radio, mobile telephones, radar, satellite services and such-like. (While those underground do not really form a building block, their placement, replacement and repair do so.)

The colour and texture of short vegetation is an important component: tundra, garigue, heather moors, the rough grass (which is grazed more than the heather), copses, tall herb patches and hedges differ. The building blocks and their combinations are innumerable.

Short-vegetation habitats on the wide scale, other than grass, agriculture or gardens, are more in extreme habitats, which are not thought to be worth cultivating.

The same processes lead to the same forms, generally. Riverscapes are formed by (rain) rivers and glaciers. Other processes lead to erosion and dissolution. On a smaller scale, biodiversity increases with the decreasing size and diversity of favourable habitats, and of propagules able to move between these habitats.

Riverscapes are resistant to change, varying with characters.

The key to the past lies in the functioning of the present (Rackham & Moody, 1996; Ihse & Lindahl, 2000). A living landscape with economic viability is the main requirement for biodiversity and cultural components. For social value, the traditional Swedish access to grass is a vital component, a part of identity.

Changes in a multifunctional landscape change multiple formations (Bakkestuen *et al.*, 2001). Old agriculture is cultural heritage. Agriculture has the functions of food, biodiversity, local landscape character and cultural identity.

11

Patterns, boundaries and fragmentation

To save the best and forget the rest leads to over-fragmentation and loss. Fragmentation is not diversity.

Connectivity for ground dwellers is the distance to the next habitat

(Vos & Chardon, 1997)

Introduction

The study of shape and pattern, of corridors, size and boundaries, is an important part of landscape ecology. At present, as with the classifications in Chapters 1, 3 and 10, methods and patterns elucidated tend to be very generalised, e.g. Bell (1999), describing the basic patterns in nature as spirals, meanders, branches and explosions. This is thought provoking and so very valuable, but difficult to apply to most riverscapes. Or they may be detailed studies of, say, the effect of a new road on a toad population, which is also valuable but also difficult to re-apply.

Fragmentation may be considered an element that degrades the overall quality of river basins (Padoa–Schioppa et al., 2006).

Scale

Scale has both an absolute and a relative effect. Figure 11.1 shows a tributary joining a meandering stream at three different scales. As a landform, scale is irrelevant, the feature is the same. There are similar erosion-sedimentation processes, similar drainage effects, and similar utilisation of the flood plain or valley bottom. However, the water space differs: (a) may support minnows, (c) should support major fish populations. A sallow bush could shade all of (a),

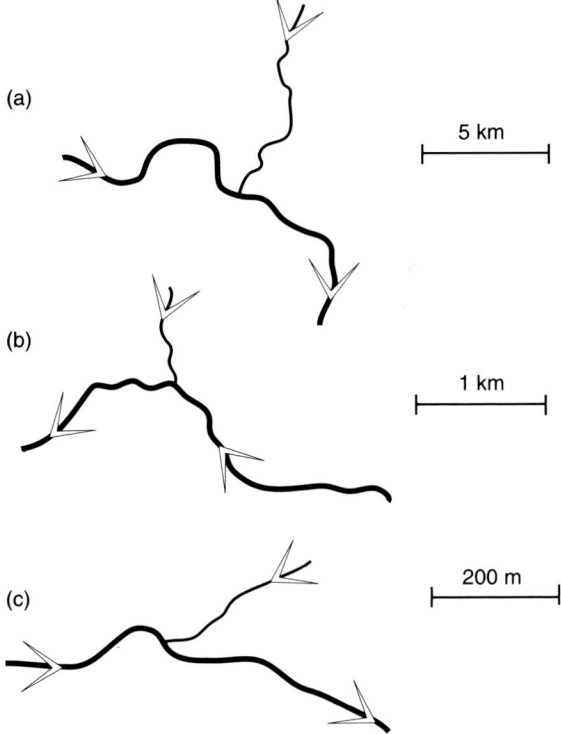

Fig. 11.1. Different scales. (a), (b) and (c) all show tributaries joining a main stream meandering in a flood plain: but at very different scales, England. (a) R. Thames near Wallingford, (b) R. Hiz near Baldock, (c) R. Stour tributary, near Haverhill.

but have a negligible effect on (c). (a) may have watered a farm and its livestock, where (c) would be too liable to flood to be safe for a farmstead. (c), though, could be a major boat highway. The flood plain of (c) may be 50 m wide and be just part of one pasture, while (a) may be several km wide, with a complex pattern of fields, ditches, hedges, woods, and maybe housing, mills, wharves.

Plateaux likewise have similarities. Streams rise on the high, near-flat land, they flow off the plateau into a self-made gully. This sheltered, V-shaped valley gradually widens as it approaches the lowlands below. This description is equally true for R. Kinzig in the Black Forest, and R. Armla in north Malta. The difference is that the latter plateau is all of 40 m high, rather than the 800 m for R. Kinzig, and the eroded gully (valley) of R. Armla has slopes nearly 4 m high rather than c. 500 m and the length is 1 km rather than c. 170 km.

The wealth and (human) resources of the Kinzig valley lie in that valley, where the village obtained water, the mills and the water drove craft, and where people lived who could exploit the valley coniferous forest on the slopes, and the lower lands as grass or arable. The Kinzig's plateau is high and exposed, and suitable in earlier times only for summer grazing (though now farmed and with a few recent settlements).

The plateau is the only similarity with R. Armla, as the plateau garigue was also used for rough grazing. The Armla ravine also has trees, but these, even though short and sparse, can fill or even overtop the valley. (They are carob and other fruit maquis species.) The present human resource is a hotel near the mouth and the tourists it attracts. The Kinzig valley is also now a tourist area, but the hotels are an integrated part of the village in the centre of the valley, not an isolated, relatively enormous block at the mouth.

Again, a field in a valley is a field in a valley. But the field may be of several hectares, with little boundary, and extremely high yield with expensive machinery, seed and agrochemicals. Or it may be a traditional field, 100 m–300 m across, with ditch, fence or hedge protecting the soil and giving corridors for wildlife, or again it may be a Mediterranean terrace only 5 m wide and 15 m long, built up on a man-made floor with strong walls downside protecting the (sloping) bank, and growing crop and wild plants, and 'ordinary' walls dividing the fields horizontally. Agri-equipment is small in size. Each field is man-made in the sense of being constructed, and the fertile soil added.

The forces determining the patterning, however, differ in more than whim. A terrace is constructed. Field history includes drainage history, and all that drying means for crops and patterns over time. Field history also depends on the density and type of population and its enterprise: for stability, for increased wealth, increased land, crop types, or whatever.

Mosaics

Riverscapes, from one point of view, are mosaics. Anywhere in Europe there is rain, therefore surface water, for part if not all the time. This ranges from the thousands of large lakes in Finland to the footprint which catches rain and does not completely dry for a week or two. Kirby (1992) describes the immense biodiversity value of tiny and fleeting, as well as large and permanent, water bodies. Some invertebrates will only survive in the former, and only if these are constantly renewed (e.g. constant new deer tracks). Here, the feature is a water body, its ecology, and the size of its biota. That is, like a mosaic they are composed of many units, which differ in shape, colour, function and size. Each piece of mosaic may be subdivided, being, say, partly black, partly yellow.

(a)

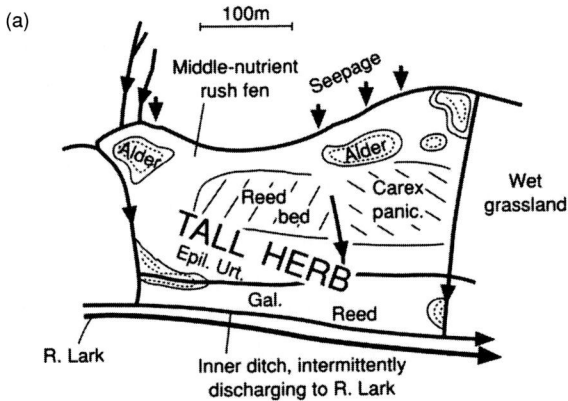

(b)

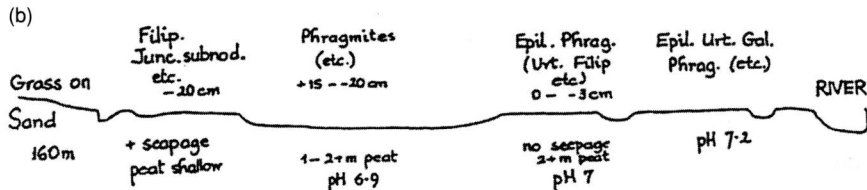

(c)

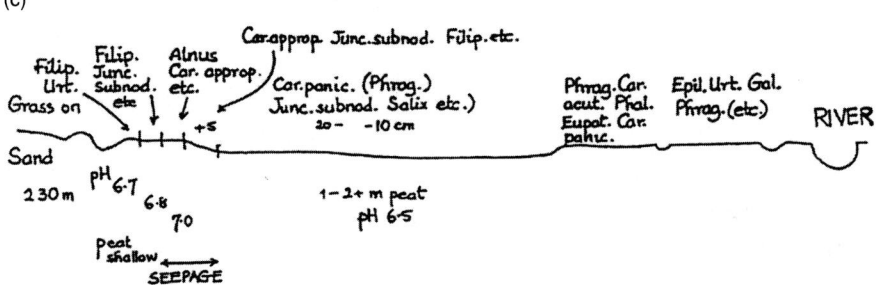

Fig. 11.2. Icklingham Poors' Fen, England, 1958 (Y. Bower in Haslam, 1994). The fen, used by the parishioners, was already a third smaller in 1950 than in 1840. Arrows show the direction of seepage flow into the fen, of ditch flow within the fen, and of river flow (which is now outside and separated from the fen). There had been some drying by abstraction, but due to the lowering of level by peat cutting in the then-wet parts, those areas were flourishing fen. The two dominants were separated by a ditch (from a fen spring), showing management was responsible. The *Carex paniculata* is dominant only in fairly nutrient-rich areas, so is unlikely to have been so pre-1600, when silty river water regularly flooded the fen: in fact, the substrate is *Phragmites* peat above, and open water organic mud below. The lower-nutrient species, e.g. *Carex appropinquata, Filipendula ulmaria, Galium uliginosus, Juncus subnodulosus, Lotus uliginosus*, are towards the outer edge where seepage water influences habitat. The high-level parts were dry (tall herb) fen by 1950, probably formerly 'marsh hay' areas. (a) Plan. (b) Profile north to south through reed bed. (c) Profile north to south through tussock sedge bed.

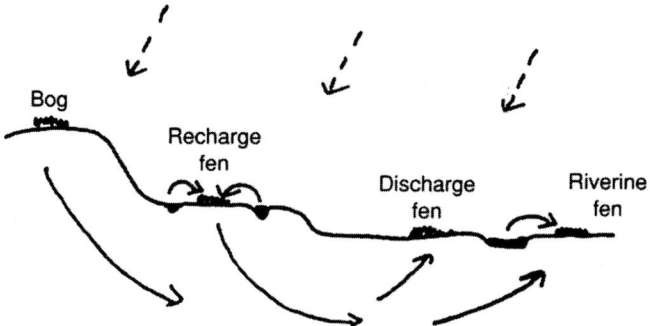

Fig. 11.3. Landscape structure showing water movement, discharge and recharge. Frequent Dutch patterns (Haslam, 1994).

Likewise, each element of the riverscape, each river, wood, construction, is part of the whole, creates the whole, but is separate, and functions by itself. Once more, this is thought provoking, therefore useful, but the principle cannot be taken too far. While the pieces of a mosaic differ in size and shape, they do so within limits. There is nothing equivalent to the narrow river winding across the whole picture (a mosaic may form a river, but *one piece* of it does not), or the chequer-board formed by fields bounded by hedges or walls. Dividing a riverscape up into different elements can be done from different perspectives (see Figs. 10.1, 11.3). These include the following.

- The river basin, the stream, its tributaries, other patterns of water movement, drainage, abstraction, alteration of surface and underground waters.
- Land use in relation to people, the field pattern, shapes, boundaries, crops, now and in the past, the position of settlements.
- Habitats for 'wild' plants and animals. Where, what size and shape, what connection to each other, boundary effects, metapopulations, over-fragmentation (if present)? Of course, each community, preferably each species, must be considered separately: watercress beds, crayfish and deer do not share the same connections, and their habitats are not the same colour in the mosaic!
- A mosaic may have different facets, e.g. in a pool landscape, dragonfly larvae find the pools as independent, separated habitats, while to the adults, they are fragments ('metafragments') of a single habitat (Gaines, 2006).
- Constructions and communications for people, settlements, bridges, communications down the footpath and sight lines, past as well as present.

- Recreation, past, present and future possibilities. Beauty and amenity value, the same.
- Conservation of natural and cultural heritage.

The initial sorting is easy, and is too easy to over-simplify. What, for instance, are the corridors along which earth-bound biota can move? The flowing river (flowing downstream only), the river bank and riverside (if allowed by planners), the paths and roads, verges, lanes, which form suitable greenways for movement, the lines of trees and hedges joining woods? Which species can use which corridor? And is there genuinely free passage along them? Is a road very broken by a cross road most destructive to frogs, and is farming a barrier? Is the stream in a pipe under the road and if so is there a fall at the downstream end preventing small biota moving upstream?

Community size and fragmentation

The size of habitat needed varies partly with species. A male otter uses up to 40 km of river, while a water shrimp, *Gammarus* (water shrimp) uses only a few metres. But the *Gammarus* may be washed downstream and use another habitat. The otter moves but is not moved by rivers. Fragmentation to small habitats may, in fact, favour some species, though decreasing others (Padoa-Schioppa, *et al.*, 2006).

The habitat differs. Species moving little must be able to spend the whole of their life within their community: feeding, moving, breeding, rearing young. This needs space. It needs space with specific habitat characters of, say, water regime, soil, disturbance. Sometimes, it is possible for metapopulations to be spread over several places, places close enough together for the relevant animal or plant species to move between them, and between them find all habitats required for long-term survival.

A young copse may have its appropriate trees, but is unlikely to have the same subsidiary fauna and flora as the ancient woodland nearby, so only for the overlappping species is it a woodland habitat. It is important to know how much communities are fragmented ecologically. If conditions are changing, how long will it be before the community changes?

Fragments

Some communities have transition zones between them (unless fence, road, etc., supervene). Passing through the transition vegetation zone, the transition animal zone may only begin when that of the vegetation ends. Are the full communities of either large enough to be breeding populations? Where communities are measured in hectares, edges are irrelevant to continuation. Somewhere like Malta, though, where fragmentation by landscape, by terracing and now by settlement, roads and recreation is extreme, size is significant. A traditional animal community may not start until 50 m from the edge, 40 m from the full plant community. In such a place, all patches under 120 m wide do not, or soon will not, have their proper invertebrate populations.

The boundaries of mosaic patches or corridors are dynamic, both in space and time, partly even when they are a road or wall, more strongly when there is a natural and gradual transition. Sarlöv-Herlin & Fry (2001) point out the importance of managing these. The better the boundary, the better the biota. Invertebrates, annual plant species, etc., should all have good habitat.

Dispersal differs with species. Each needs a habitat to spread into, and, given the immense present rate of destruction, not just their core habitat. Fungi, carabid beetles, grass snakes, oak trees and violets all need different types of linked habitats and dispersal areas, for a sustainable riverscape.

There is a danger, when considering whether a riverscape should be altered for conservation, either to plan alterations for one or a few species, or to make great efforts to preserve the highest quality area. Preserve the best, ditch the rest, in fact. The danger is that ecology and biodiversity are total, and altering to please, say, bird lovers, may lose diversity of mammals, flora and their connections. Best sites without communications may lead to its extinction either when a motorway goes through them, or when the patch is too small for sustainable populations. Many plant species are already seen to become rare in fragmented landscapes: and not just in Malta!

There are many patches of Malta maquis 10–20 m wide, few indeed over 120 m. There are many former seepage areas, where the dampness now only shows in patches of (smothering) *Arundo donax*. These may have been self-propagating vegetatively for centuries, but what about their associated, short-lived species? Can these be a metapopulation? When there are only two spring impoundments bearing *Potamogeton pectinatus* (which left the now-dried river long ago), that is no metapopulation, and the first accident (agrochemicals, dredging, fallen walls) means extinction.

While Malta is an extreme case, others may not be much better. In England corridors may be interrupted, sprayed, destroyed, the traditional community may be drained, built on, or divided by a new road. Although much is made of a few successes, reed beds for bitterns, woodland species holding their own for a whole decade (wow!), this itself exhibits the flood-tide of destruction. Looking only at this year's pattern, and without studying either connections or the reproductive capacity of both the dominant (community-shaping) and the associate species, gives a disturbing picture.

For instance, a few km of a chalk stream were enhanced with meanders and gentle edges in the 1990s. The restorers, rightly pleased, watched to see not only the common chalkstream plants already there, do well, but also the rare ones come in.

Alas:

- digging soil enhances nutrient status, and the standard chalkstream species responded and grew large and lush, instead of small, with fringing herbs of mixed dominance edging the stream; Given decades, without intervention, this will right itself. But will the pollution stay?

Except:

- how far were the missing species from the restoration site? And how easy was the line of communication?

One study on how far bird-dispersed seeds moved from forest edges showed the distance was stable, so the more tongues of woodland extended out of the wood, the greater the area covered by tree seeds, and so the faster the potential invasion by the forest. Of course, this depends on there being birds. In Malta, where nearly all birds are slaughtered, the fruits, once on the ground, are eaten, trampled, or left to rot: much less suitable for dispersal. In Lombardy, roads are the greatest agents for fragmentation (Padoa-Schioppa *et al.*, 2006).

Communication

Communications are vital, long term. Biota must be able to move. No habitat is permanent. To survive, biota must find new ones. The time-scale though may be millennia for, say, bogs; or weeks, for say, damp footprints. Reed beds in the Volga delta, and probably in many other places, also last for millennia, with the same individual plants propagating vegetatively for long periods (Rudescu *et al.*, 1965). Eventually, the delta will vanish. Ancient woodland similarly lasts long, but the individual trees live only a few centuries, and the woodland can survive only if conditions are suitable for regeneration, and regeneration of all the characteristic species. It is salutary to remember the communities that have greatly pre-dated historic Man; and how few people have permitted natural biota to survive, and none, in their original state. Fen communities in East Anglia have changed immensely in just two centuries, becoming drier and with decreased variety and biodiversity: but they are still fen communities (Table 8.3) (Haslam, 2003; Parmenter, 1995).

Fragmentation and destruction of habitat: case study, Malta

Malta's rivers, less than two centuries ago (Grech Delicata, 1853; Haslam & Borg, 1998) flowed well, spring-regulated above, the water kept up in the lowland parts by the water level just underground. The flora was a satisfactory S. European one, and so presumably the fauna was, also. They are both now on the verge of extinction:

- water loss, abstraction and drainage. Springs are a travesty of their former selves, ground water level has dropped (see Chapter 4). It would have needed careful conservation to retain some good aquatic communities.

Instead:

- bulldozing long lengths 'to prevent floods' when the bed is so dry anyway, leads to invasion by ruderals, not the retention of (long-lived) wetland species. Even dampland species like *Arundo donax* can grow only where soil is muddy, retaining water, not where this has been bull-dozed and only coarse particles remain;
- infilling the bed to make large roads is even more destructive.
- concreting watercourses for use as farm lanes: fragmenting even the ruderals of dry beds.

Worse:

- dumping quarry waste or rubble, either to make 'bridges' or as disposing of waste, causing further damage to bed and vegetation;
- weirs and other impoundments once created pools of long-term, stored water, even though separated, but the present drying mean these seldom fill and quickly empty. If water is accessible, water tankers remove it;
- building in the bed (then claiming Government compensation for flood damage);
- cultivating the valley bed, except for a narrow bed for storm flow (Fragmenting the flood plain and bed);
- failing to manage *Arundo donax*, canes. Once, this was cultivated for fencing, poles, screening, litter and earlier for furniture and thatching so that lack of harvesting and management, plus lack of scour from drying, mean that instead of being contained on river banks, it now dominates. It therefore smothers traditional biota;
- valley beds were rights of way, but new off-roading, and other recreation and farm traffic are now damaging footpaths.

Inconveniently, hunters (bird shooters) are often blocking paths and lanes as well;
- pollution is now moderate to gross, in such lengths as are wet in winter. so the little cleaner water is still more separated;
- up the slopes, terrace and other walls, and flow paths are not maintained, increasing flash floods, gullying and erosion, and decreasing water retention.
- settlement is spreading over slopes, and here run-off cannot sink into the earth, so flash floods are even worse.
- fire and other major disturbances also remove damp, and wetland species, from habitats now too dry for them to re-colonise;
- planting Eucalyptus and other exotic trees, which may (as with Acacia) shade riverbeds. This shade fragments open river bed where other species may grow. Fragments may be 1 km apart or even more. These exotics aid drying, and block traditional vegetation in their range;
- open reservoirs for irrigation do exist, but most have vertical walls and smooth floors, and are unsuitable for more than, e.g. duckweed, water boatmen, introduced goldfish;
- (marshes and other freshwater wetlands have been dried, so are no longer even fragmented.) (Also see Haslam, 1997a, b, c, 1999.)

In the 1990s, in Malta, the destruction of rivers and loss of functions was plain. A decade later, and a good deal of what then was threatened and vulnerable has gone, and the descriptions are no longer valid. This author finds studying Malta's ex-fascinating riverscapes a sad exercise in recording destruction. Other countries have damage but, because they are so much larger, the damage is proportionately less. Destroying 5 km of French river is unfortunate but trivial compared with the thousands of km of river. In Malta, 5 km is 5% of the whole.

Cultural fragmentation

Cultural fragmentation also occurs. The removal of hedges leaves valleys denuded visually, as well as biotically. The change from field tributary to wet ditch to dry ditch to no ditch has the same effect. New settlements are particularly bad when skyline becomes intrusively urban or, as Eucalyptus in Malta, alien. Old settlements tend to be clustered round the stream and the tall church tower, a farming pattern repeating over large areas of riverscape, a mosaic, connected by a road at least as old as the village. Fragmenting this with suburbs, motorways, supermarkets and other clutter, loses pattern and history.

Visual impact is too often not noticed until it has gone. Families holidaying on boats on the Norfolk rivers in 1970 would have been happy to pay to retain the much-loved reed fringes of the river: but they were lost, to the dismay of, but without reference to, the holiday makers. (Their wishes were the same as those of the conservationists.)

Sense of Place, *genius loci*, is provided by the view, with the participation of the observer. An over-fragmented view is displeasing as well as unsound. Corridors and connections add value and interest to an otherwise dull field pattern.

It is difficult in Malta to find 1 km of unfragmented bed.

Change over two decades: Gozo, Maltese Islands

Patterns can change quite fast with the impact of new or stronger socio-economic forces (Tables 11.1 and 11.2). Natural heritage deteriorated and the only betterment is that for those people who enjoy a higher material standard of living, and have no interest in cultural or natural heritage.

Land forms, fortunately, are difficult to alter apart from removing water. On them, cultivation and major settlements are superimposed.

Table 11.1 *Environmental flows in Gozo (Haslam, 2000)*

Structure	River[a]	Down-hill flows	Wall[b]	Field	Road	By road
Water	+	+	−	(+)	+	+[c]
Nutrients and Silt	+	+	−	(+)	(+)	+
Eroded land	+	+	+	(+)	(+)	−
Crop weeds	+	+	(+)	+	+	−
Wasteland spp.	+	(+)	(+)	(+)	+	−
Garigue spp.	?	?	?	−	−	−
Native trees	+	+	+	−[d]	?	(+)
Aquatic plants	+	−	−	−	−	−
Aquatic animals	+	−	−	−	−	−
Land snails, general invertebrates	+	+	+	+	+	+
Birds	+	(+)	+	+	(+)	+
Mammals	+	+	+	+	+	+
People and waste	+	+	?	(+)	+	+

[a]River corridor as well as aquatic area.
[b]Whether or not of terrace.
[c]Bowsers as well as rain-fed flow.
[d]Except abandoned.

Table 11.2 *Socio-economic forces causing change in Gozo (Haslam, 2000)*

1. **Farming**
   - Livestock in units instead of in roaming herds (pollution, less grazing).
   - Crop diversification, for sale in Gozo, Malta and further.
   - Increased irrigation (water abstraction).
   - High agrochemicals, especially on protected crops.
   - No pollution control or disposal procedures.
   - Neglect of erosion control and soil structure (greater wealth means less dependence on farming, and more Government compensation for damage).
   - Increased bird shooting and trapping (failure of Berne Convention). Planting exotic *Eucalyptus* to attract birds, which is partly toxic to invertebrates and soil organisms, and planted in obtrusive chequered patterns fitting land ownership.

2. **Tourism**
   - Increased traffic, meaning water pollution and, on minor roads, disruption and new surfaces.
   - Increased buildings: homes (including many second homes for Maltese), hotels, rented flats and houses (consequently increased quarrying), cafés, souvenir shops, etc.
   - Planned golf course in obtrusive position.
   - Pleasure boats, day trips, ice-cream selling boats (increasing litter).
   - Improved museums.

3. **Wealth and mobility**
   - Increased wealth, more and larger houses, cars, other consumer goods, more solid and liquid waste, more mobility in and outside Gozo, of people, goods and ideas, disruption of countryside, etc.
   - Increased housing and other building, infilling the eastern plateaux, spreading from other existing settlements, etc. (consequently increasing quarrying).
   - Oil drilling (one failure, at present).
   - Improved communications, roads within Gozo, ferry and heliport (later airport?) to Malta. Communications masts.
   - Increased dumping of solid waste, including in river beds.
   - Increased housing without sewers.
   - Future sewage treatment works.

By looking for different patterns using different perceptions understanding increases. The overall mosaic patterning can be considered as: land forms; cultivation (particularly as terracing is so prevalent and this is part of land form); settlements (primarily on plateaux safer from raiders) and the spaces between them (which are lessening); or of the patterns made by a single species. *Arundo donax* marks former natural springs and streams. Eucalyptus, mostly planted after 1985, for bird slaughter, is planted in fields (chequer-board effect), along

Table 11.3 Environmental effects of socio-economic forces in Gozo (Haslam, 2000)

Forces	Pollution		Water			Mobility		Ecology			
	Surface water	Ground-water	Drier rivers, springs	More floods	Loss of infiltration	Roads	Resorts	Land deterioration	Habitat loss	Habitat improvement	Excess bird shooting trapping
1. Farming											
Livestock units	+	+	+	–	–	(+)	–	–	(–)	–	–
Less grazing	–	–	–	–	–	(+)	–	–	–	+	–
More irrigation	+	+	+	?	?	–	–	?	+	–	–
Agrochemicals	+	+	–	–	–	–	–	+	+	–	–
Other chemicals[a]	+	+	–	–	–	–	–	?	?	–	–
Crop diversification	(+)	(+)	+	?	?	(+)	–	?	?	–	–
Lapsed erosion control	+	+	?	+	+	(+)	(+)	+	+	?[b]	–
Shooting, trapping	+	?	–	–	?	(+)	–	–	?	–	+
Eucalyptus for the above[c]	–	–	+	–	(+)	(+)	?	+	+	–	+
Increased wealth[d]	+	+	+	+	+	+	+	+	+	–	+

2. Tourism

Buildings	+	(+)	+	+	+	+	+[e]	−	?
Roads	+	+	+	?	+	+	+[e]	−	−
Disturbance	+	?	(+)	?	?	+	+	−	−
Golf course	+	+	(+)	−	−	?	?	−	−
Wealth[d]	+	+	+	+	+	+	+	−	+

3. Wealth, mobility

Housing, commerce, etc.	+	+	+	+	+	+	(+)	+	−	?
Dumping:										
Solid waste	+	+	−	?	+	?	+	+	−	−
Toxic waste	+	+	−	+	−	−	?	+	−	−
Roads (see above)										
Wealth, etc.[d]	+	+	+	+	+	+	+	+	+[f]	+

[a] e.g. biocides in livestock units, oil in boreholes.
[b] Some abandoned land may become of conservation value.
[c] Toxic to invertebrates and soil organisms.
[d] Less dependence in farming. More material goods, waste, mobility, pollution.
[e] Loss of land. May be deterioration of near-by land.
[f] Museums.

roads (corridor effect), on skylines and around duck decoy ponds. (All are planted, as there is no natural propagation there.) Crops also form mosaics. Irrigated crops like lettuce, strawberries, are near yet-flowing springs (e.g. Wied il-Lunziata), or by boreholes. Damp, sheltered but sunny fertile areas are good for citrus (as in upper wide north-facing valleys, e.g. San Blas), while at the other extreme, good crops of broad beans can be obtained from dry and exposed land. Here is mosaic, dependent on water regime, wind shelter and aspect.

Visible corridors connect places for linear, earth-bound movement. These may be land or water, natural or man-made. Walls, particularly if left alone (no herbicides), are good lines, except where interrupted by roads or settlements. Invisible corridors are the flyways for birds and bees, ferry ways and interconnecting mobile phone networks.

Matrices, the third element, hold the pattern together. A matrix could be the hills and valleys, or the fields, or the walls and roads (or possibly the remnants of traditional vegetation, if all else is considered as imposed upon it).

Table 11.3 shows changes with current impacts. Such garigue (and local maquis) as remains is growing taller, as no longer grazed. A less open community, though, is less satisfactory for annuals and bulbs. Degradation follows wealth, expressed as mobility, recreation and pollution. (Boreholes spread pollution too. One farmer said that, if he put oil in the borehole he need not service the pump. How many do this? This one was deterred upon learning the oil would also 'lubricate' his neighbour's borehole.)

This riverscape has nearly all boundaries sharp: Coralline mesa tops and other land forms do not, or barely, inter-grade. Terraced fields and valley floors are well demarcated. A less impacted land tends to have more interesting edges, as in Corsica and Sardinia!

Pattern in relation to habitat, Icklingham Poors' Fen, Suffolk

A local example of a single small flood plain fen peat wetland is shown in Fig. 11.2 and its table. Like so much other British wetland, there is a history of much use by villagers with rights of common, for many purposes: reed for thatch, fences, farm use; *Carex paniculata* for furniture, litter; sallow for withies; alder and sallow for timber; peat for fuel; and rush meadow at the dry end. Springs rose up-land, both giving water flowing to the corner (north east), and at the outer edge of the fen, and to a large one, within. Peat cutting lowered land level and kept the fen wetter. The cutting stopped probably before 1900, though reed harvesting continued until the 1930s. This diagram is 1950s. The then communities are determined by past management and present (and past) water and nutrient regimes. The future of these communities, given continued abandonment and no other chance, could be predicted (Table 11.4).

Table 11.4 *Past and futures of Icklingham Poors' Fen, England*

1. To about 2000

(a) Pre-1600 regularly flooded from R. Lark, mostly in winter. Fertilised from river silt. Peat building.

(b) After 1600, without river floods and silting, but with enough water for peat formation from springs and rising underground water in winter. The former water was calcium-rich, nutrient fairly low, rising from the chalk below, passing up through sands. Most spring water entered from the top of the fen, making this nearer to calcium-influenced than the rest.

(c) To about 1900, used by villagers from Icklingham as Poors' Fen, for fuel (peat, 'turf'), thatching (reeds), stools and other furniture (tussock sedges), sticks, marsh hay, etc. Use diminished though thatching reed was harvested into the 1930s. Dykes dug and maintained.

(d) To about 1950, slight drying, peat formation roughly equal to oxidation on lower levels, half of which bore reed, the other half, *Carex paniculata* (management). The high levels (less peat cutting) bore tall herb, presumably replacing harvested marsh hay, and had its black (oxidised) invertebrate-rich peat. Alder increasingly colonised *Carex appropinquata* tussocks on main spring (lower nutrient) areas, sallow colonised *Carex paniculata* tussocks on the medium-nutrient areas, and clods above water level, or surfaces in drought, in open places in the reedbeds (deer or author's tracks).

(e) To about 1970, water level stable, herb communities stable, except where shaded out by the increasing sallow. The soil (see above) of the tall herb community is less suitable for tree colonisation (Haslam, 2003).

2. To about 2005

As happened. Abstraction greatly increased. The pasture beside the river (except where interrupted by the fen) was no longer regularly flooded by rising ground water. Species such as cotton grass (*Eriophorum angustifolium*) had been lost *c*. 1900–1950, but, e.g. *Lychnis flos-cuculi* was lost now. The pasture was semi-abandoned and sedges spread. In the fen, water level dropped by over 75 cm, rare and significant frailer species such as *Galium uliginosus* were lost. Most was a tangle of carr, with tussocks, etc., dying back and unable to propagate. Reeds increased on former tall herb areas (takes time to invade dry fen). Possible conservation plans ignored the different water types, therefore the communities, and ignored the history.

3. 2005+ Possible futures

(a) Reduction of abstraction (to 1950 levels), tree removal, and a wait of several decades; restoration is perhaps possible.

(b) Addition of polluted river water and tree removal: form a polluted type wetland, probably reedswamp, without the rarer communities and species found hitherto. Heritage lost.

(c) Neglect. Dry alderwood eventually. Heritage lost – no wetland, but the habitat expected if water level had dropped naturally.

What in fact happened is that more water was abstracted and the fen was greatly dried (Table 11.4). The sallow and alder carr have spread and only relic wetland communities remain. More sensitive species (e.g. *Galium uliginosum*) are extinct. Peat is no longer formed. Mosaic, habitat pattern and community change have been drastic within a short period of c. 70 years.

The Scottish Cairngorms, change over millennia

A larger-scale example is the Scottish Cairngorms, considered 'wild', moorland and bog, uncultivable without self-defeating expense. Yet in the Bronze Age the area was open wood, with grain in small strip fields, pasture and settlements: a busy riverscape. This remained through the Roman and Anglo Saxon climate changes (Table 2.1). The sixteenth-century Agricultural revolution changed arable to sheep, with profound changes in, and expansion of, the moors. The eighteenth century, as slow warming increased, brought de-population with the Highland Clearances. This meant loss of crop yield of farming, and reversion to moor. Much wood still remained (woods sustain houses, heating, pigs, deer), but as nineteenth-century recreation developed, so the woods were lost (easier to shoot deer in the open). While climate was vital in the early stages, so that good quality farming could develop; it has been less important in the later stages than social changes. The present end is the wild grandeur of the so-called untouched moor and bog, obviously unsuited to dense farming.

Dartmoor, England, over millennia

Table 11.5 illustrates the development of Dartmoor, England. Like the Cairngorm example above, it is a warning not to accept what is, as what always has been.

Sensitivity and resistance

Communities differ in speed of change. Animals are influenced by both habitat and vegetation, plants, more by habitat. This affects speed of change. Among plants, annuals respond quicker, having to reproduce each year. Communities dependent on annual management respond quicker to its loss to those where the habitat is native to the community, and management merely preserves a 'natural phase' in succession, such as a reed bed. There are changes due to time alone: once a tree has become established, it will grow, and shade, and alter its habitat. There are changes due to people. These may be obvious,

Table 11.5 *Peat histories, England (representative of numerous sites investigated)*

1. The Fenland (Godwin, 1978)

Most recent	Raised bog	} acid bog peats
	Wood, pine, birch, Sphagnum	}
	Wood, oak, ash	}
	Wood, alder, birch	} fen peats
	Sedge (*Cladium*) fen	}
	Reedswamp (*Phragmites, Typha*)	}
	Open reedswamp (*Scirpus, Nuphar,*	}
	Sagittaria)	} organic
	Submerged aquatics	} lake muds
Oldest	Open (calcareous) water	}

2. Dartmoor (Proctor 1989) (one site)

Most recent	Sphagnum	} acid bog peats
	Carex (*Sphagnum*)	
	Carex (*Polytrichum, Maryanther*	} sedge swamp
	Calhirgon spp)	
	Carex (*Potentilla, Polytrichum, Salix*)	
	Sandy; stone	} alluvial
	Grand *Polytrichum* (sand)	
	Carex (*Polytrichum*)	} sedge swamp
Oldest	Grand, sand	} alluvial

3. Ranworth, Broadland (George, 1992)

Most recent	Reed
	Clay
	Reed
	Carr, brushwood
	Reed
	Clay
Oldest	Reed

like withdrawing management after centuries, or less obvious, like withdrawing from the wetland the water which made it and keeps it in being. Communities respond at different rates.

Therefore, there is a difference in sensitivity (see Thomas and Allison, 1993). Sensitivity is present in space and time. It can be studied at different scales. Doing so at a small scale is easiest, but it is easy to forget that, however fascinating the inter-relations of individual plants may be, this is only part of a much larger scene. A community, like a species (see Haslam, 2003, 1987) has a range of habitat in which it is a self-propagating unit, a range beyond where a relic community can exist for a while, and a range impossible. Small water regime variations within the centre of the range may not alter the community. A change of equal size at the edge of the range may move the habitat to 'impossible'. The same stress can therefore differ in its effects, in different riverscapes, and in different habitats.

Brunsden (1993) considers the types of resistance to change.

- Morphological resistance is due to smaller scale variations in slope, relief and elevation. Potential energy varies, so does its effects. Barriers such as river banks can change over shorter times than hill slopes.
- Structural resistance, or transition resistance comes from the ability to transmit change. An avalanche may start easily on one slope, but only with much difficulty, on another. The system has both 'links' and 'shape absorbers'.
- Filter resistance describes how kinetic energy is transmitted. It may have little obvious effect (if water is absorbed, there are no (or rare) flash floods), or it may have much (as when a lowland plateau river reaches a precipice edge).

This, then, is another way of looking at riverscapes, which adds to interpretations.

Practical applications may come when a degree of sensitivity can be known (Evans, 1993), and excessive erosion be prevented or dealt with. Hill slope drainage pathways are vital for drainage and erosion, and may differ from one apparently similar valley to another. These also can be discovered and managed (Hughes & Heathwaite, 1995). This subject is at a very early stage, and meanwhile, of course, fen peat still dries and flies, and a hill catchment with less absorption of rain still forms gullies.

Discussion

Most riverscapes are non-uniform, heterogeneous. Species movement cannot therefore be uniform (even though one species may use much more of a habitat than another). The diverse mosaics and corridors influence movement, some being possible for one species, some for another (rabbit and trout corridors differ).

Agricultural landscapes, which most European ones are (see Chapters 13, 14), have more stresses than unmanaged or little-impacted ones, and the dynamics of the different mosaics are therefore very complex (Bawdry & Bunel, 2001). Stone curlew nests well in fallow land in the infertile sandy Breckland. Modern agrochemicals removed the habitat by removing the fallow. Later thoughts altered management, and now both crop and bird thrive. Large reed beds harvested every year have inadequate nesting sites for high-nesting species like reed bunting. Unharvested reed beds have too little open ground (short stubble) for nesting duck. Species are as heterogeneous as riverscapes!

Species, though, need sufficient space, whichever that may be. Malta has over-fragmentation, for instance. The shape of the fragments may be crucial, Bellamy et al. (1997) find that nuthatches in Cambridgeshire consider tree lines, corridors between woods, useless. Instead, they spread if small woods occur, and are planted, around their main wood. To the nuthatches, patches are useful, corridors are not. Otters (Chapter 9) on the other hand, need corridors more than patches.

In riverscapes without much disturbance, where heterogeneity is due to varying but (locally) stable elements, if the climate warms, this means species must move to keep living in their favoured habitats: as is well documented by the north and south movements of population belts after the Ice Age (e.g. Godwin, 1978). With the impact now covering Europe, that movement is no longer possible for most species. If temperate deciduous woods are very sparse, planted and managed, how can species of deciduous woods move north to their (moved) climate when the northern woods are planted with conifers? The population belt cannot stay put, as it will become too hot, nor move north, because impact has removed suitable habitats. Lowland wetlands of the Netherlands and England cannot move far north because the physical conditions for their development do not exist there, either because landform is unsuitable, or because the area is under arable or settlement.

W. Cowper wrote, two centuries ago:

> *The poplars are felled, farewell to the shade . . .*
> *The blackbird has fled to another retreat*
> *Where the hazels afford him a screen from the heat*
> *And the scene where his melody charmed me before*
> *Resounds with his sweet flowing ditty no more*

But whether the stress is fragmentation or climate change, if the 'other retreat' no longer exists, there is population loss. Climate change just accentuates this.

Figures 10.1, 11.2 are of riverscapes with much Sense of Place, biodiversity, community diversity, and with a strong cultural *genius loci*. There are patterns of different type (wood, road, meander) patches of different relevance (visual for different species), overall continuities and discontinuities, gradients of slope and moisture, areas of cleaning ability and of pollutant entry. Cultural connections are the siting and connecting of old farming hamlets, and the motorway and suburb of the new settlement. The rural pollards enhance the scene, culturally, historically and biotically.

12

Resources III. Settlements and constructions

The power of man has grown in every sphere except over himself
(W. S. Churchill)

Changes in multifunctional landscapes change multiple functions
(Bakheshuen *et al.*, in Mander *et al.*, 2001)

Settlements

Ever since people existed, they have used rivers and used them increasingly as technology and populations increased, and the diversity of this use has been extraordinary. Recently, though, uses, particularly direct use, have declined, except for waste disposal and abstraction (Table 12.1). People have always settled by rivers (pre-mains supply, rivers or springs were essential). Rivers are the key to European development. The Danube and the Rhine opened the door to settlement from east to west, with settlements on river routes. Roman civilisation was aided by the Rhône. Towns were a legacy of Rome. The Romans used, bridged and altered rivers (and aqueducts), but their towns were sited more for military or state reasons. The river town dates from before or after Rome but may, like Colchester, London and York, have been used by Romans.

River settlements may start as an isolated homestead, and grow to a village, then a river town, but the progression is not necessary. A farm needs farm water: which may but need not be from a source large enough for a village. A river town, by definition, used river transport, so needed a river large enough for boats to bring riches. Some patterns of where there may be farms, river villages and river towns are shown in Figs. 12.1 and 12.2. Inland trade needs a good harbour (wharfs), defence if necessary, and suitable resources, e.g. near a capital, a

Table 12.1 *Some river uses for people (after Haslam, 1997a)*

Attack: by boat (primarily the Vikings); crossing rivers, moats, etc.

Cleaning: people, animals, clothes; homes, farmyards, stables, etc., and their contents; roads and other built-up and hard surfaces.

Cooking

Defence from attack: by water: river bends, marshes, lakes, moats, releasing contained water (primarily The Netherlands); by fortifications: stakes in river, chains across, forts at either side, fortified bridges, etc.

Drainage: allowing marsh hay, meadow, settlement.

Drinking: *Essential*, people, domestic and farm animals; animals used for travel (e.g. horses, camels).

Food and beverages: fish (rivers, fishponds), fowl (rivers, marshes, decoy ponds), watercress and other salad plants (rivers, marshes), alcoholic and other drinks.

Industry: Power: watermills driving machinery for grinding corn, other grain, olives, fashioning armour, jewellery, fulling, paper, gunpowder, metal products, sawing wood, etc., tanning, dyeing. Boilers (steam engines). Processing and washing for coal, tin, gold, lead, silver and other ores. Hydroelectricity.

Also, a primary use of water is cooling for electricity produced by other means. Most modern industry requires water for processes and cleaning, to a greater or lesser extent.

Irrigation: the principal use of water, exceeding all others, in many countries.

Magic: rain-making, stopping rain and flood, various other magic fountains and waters.

Materials: osiers, withies, timber (baskets, fences, houses, clogs, fishing materials and many other rural uses). Reeds (thatching, fencing, general farm use), rushes (chair seats, strewing, lights), tussock sedges (furniture), strewing plants (floors). Soaking flax, hemp, fleeces. Gravel, sand, etc., quarrying.

Medicinal: springs, spas, plants.

Punishment for crime: ducking, drowning.

Recreation and ornament: ornamental fountains, rivers, water-gardens, reedbeds. River parties, water-spectacles, boat races. Walking, picnicking and parking by waters. Model boats, Pooh sticks. Water clocks and other mechanical devices. Fishing, angling. Shooting. Irrigating gardens. Swimming, paddling, scuba diving, water skiing. (Also see Tables 9.1 and 9.6.)

Religion: baptism, holy wells and springs, ritual cleansing, pilgrimages to holy rivers. Marshes (in particular) form remote places for hermits and religious communities.

Transport: boats for trade, business and leisure activities, transport along rivers, river valleys and over ice.

Waste disposal: general waste dumped in rivers. Less than before of dead people and animals, also of mine, factory and sewage effluent. More than before of agricultural, farm and hard surface waste and run-off.

Miscellaneous: e.g. fire hydrants, fire engines, heating homes with volcanic water (Reykjavik).

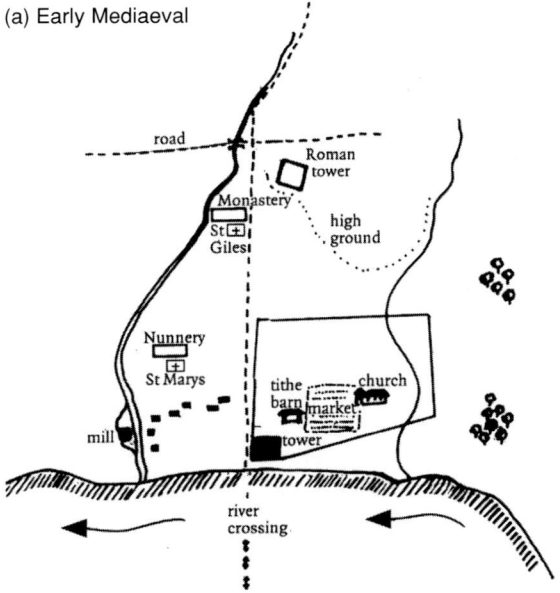

Fig. 12.1. River towns. (a)–(d) Show the general development of river towns from the Dark Ages. The fortifications of (d) are built in unsettled places, like parts of France and Germany, but were unnecessary in, say, Britain and parts of Italy. The other features, such as roads going to somewhere (e.g. London), not merely leaving the town (e.g. East) apply (Y. Bower in Haslam 1991). (e) Florence, c. 1500 (1493 *Nuremberg Chronicle*, Master and Fellows of St Catharine's College, Cambridge). This is one of the clearer pictures, and – unlike some others in the *Chronicle* – is undoubtedly Florence. It is in the stage (c) above. The first bridge is that leading to the cathedral (Duomo). Fortification is extreme, and, unlike Figs. (a)–(d) is on both sides of the river. This is an unusual feature, and is found when invasion is expected by the river. Most such cities are along the English Channel and North Sea, against the Vikings. Surprisingly, Pisa, downstream on Florence's River Arno, was sacked by the Vikings, and so Florence's pattern resembles that of Norwich, Fig. (f), except that Florence no doubt looked much finer. The Norwich plan is modern, but shows the ancient fortifications. (g) Another variant, found particularly along the Rhine, e.g. Mainz, instead of expanding outward similarly in all directions, has a repeated wharf-water street-church pattern. (h) Helmond, in The Netherlands, was built on a canal, ignoring the old river. Being built late, in settled times, fortifications were unnecessary, and the town developed on both sides of the canal (f–h, Y. Bower in Haslam, 1991).

284   The riverscape and the river

(b) Middle Mediaeval

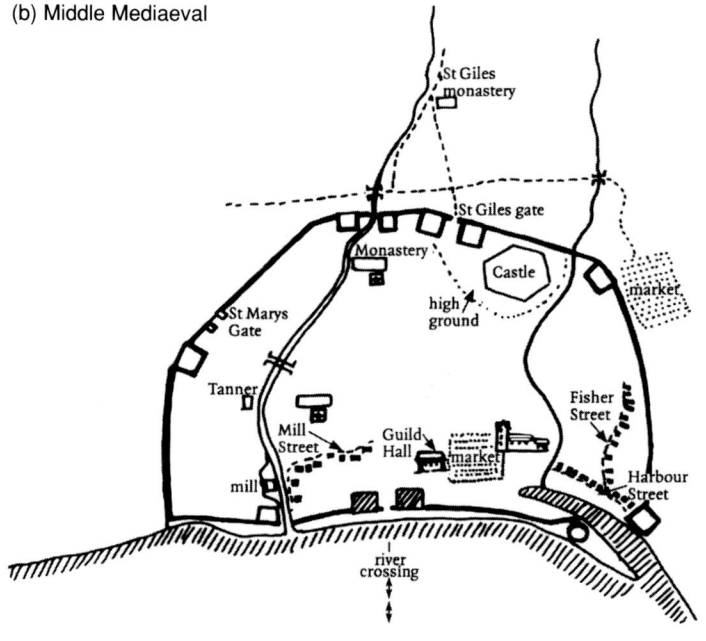

(c) Late Mediaeval

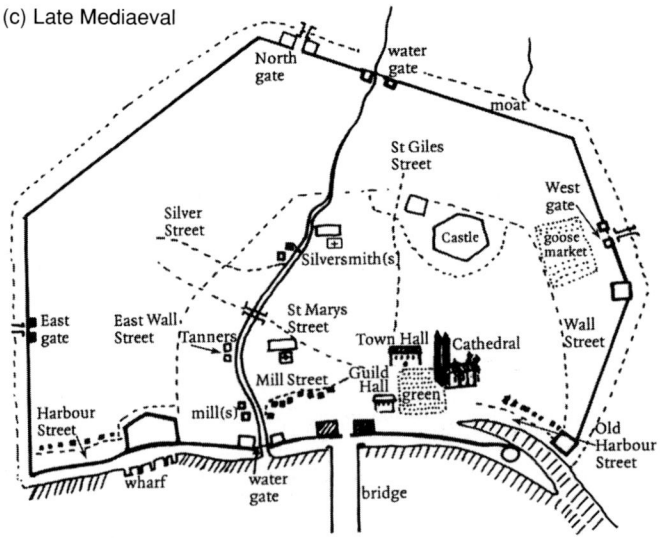

Fig. 12.1. (cont.)

Resources III. Settlements and constructions 285

(d) Late 1500s to about 1700.

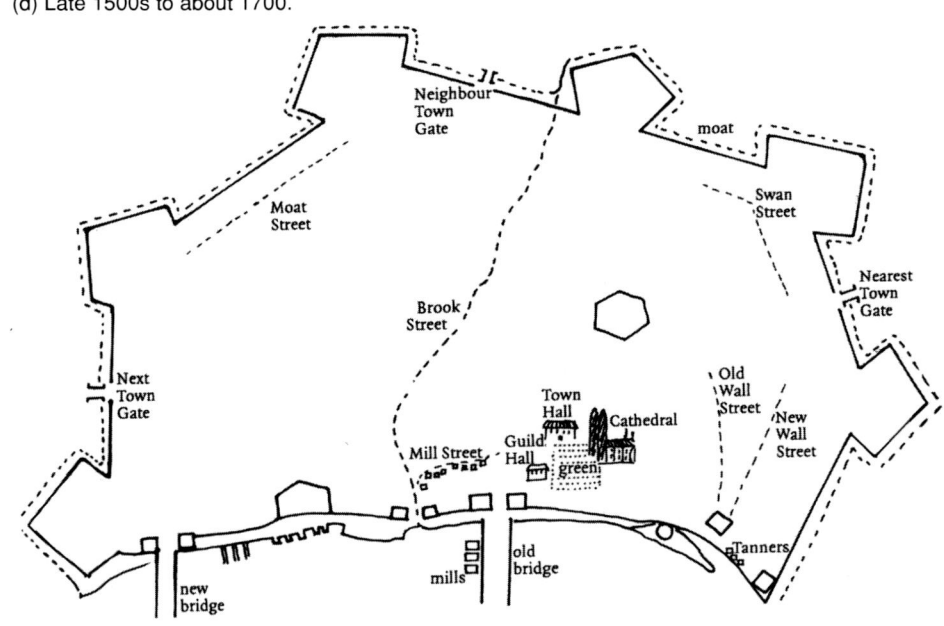

(e)

Fig. 12.1. (cont.)

286 The riverscape and the river

(f)

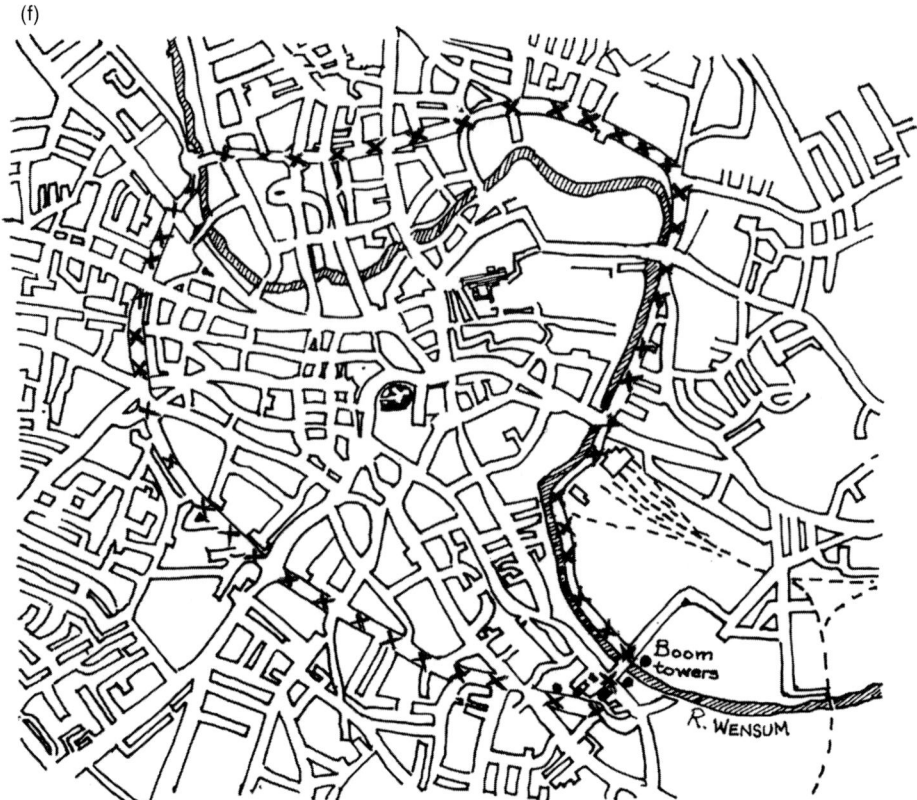

Most recent city wall × × ×
on both banks of river

(g)

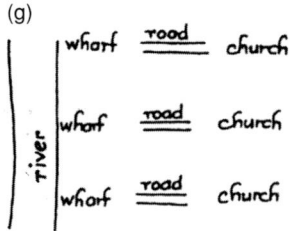

(h)

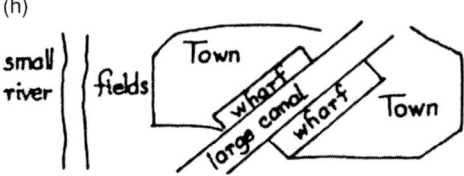

Fig. 12.1. (cont.)

Resources III. Settlements and constructions 287

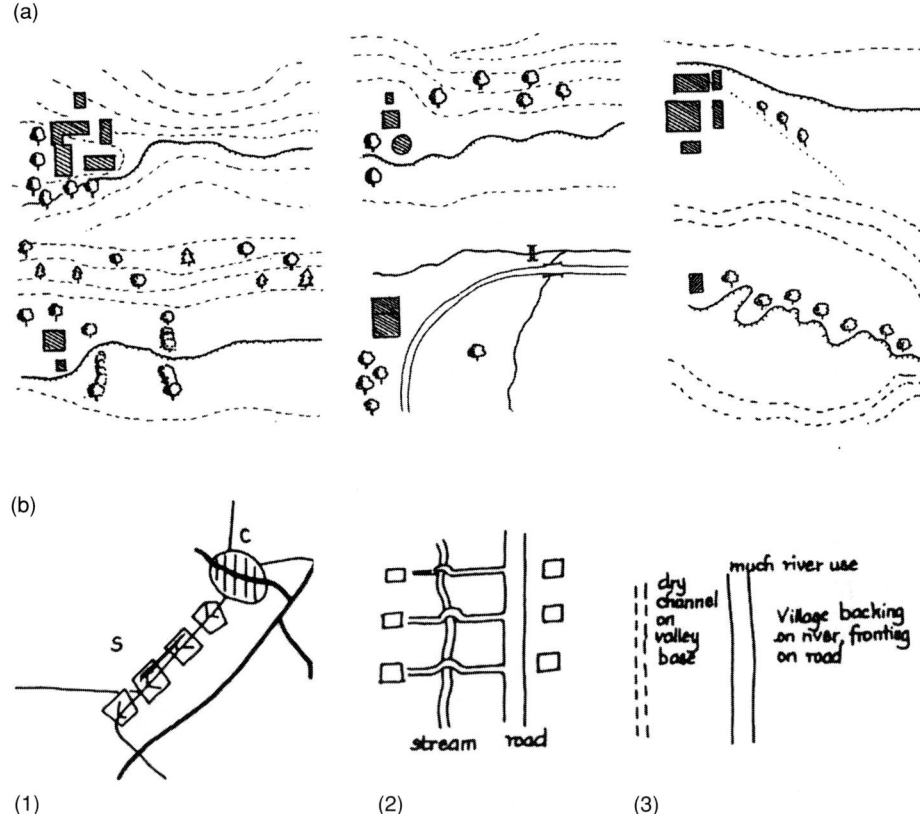

Fig. 12.2. Representative river non-trading villages (Y. Bower in Haslam, 1991). (a) Farms and farmsteads at sources, and by larger streams. (b) River villages, '1' a cluster village 'C' round a small stream, near enough to the river for access to water in drought, and for boats. Later, a street part 'S' was added, where stream-diversions were needed. '2' A street village built parallel to and along the stream and the road. '3' A street village built on a diverted stream: above flood level. (c) Also building above flood level, by a (formerly much flooded) plain. (d) Pictures of the same French village: the old centre, once dependent on the stream, and the new building independent of it.

major waterway, or the sea, or with mineral resources, or good vegetable production, or fuel. Canal towns are necessarily more recent, mostly eighteenth century – except for, say, Roman towns, like Lincoln. The towns were developed for access and trade on the canals.

Farms may be actually on flowing streams. These may be swift and perhaps used for a small water mill, be large enough for sanitation as well as supply, or form duck ponds etc. or be small, diverting water from a larger stream whether

288 The riverscape and the river

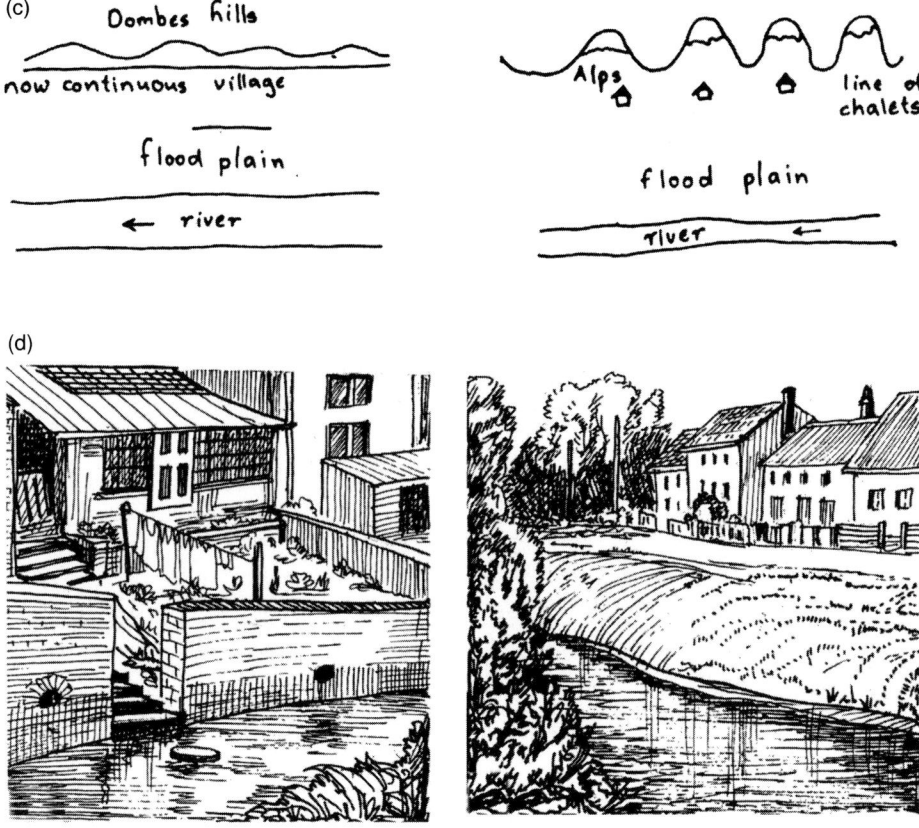

Fig. 12.2. (cont.)

natural or man-made. Small channels were dug to water several houses, or villages. They brought enough water to the (back) doors, and they, or a separate channel system, could also carry away waste.

The main village stream had enough water for the village. It may be small enough not to cause serious damage in flood. A larger stream liable to flood means buildings set back, except those requiring access (merchants' houses, wharves, watermills, bridges). To be on a minor stream just above the river flood level combines a supply of water, even in drought (since it is then possible to collect it from the river), and no flooding, since the houses are too high up.

While all old villages needed domestic water, a surprising number also used small streams for transport, by barge (in streams at least $c.$ 0.5+ m deep and 2+ m wide) or by cart, horseman and pedestrian (in streams up to $c.$ 75 cm deep, with for carts a firm, smooth bottom). Produce could go to market in the farm cart; or coals, transhipped at the junction with a larger stream, could reach the manor house.

Real trading villages, however (Fig. 12.2), obtain their wealth from boats, and were on rivers large enough to take the larger boats of the day (e.g. Standon, England; Lochem, the Netherlands), and had inland communications so goods moved in both directions (e.g. craft, ore, specialised produce out, fuel, clothing, foreign goods in). Such villages had a large wharf, where bales could be stored awaiting the next boat, and the next carter. If and when, with technological advance, boats became too large for the channel, small villages like these became by-passed, except for local traffic in the small boats. Larger towns made new channels able to manage the new boats. The large wharf, huge in, e.g. Bray-sur-Seine long in, e.g. Lyon, is a sure sign of a trading past. (These wharfs may now be roads, car parks, gardens, playgrounds), the Wharf housing estate (the name often reflects the past) and the like. Towns developing, or re-developing when communal wharfs became inconvenient, could have their merchants' houses– as before – along behind the wharf, but now with walls to the river, giving each house its private wharf or dock. The church is on the town side of the wharf, prominently seen by visitors. The building for the Wharf master and toll collector is now too often lost. Houses were behind and perhaps beyond the wharf.

River towns used, and were built on, streams other than the river. Individual houses might have natural or diverted rills for supply, or have to fetch water from stream, river, or spring. Wells are dug when clean surface water runs short. It was noted that the cholera epidemic in Ely in the 1830s mainly affected those taking water from the river, the disease being rampant in upstream towns. Those with private wells mostly escaped (Holmes, 1974). Water may have to be bought, from water carts and, later from companies which laid pipes to, eventually, every house in town. There was likely, early, to be a stream to provide the water for tanning, fulling, forging, and the other crafts wanted in a comfortable, civilised town. It might turn water mills, too. The town stream is typically a tributary to a river at the side of the town, where are the wharves: and the flooding, though this may be the main town stream too.

The basic pattern is the wharf + square+ church + town hall. Additionally, in towns built in unsettled times, there may be a fort by the wharf or main bridge, and/or one up the hill behind (if present). River forts are still numerous along, e.g. R. Rhine, R. Danube. In England, which was mostly stable after 1450, the forts are mostly national monuments (e.g. Tower of London), homes (e.g. Newark), or, and most often, ruins (e.g. Huntingdon).

A town, unlike the small village, has the market square set back from the wharf. There is often a 'Water Street' leading to the square, the square having the church, town hall, and housing. This pattern persists over the centuries. It

290   The riverscape and the river

(a)

Water power

(b) Water power developed to steam power

Fig. 12.3. Development of mills (Y. Bower in Haslam, 1991). (a) Mediaeval. (b) Steam power, early nineteenth century. (c) Electric power, late twentieth century, but built on the ancient industrial site of the town: downstream of it, by the river.

may be rebuilt larger (the church becoming a cathedral) or be repeated along the river. Large Rhine towns often have a series of these elements.

Settlements are like organisms, they have a beginning, growth, maturity, and decay. Their growth may be stopped, or they are destroyed, at any point. Growth is not inevitable. Society, technology and what at the time are resources, change (if the iron runs out, can flowers be exported instead? Or, will the settlement

Electric power, still by, and using, the river

(c)

Fig. 12.3. (*cont.*)

decay?). Craft technology may be discovered and appeal to the community (e.g. textiles) and later be superseded by better or cheaper products from elsewhere. (Belfast linen displaced by Manchester cotton displaced by Eastern manufacture). Trade comes and goes. River trade grows with population, technology and the available resources. It increased up to the nineteenth century, as navigation, boats and wealth improved, then declined with first railways, then good roads. But, as can be seen from Fig. 15.1, the heritage of the undestroyed constructions may remain.

Different types of riverscape

The purposes and so constructions and land uses to which people have put riverscapes are innumerable. It is rare to have a single purpose. The production of food and technology, the provision of homes, pollution and communications occur almost wherever people have settled (with the partial exception of Antarctica). Many other purposes occur, and are superposed or displaced.

Self-sufficient production

The riverscape designed for self-sufficient produce is one of the commonest. And, since taxes are near-universal once population is sufficient, the raising of crops direct for tax, or sold for tax money, is part of this self-sufficiency. Farming here is usually mixed, both livestock and arable, and its area is large compared with that of the settlement. The typical early pattern was crops near the settlement, meadow then rough pasture further (unless the best all-round meadows were among the in-fields).In mountain regions, livestock were taken up to mountain pastures (saeters, sheilings) in summer. Unfortunately, this practice is becoming uneconomic.

Communications were from village to field and church, and, depending on population, to the local market town, by water or land.

Water mills, spreading from the first century BC (and windmills from the twelfth century) saved the immense burden of hand (or horse, etc.)-grinding flour for bread.

Exporting produce

Riverscapes for exporting produce is the simplest specialisation, and needs only a source of demand (a town or city), and good enough communications to transport produce. This may, according to the region, be general fruit and vegetables, or be specialised in, say, meat, fruit, grain, malt (for beer), grapes (wine), olives, fodder, timber, fuel, baskets, minerals. The particular produce will cover a substantial area of the riverscape, and also may alter it by its means of production (e.g. irrigation, manure, grazing livestock, forests).

Communications

The means of communication, old and particularly new, may alter the riverscape. Rivers are straightened, shoals and other blockages are removed, banks (seventeenth century and beyond) are firmed for towing horses. Pound locks (the double locks known now just as 'locks') were introduced to make navigation smooth. These stabilise channels, so fixing in place the wetlands or dry fields beside them. Canals are straight (which is shorter), puddled (to keep water in) and, depending on period, firm-banked (horse towing) and embanked. When a canal is built, the opportunity for new trade, not only the original cause, brings new settlements. Paths, later lanes and roads run along and between riverscapes. Along the river is useful when there is dry land. Where not, the early paths run parallel but higher.

The opportunity for hospitality has (in all settled times) brought inns not just to towns and villages, but to suitable places on the various Ways between them.

Capital cities differ in two respects from lesser towns. They have or had armed forces to protect them by land and water. They have many people so many goods coming in by water but there is no need for large wharfs for storing trading goods (coals are ordered, brought and delivered). London was a trading city, with numerous wharves and docks. Close upstream was the City of Westminster, the seat of the Court, Parliament and later Government. This had well-built small wharves for transporting people and their own freight. A lesser pair are Huntingdon county capital and Godmanchester (trading), and Rastatt (capital) and Karlsruhe (industrial), and the villages opposite on the Rhine, Treutlingen (trading) and Pappenheim, a seat of a wealthy noble whose castle rises from the hill above.

In the Low Countries much wealth and consequent social status came from river trade, e.g. Namur and Donauworth. In Britain, particularly after the twelfth century, river trade came to be associated with ignorant, uneducated and vicious watermen and their little-better masters (no doubt watermens' language, dirt, and drink, at times, were deplorable. But the records do not indicate they were criminals. Just socially low). Continental towns maintained wealthy riverside houses. Trade was socially higher though not aristocratic. British nineteenth-century 'Watersides' were mostly slums. These local types of town, however, have only a small influence on the riverscape.

Industrial riverscape

Many settlements produced craft using watermill power. These included flour, woollens, paper, jewellery and armoury. Other craft just need plenty of water, like tanning, pottery and malting. From early times some areas specialised in one craft, e.g. fulling in the Quantock hills, England. Mills were built from top to tail, that is, the next mill down started holding up water for the downstream wheels as the water from the wheels above slowed. Later, Lancashire valleys became notorious for their cotton mills in the eighteenth and early nineteenth centuries, with atrocious labour conditions. Major other craft valleys included that of Bamberg, R. Main, and R. Ruhr, Germany. Good communications were needed to get the goods out, and canals could often be built to do so, when rivers or roads were inadequate (e.g. Josiah Wedgewood built a canal to transport his china; the Duke of Bridgewater, for coal). The coming of steam meant fast-flowing rivers could now be harnessed for large textile etc. factories, e.g. Lancashire, England (Fig. 12.3).

Many towns had craft areas, such as Standon, England; Megève, France; Ribe, Denmark, or just single mills. The great industrial towns may have developed from these, but they may also be due to new resources. Steam power allowed huge factories to be built in, e.g. Birmingham, and when water also was needed, the towns were by water. Steam power needed less water and the (diesel and) electrical power which followed, even less. Major industrial towns can now be sited with minor water. Light industry increasingly is replacing heavy.

Industrial towns were labour intensive, and good communications were necessary to bring in food as well as to export manufactured goods. Craft/industrial riverscapes are characterised by manufacture, good communications, and (early) access to water.

Pollution, from the coal mining which powered the industrial revolution, from the many factories, and from all the people gathering in the towns, became a blot on the riverscape, with black, filthy water.

> Dank and foul, dank and foul
> By the smoky town in its murky cowl
> Foul and dank, foul and dank
> By wharf and river and stony bank
> Danker and darker the further I go
> Baser and baser the richer I grow

So Charles Kingsley writes of R. Mersey, but the description is equally appropriate to most rivers of industrial towns from the late eighteenth until the twentieth centuries.

Gross pollution has now been much improved. Many streams formerly near-clean, though, are polluted because of the spread of good roads crowded with traffic. This characterises twenty-first century 'good' living, and widespread pollution from this and agrochemicals. Modern factories are often small, high-tech, clustered in Industrial Estates well away from the previous heavy industry and craft towns. Their pollution, from factory and, more, from all the traffic they attract, is considerable.

Industrial riverscapes are controlled by their internal resources (water, minerals, coal, peat). They may have been low housing, or the whole riverscape may also be covered by settlements.

Specialised buildings, mills and other constructions (e.g. bridges) grow to meet the demand: which varies with time as well as useable resources and communications. (Above Huy, Belgium, iron was found in the river valley, giving a railway, housing and prosperity in the nineteenth century and, because the iron ran out, and this was the only resource, abandonment in the twentieth.)

Conclusions

The valley is therefore altered for whatever is necessary for the crop concerned: forests have less erosion and good water retention, they produce low pollution (less agrochemicals). Vines need good (and southern) sunshine and aspect, so are as often grown on (sometimes terraced) slopes as on the lowlands. Terracing modifies the riverscape and alters and lessens the flow of tributaries (crop water demand). Vineyards tend to have much bare soil.

Livestock production requires either large areas of grazing (e.g. the Welsh and Scottish Highlands), or the intensive production of fodder, either in place, e.g. Swedish meadowlands, or, as often now, imported in to the livestock. The former, being the closest to natural grazing, if not overdone, produces the best conservation areas, from flower-rich lowland meadows, to the Alps of Switzerland. Over-grazing, and monospecific silage production produce degraded riverscapes.

Sacred riverscapes

Sacred riverscapes are many, but usually quite small. In literature they occur primarily in the Arthurian Cycle, either directly Christian (the mystic boat and lake), or a magic compatible with Christianity: finding another world, e.g. by going down a well or over a bridge. It is the association rather than the features which make it sacred.

Features there are, however. Holy wells are found across much of Europe. Some had the power of healing (spa waters improve many diseases, just washing in clean water helps many skin and eye troubles in dirty centuries), others could foretell the future (turn red – with algae?, boil – with underground springs?). Some were wishing wells, usually not also holy, but probably once-holy. Where, e.g. Celtic holy men and women hermits spread over the land their wells often became holy, in remembrance.

The 'Lady of the fountain' is a young (e.g. 16–25) woman often reported near small waters. She is interpreted differently in different ages, e.g. as a nymph or river goddess in classical times, as the Madonna after *c.* AD 1000. But in Hungary, she is still known as the Woman of the Wells. Where she is seen a holy place may follow, even as recently as the mid 1980s at Girgenti in Malta.

Larger riverscape features include the Pilgrim's Ways. One along the North Downs to Canterbury became major after the killing of Thomas a-Becket in 1220. It is now known as Chaucer's Way after Chaucer's poem about this pilgrimage; and the Way from near Siggiewi up to the hill Chapel of the Annunciation (and its holy well) still visited with ceremony on Good Friday, in Malta. In Ireland, various Ways of St Patrick lead to hill-tops (which ones were trodden by the Saint remains uncertain).

For whenever a saint has dwelt, wherever a martyr has given his blood for the blood of Christ
There is holy ground, and the sanctity shall not depart from it
Though armies trample over it, though sightseers come with guide-books looking over it . . .
From that ground springs that which forever renews the earth. (T. S. Eliot)

Where the holy, or doubtfully so, are murdered by river, or spring, the place often becomes sacred because a spring wells up after the event, e.g. where St Erik was killed at Uppsala. The same may occur where there was a major religious event, e.g. St Bernadette's vision, by the rubbish tip of Lourdes, led to the upwelling of a spring. Before drainage, there was much water in the land, moving in flow paths, some near the surface. The weight of many people coming to witness or gawp can alter these paths and lead to water springing up. Nature miracles may be a miracle in timing, but are likely to have a natural explanation.

St Winifrid's Well, in Wales, was said to have sprung up where Winifrid was murdered, but in fact the spring is too big, and must have been there before. The same applies to the three springs in the place outside Rome where, by tradition, St Paul was beheaded.

The greater the fame of the sacred place, the more the influence it has on the riverscape, on the hospitality industry, communications, souvenir-sellers, housing. The English local holy well may be in the churchyard wall, the church having been built by an already-holy well: Christianising the pagan. Where it is separate, it may have been dried, destroyed, forgotten: or it may still attract pilgrims. Decorating wells with flowers goes back to at least Roman times. In Derbyshire at Ascension-tide there is a special decoration, sticking petals, leaves and stones to make sacred pictures on backings of clay. This started in thanks for the lifting of a drought in 1615, but is now more for tradition and tourists. The pictures now are still on wells, but also on standpipes or other taps or just anything facing roads. Many springs and small rivers had goddesses once (while the fiercer large rivers tended to have gods).

Some cathedrals are the principal churches of river towns (e.g. Ely, London, Norwich, York). These were abbey churches, and abbeys were great enterprises, so they and their wharves and water-related activities were separate from those of the populace. On the continent, river town cathedrals include Cologne.

Invaded riverscapes

The invaded riverscape is well shown by Gozo, Maltese Islands. For a while (around 1500) raiding was so bad that the population dwelt in the heavily fortified Citadel, in the centre of the Island, on a plateau. Consequently fishing was mainly from the nearest harbours, and cultivation was within walking distance of the Citadel. Cultivation, so riverscape, was moulded by the outside (and real) threat of being carried into slavery.

A riverscape dominated by more interesting defence is R. Kbir, Malta (Chapter 2). This was never abandoned, but was both protected and threatened, for centuries. The Grand Harbour estuary which had good harbourage since sailing began, has been defended for millennia. In many periods, though, boats could slip through under cover of night, and go up the Kbir estuary, through the desolate marsh river. From this, raiders could advance, hidden, up the gorges and valleys, to two (ex-fortified, but poor) villages and their farm lands around and possibly even to the old and garrisoned capital, Mdina. Maltese criminals could also live hidden in the gorges, and steal in a lesser way. Protection was given:

- from the forts on the Great Plateau above, looking down into the valleys;
- by defensive walls and patterns of the villages and the highly defended Mdina;
- by defensive farmhouses as the country became safer. These had thick walls and arrow-slit windows and, in the most dangerous part, entry to the first floor, where people hid, was only by a removable ladder;
- by putting small horse patrols in the valley which could send for help, and deal with the trouble, if minor;
- by keeping stores, a flour mill, etc., in remote caves in the Second World War.

In the R. Kbir riverscape, the fortifications are an integral part of the riverscape. The same importance of fortifications applies to, say, R. Rhine. The gorge in the middle section, home to warring nobles, has walled river villages, resistant to attack; and also trading villages less fortified and with great wharfs. Soldiers inhabited River Towers, which were usually small and at the main point of access (so well placed for receiving tolls, also) and the main Forts above, overlooking the river and gorge. This mile after mile of steep slopes and gorges, all fortified, and the river with its boats below, makes a striking riverscape. In great contrast is the plateau above the river. This is the flat lowland, cultivation is often poor (infertile) and exposed, and there are no old villages and forts. Wealth was great. It came with the Rhine and the riverscape, not with the lowland plateau.

On a lesser scale, all river settlements liable to raids or invasion had defences when needed. Uppsala in Sweden, site of many offensive expeditions is itself defended, firstly in the old city with (as usual) the cathedral above, and secondly, downstream with the later royal castle, though the present defences of that are late, being ornamental rather than useful.

Towns where the Vikings came to (rather than from) were first razed, then defended. In England it is thought Alfred the Great (in the mid-eighth century) was the first to defend rivers with forts on both banks, and this became the standard defence against Vikings, who were the only major European invaders travelling by river. The basic river town (see above) is built on one side of the river, maybe just spilling over on to the other. Not so the towns fearing Viking attack. Whether York, Norwich or Florence, there is a small but equally fortified and equally early fortified, part on the other side. The Arno defences for Florence were mighty, including a slide passable only with a winch. The fear in Florence was justified, the Vikings having sacked downstream Pisa, but they did not in fact return for Florence. The English, with their well-known habit of being prepared to win the last war but one, also only finished their town defences after the Vikings were no longer attacking. These main trading towns contained much plunder and were rich enough to defend themselves. Lesser settlements could not do so. Monasteries usually would not defend themselves and the Viking devastation of monasteries down eastern England was enough to lose the civilised arts and delay progress.

Diversions

Rivers have been and are diverted to new channels in storms and diverted from natural to man-made channels. Obviously, this affects the riverscape, particularly where the diversions are major or in formerly-little used places. Natural diversions upset property boundaries! This may be just ordinary small movement. In 1198, though, the main entry to the east of England, R. Great Ouse, had its path diverted to bypass the important port of Wisbech and debouch at King's Lynn, formerly a fishing village, soon to be a great European port. The river to the large and excellent port of Bruges, bringing sea trade, shoaled up, and though a new channel was dug, the pre-eminence of trading there was lost, other river ports developing to take the surplus trade. Such changes have a major effect on settlements, and a lesser one on river patterns.

Diversions, or lack of them, are now done more by people, who want to keep rivers stable, and often in only one channel (though other braids may have been kept for, say, navigation).

When water mills were built they were usually on the main river, e.g. King's Mill, R. Cam. However, the town of Cambridge diverted the river to also run alongside the town and turn a Town Mill also. Such diversions reach a higher level than the main river and then drop down a weir or dam, to rejoin the main river. When a small stream was diverted to form a mill lode, of course, above the valley bottom, now often only this remains. The original stream, in the valley base, is dried and gone, but the diversion, which had been puddled and had its banks maintained well into the nineteenth century, still flows.

Quite a lot of water is needed to turn most commercial mills. Diversions may be much smaller for watering houses (Fig. 12.2) and so most were easily dried and have gone, recently. The most complex are the water meadows (see above). In these, numerous man-made rivulets, the hatches on the river, and their control of silting and water alters the riverscape: and on most counts, improves it.

Another less complex system is that found more on the continent. When a stream enters a valley, diversions are taken off to each side, at frequent intervals, at different levels. Each diversion runs along a gentle slope at the side of the valley, watering the fields. There is another irrigation diversion, a little downslope and parallel, and so on. The whole valley is thus watered: easily. The riverscape is changed, for a much greater production of crops.

Some major diversions are made to water villages. Like the mill lodes, the diversion runs at a higher level than the main stream.

The most complex system is perhaps Madeira, which has plenty of rain in its alpine centre, but little in the fertile lowlands below. A complex, interconnecting and closable system of well-made diversion channels (levadas) takes water from the alps to the coast, and waters both crops and settlements. The water is apportioned, giving one farmer's field irrigation for, say, 2 hours twice a week. This system was constructed relatively late, when the Portuguese settled the island in the sixteenth century.

Watered land, particularly in dry summers, has a very different aspect because of the difference in vegetation; so the riverscape of well-irrigated land is substantially changed, as in Madeira and Malta.

Ornamental diversions have always been made for gardens. The two main periods, though, were Arab times in Mediterranean Europe, and in a different style, the eighteenth-century ornamental, which spread across temperate (and south) Europe.

Water supply

A few of the many types of structures used to supply water are shown in Fig. 12.4. Most old and a few new ones enhance the riverscape.

River valleys are also good positions for other communications, pipes for sewage, water, oil, gas, electricity pylons, etc. Electricity generation is the largest single use of water in developed countries, not just for hydropower, but even more for cooling.

300   The riverscape and the river

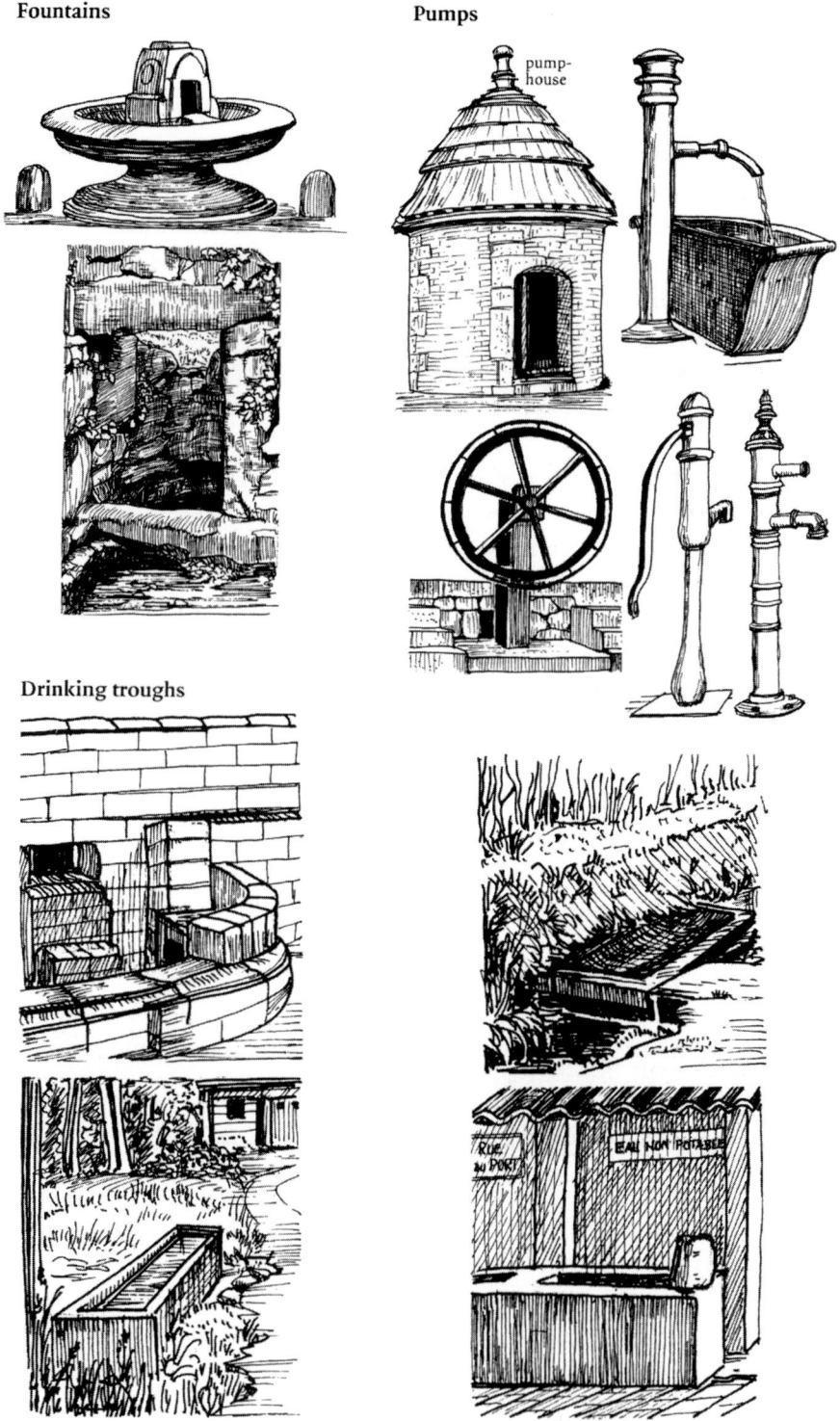

Fig. 12.4. Structures for water supply (Y. Bower in Haslam, 1991). A selection of the very wide variety of constructions delivering water (water carts omitted).

Resources III. Settlements and constructions 301

Cattle-drinkers

Laundry

Natural course to right, diversion channel to water village left

Reservoirs

Fig. 12.4. (*cont.*)

Aqueducts

Water towers

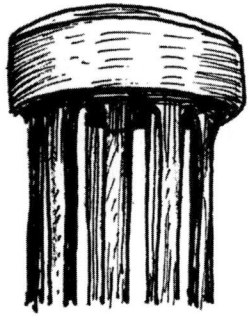  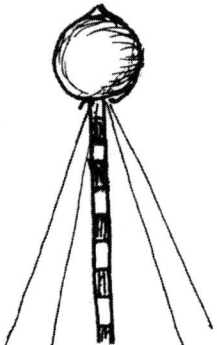

Fig. 12.4. (cont.)

Stepping Stones

Fords

Fig. 12.5. Crossing the river (Y. Bower in Haslam, 1991). A selection of the many ways: stepping stones, fords, ferries and bridges (present-day bridges date from Roman to modern).

Crossing the river

When most folk walked, and none went fast, frequent crossings of the river were necessary. They varied from the main Way out of a town, to a dairy-maid crossing to milk cows. Roman bridges are still extant, and often in places where thy are still in regular use. Stone bridges, Roman built, were not common again until later mediaeval times. Wood is, of course, still used, but for minor bridges.

Roman fords, also may still be in use (e.g. in Wiltshire). And particularly in East Anglia, there are still plenty of (now-tarmacked) fords for wheeled traffic with foot bridges beside. Hardy highland races forded rivers much later than settled and more prosperous folk. Figure 12.5 shows some ways of crossing the

304 The riverscape and the river

Ferries

Bridges

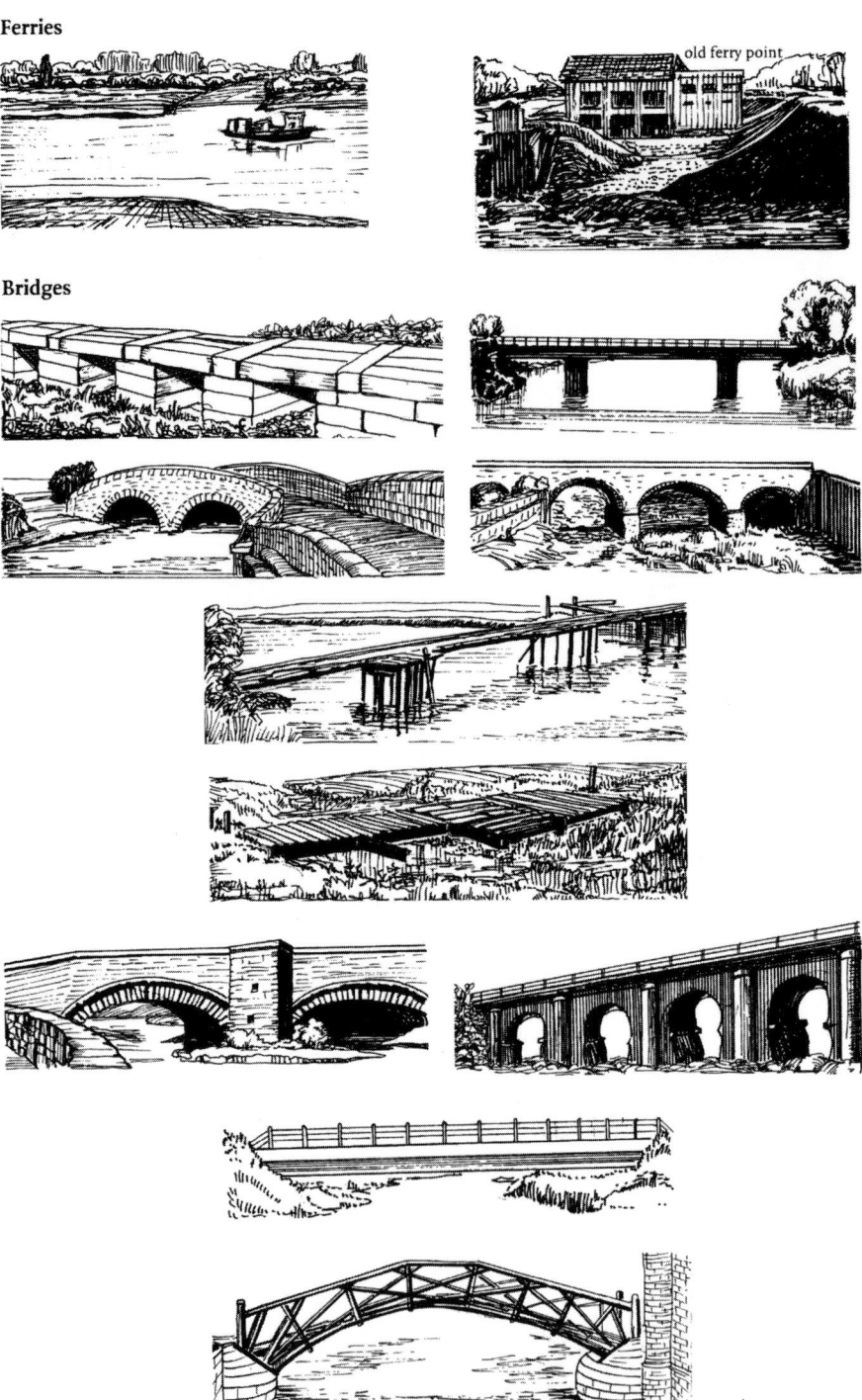

Fig. 12.5. (cont.)

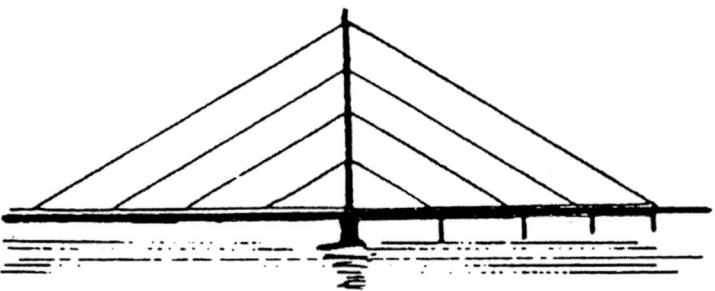

Fig. 12.5. (*cont.*)

river. Town bridges fade into the town riverscape but high modern bridges are prominent riverscape features anywhere. At the opposite extreme, small streams often flow through pipes under roads.

Ferries used to be numerous, but are increasingly replaced by bridges, as are fords. However, ferries and fords often leave traces. Ferries, as on the Rhône, Rhine and Trent, often have their ferry points left when these are no longer working: shapes cut into the bank, and inns (now sometimes houses or farms).

Bridges, both old and new can greatly enhance a riverscape, in the near and medium distance. They are a focal point over *the* focal line of the river. Contemplating a scene with a bridge, or contemplating it from the bridge, is good for mood, temper, health and clear thinking. It was most commonly done by British and Danes, but the immense increase in traffic has restricted the British to more remote bridges. The bridge, its stones, the stream, its tall emergents or rocks, its mysterious green and fishy depths, the trees and fields around: here is the riverscape to admire.

A sad tale illustrates bridge and river development in Malta. Until the seventeenth century, Mdina, in the centre, was the capital. On each stream leading from coast to garrison, a ring round Mdina, there was a foot/horse bridge for quick travel on an alarm. Two of these stand forlorn, rebuilt many times, now above the dredged, sunk and partly dried rivers and not connected to the road. One fell. Most of its stones were removed by farmers, and some concrete was poured (accidentally?) on the remainder. The stream is only storm-wet. One is quite lost. Another was quite lost in *c.* 2000 – too late to plead ignorance! – when it was unnecessarily taken away from beside the current bridge when that bridge was re-built. The last bridge awaits the same fate. (When the author explained their value to the relevant authority, it was to find no one knew or cared about ancient bridges, whose predecessors probably date from Roman, if not Punic times.)

The river unites, the land divides, is an old English saying, reflecting how much better water transport used to be, than land. Even with improved roads, in the earlier nineteenth century, English freight tended to go by water. The railways, after about 1840, then took it instead. The continent was more sensible, preserving freight transport by water on the major highways even to this day. France, in particular, built rail–river, and rail–canal links, for easy trans-shipment.

The English word 'rival' originally meant those living on opposite sides of a river: and too often arguing about riparian rights (access, fishing, boats, weirs) (see Haslam, 1991).

13

The harsh riverscape

(Cultivating a Highland croft)

> The byre and stacks in ordered row
> The means of life affording show.
> With crooked spade or coulter-vee
> Upturned the sparse deep ground
> 'Mid bog and rock so pressingly
> The run-rig strips abound.
> And lazy-beds of labour slow
> Cover the hillside slopes below . . .
> With sheep nose-down on pasture lea
> And cattle by rough bound.
> (in McLean, 1961)

Troutbeck Tongue is uncanny, a place of silences and whispering echoes. It is a mighty tableland between two streams. They rise together, north of the Tongue, in one maze of bogs and pools . . . They meet and unite below the southern crags, making the tableland almost an island, an island haunted by the sounds that creep in running water . . . From the highest point of the Tongue I could look over the whole expanse, Woundale and the Standing Stones; Sadghyll and the hut circles; the cairns built by the stone men; the Roman road; Hollilands and Swansdale named by the Norseman; and the walls of the deer park stretching for miles.

(Potter in Lane, 1968).

> O God of the heaving sea
> Give the wave fertility
> Weed for enriching the ground
> Our life-giving pouring sound
> (in McLean, 1961)

[Iona Prayer for seaweed, showing how important it was for fertilising the Scottish Highlands fields: and that the best fertiliser was from the sea, not the land]

Their slain shall fill their valleys and brooks, and the river shall be filled with their dead, till it overflow.

(Judith, 2, 8.)

Introduction

Beatrix Potter (of Peter Rabbit fame) here describes a harsh upper river in the English Lake District, the wet marsh and pools and streams on the plateau, the craggy rocks, the lack of cultivation or other land use (apart from light rough grazing), the emptiness; yet, there are the remains of the civilisations of the past, from prehistoric to Norman, which have now passed. The harshness now left is very difficult for settlement and cultivation (particularly without drainage, fertiliser and preferably a little climate warming (see Table 2.1), at the top of exposed hills, even though only half way to the north of Britain.

Harshness can, therefore, be geomorphological and climatic, and can change over time with climate and settlement. It is difficult to define a harsh riverscape, though easy to recognise it. There is difficulty in living there, it requires particularly hard work to produce a good living from the land, and consequently population is usually low. There is a concomitant wish to use any alternative resources, such as fish, minerals or timber. Most riverscapes were originally harsh for European peoples, because of the Ice Age, the later forests, heavy ground when there is no good plough, over-steep slopes, large wetlands, and other unsuitable factors. Over several millennia, most of this harshness has been reduced by the farming community.

The absence of fresh water is an absolute: the habitat is too harsh.

People may spread into harsh areas because of the spirit of adventure, of population pressure or persecution from behind, and from the decree of rulers. What happens depends partly on the place, but also on the enterprise of the people. In the R. Nene Valley, an English trading river, in the nineteenth century, mortality is six times the English average (Clarke, 1854–5): with low-lying foggy land, and houses liable to flood, disease was rife. With draining, the mortality rate in the Isle of Ely dropped, between 1796 and 1825, from 1 in 31 to 1 in 47, about the English average. Over in the trading towns of the Low Countries, where people strove for trade, and the wealth and civilisation it brings, the population was active and healthy. (The study of expanding populations, and those becoming active now, and the contrast to sleepy and decaying populations is outside the scope of this book.)

Population can increase suddenly in a bad location because a new resource, such as uranium or diamonds or inventers in Information Technology are found there. The land cannot support the new population, and either there is money from the resource for communication and imported food, or the population leaves.

Many factors affect population, including slope, aspect, geomorphology, rock type, soil and water regimes and climate. An example of lack of water is Malta. The population, up to 1800 was not over 100 000 and without modern demands, water was adequate and sustainable. By 2000, with a water-demanding population of *c.* 400 000, reverse osmosis had been invented, and supplied half the mains water. Without it, or without imported water, emigration and/or sickness would result. Malta is not an obviously harsh riverscape: but is one with a very harsh limit.

Case studies

This chapter illustrates harsh riverscapes of different kinds by means of case studies.

Sweden (Fig 13.1)

Sweden is a good example partly because of excellent descriptions (Sporrong *et al.*, 1995). Being well north (*c.* 55–66° N), unfavourable factors such as cold winters, poor soil and north aspect are more important than further south, and are more so the further north and the higher the altitude. Sweden is a prosperous, and not an industrial, country. In most of it, a good or reasonable living can be obtained from the land.

After the Ice Age, the inland ice melted, and sea level rose before again sinking, leaving a band up to 300 m wide by the sea, which is often unproductive. (This line gives an important natural feature.)

Inland, calcareous till is the earliest cultivated land, the soil being fertile and reasonably light. River and ice deposits are also easily cultivable.

Meadows (so livestock) are the motor of the Swedish landscape, (Chapter 11) and much exceed arable. Forest is also abundant, and is now used for grazing, timber, fuel and hunting. Man changes land use, and vegetation follows suit. Customs, ideas, values and decisions influence riverscapes, and, differ regionally.

- *South Skåne* is near Denmark, and like it has a chequerboard field pattern with tributaries diverted around them. Most have dried (like England, Chapter 15). This is unique in Sweden: an over-cultivated, low heritage steppe. However, the valleys remain in good condition, with

310 The riverscape and the river

(a)

Fig. 13.1. Sweden (S.E.). These are not very harsh riverscapes, but living is, in part, limited by latitude. More care is taken over aspects, soil type, easily drained soil etc., than is needed further south. (a) Meadow in valley bottom, on land (pre-drainage) fed by river sediment. Wooded above, probably on less fertile glacial till. (b) Undrained valley with lake and wetland. (c) Semi-abandoned meadow in valley base, semi-abandoned arable rising to dry wooded ground with settlement. (d) Similar but both meadow and arable are in use, and settlement is a village (with, as is typical, farms and houses separated on the crown of the rise). (e) unusually much-drained tributary leading to river at valley bottom. (f) Wider agricultural plain, rectangular fields, small, well-channelled river.

rivers dammed for meadow irrigation. The rivers are semi-channelled, and sparse, sparse because of the fertile, permeable soil allowing the water to sink. The villages are small (10–52 farms) and near water, so are often low-lying. There is the usual Swedish pattern of low meadows, medium-level crops and high-level woods. There may also be almost a pond landscape with old marl pits, dug for fertiliser. The Stone Age fields were small strips.
- *South Swedish highlands*. Here soil, excess water, and climate may be limiting. Settlements and arable are on dry warm slopes and dry hill tops with woods above agriculture. These warm slopes, hill tops and good *natural* drainage are not limiting factors met earlier in this book. Low

(b)

(c)

Fig. 13.1. (*cont.*)

(d)

(e)

Fig. 13.1. (cont.)

(f)

Fig. 13.1. *(cont.)*

land is wet meadow (unless it is drained and cultivated). Much hay and marsh hay fodder is produced.
- *The large islands in the Baltic* are interesting in having water seepage lines on the banks of sand and gravel. This water is led via underground fissures to settlements. The villages are in a fish-bone, or feather pattern, farms having land on their own side of the main road. Culture, water resources and climate therefore much influence riverscapes in their land use and settlement pattern.
- *East Sweden* is limestone, with clay till and drumlins. Villages are on south slopes in mosaics, with small winding roads. Lakes and wetlands are on the valley bottoms, meadow and arable are in the valleys, with outfields and forests above. Flood grass makes good fodder.
- *Upper Dalarn* includes the large wet silt plain of R. Dalälven, which, unlike the higher till, is fertile. Fields are and were narrow strips. Dry meadow is on the slopes, with forest above, and the hills are high enough to have saeters (summer pastures).
- *West Sweden* has drained much of its wet meadows to grow arable (like too much of the rest of Europe). The rolling landscape has the best meadow as infield. Much, however, has recently been abandoned. New farmers are arriving in parts. The main river valley has cultivable sediment.
- *Cultivated Southern Norrland* is a small piece of coast, with cultivation below the shoreline (see above, 300 m band by sea). Wet meadows are

314   The riverscape and the river

on the lowest level, then grass and arable, then, going higher, wood and pasture, with saeters at the top.

- *The river valleys of Northern Norrland* have dark mighty rivers, with splendid valleys with farms, sawmills, villages, towns and steam mills. The flat valley bottoms are arable and meadow, with forest up behind. Settlement is along the river, usually on the sunny side, and on raised (drier) levées. Moving ice keeps the landscape open. Settlement is small and local to the rivers.
- *Forests of Southern Norrland*. This is mostly forested till and clay. There is ribbon development of meadow and marsh, in open places along rivers. Settlement and arable are on warm, dry south-facing slopes. Conditions are difficult, and there is much de-population.
- *Storsjon District*, in contrast, is influenced by the Gulf Stream. With the warmer climate and calcareous soil, crops are good. Additionally, the area was Norwegian until 1645, so settlement is Norwegian. Farms are isolated, rather than grouped in villages as in Sweden, and field layout is by topography, not by local decree, as in Sweden. This shows how important culture may be, in land use. There are many saeters in the mountains.
- *Interior of North Norrland*. This is high plateau, mountains and foothills. Potatoes grow well in the restricted habitat of steep slopes, till and a suitable angle to the sun. There are vast forests, mines and water. There were flooded hay meadows which are now partly abandoned. Little agriculture remains.

Sweden has some harsh areas, some less so, but nearly all is restricted by the high latitude. Increasingly, in harsher riverscapes, cultivation is more restricted: in soil regime, water regime, aspect, altitude. With one major unfavourable factor (latitude), other potentially limiting factors become major.

A river in southern Spain (Fig. 13.2)

The Rambla del Estrecho river, in contrast, has no shortage of heat and sun, but the riverscape is harsh by lack of water and of soil. Like North Sweden, farming is less attractive than other ways of making a living, and has recently decreased.

There are bare, steep, concave gullied hills, bearing, in more shelter, short maquis and garigue and, locally, even Aleppo pine (*Pinus halepensis*) woods. Olive groves occur down in the lowland on fairly dry places, with local citrus in valleys where there is underground water (stored under the mountains).

(a)

Fig. 13.2. Arid Spain, tributary River Arigo (T. Bone). Harsh riverscape severely limited by lack of water, particularly since recent abstraction. (a) upstream, note hill gullying, general dryness, several ex-farms on the ridge, formerly spring fed. Rough grazing. (b) downstream, where even storm water is still little but substrate unstable. (c) Further downhill, where there is intermittently enough damp for patches of reedswamp: but rarely continuous water. Farm near head of tributary, on spring (main river dry).

Terraces are decaying and little cultivated. Former mining, cultivation and dwellings all used water. There used to be an irrigation system, and underground water, now decayed. Over-use of water has had its usual effect, and water is now short.

When the former care of land ended, gullying increased, rendering reclamation even more difficult.

The river (the studied tributary) now a storm water bed, rises in a high gully, then flows by a (flatter) golf course. Gully streams fall to the plain with close small meanders in grassy (formerly disturbed) garigue, and down into another gully about 15 m deep. This also carries eroding storm flows. There are some wells and a pump house, but the present water level is far down, demonstrating the now unsustainable extraction. Spring water can no longer run, so streams are without long-term, stabilising flow, and storm flows are fiercer and more gullying.

(b)

Fig. 13.2. (cont.)

The next river sector lies through abandoned land. The dryland species on the river bed show water flows seldom. Downstream, shrubby species gradually appear on the banks, these now being more stable. The hills above are more gentle here, and there are sparse farmsteads, though the farming is little. The river level drops low enough to be reached by some underground springs, and there are damp sunk patches with, e.g. *Cyperus* spp. Riversides may be marshy, or without access to water: they bear garigue, but both form a 'green corridor' along the river. Incoming tributaries are still eroding hill gullies.

Further down, the valley widens between the hills, and the river in the valley bottom is hardly drained (dredged). There are occasional pools of stagnant water, as well as marshy patches. Farms are sited above what must have been the flood plain. In only a century here, a riverscape has gone from having flowing water,

(c)

Fig. 13.2. (*cont.*)

farmed land, and flooded bottoms, to being dry and barren! Agriculture has been abandoned. The river is braided, with boulders and gravel. Downstream, signs of settlement increase, derelict farms, derelict aqueduct, and a few actual herds of sheep and goats.

Previously there was little or no gullying, a respectable river flow, and, judging by the irrigation system, both irrigated and dryland crops. This riverscape used to give a fair living from farming. (The size and type of the farmhouses show this.)

No doubt, overmuch water was taken by farmers. If farmers have to stay on the land, there is a limit to what they abstract. The nineteenth-century mineral extraction is probably most to blame, using water indiscriminately. The result was to turn a fairly harsh riverscape with adequate farming into a degraded,

318 The riverscape and the river

Fig. 13.3. Assynt area, N.W. Scotland. Hummock-and-hollow country, with infertile blanket bog, and local infertile grassland on mineral soil. Lochans abundant. Pool riverscape.

eroding, dry one, near-useless for farmers. If the aquifer is rested, and not abstracted for the golf course, farming might again be possible, and below the level of gullying and landslips, garigue, maquis, wood and marshy and grassy communities could gradually spread.

This very dry and water-depleted riverscape contrasts well with the harshness of high latitude in Sweden. (Data kindly supplied by Mrs Tina Bone.)

The north-west Scottish Highlands (Fig. 13.3)

This area is harsh in a different way. While it is north (c. 57–59° N) it has the Gulf Stream for warmth (Palms and other subtropical plants grow at Inverurie gardens), and water is ample.

The gneiss landscape is knobbly, with lumps of rock outcrop rising from a sea of blanket bog interspersed with lochans and local grassy patches. The verses at the head of the chapter illustrate how life was, here. Blanket bog peat is made of Sphagnum moss, which has large absorbent cells able to absorb and retain much water. It grows upwards, dying and compacting below. Over 90% of the bog surface may be water. The peat varies from a few centimetres to 7–8 m deep, and the oldest is probably 5000–6000 years old. The peat is basically rain-fed (and precipitation exceeds evaporation). This ground generally became wetter as the peat spread. The surface is hummock-and-hollow, the hollow being flooded, and water trickling slowly through to gradually gather and form small bog streams. These flow more quickly to form larger streams and rivers. Within the hummock-and-hollow pattern there may also be peat mounds, ridges, drought-sensitive pools and mud-bottom hollows (Haslam, 2003). Being rain-fed, and without root or other connection to mineral soil, nutrients are very low (dystrophic) and there are phenols and other toxins in the peat, so only a few other species can grow (e.g., cotton grass, *Eriophorum* spp., sundew, *Drosera* spp.).

Crofting is possible. Livestock roam the hill at a very low density, and small fields are laboriously created on slopes where mineral soil can be reached, which are preferably south-facing. Meadows, as in Sweden, are the most valuable land. They are sparse, and usually found in valleys, and (see start of chapter) may need much fertilising.

There are a few limestone outcrops, e.g. Applecross, Inchnadamph, where vegetation is green grazing, not brown bog. Cultivation is easier.

Until recently, blanket bog was so difficult to cultivate that this unique habitat was preserved. In the 1970s, it was thought 'good' to drain, fertilise and afforest bog further east, which was destructive and, fortunately not very effective. Until roads were improved after 1940, the best communications were by sea, ships joining fishing villages and isolated (seawards) crofts. Inland, some crofts had only footpaths, and their inhabitants enjoyed solitude. Most castles of clan chiefs were coastal, though one was on the limestone of Inchnadamph.

Such sparsity of inhabitants is new, resulting from the eighteenth century Highland Clearances, followed by many leaving because profitable careers were lacking. Crofting is subsistence living. Before the Clearances, cattle were the main livestock. They are more labour-intensive than the present sheep, and they allow less bog growth (their trampling allows outflow and their grazing is closer to the ground).

The nineteenth- and early twentieth-century isolation of the area was abnormal historically, as indeed is the current tourism, good roads and hotels. Tourists neither cultivate land nor refrain from degrading it.

Beautiful blanket bog and bog streams occur, and as streams get larger, the brown-tinged (peat) water swirling amidst boulders and rock, make an unusual riverscape. There is a backdrop of mountains, not cultivable (so even harsher), but providing mineral soil, and swift small streams. Trees are now infrequent, but patches of, primarily, birch may be by rivers or lochans, and on slopes steep enough to have mineral soil (or thin peat). Basically the riverscapes are bog, with higher land mountains added.

The peat is old, so there has not been large-scale 'intensive' cultivation in historic times. However, in drier (Table 2.1) and more populous times, there must have been much more than now. But cultivation is hard, with low yields. Life, and the riverscape, are harsh. It is not surprising that fighting was a favourite and probably more profitable occupation.

Quite small things can much improve life. In the 1950s, crossing into the estate of the then Duke of Westminster, the landscape changed colour, with more bright green good grassland and – less welcome to a later generation – conifer plantations. The Duke realised both the independence and the poverty of the crofter, and sent a bus round every small road every day. Any who wanted a day's work for the estate rather than his own croft, caught the bus, and worked on land improvement and for his own profit. The Duke, of all the surrounding landowners, alone saw both the potential and the means to regenerate decay. (As he left most of the blanket bog, conservation remained good.)

The harshness comes from the infertile bog and the remoteness from centres of population. Those centres were coastal, and of wealth and importance into the eighteenth century.

Alps (Fig. 13.4)

The Alps were, and are, a harsh environment, cold and snowy in winter because of the altitude, but with bright summer sun because of the latitude. Green grass grows well once forests are cut. In the past century and a half, the region has become prosperous through tourism. It was the English who first, in a big way, discovered the joys of summer scenery and climbing, and of winter snow (skiing).

The Alps now are a European playground. Technically, an alp is a cleared, grassy area high on the mountains, to which cows (and other livestock) are brought in summer, their herders and dairymaids coming too, as in the Scandinavian saeters. The name 'Alp' is now used for the mountains. Farming has continued. This is now grass and some arable (mostly) below, but even with their forests, it is less profitable. The craft towns, necessarily have diminished even more, once there was easy access to the outside world. Previously roads were poor, often closed in winter, and river trade, to places far away was hardly convenient, though regular where possible. Megéve to R. Isére is 30 km, and it is near 100 km further to R. Rhône, though towns such as Grenoble are on the route. The larger settlements are in the valleys. Hamlets and isolated chalets (and even small towns) have spread over the lower grassy slopes. There is a little cultivation, and ducks and other livestock, but most farming is cattle. The custom of taking them high in summer is decreasing. Unlike, say, England, farmers want nutritious grazing without agrochemicals. They find this in flower-rich meadow with at least a dozen species.

(a)

Fig. 13.4. Alps, France. (a) High alps (though well below the excessively harsh peaks). (b) Flower-rich grassland and woodland. Streams often marked by trees. Here all-year chalets are present: higher, there may be saeter chalets for summer use only. (c) Flood plain below forested mountain (with ski lift). Dried and cultivated, but housing on the flood plain is recent! River at far side, catchwater drain (not shown) on near side, diverting incoming stream water from plain.

The huge mountains, the higher with permanent snow and glaciers, have rivers between. Streams may rise from the usual topography patterns, but also may be draining late snowmelt in hollows, or running in permanent snows and under glaciers. Tree bands are often found along (lower altitude) streams: trees can grow, because of the warm summer. Cascades and waterfalls are frequent. Streams may be diverted to supply water for villages or chalets (and flow through chalets which may have duckponds). Due to excessive recreation, disturbance, and erosion, gullying and even land slips are increasing, giving degrading riverscapes: harsh from climate, harsh from people.

In contrast with Sweden, the Alps:

- have good light in the short days of winter
- have only some lowlands, so have less lowland meadow and crops but higher quality of these;
- more high-level grass;

(b)

(c)

Fig. 13.4. (*cont.*)

- with the worse climate, cultivation and settlement in Sweden is more dependent on aspect, soil type, etc., the Alps, on ground not too steep for good grass;
- have immense wealth and disturbance from becoming a European playground;
- use the mountains as their primary defence (Sweden was fortified for attack from the sea, with little inland defences). Large, low areas, e.g. the Lake of Geneva, have castles. The Alps are unsuitable for armies. Peasants prefer to make their own living, or fight in other nations' wars.

Similarities are present, also:

- The riverscape is the main source of wealth (excluding early looting and late tourism).
- Both have the saeter (sheiling) system, the Alps have proportionately more. This maintains grass (rather than forest) up in the mountains;
- River transport is localised. In the Alps, it is by the topography. There is usually a long distance to good navigable waterways, though Berne is on the navigable Rhine, and Geneva on the Rhône. In Sweden it is because coastal communities are easily joined by sea, and most population was there. Minor river uses there were for logging, and to connect Stockholm and Uppsala.

Iceland (Fig. 2.1)

Iceland is in the high latitude of 64–66° N. The primary colonisation was before AD 1000, and from Scandinavia (and Ireland). The soil was fertile, the crops (including grain) good, and the population flourished. Unfortunately, the Little Ice Age meant the crops failed, and grain could not grow until the warming in the mid twentieth century. Wealth, such as it was, came from fish, particularly cod (cod alone is an unsatisfactory diet). Hot volcanic areas and warmer coasts allowed farmers to grow some crops, and they herded livestock in summer up such riverscapes as had adequate grazing. Cattle were on the best grazing in the most fertile area, e.g. lava plateaux, in green oases with broad rivers and winding green corridors. There were horses on the high moors and sheep elsewhere: again, in extreme environments habitat determines the crop.

The rivers themselves, like the rest of the interior, were little altered, so snowmelt and other floods brought fertility and better grazing to the flood plains. Tundra, in life form not dissimilar to short Mediterranean garigue, is the main vegetation.

324 The riverscape and the river

(a)

Fig. 13.5. North Norway (Aüne, Kunstforlag).
(a) Very harsh!
(b) Remote farm at the base of mountains. There are a few low-quality fields, much cotton-grass and a wet sedge-marsh, harvested for general farm use.

Interestingly, most of the isolated farms had their own church, a feature not seen in the other areas considered. Defences were unnecessary in this remote and inaccessible island with little wealth.

North Norway (Fig. 13.5)

Here there are spectacular riverscapes, particularly, but not only in the Lofoten Islands. This area was populous before the Little Ice Age, producing enough food to feed surplus young men (Vikings) though not to provide careers at home. In the colder times, population dropped. Norway developed a culture of isolated farms, unlike the Swedish village. Like Iceland, there are coastal fishing villages (and the later mining town of Hammerfest). Crops are grown near settlements, with rough grazing further in the tundra. The farms are built above flood/snow melt level,. Sedge meadows and basin-mires are in the flood plains and low valleys. As in Iceland, crops are for self-sufficiency not for farming wealth. As usual, poor-quality farming means good conservation of the riverscape!

(b)

Fig. 13.5. (*cont.*)

Corsica (Fig 13.6)

Corsica is in the Mediterranean, but although there is ample water, it has a harsh environment because of its Alpine and forested centre. Unlike Iceland and north Norway, the lowland fringes can produce good crops, but do not all do so now. Inland, there is the occasional alp, as in Switzerland. Even more, though, there is abandonment in favour of coastal and tourist towns. Trees are re-invading, swallowing up the fields and hedges. In the 1790s the island was described as barren.

Rivers rise down and between mountain peaks and in the more gentle slopes of moorland high plateaux. Above perennial flow, there may be a line of bracken or shrubby vegetation marking storm flow. Because of the high rainfall, there are many tributaries at all altitudes. Fountains for man and beast were made where

Fig. 13.6. Corsica. Typical river running off mountains (Iris, Ajaccio).

these cross the steep roads. Down in the deep forests, farmsteads are scattered on flatter land, now often abandoned, with trees invading the hedged 'alps', damper meadows streamside, and irrigation systems above. Terracing occurs, but only little. Unlike Malta, there is plenty of space, and never over-population. The torrential rivers debouch into the plains, where they gradually slow and typical river vegetation appears. The coastal plains were dyked for drainage.

The great forested alpine riverscapes, over such wide areas, are now unique. Population pressure has always been low, and timber, cork and fish were more easily obtained than crops. Climate allows productive forest, steep slopes prevent easy agriculture.

Although there are some coastal town defences, Corsica's population and resources are inadequate to properly defend the island: or to give much comfort to (long-term) occupiers.

Madeira (Fig. 13.7)

This island has a sub-tropical coastal climate and highly fertile cultivation, now especially of bananas. However, these coastal regions are dry, and without human interference, harsh and uncultivable. The lower slopes are terraced, though with scrub, etc. in scarps. Inland there are high jagged mountains (to *c.* 1800 m, rising sharply from sea level). Riverscapes are therefore diverse.

(a)

Fig. 13.7. Madeira. (a) High alps, very harsh riverscape, much bare rock. (b) Mountain stream rising on small high plateau, and being diverted (far) at the start of a levada (irrigation channel). (c) Slope riverscape, levadas, houses on steep slopes and in valley, and intense terrace cultivation of these slopes. Terraces smaller on steeper slopes. (d) Fertile coastal lands, watered by levadas, mostly growing bananas. (Far, too high level for bananas.) (e) Near coast, with 'wetland' of giant reed, *Arundo donax*. River flow still swift from mountains.

Streams rise from the highest mountains and flowing down in the lowlands form jagged gullies with frequent torrential flows. There is gathered run-off on plateaux and lowlands. The high plateaux have extensive grass, lost on steep slopes below where there are forests, both Eucalyptus and traditional.

The environment is harsh because of the inland topography, and the shortage of water on the fertile coastal strip. This last was remedied in the sixteenth century, where the Portuguese not only terraced the lower slopes, but constructed an irrigation system, of open channels, levadas, collecting water from the slopes above (that otherwise going to streams) and leading it gently along contours, mostly with paths beside the channels for maintenance (and now, rambling). The water is led off as necessary, and with small oval sluice doors, allowing irrigations for different periods. In the valleys, rivers are little changed. Braiding and flooding (in suitable topography) are frequent, though, e.g. withy beds are grown. Cultivation is profitable on the terraced slopes.

(b)

Fig. 13.7. (*cont.*)

The tarn landscape of the English Lake District

The tarn landscape is part of the Lake District. The pools are topographically formed, on resistant rock, gouged out by glaciation at the bottom of shallow-soil hills. Dense pools are not in themselves a harsh environment, but usually indicate a low population and no high source of other wealth. The pool space has not been used for other purposes, and the pools are not spreading disease (by mosquitoes, sewage or other pollution, or by causing damp housing). The poolscape therefore still exists.

Wetlands (Fig. 13.8)

These form a quite different kind of harsh environment, as formerly found in the Fenland and Somerset, England, the Netherlands and large areas of France and other countries. Flood is not a good place to live, so settlements tend to be on higher ground around (e.g. Oxmoor) or on small islands rising above the wetland (Fenland). There may be summer grazing on the higher levels.

Down in the wetland there are fish, fowl, reeds for houses, furniture, litter, peat for fuel and indeed salad (watercress), reed and reedmace underground parts for drink, etc. If the wetland is large, its people are not landsmen harvesting part-time, but a separate hardy, independent, isolated, self-sufficient population.

(c)

Fig. 13.7. (*cont.*)

Strife comes when outsiders wish to drain and cultivate the land, displacing the people: who have little choice but to give up their free and independent existence and become dependent labourers.

> *They hang the man and flog the woman,*
> *Who takes the goose from off the common.*
> *But let the greater villain loose*
> *Who takes the common from the goose.* Anon.

Fought-over riverscapes (Fig. 10.2)

A harsh riverscape can also be due entirely to the unpleasantness of people. The Scottish–English border is in a range of rolling hills. For many centuries there were constant raids and invasions from both sides. In the seventeenth

330 The riverscape and the river

(d)

(e)

Fig. 13.7. (cont.)

Fig. 13.8. Wetlands (Norfolk).

century, the crowns were united and peace gradually prevailed. The large riverscapes, the deep valleys (of e.g. Annandale, Tynedale, Redesdale) were the commonest ways across country. Going was easier. There was less bog and cover from enemies. As the soil was more mineral and the valleys were the most farmed (meadow, crops, livestock), so there were also better food stocks for looting.

Defence would certainly have been possible: if one side wanted it enough. But when both sides raided, there was no will, as well as no money, for a well-defended border.

In contrast, a little further south, a wall to separate the wilder north from Roman civilisation, Hadrian's Wall, was constructed in the first century AD and was efficient: one side wanted it. It was effective, and guarded, for some 300 years. A lack of earlier development leads, without new input, to a lack of later development.

The borders have never recovered in population or in land use or wealth. though, of late years, it has been easier to move away than to intensively cultivate northern hills. The Welsh Marches, in contrast, were settled earlier, and have a smiling riverscape.

As mentioned above, around 1900 in Gozo buildings decayed as most of the population slept in the Citadel, fearing a second deportation of the people into slavery. Cultivation would have been mostly within walking distance of the Citadel.

Summary

These are just a few examples of landscapes harsh to the farming or other population there: they include:

- too cold (climatic);
- too little water (climatic and people);
- infertile, or too little soil (geographic);
- too much infertile wet bog peat (geographic: some possibly originally due to mis-management);
- too steep slopes (geographic);
- too much water (climatic or geographic);
- too hot (climatic);
- raiding by soldiers or bandits (people).

14

The tempered or smiling riverscape

A living landscape with economically viable farms is the main requirement for biodiversity and cultural components.

(Ihse & Lindall, 2000)

He looked out over a plain and saw fields and trees and woods – green and golden in the srong sunshine. He saw the silver smoke of a river wandering in a leisurely manner towards the sea, and far away over the treetops, the land tilting up gently into hills, . . . the clouds moved slowly over the shallow, tilted bowl.

(D. E. Stevenson)

I dared to rest, or wander, in a rest
Made sweeter by the step upon the grass,
And view the ground's most gentler dimplement
(As if God's finger touched, but did not press
In making England) such an up and down
A ripple of land, such little hills, the sky
can stoop to tenderly, and the wheatfields climb;
Such nooks of valleys lined with orchards,
Fed full of noises by invisible streams;
And open pastures where you scarcely tell
White daisies from white dew – at intervals.
The mythic oaks and elm-tree standing out
Self-poised upon their prodigy of shade,
I thought my father's land was worthy too
Of being my Shakespeare's

(E. B. Browning)

A little nameless brook that winds between [small meadows] with a course which, in its infinite variety, clearness and rapidity, seems to emulate the bold rivers of the north. . . . Rich tufts of golden marsh marigolds which grow on its margin . . . so clear, so wide, so shallow [and] dashing . . . in a torrent deep and narrow . . . sleeping, half-hidden beneath the alders and wild roses . . . flags, lilies and other aquatic plants almost cover the surface. Trout . . . spring to the surface for the summer flies. (The lily, as another quote shows, is . . . 'the snowy water lily, the purest of flowers', i.e. Nymphaea alba, widespread in clean nineteenth century rivers, almost vanished by the mid-twentieth century.) (Berks, Mitford, M. R., 1829–32. Our Village.)

Introduction

'Smiling' is the traditional term. Nowadays, 'by the sweat of thy hands shalt thou eat bread' (Gen. 3:19) is no longer considered a basic fact or basic good of humanity. The immensely hard work put, and sometimes still put, into keeping a riverscape fertile and productive is not thought of as 'smiling'. 'Tempered', the riverscape made more equable and pleasant for people, is perhaps the better term.

Harsh and tempered riverscapes of course intergrade, and can both occur in a small area (e.g. good crops and rich settlements in broad river valleys, and rough grazing on exposed, boggy distant hill tops).

The love of the smiling riverscape is peculiarly English. The Norwegians love and draw inspiration from their mountains (and accompanying valleys). Kilted Scots appear through mist on the purple-clad hill. It is the English who are inspired by the running stream, the green meadow, fair crops of grain and vegetable, the village nestling in the valley. An example is:

Down there in the valley, look!
Close beside the winding brook,
Sheltered warm, from the storm,
What a pretty farm house.
                    (Anon)

Here is the well-off farm, along a small stream in the valley (for watering, cooking, cleaning and for all the livestock), the implied well-farmed land. This is the lowland English riverscape. Here, and in the quotes above, is the charm of the lowland, the land dimpled with valleys, their streams, and the habitat around: flower-rich meadows, now destroyed. Just because other nations find these less inspiring, their scientific and ecological interest is no less. In fact, these days in, say, Denmark and the Netherlands, it is more.

Neolithic fields are locally frequent in many parts of Europe. These are small, oblong and narrow, on the more easily-worked ground. Some are terraced. This is the first substantial impact of people on the European riverscape. From then on, impact and changes increased. Fields spread, cultivation intensified, and water resources, rivers and settlements were more developed. There is a point where a potentially smiling riverscape is too un-tempered to be pleasant, another where it has been over-tempered (e.g. built over with rivers underground).

The cultural riverscape is a dynamic system. The Evesham site described in Chapter 12 had (1) Neolithic fields, expanded by the Romans; (2) Anglo Saxon fields; (3) eighteenth century Enclosure Act changes; and (4) twentieth century intensification of cultivation. Other alterations have indeed changed vegetation and roads (Chapter 9), but the basic pattern remained (whether wild, crops, or field weeds).

Over Europe as a whole, wealth and the comfort and pleasantness it brings, came primarily from farming. It came directly from the food grown, and indirectly, from what that food brought in craft, other goods, education and the other arts of civilisation which are found in towns, built on the wealth of the country. Since food is basic, farm wealth continues. But, its general importance to wealth lessens with time as manufactures and services increase.

The bringing of outside, or non-farming, wealth to a riverscape may make a great difference to the population it is able to support, its behaviour (standard of culture) and its function. These, in turn, greatly influence building, roads and other riverscape constructions. This may be the wealth of education of the farmers, or that from farming technology, or that from trade or the siting of a new town or industry.

Landscape does not determine human endeavour, but it has set limits to human activities and has directed human strategies (Prefill & Volkman, 1999). The limits and the strategies, though, vary over time and with technology, as well as the peoples' interests.

River trade

River towns and villages may have kept their river status (though for communications rivers are of less importance than road, rail and air), e.g. Vienna, Budapest, Lyon, Strasbourg.

Lyon exhibits a common pattern of city movement over time, as boats get bigger and wealth gets greater: (1) Old City, west of R. Saone; (2) spreading to east of the river; (3) and on to the converging Rhône. After, the railways came, downstream, on the combined river. (4) In the early stages the wealthy merchants' houses were by the river. Latterly, the wealthy merchants lived elsewhere and the trading area became a depressing industrial site. Strasbourg was similar. Originally, trade came to the city centre, later to the railway, and later still also to new docks closer to the Rhine, separate from the town. River towns may still use water transport for freight, e.g. Huy on the Meuse, and recent towns may have been built with canal and industry on one side and housing and motorway on the other, e.g. Maasland. Then there are the towns which have forgotten and ignored their trading heritage, e.g. Saffron Walden, Godmanchester, England, Itzehoe and its smaller upstream associate, Kellinghauser, N. Germany.

Another group of settlements have been by-passed (see Chapter 12). The building of the Twenthe Kanaal left Lochem as a relic, the trade moving to the new and better route. As, two centuries earlier, the Stour canal left Stoke-by-Nayland, England. Decay can also come by the lessening and stopping of river trade, as happened throughout lowland England after the *c.* 1840 coming of the railways. Former major trading towns on the continent, like Zutphen and Cologne, lost their trade gradually, keeping it longer than their upstream satellites: Namur longer than Dinant, Paris than Bray sur Seine, for example. Some of these 'lost ways' develop recreational navigation, and flourish (e.g. Ely, England, Les Roches, France). It is interesting when, of a pair of riverside villages, the trading one is now flourishing with a recreational marina, while the other, formerly a market village has not found a new rôle and is stagnant. Some villages which 'time has passed by' find a quite new rôle, say as a dormitory town or theme park. Others diminish, like Dinant, Belgium or Bray-sur-Seine.

River Thames (Fig. 14.1)

The River's Tale

I walk my beat before London Town,
Five hours up and seven down
Up I go and I end my run
At Tide–end–town which is Teddington . . .
But I'd have you know that these waters of mine
Were once a branch of the River Rhine . . .
And I remember like yesterday
The earliest Cockney who came my way . . .
He was death to feather and fin and fur
He trapped my beavers at Westminster
He netted my salmon, he hunted my deer
He killed my herons off Lambeth Pier . . .
And Norseman and Negro and Gaul and Greek
Drank with the Britons in Barking Creek,
And life was gay, and the world was new
And I was a mile across at Kew!
But the Roman came with a heavy hand
And bridged and roaded and ruled the land
Rudyard Kipling

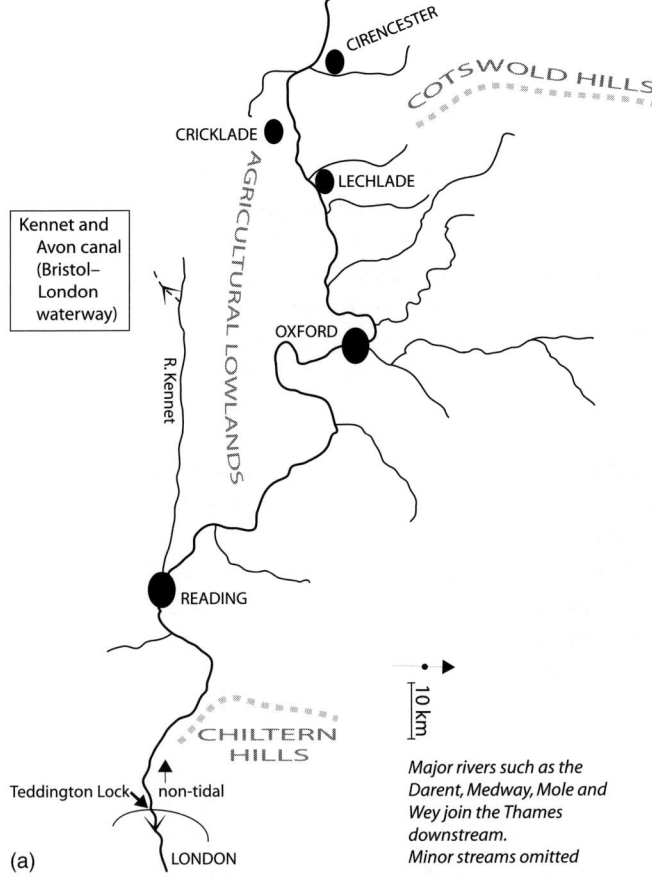

Fig. 14.1. The valley of River Thames, England. (a) One of the sources of R. Thames, a winterbourne in a (fairly flower-rich) meadow, 1971. Now dried and gone. (b) Upper river, little-drained, not straightened (SKYSCAN). (c) Drained tributary (R. Cole), Cotswolds, settlement above. (d) Well-drained, smooth meanders, riverside ploughed (SKYSCAN). (e) Less-drained, wetland (ex-meadow?) foreground, pasture centre, arable – and farm – away from river. (f) Godstow, with (right) ancient nunnery and its former wharf present lock, and island perhaps natural, perhaps a 'City Island' made by the boats eroding the wharf. Arable behind. On the right, Port Meadows is ancient and protected common land (SKYSCAN). (g) Near the Chiltern Hills.

The Reeds of Runnymede

At Runnymede, at Runnymede
   What say the reeds at Runnymede?
The lissom reeds that give and take,
That bend so far, but never break,
They keeps the sleepy Thames awake
   With tales of John at Runnymede.

The riverscape and the river

(b)

Fig. 14.1. (cont.)

> At Runnymede, at Runnymede,
> Your rights were won at Runnymede!
> No freeman shall be fined or bound,
>   Or dispossessed of freehold ground,
> Except by lawful judgment found
> And passed upon him by his peers.
> Forget not, after all these years,
>   The Charter Signed at Runnymede.
>   Rudyard Kipling

The R. Thames, England's best known river, has been a major highway throughout historical times, until recently. From London, the capital City since the later Roman period, the Thames leads both seawards to the North Sea

(c)

Fig. 14.1. (*cont.*)

(St George's Channel) and coastal towns in England and overseas, and inland and westwards through settled country and towns like Windsor, Oxford, Reading, and Henley. The 'Navigation', with tow path and early locks, was constructed in the seventeenth and eighteenth centuries up to Cricklade and Lechlade, only *c.* 50 km from the west coast. Smaller boats could travel nearly to the sources, up to 15 km further along various tributaries. It was only *c.* 20–30 km from the Avon, leading to Bath and Bristol and the ocean trade. This was the east–west crossing of the south of the kingdom. Much has been written on the Thames, its usefulness, its beauty and its history (e.g. Thacker, 1909, 1914; Mackay, 1992).

A stone monument marks the Official Source of R. Thames: in a now-dry field. A 1970s source in pleasing green meadows was a winterbourne, flowing all winter and parts of summers. This little stream had not then been dredged. This deplorable water loss is, of course, due to abstraction from the aquifer and drainage of the land. The hills of the (oolite) Cotswolds typically have gentle valleys, with good limestone streams (unless dredged and polluted). They have immense charm, and this is added to by the buildings in yellow Cotswold stone. Typical village names include: Stow-on-the-Wold, Midsomer Norton, Duntisbourne, Abbots Frampton, Mansell and Bourton-on-the-Water. Most still

340   The riverscape and the river

(d)

Fig. 14.1. (*cont.*)

have streams, and most east-flowing brooks eventually join the Thames, near Oxford. The main Thames, rising south and east, is dying.

From the Cotswold hills, the Thames flows down into lowlands, where it stays, except when passing through the chalk Chiltern hills, for its course to the sea. Grass and sheep are typical here: together, by the river, with the riverside gravel extraction works, extracting huge amounts. These affect the valley bottom and riverscape, but not, fortunately, the river.

The Thames was highly developed. It carried food, other freight and people. Weirs and mills were numerous, holding up water, helping boat passage. When

(e)

Fig. 14.1. (*cont.*)

these were not enough, and boats were held up by shoals, cattle could be hired to stand in the water and raise its level.

Ferries were also numerous, since most people walked, and even horse power is much slower than motor power. Ferries only decreased when roads became better and traffic faster (it is slow unloading and loading a ferry). Fords were made wherever the river was sufficiently shallow. (Undredged rivers can be surprisingly shallow, even where not shoaled.) Bridges were few and mostly in towns. There were enough ferries. More recently, motorway and railway bridges have been built.

Inns, hotels, restaurants peppered the riverside, offering meals and beds to all classes of people from gentry to the unfortunate much-despised watermen. Trading boats continued on the Thames into the twentieth century, longer than main freight in most of England, as the highway was such a major one. Unfortunately, drastic twentieth-century channel works mean only a few riverside constructions remain.

In Cricklade, the trading part of the town is, of course, by the river, and the manor house and others are further off, which is typical for England. An eighteenth-century towpath runs downstream from Cricklade. Lydwell mostly

(f)

Fig. 14.1. (cont.)

still has water (though it is now pumped up) in a marsh recorded in 931 as 'swampy and watery, giving grazing for up to 3000 ewes'. Many springs rose from the aquifer. Now the marshes are dry, from abstraction and drainage.

Nar Meadow is a relic flower-rich meadow.

The next stretch has, typically for a small river, a small flood plain. Much of this is drained, its channels are deepened, and the plain is used for arable. More

(g)

Fig. 14.1. (*cont.*)

abstraction and draining would be unnecessary. Because of the plain, villages and farms, in contrast to further upstream, are no longer on the river, but just up the slope at the edge of the plain above the flood level. The land rises only slightly, and has (over-drained but good-quality) streams winding to the Thames, and bushes, copses and isolated trees beside them. The Thames itself has over-many alien weeping willows.

As the river gets larger, it becomes too expensive to straighten and so it still meanders in its now wide plain. Hedges, trees and mixed farming (crops, ley, a little meadow) are on and above the plain. Villages are usually above; though where possible, they are close to the (former) ford or ferry. Flood protection has removed wetlands and reedswamps.

Downstream the enlarged river used to flood more, so settlements were sited yet higher on the slope, to keep above flood level. River trading villages (e.g. Stanton Harcourt) and trading towns (e.g. Maidenhead, Wallingford) fringe the Thames intermittently. Some were partly craft towns (e.g. Henley). Good cultivation, traded wealth and easy access to London made this, the middle of England, a centre of elegance and culture. The mediaeval University of Oxford is the oldest in England. Wallingford contains the memorial to the king who 'made' England, Alfred the Great.

Braiding in the river may mean one channel had a mill or lock, and a second channel was made use of to prevent blocking boats. Or a second channel may have been dug to bypass the block.

Farming is excellent, but the river is over-managed. Pollards are present.

The Thames next runs in a groove in the Chiltern hills. The land is pleasantly wooded, and pleasantly farmed, but the impact of increased building and, importantly, recreation on the river are significant. Riparian trees are mostly by villages, having been cleared off, in the country. Behind, villages are sited beside streams in the little valleys above, so getting the advantages of both river and stream (except that of trading). Recent building in the villages is down on the drained plain. The old centres of town, village, hamlet and isolated farm are all related to the stream, whatever may have happened in the twentieth century. In the Chiltern hills, tributaries are good chalk streams above, but in the plain are severely drained.

The suburbs of Reading start all too soon, ending the high-quality part of the rural Thames. From here, suburbs and towns extend most of the way to London. There are still flood meadows and the, here very characteristic, eyots (islets) in the river.

Downstream, the river is recreational, with numerous summer houses, moorings, managed banks. Hampton Court Palace (sixteenth century) was designed for entry by river from London, and still looks magnificent. London approaches, and Teddington Lock now separates the freshwater Thames (above) from the tidal Thames. Old village centres (e.g. Putney) and large green areas (e.g. Kew Gardens) disappear as the river flows to central Westminster and London. London was once the main seaport of the kingdom. Now the dock areas are partly re-built as offices and dwellings. Here is an Awful Warning. When container shipping came in, the London dockers refused to handle them. Thus much of the trade moved elsewhere, largely to Southampton and Felixstowe. Ships then became larger, and the largest could not now go up the Thames. In spite of the loss, tens of thousands of ships still come to the Port of London, and the dense shipping needs one of the most sophisticated control systems in the world (cf. Bruges some 700 years before!). There are far fewer and mostly recreational boats on the capital's river above the Port of London. Much money was made from the river trade; as appropriate to the Capital. The first Custom House is recorded in AD 870, though no doubt the Romans had an earlier one.

London's flood plain is built on, and is still sinking after the Ice Age, quite apart from any sea rise from Global Warming. To meet this, the Thames Barrier was built in 1982, to prevent London flooding from high seas. It is only 25 years old, and a new and higher barrier will soon be needed.

Downstream, in the Thames estuary, industry pervades the region, and there is the holiday town of Southend-on-Sea. River sediment is building sunken flats. Intensive farming upstream has increased erosion, and therefore deposition downstream. On the Kent side, there are ex-marshes, now mostly drained, and over-grazed. Finally, the wide estuary joins the North Sea.

The south of England has been almost stable for a millennium, and consequently there is little in the way of defence. The Romans built a fort in London to guard their bridge. The Tower of London was fully fortified by William the Conqueror (1066) but it has been used more as a palace and prison than to defend the town. Windsor Castle is another of the Conqueror's river forts, again a palace now.

This description indicates uniformity, but in fact there is much diversity in:

- topography
- floodplain
- drainage, channelling, etc.
- woods, groves, isolated trees
- material used for housing
- style of housing
- river trading villages, farming villages trading towns, market towns, craft-mixed towns
- the means of communicating along and across the river, and the constructions associated
- the resources available: (1) *Produce*, country and river. In the river fish was an important source of food. Duck, swans, and geese were once abundant. Plants could be used for salad, drink, furnishings, fencing; (2) *Navigation*, boat building and maintenance; (3) *Accommodation*, inns, hotels, restaurants and other eating places; (4) *Craft towns*; (5) *gravel and sand extraction*; (6) *timber*, fuel, fencing, etc.

While there is this variety (e.g. Fig. 14.1), most is immediately recognisable as England. Figures 14.2 and 14.3 show rather similar riverscapes from other countries, and there are significant differences, not just in buildings, but in the pattern of fields, small tributaries, trees, and even the shape of the same species of tree. Culture and climate have subtle, as well as major, effects.

Tributaries enter, in their own riverscapes, all the length of the Thames. Some are large, like the Medway, most are medium or small, but all are lowland. As usual, those near the source are generally similar to the small main Thames, swift low tributaries from the limestone hills, in small attractive valleys. Lower, small tributaries differ greatly to the large Thames in its flood plain, and have their separate distinctive riverscapes. The flood plain is mainly drained, and

346 The riverscape and the river

(a)

Fig. 14.2. Tempered or smiling riverscapes across Europe. Prosperous agricultural riverscapes. Note variation in landscape, positions of settlements, size, shape and structure of fields, position and management of streams, etc. Old settlements must be, or have been, with water. (a) Sixteenth century, Germany: remarkably similar to now (except for tall corn, small village and more harvesters (New York Metropolitan Museum of Art). (b) Germany. Straightened stream. Settlement under slope. Forested hills. (c) France. Canal far left. Willows and wetland centre (see Fig. 6.1). Settlement well up slope (Draeger, Imp.). (d) Denmark. Straightened streams. Farms on slight elevations. (e) Belgium. Farming hamlet on stream. (f) The Netherlands. Note road is raised above farmed level. (g) Hungary. Settlements on slopes above flood plain. (h) Wales. Fertile valley, rough grazing hills. Isolated farms. (i) England. Settlements on low slopes.

the original channels, are lost, replaced by dykes, ditches or not even those, depending on the drainage.

Drainage of the flood plain, the wet tributary valleys and abstraction from aquifers have dried the riverscapes allowing crops to grow well. Marshes and flower-rich meadows have nearly gone, but the riverscape still 'smiles'. It is good to live in. It gives a good living to the people here (partly from Mackay, 1992).

The tempered or smiling riverscape 347

(b)

(c)

Fig. 14.2. (cont.)

348 The riverscape and the river

(d)

(e)

Fig. 14.2. (cont.)

The tempered or smiling riverscape 349

(f)

(g)

Fig. 14.2. (*cont.*)

(h)

(i)

Fig. 14.2. (cont.)

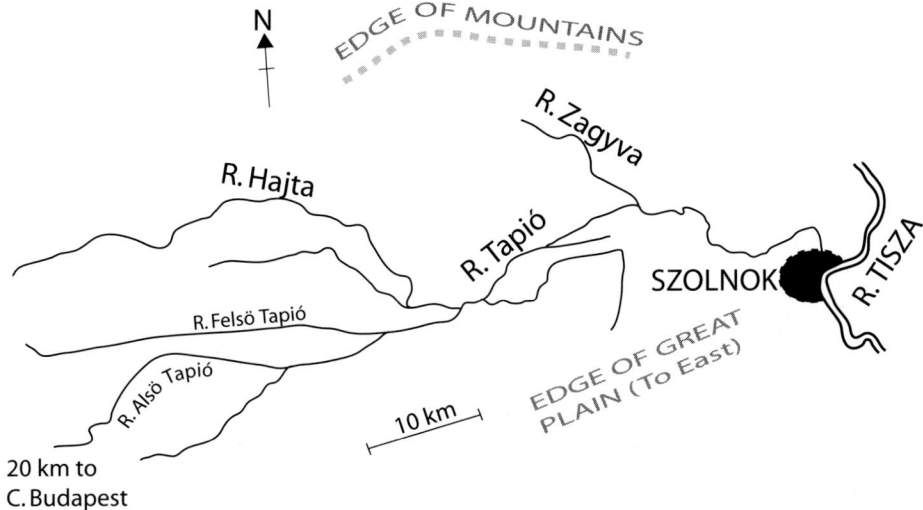

Fig. 14.3. River Tapio, east of Budapest, Hungary. This lowland river lies between the northern mountains and the Danube, on an alluvial plain with some variation in level (terraces, etc.). Most settlement is on the lower slopes of the hills to the north, above the former flood level. For landscape type, see Fig. 8.2d.

R. Tapio (Fig. 14.3)

Another tempered riverscape is that of the Tapio in the west of the Hungarian Great (Danube) Plain (Fig. 14.2). Hills and mountains lie to the north, with streams flowing down. The main rivers and other tributaries rise within the low rolling lowland. This is fertile, growing grain, vegetables, and sunflowers. Most is open field, unlike England post-eighteenth century. The former wetness is shown by the villages. Old villages are on raised ground, either on ridges in the plain, or along the lower slope of the hills nicely above flood level, but with easy access to what was the wetland. (A few newer villages are on the plain: flooding is no longer expected.) Trees are on steeper ridges, by roads, and as field-dividers. Poplar groves are planted. Willows, however, grow on lower levels. Riversides may have willow and reed (*Phragmites*) bands, which also occur on streams running down slopes.

Willow-reed bands in the bottom of small valleys, and along lowland streams, are frequent throughout temperate Europe, and especially so, perhaps, in Hungary. In the west, where snow lies little in lowlands, such bands are wet most of the year. In Hungary, with ample snowmelt in spring, they may be quite dry in summer. Reeds grow well in a wide variety of water regimes, as long as that regime is stable and repetitive: the rhizomes getting water in spring is sufficient,

352   The riverscape and the river

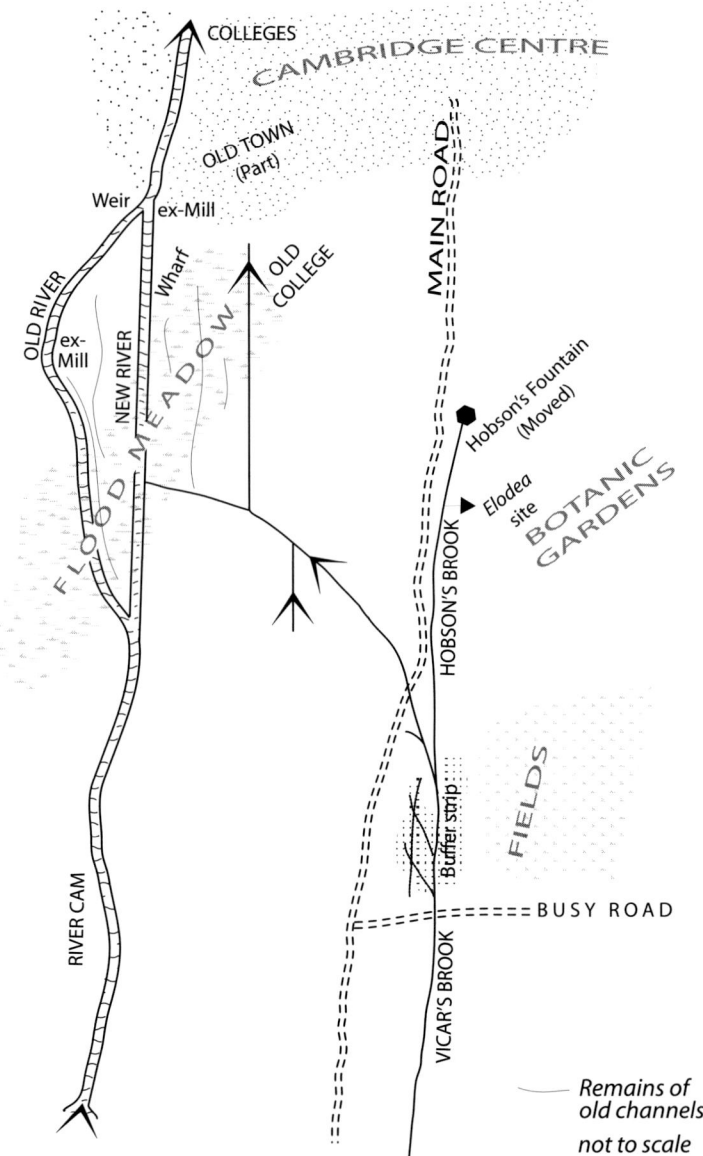

Fig. 14.4. Watercourses by the south edge of Cambridge, England. (Much simplified, not to scale, omitting those lost and some remaining flood meadow channels.) The River Cam flows to Cambridge, where it was formerly the main communication route for freight and foreign travel. After King Henry VI (fifteenth century) removed the town centre, including the wharf to make room for his King's College, wharfs were made at both ends of the town. The one marked here was mainly for freight. The primary mill was that on the Old River. The New River was constructed to run direct to the town, almost along the contour, giving enough head by where

provided the water recurs each year. The willow-reed bands look much the same in east and west, but water regime may differ.

Larger streams are dredged and channelled, so tall herbs grow on the banks. River vegetation is generally poor, reflecting the channelling, shallowing and pollution. Going up the hills, arable is usually found on the lower slopes, overlapping with grass above, and then grass giving way to the forests of the mountains. This influences the streams. Agrochemical pollution is severe only low down, and village pollution enters only at low levels, and up valleys further away. Pools and ponds are sparse. Some villages and river farms are joined directly by the river, but only indirectly by roads.

This is another 'smiling' riverscape. For conservation, some wetland should have been left, for biodiversity, habitat, and great numbers of wild fowl. But for people and crops (especially for those who have never known better) the riverscape gives good crops, and 'smiles'. More effort (more destruction) was put into this riverscape than into that of the Thames. In the Thames valley only the flood plain was severely altered: and there the crop production merely went up, from rich wet meadow to arable.

Fig. 14.4. (*cont.*)
the rivers meet to power another (and town) mill. Vicar's brook passes under a busy road, and receives, after storms, enough run-off pollution to turn the water dark, and, cumulatively over 30 years, skew and reduce the vegetation. Many small irrigation/drainage channels used to be diverted off from the brook, which have mostly dried. Once in the flood meadow, there were numerous watercourses in a network, of which few remain. The water flows down to the river. Of the constructed channels remaining, one runs to a late mediaeval College. In an allotment area, a diversion brook ran to the town centre, where it ended in a fountain in the market place, supplying clean water for all. This is named after the seventeenth-century constructor, Mr Tobias Hobson, who originated the saying 'Hobson's Choice' meaning 'No Choice'. He ran a livery stable, and those wanting to hire a horse could not, as was usual, choose which. They had to take the horse which was most rested, or go without. Hobson's brook now ends by the town, and the fountain has been moved there. Mr Hobson's brook also supplied water running down the sides of the main roads, to clean them. The remnants of these are used as a tourist attraction. There was a side tributary into the (nineteenth-century) Botanic Garden. The highly respected Professor Babington planted, within the garden, some *Elodea canadensis* from North America which escaped, and is now found throughout temperate Europe.

Old edge of Cambridge, R. Cam (Fig. 14.4)

Figure 14.4 shows a small riverscape, largely shaped in early modern times, but also altered since.

- The main river with an ancient (King's) mill.
- The main river with a large diversion to turn the town mill. This also brought freight to the wharf by the mill from downstream. (The Cam brought shipping from, e.g. Ely, Bedford, Huntingdon, Kings Lynn, The Wash and the continent.)
- The main river navigable formerly for general transport, now for recreation.
- The minor watercourses diverted to better water the town and Colleges of the University (from late mediaeval times).
- Wet, now dry grazing, close to town.
- The loss of the watercourses formerly used to flood and fertilise (storm water) the meadow and to stabilise the water level, giving the best grass.
- Pollards along watercourses and dried watercourses.
- Other trees along watercourses and in copses.
- The riverside and the (twentieth-century) roadside both have side ditches to stabilise water regime.

Pond landscape (Fig. 14.5)

Pond landscapes, like the pool ones of the harsh riverscapes, are a separate category, but perhaps best fit here. Ponds have been dug over the ages, and some natural pools have been converted to ponds for human use. When ponds are no longer needed, they may be filled, drained or abandoned. The last usually become a good-quality aquatic habitat, often some of the best in the region (see Boothby, 1998a, b; Boothby *et al.*, 2001).

In that ponds needed to be dug by hand until recently, dense ponds mean a substantial value to the ponds. The remaining ponds are estimated at 1 million ha in Western Europe, much more in Eastern Europe. Even though they are disappearing fast, this is a substantial area, a substantial resource, whether for former or present economic use or present conservation or, and ideally, both (a pond producing a crop although having high biodiversity is more likely to be retained). Ponds, like pools, can form a visual focus, and, when many, form a distinctive pondscape. Unless well puddled and maintained, ponds survive only if groundwater is high, river water flows in, or springs rise.

Fig. 14.5. Pond landscape, Cheshire, England.

Fish ponds expanded in the early Christian centuries. They provided food in inland areas, and specifically protein (for Lent and fast days, in mostly Roman Catholic countries until recently). They were unnecessary in coastal areas, e.g. Iceland, as freshwater fish merely added variety to marine ones. In most countries fishponds produced fish for local consumption. English monasteries, villages and manors all had their fish ponds, though abbey ponds may have been lost after the Reformation. Food was still needed.

Village fish ponds were typically downstream of villages to avoid polluting the drinking water With increasing wealth, the ponds could be disused, be turned into, say, watercress ponds. Later, there could be modern container fish ponds. Manor ponds, in particular, might be turned into ornamental ponds (as in eighteenth-century landscaping).

The importance of the manor and castle fish ponds is shown by the standing of the Master of the Fish Ponds, who in the seventeenth century, ate at the same table as the Master of the Horse in Raglan Castle. It is easy to forget that food is as important as horses!

Large fishponds for exporting fish were constructed in parts of the continent. In Hungary they were much expanded in the Communist years (1950s+). In the south Czech Republic they date from in and around the sixteenth century. Those in the Dombes region of eastern France are older again. These are truly pond landscapes.

The lakes, Broads, of Norfolk are even more distinctive, with their wetlands and wet woodlands. Until the 1950s (Lambert, 1951; Lambert & Jennings, 1951) they were thought natural. Then it was found – as in the Netherlands – that they were dug for peat, for export to towns as well as local use. This peat digging was a Danish invention, brought to Britain by them, so starting in the eighth century. It reached its maximum in the thirteenth century. Then water level rose, and the pits became fisheries (George, 1992).

Ploughed land needed water for horse and ox, and many small ponds were made or retained for this. Most have gone, since upkeep was laborious and the land of the pond, ploughable. They could still be seen, scattered over the land, in the 1950s, but few are now visible. All ploughed land without other surface water needed ponds. There could be dewponds in limestone hills, lined with hard limestone fragments and flints, then puddled. These provided water for the huge flocks of sheep and other livestock roaming over the English chalk Downs. Ponds in which cattle could cool off during the summer heat were much appreciated (White, 1788).

Every village had riders and ploughmen passing through, so a village pond was necessary. (It could also be used for duck.) Now that water comes from pipes, and power from the combustion engine, it is near-impossible to imagine the vital need for water pre-1900, water for travel, water for farm production, just water. It was therefore impossible to drain the land dry for extra food. (Much was drained, especially in the nineteenth century: but water had to be left.)

Table 14.1 lists types of ponds, some sparse, some dense.

Table 14.1 *Some origins of ponds (modified from Boothby, 1998a, b).*

Industrial ponds:	Water mills (e.g. corn, cotton), turf ponds (e.g. Norfolk Broads), retting flax; 'beavering' woad for dye extraction; ice-harvesting; swans, furnaces, forges, canals; cooling ponds; extraction of sediment; marl; coprolite digging; formed in quarries, sawpits, charcoal pits.
Field ponds:	Stock watering, irrigation, dewpond construction.
Specialist ponds:	For fish, watercress; duck (decoys); curling; ice; hammer-making, garden ponds and ornamental lakes, moats.
'Accidental' ponds:	Bomb craters; subsidence of salt, coal mining.
Ornamental ponds:	Landscaped ponds on great estates or business parks; garden ponds; moats.
Village ponds:	Water supply for man and beast, fire-fighting, for swelling cartwheels; washing horses; ducks and fish for food; willow used for baskets; geese, skating in winter, and other craft, farm and garden uses.

In the NW of England, round Cheshire, some 30 000 ponds remain out of *c*. 80 000 in the 1870s. This is undoubtedly a visual pondscape! (Boothby *et al.*, 2001). They form mosaics of clusters of ecosystems over some miles (metapopulations), so there is good connectivity for many species. The land is tempered to make the ponds; and the wealth they bring when in full use should make the people smile.

Discussion

The differences between tempered riverscapes are clearly less than between harsh ones. They are subtle and difficult to characterise in words. Fig. 14.2 shows a variety of 'smiling' riverscapes across Europe. All provide a good living.

As Rackham (1986) points out, wood-pasture goes back to prehistoric times, so is probably the earliest managed landscape. Wood pasture gave a good living for a small population, and from this, and small strip fields, our present tempered, industrially farmed, riverscapes have evolved. They are over-managed, for all purposes except food quantity (not quality). They are over-drained, especially in England, where there is more riverside arable. Sweden, for instance being constrained by climate, has plenty of riverside meadow.

Industrial farmland loses the invisible heritage, the Ways, holy wells, historical features, and the historic and natural heritage of birds, mammals, soil, field plants. The topography of the valleys remains, but the riverscape is drained, the river diminished, damaged or even destroyed.

Crops change with culture, time and technology. Cattle bring milk, meat, leather, but are labour intensive, particularly for milk. There have been frequent changes between cattle and sheep, with distress among those unemployed thereby. In England in the sixteenth century, in Scotland in the nineteenth, this change was made. The former, in a more populous and diverse country, could better (with time) absorb the unemployed. In the Middle Ages, Britain produced huge numbers of sheep. The wool areas of, e.g. East Anglia and the Cotswolds, were very wealthy, as can be seen by their mediaeval village churches. Crop and other changes are too numerous to describe here, but while they produced wealth, the land 'smiled'. Land has, however, a limited area, so total production is limited (in the technology of the day), so any excess population must leave or starve.

Such complexity of history (merely summarised here) is the usual, not the unusual. Even out in the country, the record of rivalry, folk customs, and use of all resources, once investigated, is as interesting.

Riverscapes, while unique, are often repetitive in a general sense. The landscape elements are repeated, such mosaics and corridors as there are, stretch for many miles. Other riverscapes are small and distinctive, but even these may have corridors and metapopulation patches if looked for.

The riverscape can, as has been shown in this book, be looked at from many different perspectives. Yet all is one riverscape.

For millennia, people have – in the more suitable lands – tempered the riverscape to give maximum protection for people. Technology, until very recently, required that people worked in association with natural heritage. To get best production, this was necessary.

Recent changes to industrial farming and high demand for water, communications and buildings, has led to damage to the water resources, and the land. The worse the damage, the longer, probably, the recuperative time – if recuperation be possible. London's underground water is recovering in quantity: but is still polluted.

A major difference between the harsh and the tempered riverscape is that in the former most time and labour is spent by wresting a living from the soil. The higher arts of civilisation and science and technology generally come from people of the tempered riverscapes, where enough surplus food is produced for much of the population to be engaged in non-farming, non-labouring, pursuits.

What will happen to the potential recovery envisaged by the Water Framework Directive?

European riverscapes approach a crossroads. Will working once more with natural processes, aiming (long term) at sustainability prevail, or will the 'developers' succeed in destroying the potential for water, food and other resources?

15

Envoi

The tale of the cave settlement of Ta' Baldu, Malta, and its water relations (Fig. 15.1)

The water features in the riverscape

- Stream rising in depression in plateau, with springs and winter run-off (semi(?)-wetland).
- Stream flowing down off plateau, shallow ravine widening downstream, very fertile valley bottom.
- Stream used for irrigation. High walls give shelter, with weeping holes and stream holes for the passage of water.
- Stream dries with abstraction and drainage. Gallery tunnels have been excavated below. Wind pumps now abstract water near (not at) where the stream rose.
- Springs, large and small, rise at base of bedding planes in the hard limestone cliffs under the plateau, bounding the valley.
- One spring rises in the larger of the two cave rooms of Ta' Baldu.
- Springs were used for domestic supply and irrigation.
- Stone irrigation channels were built to convey water. These are still extant downstream leading from the next large spring.
- Gallery (*c.* 1.5 m × 0.8 m) dug in the limestone to bring out more water, into the cave room. (This is thought to be mediaeval.)
- Ancient path leads down into valley, crossing a (tributary) stream by a bridge to reach the 'larger' settlement of is-Simblija.
- Arab bath, like a Malta reservoir, inside cave room.
- So, several layers of water use within the cave rooms.
- Access to area is now restricted, in case men with bowsers (water tankers) come to steal water. (This could be reached, by a long pipe hanging down, with a pump.)

(a)

Fig. 15.1. Ta' Baldu cave settlement, Malta. (a) Upper valley, just downstream of main ex-marsh (delta-marsh), formerly wet from springs and the run-off. Fairly exposed. Beyond, to the right, is a sharp drop down a rock layer, forming a new head (see (c)). (b) Main very fertile valley below the head from (a). There is a high wall providing shelter for the former excellent fruit. Springs arise from sides (between beds of hard limestone). The wall has 'weeping holes' to let water through from the section above. Note old archway in wall. (c) Looking down the valley to the sea: from whence comes fertile red soil blown from North Africa. The cross wall in the centre is another high one, protecting the section above from the wind. Note olives on the dry ground above the fruit. (d) The major cave. Inside is a sunk Arab bath (like a tank, not shown), a probably mediaeval (ex) water-gathering gallery. (e) Centre back of cave with various pipes and channels, a Roman olive press used as a water barrel (front left centre), half of the old stone table (the other half being used for picnics further away (not shown): and of course space for a family to live. (Other caves along this rock bed were, and sometimes are, still used.) The 1649 sketch shows the stone table outside, the low wall now seen in front built high, to shelter and protect the family, and a sun-screen of branches and reeds above, giving a cool outside room in the dry Mediterranean summer. Water is now being led in from another spring, by an old but, within the cave, comparatively recent channel ('e' across centre).

Envoi 361

(b)

(c)

Fig. 15.1. (cont.)

(d)

(e)

Fig. 15.1. (*cont.*)

- Good irrigation (as well as shelter, from valley and walls, and fertile soil) gives very fertile cultivation. In the seventeenth century, fruit from here was said to be the best in Malta. The fields are still very fertile.

The stream is now dried and gone at this level. It rises a couple of hundred metres downstream, in a large spring on the other side of the valley. A complex of reservoir, channels and pipes ensures:

- abstracted water is now contaminated by agrochemicals and unfit for human consumption;
- water use by farmers for a long time (a millennium, probably more). The pattern of use has changed but irrigation continues. Over-use of farming chemicals means abstracted water is no longer fit for drinking.

There are other habitable caves near.

Description

The R. Rum rises in the west of Malta, on an Upper Coralline (hard) limestone (like R. Kbir, Chapter 2). It rose in a depression in the plateau, certainly often wet, possibly a wetland. With the strong bedding of the rock, the stream dropped down, and into a (semi-ravine) head, a narrow cone-shape. This has good fields on the valley floor, and drops, with wide (and not deep) terraces, with the typical cliffy limestone at the sides. R. Rum, in the early nineteenth century, was enough of a stream to be marked on the OS map. It flowed down the valley floor, rising from springs as well as marsh and run-off. The stream would have flowed most or more likely, all of the year, and been available for irrigation.

Ta' Baldu is in a very remote area, away from villages both inland and coastal. After the Norman invasion of 1090, and particularly after the 'official' expulsion of the still-Muslim Arabs a couple of centuries later, the remaining Muslims were pushed away from the major settlements, and lived as they could in land unwanted by the Christians. Over centuries, and with aid of small monasteries, all became Christian.

The fields of the valley floor were probably already terraced and cultivated at this stage. In the seventeenth century there was 'all manner of fruit'. In the twenty-first century, fruit is mainly citrus and olive, though also vine, peach, pomegranate and others. Citrus requires the most water. And water was there. Shelter was there. It came from the high steep sides of the narrow valley, and, across the valley, by extraordinary high and well-built walls, which are near-unique in the Islands. They are probably seventeenth or eighteenth century, and not associated with the monastery. Citrus requires the most shelter; olive the least, and is planted on the more exposed places. And some fertiliser was there. Facing east, winds brought and bring red nutrient-rich particles from North Africa. These are funnelled up the valley, where the cliff lessened wind speed and allowed deposition. Most walls in the valley were the usual short terraces. Three cross-walls, however, were built up to 10 m high, giving shelter from the sea winds blowing up the valley. The fruit trees had shelter, water and nutrients: no wonder the 1649 description is of bearing the best fruit in the Island!

The cliffs of the enclosing walls have a number of caves (they are in the lower part of a bed, their floors being on top of the bed below). No doubt all caves that were large enough were used for storage, stables or housing other livestock. Two room-sized caves occur side-by-side on the north rock face and here the (known) inhabitants lived. Over a kilometre across the next valley is a larger settlement, is-Simblija, and this is considered at least mediaeval. The ta'-Baldu farm may be this or older, as it contains a Roman olive press. Later on, the press was – Roman technology having been lost – used as a water basin for incoming water. The water here (as R. Kbir, Chapter 2) is perched in the aquifer above a clay layer.

While the stream in the middle of the valley would have watered the fields and, if necessary, livestock, the cave inhabitants would have found it more convenient to use their own spring water. This, the smaller but more steady flow, could also be used for watering, as needed, though not for much irrigation. There is a natural spring in this as in other caves. This one is unusually large: it still flows substantially, enough for its owners to fear water theft. Commonly, springs occur where a bed of softer rock overlies a harder one.

Along the contour which is the bedding plane, a water-collecting gallery has been constructed, leading into the cave room. This is thought to be mediaeval, indicating farming and settlement then. This added considerably to the available (spring) water and could be used for domestic or irrigation water. The standard of the masonry is high. At the back of the room, the Arab bath was altered, later used for storing water.

From the opposite side of the valley, spring water was led, by water channel, to the cave room, to join the existing water source. This suggests water ran short at some point.

There are other cave rooms and, as at is-Simblija and elsewhere, also rooms above ground. These built rooms are both directly above caves, and separate, and occur in similar places on the plateau edges. Ta' Baldu is on an upper valley. More rooms are on headlands further away in the valley.

A drawing of 1664 shows the home, with the two caves. The family is outside, using what was probably the same stone table as is now present. This 'outside room' was enclosed on the far side by a wall, and above, by a light screen of branches, greenery, and cane, *Arundo donax*. Cane now grows only downstream of here (stream-side and marking small springs) – but if not available on this farmer's property, doubtless it could be collected from below. If the drawing is correct, this farming family lived in at least as civilised and healthy a manner as did those in houses (from later descriptions, probably more so!).

It is surprising that, if there were any sacred springs, they have not survived as such. Malta has many spring and river chapels. The nearest chapel was the mediaeval one at is-Simblija (which, at present, has no spring).

Communications were good. A track lies above the cave, leading to more settlements along the plateau (the rooms referred to above). This track, in the other direction upstream, divides. One fork leads to the capital, Mdina, via another valley with a larger river. There is a side lane to the nearest village (Dingli, the main centre of the area). (There are other, but perhaps newer tracks.) In addition, going under the plateau then down the valley, bridging a stream, is the ancient track to the large is-Simblija settlement on the headland opposite. The bridge existed in 1718–20.

Now, these 'ways' are lanes (except part of the one to is-Simblija is still a path) and are carrying ever more traffic. Farmers want access by car. So do the more remote houses: the ta'-Baldu home is, however, abandoned. Elsewhere, extension building may turn caves into a room or two at the back of the house, shaped and furnished like any other room. The rock insulates, the rooms are warm in winter, cool in summer. Other caves may have had doors fixed. A purpose was found for all useful space.

Over the centuries, settlements and water use changed. There are layers of constructions for stream abstraction and for spring use. Being remote, springs and wells are – though diminished – more frequent than in more populous areas.

For many, many centuries the ta'-Baldu river and riverscape was used sustainably. There was plenty of natural biodiversity on the plateau, the steep valleys, in fields (pre-biocides), and in and by water bodies. There were fertile fields and shelter.

And now? Drying leaves no water for the river (except in major storms), most walls are not properly maintained, some farming has excess agrochemicals, and no water is left for the river (except in major storms), tracks and paths become roads both tarmacked and wider, traffic increases with new houses and all the disruption this entails, biodiversity is less. Recently, ownership changed, and at the time of writing (in 2006) alterations were incomplete. All has been tidied, with new fenced paths not on the old. The two largest caves have been lit (with what damage to cave biota?), spring water is used to irrigate, among others, a new lawn, part of an old wall has been taken down, and half the old stone table has been moved for a picnic site. New housing is being built above. Sadly, care and much money without environmental and cultural knowledge produces mixed results, and here has already skewed and partly destroyed a site of extraordinary interest. Rumour has it that the site will be a nightclub or disco: than which only bulldozers could be more damaging.

The river has gone, the riverscape remains, but damage creeps on, and on. The heritage, natural and cultural, is still superb! But for how long will it remain? (See Abela, 1647; Saliba *et al.*, 2002; and with thanks to Mr C. Buhagiar.)

Bibliography

This is a small book on a large subject. Its first draft was nearly double the contracted length. Therefore, much of the detail and examples, even of principles, which fill out and interpret rather bald statements, had to be omitted.

For those who want to go further, however, most of the omitted references are included here. Those used in the book are marked with an asterisk. All are of interest, for principle or detail. Fortunately, the titles describe the subject matter, and so, in a way, form part of the coverage of the book.

Aalen, F. H. R. (1978). *Man and the Landscape in Ireland*. London: Academic Press.

*Abela, G. F. (1647). *Della Descrtione di Malta*, Malta.

Allison, R. J. & Thomas, D. S. G. (1993). The sensitivity of landscapes. In *Landscape Sensitivity*, ed. D. S. A. Thomas & R. J. Allison. Chichester: John Wiley & Sons, pp. 1–6.

*Alumäe, H., Palang, H. & Printsmann, A. (2001). Cultural and historical values in landscape planning. In *Development of European Landscapes*, ed. Ü Mander, A. Rintsmann & H. Palang, vol. 1, University of Tartu, pp. 183–8.

Alumäe, H., Printsmann, A. & Palang, H. (2003). Cultural and historic values in landscape planning. In *Landscape Interfaces*, ed. H. Palang & G. Fry. Dordrecht: Kluwer Academic Publishers, pp. 125–45.

*Andressen, T. & Curado, M. J. (2001). The shaping of the future of a cultural landscape. In *Development of European Landscapes*, ed. Ü Mander, A. Rintsmann & H. Palang, vol. 1, University of Tartu, pp. 313–16.

Andressen, T. & Curado, M. J. (2003). Shaping the future of a cultural landscape. The Douro valley wine region. In *Landscape Interfaces*, ed. H. Palang & G. Fry. Dordrecht: Kluwer Academic Publishers, pp. 109–24.

*Andrew, J. & Kinsman, D. (1990). *Gravel Pit Restoration for Wildlife*. Sandy, Bedfordshire: Royal Society for the Protection of Birds.

Andrews, J. H. (1988). The development of wildlife conservation on rivers. *Conservation Review*, 2, 78–80. Sandy, Bedfordshire: Royal Society for the Protection of Birds.

Anon. (1991). *Nature conservation and pollution from farm wastes*. Peterborough: Nature Conservancy Council.

Anon. (1994). *Biodiversity*. London: The UK Action Plan. HMSO.

Anon. (2000). *Hedgerows of England*. Cheltenham: The Countryside Agency.

Antrap, M. (1987). *Invisible connectivity in rural landscapes.* International Association for Landscape Ecology (IALE), pp. 57–62.

Antrap, M. (1988). Invisible connectivity in rural landscapes. In *Conductivity in Landscape Ecology*, ed. K. F. Schreiber, pp. 57–62.

Arheimer, B. & Andersson, L. (2001). Landscape wetness and nitrogen transport 1885–94. In *Development of European Landscapes*, ed. Ü Mander, A. Rintsmann & H. Palang, vol. 1, University of Tartu, Tartu.

*Association Française de Normalisation (2003). NF T90–395. Determination de l'indice biologique macrophytique en rivière. AFNOR.

*Athie, D. & Cerri, C. C., eds. (1987). *The Use of Macrophytes in Water Pollution Control*. Oxford: Pergamon Press.

Aubrecht, G., Dick, G. & Prentice, C. (1994). Monitoring of ecological change in wetlands of middle Europe. *Stapfia*, **31**.

Bailey, R. G., José, P. V. & Sherwood, B. R. (1998). *United Kingdom Floodplains*. Otley: Westbury.

*Baker, A. R. H. (1992a). Collective consciousness and the local landscape. In *Ideology and Landscape in Historical Perspective*, ed. A. R. H. Baker & G. Biger. Cambridge: University Press, pp. 255–88.

Baker, A. R. H. (1992b). Introduction. In *Ideology and Landscape in Historical Perspective*, ed. A. R. H. Baker & G. Biger. Cambridge: University Press, pp. 1–24.

*Baker, A. R. H. & Biger, G., eds. (1992). *Ideology and Landscape in Historical Perspective*. Cambridge: Cambridge University Press.

Baker, C. D., Casey, H., Castellano, E. R., *et al.* (1973). *The chalk stream ecosystem, Bere Stream, Bere Heath*. International Biological Progamme – UNESCO Production–Freshwaters sectional Symposium on Synthesis of P-F results, Report 40.

*Bakkestuen, V., Dramstad, W. D. & Fjellstad, W. J. (2001). Landscape changes in multifunctional landscapes change multiple function. In *Development of European Landscapes*, ed. Ü Mander, A. Rintsmann & H. Palang. vol. 1, University of Tartu, pp. 378–82.

*Barr, C. & Petit, S., eds. (2001). Hedgerows of the World. *Proceedings of the 10th annual IALE (UK) conference*. Chapter: International Association of Landscape Ecology, UK.

Barr, C. J., Birtt, C. P. & Sparks, T. H. (1995). *Hedgerow management and wildlife*. Grange-over-Sands: ADAS and Institute of Terrestrial Ecology.

Barrett, P. R. F., Greaves, M. P., Murphy, K. J. *et al.*, eds. (1990). European Weed Research Society, 8th International Symposium on Aquatic Weeds Sweden, 1990. EWRS, Wageningen.

*Baudry, J. & Bunce, R. G. H. (2001). An overview of the landscape ecology of hedgerows. In *Hedgerows of the World,*. ed. C. Barr & S. Petit. International Association of Landscape Ecology, UK Branch IALE (UK), pp. 3–16.

*Baudry, J. & Bunel, F. (2001). Agricultural landscape dynamics. In Species dispersal and land use processes. *Proceedings of the 6th annual conference of IALE (UK,)*. ed. A. Cooper & J. Power. International Association of Landscape Ecology, UK Branch, pp. 3–16.

Baudry, J. & Merriam, H. G. (1988). Connectivity and connectedness: functional versus structural patterns in landscape. In *Conductivity in Landscape Ecology*, ed. K. F. Schreiber, pp. 23–8.

Beardall, C. H. (1992). *Water for Wildlife*. A review of water resource management issues in the Anglian region, Anglian Region Wildlife Trusts.

*Bell, S. (1999). *Landscape: Pattern, Perception and Process*. London: Span.

*Bellamy, P. E., Brown, N. J., Enoksson, B. et al. (1997). The role of landscape structure and dispersal in limiting nuthatch distribution. In Species dispersal and land use processes. *Proceedings of the 6th annual conference of IALE (UK)*, ed. A. Cooper & J. Power. International Association of Landscape Ecology, UK Branch, pp. 151–8.

Ben-Artzi, Y. (1993). Religious ideology and landscape formation. In *Landscape Sensitivity*, ed. D. S. A. Thomas & R. J. Allison. Chichester: John Wiley & Sons, pp. 83–106.

Bernez, I., Haniel, H., Haury, J. & Ferreira, M. T. (2004). Combined effects of environmental factors and regulation on macrophyte vegetation along three rivers in Western France. *River Research and Applications*, **20**, 43–59.

Bill, H. C., Peschled, P., Reich, M. & Plachter, H. (1999). Experiments and observations on seed dispersal by running water in an Alpine floodplain. *Bulletin of the Geobotanical Institute ETH*, **65**, 13–28.

Blasi, C., Carranza, M. L. Di Marzio, P. & Frondini, R. (1998). Landscape ecology and biodiversity for defining a sustainable management model. *Fresenius Environmental Bulletin*, **7**, 175–82.

Boardman, J. (1993). The sensitivity of Downland arable land to erosion by water. In *Landscape Sensitivity*, ed. D. S. A. Thomas & R. J. Allison, Chichester: John Wiley & Sons, pp. 211–28.

*Boatman, N. D., Clay, D. V., Goodman, A. et al., eds. (2000). Vegetation management in changing landscapes. *Aspects of Applied Biology*, **58**.

*Boeye, D. (1992). Hydrologie, hydrochemie en ecologie van een grundwater afhankelijk veen. Ph.D. Thesis, University of Antwerp.

Bold, R. (2002). The wonderful water world of wood. *FBA News*, **20**, 10–11.

Bollens, U. & Ramseier, D. (2001). Shifts in abundance of fen-meadow species along a nutrient gradient in a field experiment. *Bulletin of the Geobotanical Institute ETH*, **67**, 57–72.

Bolton, P. & Dawson, F. H. (1992). The use of a check-list in assessing possible environmental impacts in planning watercourse improvements. *Final Proceedings of the International Symposium on Effects of Watercourse Improvements*. 10–12 September 1991, Wpion, Namur, Belgium, pp. 29–42.

Boon, P. J. (1991). The role of Sites of Special Scientific Interest (SSSIs) in the conservation of British rivers. *Freshwater Forum*, **1**(2), 95–108.

Boon, P. J. & Lee, A. (2005). Falling through the cracks: are European directives and international conventions the panacea for freshwater nature conservation? *Freshwater Forum*, **24**, 24–37.

Boon, P. J. & Raven, P. J. (1948). The application of classification and assessment methods to river management in the UK. *Aquatic Conservation*, **8(4)**, special issue.

Boon, P. J., Calow, P. & Petts, G. E., eds. (1991). *River Conservation and Management*. Chichester: John Wiley & Sons.

*Boon, P. J., Calow, P. & Petts, G. E., eds. (1992). *River Conservation and Management*. Chichester: John Wiley & Sons.

*Boothby, J., ed. (1997a). British pond landscapes. *Proceedings of the UK Conference of the PondLife Project*, 1997. John Moores University, Liverpool.

Boothby, J. (1997b). Ponds and pondscape conservation strategy. *Proceedings of the International Conference of the PondLife Project*. John Moores University, Liverpool.

*Boothby, J. (1998a). Pond and pond landscapes of Europe. *Proceedings of the International Conference of the PondLife Project*. John Moores University, Liverpool.

*Boothby, J. (1998b). Ponds, a search for significance. In (1998a). *Ponds and Pond Landscapes of Europe*. PondLife Project, ed. J. Boothby, John Moores University, Liverpool, pp. 1–9.

*Boothby, J. (2006). Stability in pond networks. In Water and the landscape. *Proceedings of the 19th annual IALE (UK) conference*, ed. B. Davies & S. Thompson, International Association for Landscape Ecology, UK Branch, pp. 93–101.

*Boothby, J., Guest, J. P. & Bentley, D. (2001). *A landscape worth saving*. Final report of the pond biodiversity survey of north west England. PondLife Project, John Moores University, Liverpool.

*Borg. J. (1927). *Descriptive Flora of the Maltese Islands*. Government Press, Malta.

Borman, F. H. & Likens, G. E. (1979). *Pattern and Process in a Forested Ecosystem*. New York: Springer-Verlag.

Bornette, G. & Amoros, C. & Collilieux, G. (1994). Role of seepage supply in aquatic vegetation dynamics in former river channels: prediction testing using a hydroelectric construction. *Environmental Management*, **18**, 223–34.

Bornette, G., & Amoros, C. (1991). Aquatic vegetation and hydrology of a braided river floodplain. *Journal of Vegetation Science*, **2**, 497–512.

*Botaman, N. D., Clay, D. V., Goodman, A. et al., eds. (2000).

Bowen, H. G. (1961). *Ancient Fields*. British Association for the Advancement of Science.

Bowen-Jones, H. Dewdney, H. C. & Fisher, W. B. (1961). Malta: background for development. Department of Geography, University of Durham.

Breugnot, E., Dutartre, A., Laplace-Tryture, C. & Haury, J. (2004). Variabilitédes peuplements de macrophytes en grands cours d'eau – Premiers résultats sur l'hydrosystème Adour-Garonne. *Ingénieries*, **37**, 37–50.

*Brewer, E. C. (1881). *Dictionary of Phrase and Fable*. 12th edn. London: Cassells & Co.

Brookes, A., Gregory, K. J. & Dawson, F. H. (1983). An assessment of river channelization in England and Wales. *Science of the Total Environment*, **27**, 97–111.

Brookes, A. (1988). *Channelized Rivers. Perspective for Environmental Management.* Chichester: John Wiley & Sons.

Brookes, A. & Shields, F. D., eds. (1996). *River Channel Restoration: Guiding Principles for Sustainable Projects.* Chichester: John Wiley & Sons.

Brooks, S. (2004). The restoration of Scottish raised bogs (2001–2003). Successful conclusion of latest peatland LIFE Nature Project. *IMCG Newsletter,* p. 23.

Brown, A. G. Harper, D. & Peterken, G. F. (1997b). European floodplain forests: structure, functioning and management. *Floodplain Forests* (special issue), pp. 169–78.

Brown, P. M. J. & Doberski J. (2005). Ground beetle succession and the conservation status of High Fen (Kingfisher Bridge). *Nature in Cambridgeshire,* **47**, 23–30.

Brunsden, D. (1993). In *Landscape Sensitivity,* ed. *D. S. G. Thomas & R. J. Allison. Chichester: John Wiley & Sons, pp. 7–12.

*Buhagiar, K. (2003). L-Ghar ta' Baldu water gallery. *The Sunday Times of Malta,* 44–5.

*Buhagiar, K. (2003). Personal communication.

*Bunyan, J. (1682). *The Pilgrim's Progress.* London: Jarrold (reprinted).

Burt, T. P. & Haycock, N. E. (1991). Farming and nitrate pollution. *Geography,* **76**, 60–3.

*Burt, T. P. & Haycock, N. E. (1993). Catchment sensitivity to nitrate leaching: land use controls. In *Landscape Sensitivity,* ed. D. S. G. Thomas & R. J. Allison. Chichester: John Wiley & Sons, pp. 229–40.

Burt, T. P., Heathwaite, A. L. & Trudgill, S. T. (1943). Catchment sensitivity to land use controls. In *Landscape Sensitivity,* ed. D. S. A. Thomas & R. J. Allison, Chichester: John Wiley & Sons, pp. 229–40.

*Butcher, R. W. (1927). A preliminary account of the vegetation of the river Itchen. *Journal of Ecology,* **15**, 55–65.

*Butcher, R. W. (1933). Studies on the ecology of rivers. I. On the distribution of macrophytic vegetation in the rivers of Britain. *Journal of Ecology,* **21**, 58–91.

Butcher, R. W., Longwell, J. & Pentelow, F. T. K. (1951). A biological investigation of the River Lark and the effect of beet sugar pollution. Fishery Investigations Land, 3.

Caffrey, J. M. (1993a). Aquatic plant management in relation to Irish recreational fisheries development. *Journal of Aquatic Plant Management,* **31**, 162–8.

Caffrey, J. M. (1993b). Plant management as an integrated part of Ireland's aquatic resources. *Hydroecologie appliqué,* **5**, 77–96.

Caffrey, J. M. & Beglin, T. (1996). Bankside stabilisation through reed transplantation in a newly constructed Irish canal habitat. *Hydrobiologia,* **340**, 349–54.

Caffrey, J. M., Barrett, P. R. F., Murphy, K. J. & Wade, P. M. (1996). *Management and Ecology of Freshwater Plants.* Dordrecht: Klewer Academic Publishers.

*Calow, P. (1998). *Handbook of Environmental Risk Assessment and Management.* Oxford: Blackwell Science.

Canadian Heritage Rivers System (N. Coomber, *et al.*) (2001). A cultural framework for the national values of Canadian heritage rivers. Minister of Public Works and Government Services, Ottawa.

*Carbiener, R. Trémolières, M., Mercier, J. L. & Ortscheit, A. (1990). Aquatic macrophyte communities as bioindicators of eutrophication in calcareous oligotrophic stream water (Upper Rhine plain, Alsace). *Vegetatio*, **86**, 71–88.

Carter, M. (2005). Identifying and prioritising opportunities to improve fish populations in the rivers of London. River Restoration Centre, Silsoe, Bedfordshire, **25**.

*Cassar, P. (1965). *Medical History of Malta*. Wellcome Historical Medical Library, Publ. New Series **6**, London.

Claassen, T. H. L. (1997). Ecological water quality objectives in the Netherlands, especially in the province of Friesland. *European Water Pollution Control*, **7**, 36–95.

Clare, T. (1996). Archaeology, conservation and the late twentieth century village landscape. *Conservation and Management of Archaeological Sites*, **1**, 169–88.

Clare, T. (2000). An assessment of the potential of the TWINSPAN program of multivariate analysis to contribute to the classification and management of village landscape, with reference to historical features. *Landscape Research*, **25**, 117–39.

*Clare, T. & Howard, D., eds. (2000). Quantitative approaches to landscape ecology. *Proceedings of the 2000 Animal IALE (UK) Conference*. International Association of Landscape Ecology, UK Branch.

*Clarke, J. A. (1854–5). On trunk drainage. *Journal of the Royal Agricultural Society*, **15** (1st series), 1–73.

*Cobham Resource Consultants (1992). The Tamar Valley Landscape. Countryside Commission, Cheltenham.

Collins, A. (2000). The effect of willow root architecture on riverbank stability. The Robson Meeting, *Abstracts*, p. 8.

*Commission Européen neu de Normalisation (2003). CEN/TC 230 N 0429 – EN 14184 Water quality. Guidance standard for the surveying of aquatic macrophytes in running water. Guide pour l'étude des macrophytes aquatiques dans les cours d'eau. AFNOR.

*Commission of the European Union (1992). The CORINE Biotype Project, Brussels.

Chadwick, O. (1894) *Water Supply of Malta*, Malta: Government Printing Press.

*Cook, H. & Williamson, T. (1999). *Water Management in the English Landscape*. Edinburgh: University Press.

*Cooper, P. F. & Findlater, P. C., eds. (1990). *Constructed Wetlands in Water Pollution Control*. Oxford: Pergamon Press.

*Cooper, A. & Power, J. (1997). Species dispersal and land use processes. *Proceedings of the 6th annual conference of IALE (UK)*. International Association of Landscape Ecology, UK Branch.

Council Directive 91/271/EEC of 21 May 1991 concerning urban waste-water treatment.

Council Directive 92/93/EEC of 21 May 1992 on the conservation of natural habitats and of wild fauna and flora.

Countryside Agency (2000). *Hedgerows of England*. Wetherby: Countryside Agency.

*Countryside Commission (1991a). *Assessment and conservation of landscape character*, Cheltenham.
*Countryside Commission (1991b). *The Warwickshire Landscapes Project Approach*, Cheltenham.
*Countryside Commission (1993). Central Lincolnshire Vale. *English Nature*, **44**, Cheltenham.
*Countryside Commission (1994). *The Isle of Wight Landscape*. Cheltenham: Nicholas Pearson Associates Ltd.
*Countryside Commission (1995a). Lincolnshire coast and marshes. *English Nature*, **42**, Cheltenham.
*Countryside Commission (1995b). *The Cannock Chase Landscape*. Countryside Commission, Cheltenham.
Countryside Focus (2004). *Countryside Quality Counts*. Cheltenham: Countryside Agency.
Cox, M., Straken, U. & Taylor, D., eds. (1996). Wetlands: archaeology and nature conservation. *English Nature*. London: English Heritage.
Daniel, H., Bernez, I. & Haury, J. (2002). Relations entre la morphologie des macrophytes et les caractéristiques physiques des habitats en rivière. In Gestion des Plantes Aquatiques. *Proceedings of the 11th European Weed Research Society International Symposium on Aquatic Weeds,* ed. A. Dutartre & M. H. N. Montel, September 2–6. Moliets et Maâ, France, pp. 115–18.
Darby, H. C. (1968). *The Drainage of the Fens*. Cambridge: Cambridge University Press.
*Darby, H. C. (1971). *The Domesday Geography of Eastern England*. 3rd edn. Cambridge: Cambridge University Press.
*Darby, H. C. (1983). *The Changing Fenland*. Cambridge: Cambridge University Press.
Davies, B. & Thompson, S., eds. (2006). Water and the landscape. *Proceedings of the 19th annual IALE (UK) conference*. International Association of Landscape Ecology, UK Chapter.
*Davies, B. R., Biggs, J. & Williams, P. (2006). Towards achieving sustainability for the biodiversity of aquatic habitats in UK agricultural landscapes. In Water and the landscape. *Proceedings of the 19th annual IALE (UK) conference*, ed. B. Davies, & S. Thompson, International Association of Landscape Ecology, UK Chapter, pp. 146–53.
Dawson, F. H. (1978). The seasonal effects of aquatic plant growth on the flow of water in a stream. *Proceedings of the 5th European Weed Research Council Symposium on Aquatic Weeds*, pp. 71–8.
*Dawson, F. H. (1980). The flowering of *Ranunculus penicillatus* var. *calcareus* in the River Piddle, Dorset. *Aquatic Botany*, **9**, 145–57.
Dawson, F. H. (1981). The downstream transport of fine material and organic balance for a section of a small chalk stream in southern England. *Journal of Ecology*, **69**, 367–80.
Dawson, F. H. (1988). Water flow and the vegetation of running waters. In *Handbook of Vegetation Sciences, series 15: Vegetation of Inland Waters*, ed. J. J. Symoens. The Hague: Junk, pp. 283–309.

*Dawson, F. H. (1994). The spread of *Crassula helmsii* (Kirk) Cockayne in Britain. In *Ecology and Management of Invasive Riverside Plants*, ed. L. C. de Waal, L. E. Child, P. M. Wade & J. H. Brock. Chichester: John Wiley & Sons, pp. 1–14.

Dawson, F. H. & Newman, J. R. (1998). Decline of *Ranunculus* in British rivers: true or false? *Proceedings of the 10th European Weed Research Society International Symposium of Aquatic Weeds*, Lisbon, pp. 95–8.

Dawson, F. H. & Szoszkiewicz, K. (1998). Ecological factors and the associations of aquatic vegetation in the British rivers. *Proceedings of the 10th European Weed Research Society International Symposium of Aquatic Weeds, Lisbon*. pp. 179–82.

Dawson, F. H., Castellano, E. & Ladle, M. (1978). The concept of species succession in relation to river vegetation and management. *Verhandlung international Vereinung theoretische angewandte Limnologie*, **20**, 1451–56.

Dawson, F. H., Clinton, E. M. F. & Ladle, M. (1991). Invertebrates on cut-weed removed during a weed-cut operation along an English river, the River Frome, Dorset. *Aquaculture & Fisheries Management*, **22**, 113–21.

Dawson, F. H., Raven, P. J. & Holmes, N. T. H. (1998). The distribution of aquatic plants by morphological group for rivers in the UK. *Proceedings of the 10th European Weed Research Society International Symposium of Aquatic Weeds*, Lisbon, pp. 183–6.

de Lange, L. (1975). Gibbosity in the complex *Lemna gibba/minor*: literature survey and ecological aspects. *Veroffrungun des Geobotanisches Institut*, Zurich, **49**, 127–44.

de Waal, L. C., Child, L. E., Wade, P. M. & Brock, J. H., eds. (1994). *Ecology and Management of Invasive Riverside Plants*. Chichester: John Wiley & Sons.

Décamps, H. & D'Camps, O. (2002). Mediterranean riparian woodlands, an example of a successful study of landscape ecological research for planning. *IALE Bulletin*, **20**, 1–2.

*Defoe, D. (1724–7). *A Tour through the Whole Island of Great Britain*. London (1974): Everyman, J. M. Dent.

den Hartez, C. (1982). Architecture of macrophyte-dominated aquatic communities. In *Studies on Aquatic Vascular Plants*, ed. J. J. Symvens, S. S. Hooper & P. Compère, Royal Botanical Society of Belgium, Brussels, pp. 222–39.

Denecke, D. (1992). Ideology in the planned order upon the land. In *Ideology and Landscape in Historical Perspective*, ed. A. R. H. Baker, & G. Biger. Cambridge: Cambridge University Press, pp. 303–29.

*Dennis, P., Beaton, K., Langan, S. & Stockan, J. P. (2006). Accumulated landscape ecological effects of riparian management in river catchments used for agriculture. Water and the landscape. *Proceedings of the 19th annual IALE (UK) conference*, ed. B. Davies, & S. Thompson, International Association for Landscape Ecology, UK Chapter, pp. 155–62.

Department of the Environment, Transport and the Regions (2000). *Our Countryside: The Future. Rural White Paper*. London: HMSO.

Dick, Th., Melman, C. P. & van Strien, A. J. (1993). Ditchbanks as a conservation focus in intensively farmed exploited peat farmland. In *Landscape Ecology of Stressed Environments*, ed. C. C. Vos & P. Opdam. London: Chapman & Hall, pp. 122–42.

*Dickens, C. (1868). *Martin Chuzzlewit*. London: Chapman & Hall.

Dobson, M., Cariss, H. & Murray, B. (1997). Effects of a flash flood on channel morphology and some insects of a small stony stream in the Peak District, Derbyshire. *Freshwater Forum*, **9**, 2–13.

Dokulil, M. & Janauer, G. A. (2000). Alternative stable states of macrophytes versus phytoplankton in two interconnected impoundments of the New Danube (Vienna, Austria). *Archivum Hydrobiologia* (Supplement, Large Rivers), **12/1**, 75–83.

*Downs, P. W. & Gregory, K. J. (1993). The sensitivity of river channels in the landscape system. In *Landscape Sensitivity*, ed. D. S. G. Thomas & R. J. Allison. Chichester: John Wiley & Sons, pp. 15–30.

*Drake, M. (1995). A brief survey of the insects of river banks with or without grazing along the River Itchen. *English Nature Research Reports*, **135**.

Drongvang, B. (1998). Restoration of the rivers Brede, Cole and Skerne, III. *Aquatic Conservation*, **8**, 209–22.

Dudgeon, D. & Corbett, C. (1995). *Hills and Streams. An Ecology of Hong Kong*. Hong Kong: University Press.

*Eaton, J. W. & Freeman, J. (1982). Ten years' experience of weed control in the Leeds and Liverpool Canal. *Proceedings of the European Weed Research Society 6th International Symposium on Aquatic Weeds*. EWRS, pp. 96–104.

Economic Commission for Europe (1993). Protection of water resources and aquatic ecosystems. *Water Series*, United Nations, New York: **1**.

Edelkraut, K. & Güsewelt, S. (2001). Effects of light and nutrient supply on the growth and competitive ability of five *Carex* species. *Bulletin of the Geobotanical Institute ETH*, **67**, 57–72.

Edward-Jones, E. (1993). The Water of Leith integrated environment action plan. Edinburgh District Council.

*Edwards, P. (1962). *Trees and the English Landscape*. London: Bell & Sons.

Edwards, R. R., Greaves, M. P. & Jackson, M. P. (2000). The potential for use of willows as components of practical buffer zones. Department of Agricultural Sciences, IACR, Long Ashton, University of Bristol.

Eiseltova, M. & Biggs, J., eds. (1995). *Restoration of Stream Ecosystems*. Slimbridge: International Waterfowl and Wetlands Research Bureau.

Environment Agency (1998). A. M. Walker. Audit surveys in the Environment Agency, Thames Region.

*Ernier, C. & Gutestarz, B., eds. (1991). *Ecological Engineering for Wastewater Treatment*. Germany: Boksgogen.

*Evans, R. (1993). Sensitivity of the British landscape to erosion. In *Landscape Sensitivity*, D. S. G. Thomas & R. J. Allison. Chichester: John Wiley & Sons, pp. 189–210.

*Everard, M. (2005). *Water Meadows*. Cardigan: Forrest Text.

Everard, M. (2000). Aquatic ecology, economy and society: the place of aquatic ecology in the sustainability agenda. *Freshwater Forum*, **13**, 31–46.

Everard, M. (2001). Taking a systems-orientated view of phosphorus enrichment in fresh waters. *Freshwater Forum*, **15**, 35.

Everard, M., James, B., Carty, P. & Powell, A. (2002). Implementing the water framework directive. *FBA News*, **17**, 1–5.

Fairbrother, N. (1970). *New Lives, New Landscapes*. London: Architectural Press.

Fairclough, G. (2003). The long chain: archaeology, historical landscape characterisation and time depth in the landscape. In *Landscape Interfaces*, ed. H. Palang & G. Fry. Dordrecht: Kluwer Academic Publishers, pp. 295–318.

*Feld, S. & Basso, K. H. (1996). *Sense of Place*. Santa Fe: School of American Research Press.

Feureira, T., Moreira, I., Wade, P. M. Pieterse, A. H., Caffrey, J. & Barrett, P. R. F. (1999). Advances in aquatic weed ecology and management: issues for the next millennium. *Developments in Hydrobiology Series*.

Finlayson, M., ed. (1992). Integrated management and conservation of wetlands in agricultural and forested landscapes. Wetlands Research Bureau, Slimbridge, **22**.

Floodplain Forests (1997). Special Issue. *Global Ecology and Biography Letters*, **6**.

Fokkens, B. & Monk, U. (2004). Using river restoration as a focus to guide river basin management. Restoration Centre, Silsoe, Bedfordshire.

*Forman, R. T. T. & Godron, M. (1986). *Landscape Ecology*. New York: John Wiley & Sons.

Friday, L., ed. (1998). *Wicken Fen, the Making of a Nature Reserve*. Colchester: Harley Books.

Fukamachi, K., Oku, H. & Rackham, O. (2003). A comparative study on trees and hedgerows in Japan and England. In *Landscape Interfaces*, ed. H. Palang & G. Fry. Dordrecht: Kluwer Academic Publishers, pp. 53–69.

*Gaines, K. H. (2006). Does the equilibrium theory of island biogeography apply to dragonfly breeding ecology in a desert sinkhole complex? In Water and the landscape. *Proceedings of the 19th annual IALE (UK) conference*, ed. B. Davies & S. Thompson, International Association of Landscape Ecology, UK Chapter, pp. 64–71.

Gardiner, J. L. (1991). *River Projects and Conservation*. Chichester: John Wiley & Sons.

Garred, G. D. & Willis, K. G. (1996). Estimating the benefits of environmental enhancement: a case study of the River Darent. *Journal of Environmental Planning and Management*, **39**, 189–203.

*George, M. (1992). *The Land Use, Ecology and Conservation of Broadland*. Chichester: Packard.

*Gerald of Wales (*Giraldus Cambrensis*, Twelfth Century). *Travels Through Wales*. London: Penguin.

Gerrard, A. J. W. (1993). Landscape sensitivity and change on Dartmoor. In *Landscape Sensitivity*, ed. D. S. G. Thomas & R. J. Allison. Chichester: John Wiley & Sons, pp. 49–64.

Giles, N. & Summers, D. (1996). Helping fish in lowland streams. Fordingbridge (Hants): Game Conservancy.

Gill, C. J. (1970). The flooding tolerance of woody species – a review. *Forestry Abstracts*, **31**, 671–88.

*Gilman, K. (1994). *Hydrology and Wetland Conservation*. Chichester: John Wiley & Sons.

Gilver, D., Davids, C., Tyler, A., Corbelli, D. & Thorburn, K. (2003). Assessing the feasibility of using remotely sensed data to date river hydromorphology and hydromorphic alteration to meet WFD obligations. Robson Meeting, IACR, Sonning on Thames.

*Godwin, H. (1978). *Fenland: the Ancient Past and Uncertain Future*. Cambridge: Cambridge University Press.

Golterman, H. L. (2004). *The Chemistry of Phosphate and Nitrogen Compounds in Sediments*. Dordrecht: Kluwer Academic Publishers.

Goodson, J. (2003). Sediment and seed dynamics along rivers. Robson Meeting, IACR, Sonning on Thames.

Gopal, B. Junk, W. J. & Davis, J. A. (2001). *Biodiversity in Wetlands: Assessment, Function and Conservation*. Leiden: Backhuys Publishers.

*Grech Delicata, J. C. (1853). *Flora Melitensis*. Malta.

Grech, H. (2003). Dingli Cliffs score high in coastal evaluation study. *The Times of Malta*, 9 June.

Gregory, K. J., ed. (1983). *Background to Palaeohydrology*. Chichester: John Wiley & Sons.

Grison, R. (2001). A study of the significance of newly established hay meadows as a habitat for butterflies by means of a quantitative inventory of caterpillars and imagines. *Bulletin of the Geobotanical Institute ETH*, **68**, 109.

Grootjans, A. P. (1985). Changes of groundwater regime in wet meadows. Ph.D. Thesis, University of Groningen.

Gunnison, D. & Baoko, J. W. (1987). The rhizosphere ecology of submerged macrophytes. *Water Resource Bulletin*, **25**, 193–202.

Gurnell, A. M. (1998). The hydrogeomorphological effects of beaver dam building activity. *Progress in Physical Geography*, **22**, 167–84.

*Hammer, D. A., ed. (1989). *Constructed Wetlands for Wastewater Treatment*. Chelsea, Michigan: Lewis.

Hansson, L., Fahrig, L. & Merriam, L., eds. (1995). *Mosaic Landscapes and Ecological Processes. IALE Studies in Landscape Ecology 2*. London: Chapman & Hall.

Harnung, M. & Newson, M. D. (1986). Upland afforestation: influences on stream hydrology and chemistry. *Soil Use and Management*, **2**, 61–5.

Harper, D. M. & Ferguson, A. J. D., eds. (1995). *The Ecological Basis of River Management*. Chichester: John Wiley & Sons.

*Harper, D. M. & Smith, C. D. (1992). Habitats as the building blocks for river conservation assessment. In *River Conservation and Management*. P. J. Boon, P. Calow & G. E. Petts. Chichester: John Wiley & Sons, pp. 311–19.

Harper, D., Witkowski, F., Kemp-McCarthy, D. & Crabb, J. (1997). The distribution and abundance of riparian trees in English lowland floodplains. *Global Ecology and Biography Letters*, **6**, 297–306.

Harrison, S. S. C., Harris, I. T. B. & Armitage, P. D. (2000). The role of bankside habitat in river ecology: the importance of riparian vegetation on the distribution and abundance of aquatic invertebrates. Institute of Freshwater Ecology, Blandford Forum.

Haslam, H., ed. (1999). Regional geochemistry of Wales and part of west central England: stream water. British Geological Survey, Nottingham.

Haslam, S. M. (1960). The vegetation of the Breck–Fen margin. Ph. D. Thesis University of Cambridge.

Haslam, S. M. (1973a). The management of British wetlands. I. Economic and amenity use. *Journal of Environmental Management*, **1**, 303–2.

Haslam, S. M. (1973b). The management of British wetlands. II. Conservation. *Journal of Environmental Management*, **1**, 345–61.

*Haslam, S. M. (1978). *River Plants*. Cambridge: University Press.

*Haslam, S. M. (1982). *Vegetation in British Rivers*. Nature Conservancy Council, 2 vols., pp. 203–5.

Haslam, S. M. (1986). Causes of changes in river vegetation giving rise to complaints. *Proceedings of the European Weed Research Society 7th International Symposium on Aquatic Weeds*, pp. 151–6.

*Haslam, S. M. (1987). *River Plants of Western Europe*. Cambridge: University Press.

*Haslam, S. M.(1990). *River Pollution: An Ecological Perspective*. London: Belhaven Press.

*Haslam, S. M. (1991). *The Historic River*. Cambridge: Cobden of Cambridge Press.

*Haslam, S. M. (1994). Wetland habitat differentiation and sensitivity to chemical pollutants (non-open water wetlands). London: HMSO, 2 vols.

Haslam, S. M. (1995). Cultural variation in river quality and macrophyte response. *Acta Botanica Gallica*, **142**, 345–8.

Haslam, S. M. (1996). Enhancing river vegetation: conservation, development and restoration. *Hydrobiologia*, **340**, 345–8.

*Haslam, S. M. (1997a). *The River Scene: Ecology and Cultural Heritage*. Cambridge: Cambridge University Press.

*Haslam, S. M. (1997b). River habitat fragmentation in Malta: a danger needing investigation. *Fresenius Environmental Bulletin*, **6**, 43–7.

*Haslam, S. M. (1997c). Deterioration and fragmentation of rivers in Malta. *Freshwater Forum*, **9**, 55–61.

Haslam, S. M. (1997d). The precarious state of the rivers of Malta. *Fresenius Environmental Bulletin*, **6**, 343–8.

Haslam, S. M. (1998). The deterioration of water quality in Malta. *Fresenius Environmental Bulletin*, **7**, 96–9.

Haslam, S. M. (1999a). River patterns in landscapes. In *Heterogeneity in Landscape Ecology Pattern and Scale*. IALE (UK) ed. M. Maudsley & J. Marshall, International Association of Landscape Ecology, UK Branch, pp. 169–75.

Haslam, S. M. (1999b). Ponds and pools of Malta: past and present. In *Ponds and Pond Landscape of Europe. Pond*Life, ed. J. Boothby. Liverpool: John Moores University, pp. 117–24.

*Haslam, S. M. (2000a). Socio-economic forces in Gozo (Maltese Islands) and landscape ecology analysis. In *Quantitative Approaches to Landscape Ecology*, ed. T. Clare & D. Howard, International Association of Landscape Ecology, UK Branch, pp. 25–32.

Haslam, S. M. (2000b). Impact of land use changes on rivers. *Aspects of Applied Biology*, **58**, 197–204.

Haslam, S. M. (2000c). The evaluation of river pollution in the Maltese Islands. *Fresenius Environmental Bulletin*, **9**, 347–51.

Haslam, S. M. (2001). Retaining the cultural heritage of rivers? In *Development of European Landscapes*, ed. Ü Mander, A. Rintsmann & H. Palang vol. 1, University of Tartu Press, pp. 206–9.

*Haslam, S. M. (2002). Stream community lists as bioindicators. *Proceedings of the 11th European Weed Research Society International Symposium on Aquatic Weeds*, September 2–6. Moliets et Maâ, France, pp. 243–6.

*Haslam, S. M. (2003). *Understanding Wetlands: Fen, Bog and Marsh*. London: Taylor & Francis.

*Haslam, S. M. (2006). *River Plants*. 2nd edn. Cardigan: Forrest Text.

*Haslam, S. M. & Borg, J. (1998). *The River Valleys of the Maltese Islands*. Malta: Ciheam, Bari and Islands and Small States Institute, Foundation of International Studies.

*Haslam, S. M. & Wolseley, P. A. (1981). *River Vegetation: Its Identification, Assessment and Management*. Cambridge: Cambridge University Press.

*Haslam, S. M., Sell, P. D. & Wolseley, P. A. (1977). *A Flora of the Maltese Islands*. Malta: University Press.

Haslam, S. M., Sinker, C. A. & Wolseley, P. A. (1982). *British Water Plants*. Field Studies Council Publication S10, 2nd edn.

*Haslam, S. M., Klötzli, F., Sukopp, H. & Szczepanski, A. (1998). The management of wetlands. In *The Production Ecology of Wetlands*. ed. D. F. Westlake, J. Kvet and A. Szczepanski. Cambridge: Cambridge University Press, pp. 405–64.

*Haslam, S. M., Borg, J. & Psaila, J. M. (2004). *River Kbir: The Hidden Wonder*. Zabbar, Malta: Veritas Press.

Haury, J. (1995). Patterns of macrophyte distribution within a Breton brook compared with other study scales. *Landscape and Urban Planning*, **31**, 349–61.

Haury, J. (1996a). Macrophytes des cours d'eau: bioindication et habitat piscicole. Thèse d'Habilitation a Diriger des Recherches, Universitéde Rennes, I. vol. 3.

*Haury, J. (1996b). Assessing function typology involving water quality, physical features and macrophytes in a Normandy river. *Hydrobiologia*, **340**, 43–9.

*Haury, J. & Aidara, L. G. (1999). Macrophyte cover and standing crop in the River Scorff and its tributaries (Brittany, north western France): scale, patterns and process. *Hydrobiologia*, **415**, 109–15.

*Haury, J. & Muller, S. (1991). Variations écologiques et chorologiques de la végétation macrophytique des rivières acides du Massif Armoricain et des Vosges du Nord (France). *Review Science Eau*, **4(4)**, 463–82.

*Haury, J., Peltre, M. C., Muller, S. et al., (1996). Des indices macrophytiques pour estimer la qualitédes cours d'eau fraînçais: premières propositions. *Ecologie*, **27(4)**, 79–90.

*Haury, J. Jaffre, M., Dutartre, A. et al. (1998). Application de l a méthode 'Milieu Et Végétaux aquatiques fixés' a 12 rivières françaises: typologie foristique préliminaire. *Annales Limnologie*, **34**, 1–11.

*Haury, J., Dutartre, A., Binesse, F., Codhant, H. & Valkman, G. (2001). Macrophyte biotypologies of rivers in Lozère, France. *Verbandlung Internationale Vereinung fur Theoretische und Angewandte Limnologie* (Dublin 1998), **27**(6), 3510–17.

*Haury, J. Peltre, M.-C., Trémolières, M. (2002). A method involving macrophytes to assess water trophy and organic pollution: the Macrophyte Biological Index for Rivers – application to different types of rivers and pollutions. In Gestion des plantes aquatiques. *Proceedings of the 11th European Weed Research Society International Symposium on Aquatic Weeds*, A. Dutartre & M. H. N. Montel, 3–7 September 2002. Moliets et Maâ, France, pp. 247–50.

*Haworth, E., de Boar, G., Evans, I. et al. (2003). *Tarns of the Central Lake District*. Brathay Exploration Group Trust, Ambleside.

*Haycock, N. E. & Burt, T. P. (1993a). Catchment sensitivity to nitrate leaching: the effectiveness of riparian zones in protecting stream ecosystems. In *Landscape Sensitivity*, ed. D. S. G. Thomas & R. J. Allison. Chichester: John Wiley & Sons, pp. 261–72.

*Haycock, N. E. & Burt, T. P. (1993b). Role of floodplain sediments in reducing the nitrate concentration of subsurface run-off: a case study in the Cotswolds, UK. *Hydrology Processes*, **7**, 287–93.

Haycock, N. E. & Burt, T. P. (1993c). The sensitivity of rivers to nitrate leaching. In *Landscape Sensitivity*, ed. D. S. G. Thomas & R. J. Allison. Chichester: John Wiley & Sons, pp. 261–72.

*Haycock, N. E. & Pinay, G. (1993). Nitrate retention in grass and poplar vegetated riparian buffer strips during the winter. *Journal of Environmental Quality*, **22**, 273–8.

Haycock, N. E., Pinay, G. & Walker, C. (1993). Nitrogen retention in river corridors: European perspective. *Ambio*, **22**, 340–6.

Heath, D. (1991). River corridor surveys in Devon. *Nature in Devon*, **11**, 4–11.

Henderson, C. L., Dindorf, C. J. & Rozumalski, F. J. (2002). *Landscaping for Wildlife and Water Quality*. Department of Natural Resources, Minnesota.

*Higham, N. (1986). *The Northern Counties to AD 1000*. London: Longman.

Hill, M. O. (1978). Vegetation changes resulting from afforestation of British uplands and bogs. *Chief Scientists Team Report*, Institute of Terrestrial Ecology, **204**.

*Hofmann, K. (1991). The role of plants in subsurface flow constructed wetlands. In *Ecological Engineering for Wastewater Treatment*, ed. C. Ernier & B. Guterstam, Gothenburg: Bokskogen, pp. 248–50.

*Holloway, R. (2003). A river keeper's observations on invertebrate populations over 34 winters. *FBA News*, **23**, 5–6.

Holmes, N. T. H. (1983a). Focus on nature conservation. 3. Classification of British rivers according to the flora. Nature Conservancy Council, Peterborough.

Holmes, N. T. H. (1983b). Focus on nature conservation. 4. Typing British rivers according to their macrophytic flora. Nature Conservancy Council, Peterborough.

Holmes, N. & Bradbrook, E. (2005). The river Darent: a strategy for recovery. River Restoration Centre, Silsoe, Bedfordshire, **27**.

*Holmes, P. (1974). *That Alarming Malady*. Cambridge Education Authority, Ely.

Hoskins, W. G. (1953). *The Making of the English Landscape*. London: Penguin.

Hoskins, W. G. (1973). *English Landscapes*. London: BBC.

*Howorth, R. & Manning, C. (2006). Land use change and the water environment of the West Weald over a 30-year period, 1971–2001. In Water and the landscape. *Proceedings of the 19th annual IALE (UK) conference*, ed. B. Davies & S. Thompson, International Association for Landscape Ecology, UK Chapter, pp. 126–33.

Hughes, J. M. R. & Heathwaite, A. L., eds. (1995). *Hydrology and Hydrochemistry of British Wetlands*. Chichester: John Wiley & Sons.

*Ihse, M. & Lindahl, C. (2000). A holistic model for landscape ecology in practice: the Swedish survey and management of ancient meadows and pastures. *Landscape and Urban Planning*, **50**, 59–84.

Janauer, G. A. (2000). Ecohydrology: fusing concepts and scales. *Ecological Engineering*, **16**, 9–16.

Janauer, G. A. (2002a). Water framework directive, European standards and the assessment of macrophytes in lakes: a methodology for scientific and practical application. *Verh. Zool. Ges. Osterreich*, **139**, 143–7.

Janauer, G. A. (2002b). Establishing ecohydrology in the real world: the Lobau Biosphere Reserve and the integrated water scheme in Vienna. In Ecohydrology and hydrobiology. The application of ecohydrology in water resources development and management. *Proceedings of the final conference of the first phase of the IHP-V Project 2.3/2.4 on Ecohydrology*, ed. M. Zalewski, D. M. Harper, Venice, September 2001, pp. 120–5.

Janauer, G. A. & Exler, N. (2003). Aquatic plants in the spotlight of international research. *Danube Watch*, **2**, 26–28.

*Janauer, G. A. & Exler, N. (2004). Distribution and habitat conditions of the six most frequent hydrophytes in the Danube River corridor: status 2002. *Proceedings of the 35th IAD Conference*. Novi Sad, Montenegro, pp. 407–12.

Janauer, G. A. & Wychera, U. (2000). Biodiversity, succession and the functioning role of macrophytes in the New Danube. *Archivum Hydrobiologia* (Supplement, Large Rivers), **12/1**, 61–74.

Jefferies, D. J., Strachan, R. & Strachan, C. (2004). The catastrophic 99.8% crash of the water vole *Arvicola terrestris* population of Cambridgeshire (v.c. 29) between 1989 and 1997. *Nature in Cambridgeshire*, **46**, 3–8.

Jeppesen, E., Søndergaard, M., Søndergaard, Marten & Christoffersen, K., eds. (1998). *The Structuring Role of Submerged Macrophytes in Lakes*. New York: Springer.

Johnes-Wright, G. & Gerrard, R. (2005). Strategic approach to flood risk management and habitat creation. River Restoration Centre, Silsoe, Bedfordshire, **26**.

Jones, J. M. (1963). Local rivers as sources of power. *Proceedings of the Birmingham Natural History and Philosophical Society*, **20**, 22–36.

Jones, M. (2003). The concept of cultural landscape. In *Landscape Interfaces*, ed. H. Palang & G. Fry. Dordrecht: Kluwer Academic Publishers, pp. 21–51.

Jousten, H. (2003). Perspectives of global peatland use and conservation. *IMCG Newsletter*, pp. 14–19.

Joyce, C. B. & Wade, P. M. (1998). *European Wet Grasslands*. Chichester, John Wiley & Sons.

Kark, R. (1992). Land–God–Man. In *Ideology and Landscape in Historical Perspective*, ed. A. R. H. Baker & G. Biger. Cambridge: Cambridge University Press, pp. 63–82.

Keddy, P., Fraser, L. H. & Keaugh, T. A. (2001). Response of 21 wetland species to shortage of light, nitrogen and phosphorus. *Bulletin of the Geobotanical Institute ETH*, **67**, 13–26.

Keddy, P. A. (2000). *Wetland Ecology: Principles and Conservation*. Cambridge: Cambridge University Press.

King, J. J. (1996). The impact of drainage maintenance strategies on the flora of a low gradient, drained Irish salmonid river. *Hydrobiologia*, **340**, 197–203.

*Kingsley, C. (1882). *The Water Babies*. London: Macmillan & Co.

*Kirby, P. (1992). *Habitat Management for Invertebrates*. Sandy, Bedfordshire: Royal Society for the Protection of Birds.

Klaas, D. (2003). Integrated river basin management in Air Hitam Laut River Basin, Sumatra. *Newsletter 3*. International Mire Conservation Group.

Kohler, A. & Janauer, G. A. (1995). Zur Methodik der Untersuchung von aquatischen Makrophyten in Fließgewässern. In *Handbuch Angewandte Limnologie*, ed. Ch. Steinberg, H. Bernhardt & H. Klapper, Landsberg: Ecomed Verlag.

*Kohler, A. & Labus, B. C. (1983). Eutrophication process and pollution of freshwater ecosystems including waste heat. *Physiological plant ecology* (*Encyclopedia of Plant Physiology*. New series. vol. 12D), **4**, 413–64.

*Kohler, A. & Schneider, S. (2003). Macrophytes as bioindicators. *Archivum Hydrobiologia* (Supplement, *Large Rivers*. **14**, 1–2).

*Kohler, A. & Veit, U. (2003a). Makrophyten als biolgische Qualitätskomponente bei den Fließgewässern. Bewertun – Anmerkungen zur EU Wasserrahmenrichtlinie. *Naturschutz und Landschaftsplanung*, **35**(12), 357–63.

*Kohler, A. & Veit, U. (2003b). Die EU-Wasserrahmenrichtlinie – Anmerkungen aus der Sicht der Makrophytenforschung in Fließgewässern. Stuttgart

*Kohler, A., Sipos, V. & Björk, S. (1996). Makrophytenvegetation und Standorte im humosen Bräkne Fluß(Südschweden). *Bot. Jahrb. Syst.*, **118**, 451–503.

*Kohler, A., Sipos, V., Sonntag, E., Penksza, K., Pozzi, D. & Veit, U. (2000). Makrophytenverbreitung und Standortqualität im Bjorka-Kävlinge Fluß(Skåne, Südschweden). *Hydrobiologia*, **30**, 281–98.

*Kohler, A., Sonntag, E., Köhler, M. *et al.* (2003). Macrophyte distribution in the River Vils (Oberpfalz, Bavaria). *Archivum Hydrobiologia* (Supplement, Large Rivers 14, no. 1–2), **147**/1–2, 33–53.

*Kohler, A. (1978). Methoden der Katierung von Flora und Vegetation von Süsswassertiotopen. *Land Schaft und Stadt*, **10**, 23–85.

Kondolf, G. M. (1998). Environmental effects of aggregate extraction from river channels and floodplains. In *Aggregate Resources: A Global Perspective*, ed. P. T. Bobrowsky, Vermont: A. A. Balkema, Brookfield, pp. 113–29.

*Lachat, B. (1994). Guide de protection des berges de cours d'eau au techniques végétales. Ministère de L'Environment, Dirron Rhone Alpes.

Lambert, J. M. & Jennings, J. M. (1951). Alluvial stratigraphy and vegetational succession in the region of the Bure Valley broads: II. *Journal of Ecology*, **39**, 149–70.

Landolt, E. (1975). Morphological differentiation and geographical distribution of the *Lemna gibba–Lemna minor* group. *Aquatic Botany*, **1**, 345–63.

*Lane, M. (1968). *The Tale of Beatrix Potter*. (Amazon Books) London: F. Warne & Co.

*Leach, J. & Dawson F. H. (1999). *Crassula helmsii*: an unwelcome invader. *British Wildlife*, April, pp. 115–19 & 145–9.

*Lewan, L. (2001). Land use and natural resources. In *Development of European Landscapes*, Ü Mander, A. Rintsmann & H. Palang, vol. 1, University of Tartu, pp. 337–42.

Limbrey, S. (1983). Archaeology and Palaeohydrology. In *Background to Palaeohydrology*, ed. K. J. Gregory. Chichester: John Wiley & Sons, pp. 189–212.

Linløkken, A. (1997). Effects of in-stream habitat enhancement on fish populations of a small Norwegian stream. *Nordic Journal of Freshwater Research*, **73**, 50–9.

Maaranen, P. (2003). Landscape archaeology and management of ancient cultural heritage sites. In *Landscape Interfaces*, ed. H. Palang & G. Fry. Dordrecht: Kluwer Academic Publishers, pp. 255–71.

Mackay, J. (1992). *The Secret Thames*. London: Ebury Press.

Maddock, I. (1999). The importance of physical habitat assessment for evaluating river health. *Freshwater Biology*, **41**, 373–91.

*Madsen, B. L. (1995). Danish Watercourses. Ten years with the new Watercourse Act. Danish Environment Protection Agency, Copenhagen, *Miljønyt*, **11**.

Maitland, P. S. (1996). The River Endrick – then and now – monitoring by photography. *Freshwater Forum*, **7**, 7–22.

*Malanson, G. P. (1993). *Riparian Landscapes*. Cambridge: Cambridge University Press.

*Mander, U. Printsmann, A., Palang, H., eds. (2001). *Development of European Landscape*. IALE European Conference (2001). Institute of Geography, University of Tartu. Vols. 1, 2.

Maquire, C. & Gibson, C. (2005). Ecological change in Lough Erne: influence of catchment changes and species invasions. *Freshwater Forum*, **24**, 38–58.

Maudsley, M. & Marshall, J., eds. (1999). Heterogeneity in landscape ecology. *Proceedings of the 1999 annual IALE (UK) conference*. International Association of Landscape Ecology, UK Branch.

*Maxwell, G. (1960). *Ring of Bright Water*. Longmans, Green & Company Ltd.

Maxwell, J. (1993). Ecosystem management by watersheds. *NPS Newsletter*, **32**, 6–8.

McCauley, D. E. (1995). Effects of population dynamics on genetics in mosaic landscapes. In *Mosaic Landscapes and Ecological Processes. IALE Studies in Landscape Ecology 2*, ed. L. Hansson, L. Fahrig, & L. Merriam. London: Chapman & Hall, pp. 179–98.

McCollin, D. (2001). Contemporary themes in hedgerow research in the UK. In *Hedgerows of the World*, ed. C. Barr, & S. Petit, International Association of Landscape Ecology (IALE, UK), UK Branch, pp. 17–29.

*McFarlane, R. (1999). Linking socio-economic driving forces to landscape ecology. In Quantitative approaches to landscape ecology. *Proceedings of the 2000 Animal IALE (UK) conference*, ed. T. Clare & D. Howard, International Association of Landscape Ecology, UK Branch, pp. 3–14.

*McLean, G. R. D. (1961). *Celtic Spiritual Verse*. Imprint SPCK (Society for Promoting Christian Knowledge): 22 November 2002.

Melman, P. J. M., Verkaar, H. G. & Heemsbergen, H. (1987). The maintenance of road verges as possible ecological corridors of grassland plants. In Conductivity in landscape ecology. *Proceedings of the 2nd International Seminar of IALE, Munster*, ed. K. F. Schreiber, Schörurgh, Paderborn, (1988) pp. 131–4.

Mesters, C. M. L. (1997). Polluted Dutch transboundary streams: effects on aquatic macrophytes. Ph.D. thesis, University of Utrecht.

Miller, S. H. & Skertchley, S. B. J. (1878). *The Fenland, Past and Present*. Wisbech: Leach & Sons.

Mineava, T. & Sirin, A. (2004). Climate change and peatlands, biodiversity aspects. *IMCG Newsletter*, p. 22.

*Mitford, M. R. (1829). *Our Village*. (Sketches of rural character and scenery). Ave-Maria-Lane, London (1824/32): G. & W. B. Whittaker.

*Mitsch, W., ed. (1994). *Global Wetlands, Old World and New*. Amsterdam: Elsevier Publications.

*Mitsch, W. J. & Gosselink, J. G. (1993). *Wetlands*, 2nd edn. New York: Van Nostrand Reinhold.

Monteiro, A., Vasconselos, T. & Catarine, L. (1998). Management and ecology of aquatic plants. *Proceedings of the 10th European Weed Research Society International Symposium of Aquatic Weeds*.

Moore, P. D. & Bellamy, D. J. (1974). *Peat Lands*. New York: Springer-Verlag.

Morris, J. (2002). Economics of Washland creation. River Restoration Centre Conference Abstract.

*Moshiri, G. A., ed. (1993). *Constructed Wetlands for Water Quality Improvement*. Boca Raton, Florida: Lewis Publishers.

Moss, D. (1979). Changes in songbird populations associated with the conversion of open hill ground to forest. *Chief Scientists Team Report*, Institute of Terrestrial Ecology, **239**.

Mountford, J. & Sheail, J. (1987). The Pembrokeshire valleys as baseline for reading future changes in plant life. NCC Research Contract HF3/08/09. Nature Conservancy Council.

Mountford, O., Goodson, J., Gurnell, A. Thompson, K. & Clifford, N. (2001). Seeds and sediment. Quantifying the sources for riparian restoration. Poster. In *Development of European Landscapes*, ed. Ü Mander, A. Rintsmann & H. Palang, vol. 1, University of Tartu, pp. 206–9.

Munshower, F. F. (1993). *Practical Handbook of Disturbed Land Vegetation*. Boca Raton, Florida: Lewis Publishers.

National Rivers Authority (1992). Blackwater river catchment management plan: consultation draft. Reading.

National Rivers Authority (1994). Guidance for the control of invasive plants near watercourses. Bristol: National Rivers Authority.

National Rivers Authority (1996). River habitats in England and Wales. River Habitat Survey Report, 1.

National Rivers Authority (1996). *River Habitats in England and Wales*. Bristol: National Rivers Authority.

National Rivers Authority (1995). *River Pollution from Farms in England*. London: HMSO.

*Neori, A. Reddy, K. R., Cisková-Koncalová, H. & Agami, M. (2000). Bioactive chemicals and biological–biochemical activities and their functions in rhizospheres of wetland plants. *The Botanic Review*, **66**, 350–78.

Newbold, C., Purseglove, J. & Holmes, N. (1983). *Nature Conservation and River Engineering*. London: Nature Conservancy Council.

*Newbold, C., Honnor, I. & Buckley, K. (1989). *Nature Conservation and the Management of Drainage Channels*. Peterborough: Nature Conservancy Council.

*Nisbet, T. R. & Thomas, H. (2006). The role of woodland in flood control. In Water and the landscape. *Proceedings of the 19th annual IALE (UK) conference*, ed. B. Davies, & S. Thompson, International Association of Landscape Ecology, UK Chapter, pp. 118–25.

Nolet, B. A. (1997). Management of the beaver (*Castor fiber*). Nature and Environment Series. Strasbourg: Council of Europe.

*Norden, J. (1610). *The Surveiors Dialogue, Very Profitable for all Men to Peruse*. London: Montague, 1739.

Norotny, V. & Olem, (1994). *Water Quality: Prevention, Identification and Management of Defense Pollution*. New York: Van Nostrand Reinhal.

Nuremberg Chronicle (1493). Schedel, H. Liber cronicarum, Nuremberg.

*O'Hallaran, D. et al., eds. (1994). Geological and landscape conservation. *Proceedings of the Malvern International Conference, 1993*. London: Joint Nature Conservation Committee and others.

*Olsen, O. R. K. (1993). *Created and Natural Wetlands for Controlling non-point Source Pollution*. Boca Raton, Florida: Smoley, CRC.

Opdam, P., Van Apeldoorn, R., Schotman, A. & Kalkhoven, J. (2001). Population responses to landscape fragmentation. In *Landscape Ecology of a Stressed Environment*, ed. C. C. Vos, & P. Opdam, (1993). London: Chapman & Hall.

Oxford Department of External Studies (1981). *The Evolution of Marshland Studies*. Oxford: Oxford University Press.

*Padoa-Schioppa, E., Poggesi, M. C. & Bottoni, L. (2006). Using river basins as ecological units to evaluate landscape fragmentation. In Water and the landscape. *Proceedings of the 19th annual IALE (UK) conference*, B. Davies & S. Thompson, International Association of Landscape Ecology, UK Chapter, pp. 77–84.

*Paetzold, A. & Tockner, K. (2006). Aquatic–terrestrial food web linkages along rivers. In Water and the landscape. *Proceedings of the 19th annual IALE (UK) conference*, ed. B. Davies & S. Thompson, International Association of Landscape Ecology, UK Chapter, pp. 201–7.

*Page, S. E. & Rieley, J. O. (1992). Eutrophication and rehabilitation of Wybungurg Moss National Nature Reserve, Cheshire. In *Peatland Ecosystems and Man*, ed. E. M. Bragg, P. D. Hulme, H. A. P. Ingram & R. A. Robertson, British Ecological Society, International Peat Society.

Palang, H. & Fry, G., eds. (2003). *Landscape Interfaces*. Dordrecht: Kluwer Academic Publishers.

Palmer, M. & Newbold, C. (1983). Wetland and riparian plants in Great Britain: an assessment of their status. *Focus on Nature Conservation*, **1**.

Pan-European biological and landscape diversity strategy (1995). *Nature and Environment*, **74**. Council of Europe, Strasbourg.

Parker, D. M. (1992). Habitat Creation – a critical guide. *English Nature Science*, Peterborough, **21**.

*Parker, R. (1975). *The Common Stream*. London: Collins.

Parmenter, J. (1995). The Broadland fen resource survey. Broads Authority and English Nature, Norwich.

Patten, B. C., ed. (1990). *Wetlands and Shallow Continental Water Bodies*, vol 1. *Natural and Human Relationships*. Amsterdam: SPB Academic Publishing.

Patten, B. C., ed. (1994). *Wetlands and Shallow Continental Water Bodies* vol. 2 *Case Studies*. Amsterdam: SPB Academic Publishing.

Pearson, G. & Frear, P. (2003). Use of angler catches to appraise the effectiveness of river habitat restoration on fish stocks. Robson Meeting, IACR, Sonning on Thames.

Peat, N. & Patrick, B. (2001). *Wild Rivers*. Dunedin: University of Otago Press.

Peter, A. & Woolsey, S. (2005). Importance of local river widenings as rehabilitation measures: experiences from Switzerland. River Restoration Centre, Silsoe, Bedfordshire, **35**.

*Peterken, G. F. & Hughes, F. M. R. (1995). Restoration of floodplain forests in Britain. *Forestry*, **68**, 187–202.

*Peterken, G. F. (1996). *Natural Woodland*. Cambridge: University Press.

*Petts, G. & Calow, P. (1992). *The Rivers Handbook*. Oxford: Blackwell Science.

*Petts, G. & Foster, I. (1985). *Rivers and Landscape*. London: Edward Arnold.

Piccolo, A., Celano, G. & Conte, P. (1996). Interactions between herbicides and humic substances. *Pesticide Outlook*, 1996, pp. 21–4.

Pieterse, A. H. (1975). Physiological, morphological and anatomical aspects of gibbosity in *Lemna gibba*. *Aquatic Botany*, **1**, 333–44.

Planteijilt, R., Johngman, R. H. G. & Kerkstra, K. (2005). The future landscape of the River Aa. In (1988). *Conductivity in Landscape Ecology*, ed. K. F. Schreiber, pp. 141–4.

*Porter, E. (1969). The river trade of old Cambridgeshire. *Cambs Hunts and Peterborough Life*. October, pp. 24–6 & 317–44.

*Potter, B. (1906). *The Tale of Mr Jeremy Fisher*. London: F. Warne & Co.

*Prach, K. (1992). Vegetation, microtopography and water table in the Luznice River flood plain, South Bohemia, Czechoslovakia. *Preslia*, Prague, **64**, 357–67.

*Prach, K. (1993). Vegetation changes in a wet meadow complex, South Bohemia, Czech Republic. *Folia Geobotanica Phytotaxonomica*, Prague, **28**, 1–13.

*Prach, K. & Rauch, O. (1992). On filter effects of ecotones. *Ekologia (CSFR)*, **11**, 293–8.

*Prach, K., Jeník, J. & Large, A. R. G. eds. (1997). *Floodplain Ecology and Management*. Amsterdam: SPB Academic Publishing.

*Prefill, P. P. & Volkman, N. (1999). *Landscape in History: Design and Planning in the Eastern and Western Traditions*. New York: John Wiley & Sons.

Purseglove, J. (1989). *Taming the Flood*. Oxford: Oxford University Press.

Pysek, P., Prach, K. Rejmánek, M. & Wade, M. (1995). *Plant Invasions*. Amsterdam: SPB Academic Publishing.

Rackham, O. (1976). *Trees and Woodland in the British Landscape*. London: J. M. Dent & Sons.

*Rackham, O. (1986). *The History of the Countryside*. London: J. M. Dent & Sons.

*Rackham, O. & Moody, J. (1996). *The Making of the Cretan Landscape*. Manchester: University Press.

Rath, B., Janauer, G. A., Pall, K. & Berczik, A. (2003). The aquatic macrophyte vegetation in the Old Danube/Hungarian bank, and other water bodies of the Szigetköz wetlands. *Archivum Hydrobiologia* (Supplement, Large Rivers), **14/1–2**, 129–42.

*Raven, P. J., Fox, P., Everard, M., Holmes, H. T. H., & Dawson, F. H. (1997). River habitat survey: a new system to classify rivers according to their habitat quality. In *Freshwater Quality: Defining the indefinable*, ed. P. J. Boon. London: HMSO, pp. 215–34.

*Raven, P. J., Boon, P. J., Dawson, F. H. & Ferguson, A. J. D. (1998a). Towards an integrated approach to classifying and evaluating rivers in the UK. Special Issue: the application of classification and assessment methods to river management in the UK. *Aquatic Conservation: Marine and Freshwater Ecosystems*, **8(4)**, 383–93.

*Raven, P. J., Holmes, N. T. H., Dawson, F. H. & Everard, M. (1998b). Quality assessment using river habitat survey data. Special issue: the application of classification and assessment methods to river management in the UK. *Aquatic Conservation: Marine and Freshwater Ecosystems*, **8(4)**, 477–99.

*Raven, P. J., Holmes, N. T. H., Dawson, F. H., Fox, P. J. A., Everard, M., Fozzard, I. & Rouen, K. J. (1998c). River habitat quality: the physical character of rivers and streams in the UK and Isle of Man. River Habitat Survey Report No. 2. Environment Agency, Bristol.

Raven, P. J., Holmes, N. T. H., Dawson, F. H. et al., eds. (1998d). River habitat quality. *Aquatic Conservation*, **8**.

Raven, P. J., Holmes, N. T. H., Naura, M. & Dawson, F. H. (1999). River habitat survey and its use in environmental assessment and integrated river basin management in the UK. International conference on assessing the ecological integrity of running waters, Vienna, 1998.

Read, K. Fermar, P. & Bundy, C. (2005). Riverine and floodplain rehabilitation best practice: a case study at Aston Hall Farm. River Restoration Centre, Silsoe, Bedfordshire, **36**.

*Reddy, K. R. & Smith, W. H., eds. (1987). *Aquatic Plants for Water Treatment and Resource Recovery*. Orlando, Florida: Magnolia Publishers.

Regional Flood Defence Committee (1997). Flood defence policy on environmental enhancement. Environment Agency, Thames Region.

*Richardson, P. (2003). New echoes from Batworld. *Natural World*, **19**, 22–4.

*Rieley, J. & Page, S. (1990). *Ecology of Plant Communities*. London: Longman.

*River Restoration Centre [various dates]. Manual of Techniques, Newsletters, Database, River Restoration Project, etc., Silsoe, Bedfordshire.

Robach, F., Eglin, I. & Trémolières, M. (1997). Species richness of aquatic macrophytes in former channels connected to a river: a comparison between two fluvial hydrosystems differing in their regime and regulation. *Global Ecology and Biogeography Letters*, **6**, 267–74.

Röck, S. & Kaiser, O. (2005). Assessment of stream passage obstructions caused by flood detention basins. River Restoration Centre, Silsoe, Bedfordshire, **43**.

Rodwell, J. S., ed. (1991). *British Plant Communities. Woodlands and Scrub*. Cambridge: Cambridge University Press.

*Rodwell, J. S., ed. (1992). *British Plant Communities, Grasslands and Mountain Communities*. Cambridge: Cambridge University Press.

*Rodwell, J. S., ed. (1995). *British Plant Communities, Aquatic Communities, Swamps and Tall-herb Fens*. Cambridge: Cambridge University Press.

Rukec, C. D. A. & Overend, R. P., eds. (1987). *Proceedings of Symposium 1987. Wetlands / peatlands*. Edmonton, Alberta.

Sabater, F., Sabater, S. & Armengol, J. (1990). Chemical characteristics of a Mediterranean river as influenced by land uses in the watershed. *Water Research*, **24**, 143–55.

Said, S. & Delcross, P. (2002). Using the hedges and spatial analysis for studying vegetation (laricio pine and beech) dynamics in Corsica (France). 11th European Weed Research Society International Symposium, Landes, France, poster.

*Saliba, P. C., Magro Conti, J. & Borg, C. (2002). A study of landscape and irrigation systems at is-Simblija, limits of Dingli. Malta and Conservation project. Consiglio Nazionale delle Ricerche, ARAMIS, Malta.

Sand-Jensen, K. & Rasmussen, L. (1978). Macrophytes and chemistry of acidic streams from lignite mining areas. *Bot. Tideskr.*, **72**, 105–12.

Sansom, A. (1993). *Ponds and Conservation*. York: National Rivers Authority.

Sarlöv-Herlin, I. & Fry, G. (2001). Managing wooded boundaries to improve wildlife experience in near-urban areas. In *Development of European Landscapes*, Ü Mander, A. Rintsmann & H. Palang, vol. 1, University of Tartu, pp. 486–90.

Schneeweiss, N. & Beckmann, H. (1998). The ponds of the young-moraine-landscape: habitats and centres of distribution of amphibians in Brandenberg (NE Germany). In *Ponds and Pond Landscape of Europe. Pond*Life, ed. J. Boothby. John Moores University, Liverpool, pp. 197–202.

Schreiber, K. F. ed. (1988). Connectivity in landscape ecology. *Proceedings of the 2nd International Seminar of International Association for Landscape Ecology, Munster 1987.* Schörurgh, Paderborn, pp. 11–16.

Schropp, M. H. & Babber, C. (1998). Secondary channels as a basis for the ecological rehabilitation of Dutch rivers. *Aquatic Conservation*, **8**, 53–9.

Scott, S. & Angell, G. (2005). Implementing the biodiversity strategy and action plans for the Environment Agency (Thames Region) through partnership. River Restoration Centre, Silsoe, Bedfordshire, **45**.

Sear, D. & Elliott, M. (2005). Sustainable wetland restoration in the New Forest. River Restoration Centre, Silsoe, Bedfordshire, **44**.

Sear, D., Armitage, P. D. & Dawson, F. H. (1999). Groundwater dominated rivers. *Hydrological Processes*, **13**, 255–77.

Sear, D. A. (1994). River restoration and geomorphology. *Aquatic Conservation*, **4**, 169–77.

Seidel, K. (1967). Aquatic plants purify sewage. *Umschau*, **67**, 565.

Seidel, K. (1968). Eliminatio van Schmitz- und Balastoffen aus belustaten Gewässern durch höhere pflanzen, *Zeitschrift Nitalstoffen-zwilisations krankheitan*, **4**.

Shafer, E. L. & Brush, R. O. (1977). How to measure preferences for photographs of natural landscape. *Landscape Planning*, **4**, 237–56.

Shafer, E. L., Hamilton, J. F. & Schmidt, E. A. (1969). Natural landscape preferences: a predictive model. *Journal of Leisure Research*, **1**, 1–19.

Sheail, J. (1976). The land use history of the Huntingdonshire fenland, with special reference to the Holme Fen and Woodwalton Fen NNRs. NCC Research Contract F3/03/27. Institute of Terrestrial Ecology.

Sipes, U. K. (2001). Makrophyten-vegetation und standarb in eutrophen und humosum fliesege-wässen. Benichte des Institutle foir Landschafts-und Pflanzenökalogie den Universität Hohenheim, **13**.

*Sipos, V., Kohler, A. & Björk, S. (2000). Makrophytenvegetation und Standorte im eutrophen Björka Fluß(Südschweden). *Botanisches Jahrbuch Systematicsche*, **122**, 93–152.

Sipos, V. K., Kohler, A. & Veit, U. (2001). Vergleichende Kennzeichnung der Makrophytenvegetation verschiedener Fliessgewässertypen anhand quantitativer Kenngrössen. *Berichte: Institut fur Landschafts- und Pflanzenokologie Universität Hobenheim*, **10**, 33–56.

*Skowronek, E., Krükowska, R. & Swieca, A. (2003). Transformations of cultural landscape. In *Landscape Interfaces*, ed. H. Palang & G. Fry. Dordrecht: Kluwer Academic Publishers, pp. 71–89.

SKYSCAN Mackay, J. (1992). *The Secret Thames.* London: Ebury Press.

Smith, A. G. & Morgan, L. A. (1989). A succession to ombiotrophic bog in the Gwent Levels and its demise. *New Phytologist*, **112**, 195–6.

Sønderjyllend Amtskommune (1982). Undersøgelse of okkarindholdets in Flydelse på invertebratfaunen i vida system at 1979–80. Teknisk Forvaltning Miljøfdelingen.

Spink, A. J., Murphy, K. J. & Westlake, D. R. F. (1997). Distribution and environmental regulation of species of *Ranunculus* subgenus *Batrachium* in British rivers. *Archivum Hydrobiologica*, **139**, 509–25.

*Sporrong, O., Ekstam, U. & Samudesan, K. (1995). *Swedish Landscapes*. Stockholm: Swedish Environment Protection Agency.

Ssymonk, A. & Hauho, U. (1998). Landscape ecology of calcareous fens (*Caricion davallianae*) and the *Cladicetum marisci* in the lowlands of N E Germany and their relevance for nature conservation in the European Union Habitats Directive. *Phytocoenelogia*, **28**, 105–42.

Sterba, O. Melotova, J., Krskova, M., Samsonova, P. & Harker, D. (1997). Floodplain forests and river restoration. *Global Ecology and Biography Letter*, **6**, 331–7.

*Stoate, C., Whitfield, M., Williams, P. & Driver, K. (2006). Wetland habitat creation and mitigation of water pollution from field drains: use of buffer strip pods within an arable landscape. In Water and the landscape. *Proceedings of the 19th annual IALE (UK) conference*, B. Davies & S. Thompson, International Association of Landscape Ecology, UK Chapter, pp. 331–4.

*Storey, E. (1993). *The Winter Fens*. Oxford: Isis.

Sutcliffe, D., ed. (2001). Lakes assessment and the EU Water Framework Directive. *Freshwater Forum*, **16**.

Suwannee 1985 (1985). State of Florida, Department of Environmental Regulation.

Swale and Ure Washlands Project (2001). A future for the Washlands. North Yorkshire County Council.

*Swanwick, C. (2002). *Landscape Character Assessment*. Wetherby: Countryside Agency and Scottish Natural Heritage.

Symoens, J. J., Hooper, S. S. & Compère, P., eds. (1982). *Studies on Aquatic Vascular Plants*. Brussels: Royal Botanical Society of Belgium.

Tabacchi, E. & Planty-Tabaichi, A. M. (2002). Changes in alien and native weedy vegetation along rivers. What's new? *11th European Weed Research Society International Symposium*, Landes, France, pp. 439–42.

*Tansley, A. G. (1911). *Types of British Vegetation*. Cambridge: Cambridge University Press.

Tapsell, S. M. (1995). River restoration: what are we restoring to? A case study of the Ravensbourne River, London. *Landscape Research*, **20**, 98–11.

Thacker, F. S. (1909). *The Stripling Thames*. London: Fred S. Thacker, Holborn.

Thacker, F. S. (1914). *The Thames Highway*. London: Fred S. Thacker, Holborn.

*Thomas, D. S. A. & Allison, R. J., eds. (1993). *Landscape Sensitivity*. Chichester: John Wiley & Sons.

Thorne, C. J. R. (1995). *A Summary Checklist of the Birds of Wicken Fen*. Guides to Wicken Fen.

Thorne, C. R. (1996). *Stream Reconnaissance Handbook*. Chichester: John Wiley & Sons.

Ticehurst, N. F. (1957). *The Mute Swan in England*. London: Cleaver Hume.

Trémolières, M. & Mullen, S., eds. (1995). Macrophytes aquatique et qualitéde l'eau. *Acta Botanica Gallia*, **142** (6).

*Trémolières, M., Carbiener, R. Urtscheit, A. & Klein, J. P. (1944). Change in aquatic vegetation in Rhine floodplains in Alsace in relation to disturbance. *Journal of Vegetation Science*, **5**, 169–78.

*Trémolières, M., Carbiener, D., Carbiener, R. *et al.* (1991). Zones inondable, végétation et qualitéde l'eau en milieu alluvial Rhonen: e'lle de Rhinan, un site de recherches integrées. *Bulletin Ecologique*, **22**, 317–36.

Trémolières, M., Eglin, I., Roeck, U. & Carbiener, R. (1993a). The exchange process between river and groundwater on the Central Alsace flood plain (Eastern France). I. *Hydrobiologia*, **254**, 133–48.

Trémolières, M., Eglin, I., Roeck, U. & Carbiener, R. (1993b). The exchange process between river and groundwater on the Central Alsace floodplain (Eastern France). II. The case of the canalised river Rhine. *Hydrobiologia*, **259**, 133–42.

*Trémolières, M., Roeck, U., Klein, J. P. & Carbiener, R. (1994). The exchange process between river and groundwater on the Central Alsace flood plain (Eastern France). III. The case of a river with functional flood plain. *Hydrobiologia*, **273**, 19–36.

Tremp, H. & Kohler, A. (1995). The usefulness of macrophyte monitoring-systems, exemplified on eutrophication and acidification of running waters. *Acta Botanica Gallica*, **142**, 541–50.

*Triest, L. (2002). Macrophytes as biological indicators of Belgian rivers: a comparison of macrophyte indices with those of other organisms in high quality headwaters. *Proceedings of the 11th European Weed Research Society International Symposium on Aquatic Weeds*. September 2–6. Moliets et Maâ, France, pp. 263–66.

Ullrich, K. S. (2001). The influence of wildflower strips on plant and insect (heteroptera) diversity in an arable landscape. *Bulletin of the Geobotanical Institute ETH*, **68**, 121–2.

Urciuolo, A. & Iturrapse, R. (2004). Workshop management of water basis regulated by peatland. *IMCG Newsletter*, pp. 13–14.

Van Buuren, M. & Kerkstra, K. (1993). The framework concept and the hydrological landscape structure. In *Landscape Ecology of a Stressed Environment*, ed. C. C. Vos, & P. Opdam. London: Chapman & Hall, pp. 219–43.

*Veit, U. & Kohler, A. (2003). Long-term study of the macrophytic vegetation in the running waters of the friedberger Au (near Augsburg, Germany). *Archivum Hydrobiol* (Supplement, Large Rivers, 14/1–2), **147/1–2**, 65–86.

*Veit, U., Zeltner, G.-H. & Kohler, A. (1997). Die Makrophytenvegetation des Fließgewässersystems der Friedberger Au (bei Augsburg) – Ihre Entwicklung von 1972 bis 1996. *Berlin Institut Landschafts- Pflanzenokologie* (Univ. Hohenheim), **4**, 7–241.

*Verhoeven, J. T. A. (1992). *Fens and bogs in The Netherlands: history, nutrient dynamics and conservation*. Dordrecht: Kluwer.

*Vink, A. P. A. (1983). *Landscape Ecology and Land Use*. London: Longman.

Von Ax, G. (2001). Nature meets Pasture. *Bulletin of the Geobotanical Institute ETH*, **68**, 111.

Vos, C. C. & Chardon, J. P. (1997). Landscape resistance and dispersal in fragmented populations. In Species dispersal and land use processes. *Proceedings of the 6th annual conference of IALE (UK)*, ed. A. Cooper & J. Power, International Association of Landscape Ecology, UK Branch, pp. 19–26.

*Vos, C. C. & Opdam, P., eds. (1993). *Landscape Ecology of a Stressed Environment*. London: Chapman & Hall.

*Vymazal, J. Brix, H., Cooper, P. F., Green, M. B. & Hobert, R., eds. (1998). *Constructed Wetlands for Wastewater Treatment in Europe*. Leiden: Backhuys.

*Vymazal, J. ed. (2001). *Transformations of Nutrients in Natural and Constructed Wetlands*. Leiden: Backhuys.

Waal, L. C. de *et al.*, eds. (1994). *Ecology and Management of Invasive Riverside Plants*. Chichester: John Wiley & Sons.

*Wait, G. A. 1997. Archaeological Heritage. In *The River Scene*, ed. S. M. Haslam. Cambridge: University Press, pp. 297–302.

Walker, J. & Reuter, D. J., eds. (1996). *Indicators of Catchment Health*. Victoria: CSIRO.

Ward, D. (1991). River banks and their bird communities. Occasional papers in environmental studies. *Riverbank Conservation*, **11**, Hatfield Polytechnic.

Ward, D. Holmes, N. T. H. & José, P., eds. (1994). *The New Rivers and Wildlife Handbook*. Sandy, Bedfordshire: Royal Society for the Protection of Birds.

Ward, J. V. (1989). The four-dimensional nature of tolic ecosystems. *Journal of the North American Benthological Society*, **8**, 2–8.

*Warnock, S., Griffiths, G., Porter, J. & Simmons, E. (2001). The cultural component of landscape character assessment. In *Development of European Landscapes*, ed. Ü Mander, A. Rintsmann & H. Palang, vol. 1, University of Tartu, pp. 229–32.

Westlake, D. F. & Dawson, F. H. (1982). Thirty years of weed cutting on a chalk stream. *Proceedings of the 6th European Weed Research Council Symposium on Aquatic Weeds*, pp. 132–40.

Westlake, D. F. & Dawson, F. H. (1986). The management of *Ranunculus calcareus* by pre-emptive cutting in southern England. European Weed Research Society, Association of Applied Biologists, *7th International Symposium on Aquatic Weeds*, pp. 395–400.

Westlake, D. F. & Dawson, F. H. (1988). The effects of autumnal weed cuts in a lowland stream on water levels and flooding in the following springs. *Verhandlung international Vereinung theoretische angewante Limnologiae*, **23**, 1273–77.

Westlake, D. F., Casey, H., Dawson, F. H., Ladle, M., Mann, R. H. K. & Marker, A. F. H. (1972). The chalk stream ecosystem. In *Productivity Problems of Freshwaters Warsaw-Kracov*, ed. Z. Kajak & A. Hillbricht-Ilkowska, pp. 615–635.

*Westlake, D. F., Kvet, J. & Sczepanski, A., eds. (1998). *The Production Ecology of Wetlands*. Cambridge: Cambridge University Press.

Weston, D. E. (no date). *The Lark Navigation*. Bury St Edmunds: D. W. Weston.

Wheeldon, J. & Dagmar, J. (2004). Stream-restoring a chalk river system on a catchment scale. River Restoration Centre, Silsoe, Bedfordshire.

*Wheeler, B. D. & Shaw, S. C. (1992). Biological indicators of the dehydration and changes to East Anglian fens past and present. *English Nature Research Reports*, **20**.

Wheeler, B. D., Shaw, S. C., Fojt, W. J. & Robertson, R. A. (1995). *Restoration of Temperate Wetlands*. Chichester: John Wiley & Sons.

*White, G. (1788). *The Natural History of Selbourne*. London (1977): Penguin.

White, P. C. L., Gregory, K. W., Lindley, P. J. & Richards, G. (1997). Economic values of threatened mammals in Britain: A case study of the otter *Lutra lutra* and the water vole *Arvicola terrestris*. *Biological Conservation*, **82**, 345–59.

Whitton, B. A., Boulton, P. N. G., Clegg, E. M. *et al.* (1998). Long-term changes in macrophytes of British rivers: 1. River Wear. *The Science of the Total Environment*, **210/11**, 411–26.

Whyle, L. (1962). *Medieval Technology and Social Change*. Oxford: Oxford University Press.

*Wildig, J. (2000). Mynydd y ffynnon. *Aspects of Applied Biology*, **58**, 159–66.

*Williams, J. H., Kingham, H. G., Cooper, D. J. & Regle, S. J. (1977). Growth regulator injury to tomatoes in Essex, England. *Environmental Pollution*, **12**, 145–57.

*Williams, M. (1970). *The Draining of the Somerset Levels*. Cambridge: University Press.

*Williams M. (1974). *The Making of the South Australian Landscape*. London: Academic Press.

Winteler, M. (2001). Fen rotation fallow near lake Gneifenses (2H) *Bulletin of the Geobotanical Institute ETH*, **68**, 112.

Wolseley, P. A., James, P. W., Theobald, M. R. & Sutton, M. A. (2006). Detecting changes in epiphytic lichen communities at site affected by atmospheric ammonia from agricultural sources. *The Lichenologist*, **38**, 161–76.

Wolseley, P. A., Stafor, S., Mitchell, R. *et al.* (2006). Variation of lichen communities with land use in Aberdeenshire, UK. *The Lichenologist*, **38**, 307–22.

Worall, P. (2002). Putting function back into the flood plain. River Restoration Centre Conference Abstract.

Wright, J. F., Sutcliffe, D. W., Furse, M. Y., eds. (2000). Assessing the biological quality of freshwater s-c rivpace and other techniques. Freshwater Biological Association, Ambleside.

*Yonge, C. M. (1864). *The Trial*. London: Macmillan.

Index to plant and animal vernacular and taxonomic names

Achillea millefolium, 173
Acorus calamus, 164, 165, 227
Agrostis
    capillaris, 172
    castellana, 172
    stolonifera, 31, 34, 39, 40, 41, 133, 171
Alisma, 162
    plantago, 39
    plantago-aquatica, 30, 31, 34, 46, 75, 78, 119, 169, 171
Alnus, 154
    glutinosa, 173
amphibians, 5
Anthoxanthum odoratum, 172
Apium
    graveolens, 75
    inundatum, 75
    nodiflorum, 31, 33, 38, 39, 41, 44, 46, 75, 118, 120, 133, 162, 165, 169, 170
Arundo donax, 31, 34, 75, 76, 230, 268
Azolla, 162, 165, 176
    filiculoides, 169

bats, 251, 263
beavers, 186, 218, 220, 224–5
bees, 225
beetles, 254
Berula
    aquatica, 46
    erecta, 31, 33, 35, 36, 38, 40, 113, 120, 130, 133, 162, 169, 170
Betula, 173
Bidens cernua, 31, 33
birds, 221–3, 224
    see also individual types
bitterns, 254
Blanket weed, 32, 34, 35, 120, 162
Butomus umbellatus, 31, 34, 164

Cabomba, 162
    caroliniana, 176
Calamagrostis striata, 199
Callitriche, 31, 38, 39, 40, 41, 44, 78, 117, 120, 125, 130, 133, 162, 176
    brutia, 75
    cophocarpa, 33, 46, 169
    hamulata, 31
    obtusangula, 33, 46, 169
    palustris, 75
    platycarpa, 33, 46, 169
    stagnalis, 33, 46, 75, 169
    truncata, 75
Calluna, 194

Caltha palustris, 31, 33
Canna, 162
Carex, 39, 40, 162, 199
    acutiformis, 31, 34, 38, 39, 46, 120, 164, 169
    appropinquata, 264, 275
    elata, 198
    palustris, 169
    paniculata, 198, 264, 275
    riparia, 34, 164
    rostrata, 31, 33
    stricta, 169
Catabrosa aquatica, 118
Ceratophyllum demersum, 31, 34, 40, 120, 169
Chara hispida, 33, 186, 210
Cladium, 162, 165
    mariscoides, 169
    mariscus, 169, 216, 228
Cladophora glomerata, 40, 75
Colocasia
    antiqua, 162, 226
    esculenta, 75
Corylus avellana, 172
cotton grass, 319
coypus, 225
Crassula
    helmsii, 47, 162, 177
    vaillanti, 75
Crataegus monogyna, 172
curlews, 279

Index to plant and animal vernacular and taxonomic names

Cynosurus cristatus, 172
Cyperus, 78, 162, 165, 195, 316
   badius, 75
   bardii, 31, 34
   longus, 75, 164

Damasonium bourgaeli, 75
Danous carota, 173
Drosera, 194, 196, 319
ducks, 221, 222–3

eels, 219, 220
Egeria, 167, 177
Eichornia, 176
   crassipes, 232
Elatine
   gussonei, 75
   macropoda, 75
Elodea, 162, 177
   canadensis, 31, 34, 38, 39, 43, 46, 47, 113, 119, 120, 125, 127, 130, 133, 169
   nuttallia, 31, 47, 169
Enteromorpha, 32, 34, 39
   intestinalis, 40
Epilobium
   hirsutum, 31, 34, 38, 39, 171, 172
   tetragonum, 75
Equisetum, 31, 162, 171
   fluviatile, 33, 169, 171
   palustre, 33, 169
Eriophorum, 194, 319
   angustifolium, 275
   vaginatum, 199
   scheuchzeria, 198
eucalypts, 77, 243, 250, 271

Fallopia japonica, 173
Festuca
   ovina, 172
   rubra, 173

Filipendula ulmaria, 171, 264
fish, habitat requirements, 222

Galium uliginosum, 276
   uliginosus, 264, 275
Gammarus, 42, 265
geese, 221–4
Glyceria, 31, 162
   canadensis, 169
   declinata, 34
   fluitans, 31, 33, 34, 40, 130, 171
   grandis, 169
   maxima, 31, 34, 36, 38, 39, 41, 46, 75, 94, 119, 120, 130, 160, 163, 164, 169, 170
   plicata, 34, 75
grasses, 163, 168, 169, 171, 172
grebes, 222
Groenlandia densa, 38, 118, 130, 133

Heracleum mantegazzianum, 173
herons, 222
Hippuris vulgaris, 169
horsetails, 162, 171
Hydrocharis, 162
   morsus-ranae, 31, 33, 176
Hydrocotyle, 162
   ranunculoides, 162
Hypochaeris radicata, 173

Impatiens glandula, 173
invertebrates, 137–8, 174–5, 222
Iris, 162
   pseudacorus, 31, 33, 41, 46
Isoetes hystrix, 75

Juncus, 162, 164, 171, 177, 198
   articulatus, 20, 31, 33, 75, 81, 171
   bufonius, 75
   bulbosus, 31, 33, 40
   capitatus, 75
   effusus, 31, 34, 169, 171, 230
   subnodulosus, 33, 186, 264

leeches, 13, 225–6
Lemna, 162, 165, 167, 176
   gibba, 34
   minor, 31, 34, 38, 39, 40, 41, 75, 169
   minuta, 169
   polyrhiza, 33
   trisulca, 31, 33, 130
Leucanthemum vulgare, 173
Littorella, 162, 167
Lobelia, 162
Lotus
   corniculatus, 173
   uligonosus, 264
Luzula sylvatica, 31, 33
Lychnis flos-cuculi, 275
Lythrum junceum, 75

Malus sylvestris, 172
mammals, 224–5
Mentha, 162
   aquatica, 31, 33, 38, 46, 75, 118, 130, 169
   piperita, 169
Menyanthes trifoliata, 31
Mimulus, 162, 170
   guttatus, 31, 33, 38, 39, 130, 133, 169
mink, 174, 220, 225
Miranthemum umbrosum, 177
Molinia caerulea, 199
mosses, 32, 33, 39, 78, 133, 162, 177
muskrats, 220, 225

mussels, 47
Myosotis scorpioides, 31, 33, 38, 39, 44, 46, 130, 133, 170
Myosoton aquaticum, 75
Myriophyllum, 129, 162, 177
   alterniflorum, 31, 33, 39, 127
   exalbescens, 169
   spicatum, 31, 34, 38, 78, 120, 133, 169
   verticillatum, 75

Nelumbo, 162
Nuphar, 22, 162
   lutea, 32, 34, 39, 40, 46, 119, 120, 132, 169
nuthatches, 279
Nymphaea, 162
   advena, 169
   alba, 169
   odorata, 169
   tuberosa, 169
   variegata, 169
Nymphoides peltata, 32, 33
Nyssa, 56

Oenanthe
   crocata, 32, 33
   fluviatilis, 19, 38, 44, 120
   globulosus, 75
Osmunda regalis, 32, 34, 78
otters, 220, 223, 225, 239, 252, 263, 265

Panicum, 162
perch, 218
Petasites hybridus, 32, 33, 39, 127
Phalaris, 162
   arundinacea, 32, 33, 34, 36, 38, 39, 40, 41, 44, 46, 120, 125, 130, 133, 163, 164, 169, 170
   australis, 163

Quercus, 172

Ranunculus, 32, 33, 36, 38, 39, 41, 44, 78, 113, 119, 120, 129, 130, 162, 169, 239, 254
   spp. *Batrachium*, 46, 254
   aquatilis, 43, 125
   baudoti, 75
   flammula, 32, 33, 127
   fluitans, 20, 43, 75, 94, 120, 125, 127, 133
   longirostris, 169
   peltatus, 43, 75, 118, 120
   pencillatus ssp. *pseudifluitans*, 118
   pseudofluitans, 120
   trichophyllus, 30, 75, 169
reed bunting, 279
Rhynchospora, 162
Riccia, 162
Rorippa, 162, 170
   amphibia, 32, 34, 38, 39
   austriaca, 32
   microphylla, 33
   nasturtium-aquaticum, 32, 33, 38, 39, 44, 46, 75, 118, 120, 125, 169, 171
Rumex, 162
   conglomeratus, 171
   hydrolapathum, 32, 34, 41, 171

Sagittaria, 162, 177
   cuneata, 169
   sagittifolia, 22, 32, 34, 39, 40, 43, 44, 120, 129, 169

Salix, 36, 78, 154, 172
   alba, 14, 145, 154
   alba caerulaea, 14
   purpurea, 14
   triandra, 14
   viminalis, 14
Salvinia, 176
Schoenoplectus
   lacustris, 34, 40, 75, 113, 120, 169, 176
   validus, 169
Schoenus nigricans, 94, 195, 196, 198, 216
Scirpus, 162, 164, 171
   fluitans, 33
   lacustris, 32, 38, 39, 40, 43, 118, 164, 227
   maritimus, 32, 34, 75
Scorpioides haloschoenus, 75
sedges, 163
shrimps, 42, 265
Solanum dulcamora, 169
Sparganium, 162
   americanum, 169
   angustifolium, 176
   chlorocarpum, 169, 176
   emersum, 32, 33, 34, 35, 36, 38, 39, 40, 41, 43, 44, 46, 75, 78, 94, 113, 118, 119, 120, 121, 125, 129, 130, 133, 160, 163, 164, 169
   erectum, 170
   eurycarpum, 169
Sphagnum, 32, 33, 194, 318
Spirodela polyrhiza, 32, 33
Stratiotes aloides, 176
sundew see *Drosera*
swans, 175, 222, 224
sweet flag, 227

Taxodium, 56
   distichum, 36

Trapa, 162, 176
Trisetum flavenscens, 173
Typha, 39, 46, 120, 162, 164, 228, 232
    angustifolia, 169
    domingensis, 75, 160
    latifolia, 32, 34, 160, 169

Urtica dioica, 171, 172
Utricularia, 162, 186
    vulgaris, 169

Vallisneria, 162
Veronica, 162
    anagallis-aquatic, 32, 33, 38, 39, 46, 75, 130, 133, 169
    beccabunga, 32, 33, 38, 39, 44, 46, 75, 125, 130, 133, 165, 169, 170
    catenata, 33
voles *see* water voles

water shrimps, 42, 265
water voles, 174, 223, 225
watercress, 226, 355
waterfowl, 221–4, 231

Zannichellia, 177
    palustris, 32, 34, 36, 75, 118, 169
zebra mussel, 47

General subject index

Aberdeen, 81
abstraction, 48, 102–4, 243
acidic fens, 191, 198
aesthetic values, 15
alien species, 47, 162
alluvial forest, 192, 199
Alps, 321–3
Altnacealga, 10
Amstel, River, 247
Amsterdam, 247
ancient countryside, 246
animals, 174–5, 257
    habitats, 41–2, 222–3
    see also individual types
Applecross, 319
aquatic trees, 168
aquifers, 12, 94, 103–4, 108, 249
areas, 6
Arigo, River, 315
Armier, River, 7
Armla, River, 261–2
Arthurian Legends, 11, 295
artists, 11
Ashby Warren, 215
Assynt, 318
Athelney, 187
Avon, River, 117, 119, 255

Baltic islands, 313
Bamberg, 247, 293
bank vegetation, 172–3
bedrock, 54
Beeston Bog, 95
Beetley Meadow, 95
Bernadette, Saint, 296
blanket bog, 189, 318–19
bogs, 194–5
borders, 148–9, 266
Boudewijn, River, 247
boundaries, 148–9, 266
Bourn, River, 62, 118
braiding, 112–13, 119, 343
Bray-sur-Seine, 289, 336
Breckland, 279
Bressingham Fen, 95
bridges, 303, 305
Briston Common, 95
Britain
    climatic changes, 55–6
    common riverine plants, 120
    landscape classifications, 243–5
    pollution, 49
    post-glacial era changes, 18
    restoration finance, 51
Broads, 214–15, 356
Brock's watering, 95
Bruges, 247
buffer strips, 234–5, 254–5

building blocks, 160, 162, 165, 169
Burwell, 59, 64
Bury St Edmunds, 204, 207
Buxton Heath, 95
bylaws, water usage, 62–3

Cairngorm Mountains, 20, 81, 82, 276
calcium, and wetlands, 196
Cam, River, 58–67, 352
    conservation, 49
    diversions, 298, 354
    pollution, 66
    trade, 63
Cambridge, 62, 63–4, 298–9, 352, 354
canals, 292, 293
Canterbury, 295
carbon, in rivers, 36
carrs, 199
catchments, 6–8, 88–9
catchment-scale approach, 244
cathedrals, 296
Cavenham Poors' Fen, 95
caves, 364–5
chalk streams, 19, 24, 38, 118
chalk valleys, 124
change of species, 37–9

channelling, 113
character, 5
characteristic, 5
Cheshire, ponds, 353, 357
Chiltern Hills, 337, 340, 344
cities, 247, 293
citrus, Malta, 243
classification, of riverscapes, 144
clay streams, 39, 119
climate change, 135
Clyde, River, 17
CoDi *see* Cover-Diversity number
Cole, River, 266, 337
Cologne, 336
Comberton, 59
communication (biotic), 266, 267
communications (human), 239, 258, 292–3
    Alpine, 320
    Fenlands, 65
    Malta, 74, 76, 109, 365
    River Eger, 143
    Scottish Highlands, 319
communities, size, 265
composers, 11
conifers, 320
connectivity, 42, 139–40, 153
conservation of riverscapes, 4–5, 23, 51
Constable, John, 9
CORINE Vegetation Classification, 189–93, 197
corridors, 42, 147–8, 150, 264
    boundaries, 265
    in England, 266
    in Gozo, 274
    for nuthatches, 279

Corsica, 78, 325–6
    rainfall, 77
    riverscapes, 245
    settlement, 77
    vegetation, 80
Costa, Lake, 68, 76
Costa, River, 73
Cotswolds, 339–40
Countryside Commission, 243–4
Cover-Diversity number, 131–2, 134
Cowper, William, 279
Crete, fishing, 220
Crickdale, 341
crofting, 319
crossings, of rivers, 303–5
Crostwick Marsh, 95
Czech Republic, fishponds, 355

Dalä Loen, River, 313
Dalama, 313
Danube, 180
Dartmoor, 276
Decoy Carr, 215
defences, 283, 289, 296–8
    Anglo-Scottish border, 329–31
    Corsica, 326
    London, 345
    Malta, 296–8
    River Eger, 143
deities, 296
Denmark, conservation, 49, 50
Denver Sluice, 65
depth of water, 25
Derbyshire Wells, 256
destruction of riverscapes, 4–5
diagnostic species, 31–4
Dickens, Charles, 11
Dilham Broad, 215

Dinant, 336
Dingli, 365
disease, 308
ditches, 256
diversion of rivers, 99–100, 102–3, 298–9
Don, River (Scotland), 36, 81–4
Donausworth, 247, 293
Dove, River, 133, 139
Downland rivers, 123
downstream development, 25–7, 30, 45, 107–14, 115, 117, 127–36
Drainage Order, 121–3
Ducan's Marsh, 95

Eamont, River, 126
East Ruston Common, 95, 214
Ebble, River, 117, 118, 119
Eden, River (Cumberland), 126–7
Eger, River, 142–3, 201
Eköln, River, 247
elements of riverscapes, 5–6
Eliot, George, 11
Ely, 59, 64–5, 66, 75, 289, 336
Ely, Isle of, 308
embanking, 104–5
emergents, 43, 162, 163, 165–7, 168
England *see* Britain
English Nature, 243–4
Environmental Impact Assessments, 88
Erik, *Saint*, 296
European Union, conservation policies, 199, 213
    see also CORINE Vegetation Classification

Europe and North America
geochemical differences, 27
plant similarities, 168, 169
Evesham, Vale of, 255, 335

farming
abandonment, 316–18
for export, 292
Malta, 109
Norway, 324
requirements, 253
riverside, 287–8
self-sufficient, 292
features, 5
Feltorpe bogs, 95
fen peat, 196
Fenlands, The, 56, 64–7
communications, 65
damage to, 95
diversions, 64, 65
eels, 219
exports, 66
farming, 65–6
peat, 59, 65, 277
pollution, 66
population, 64
post-glacial era changes, 18
village sites, 187, 328
fens, 190–1, 195, 198
ferries, 303, 305, 341
fields, 262
and river patterns, 124
dividers, 249–50
drainage, 100–1
filter resistance, 278
fish farms, 220
fisheries, pollution, 219
fishing, 217–20
fishponds, 354–5
flax, 227
Fleet, River, 7

floating rooted species, 46, 162, 168, 169
flood plains, 90, 91
building on, 188–94
diversity of, 209–16
estuarine, 196
fertility, 188
and flooding, 187–8
form of, 238, 247
London, 344
pollution, 186
River Thames, 342–4
size, 180
substrate, 180
and tributaries, 261
vegetation, 188, 194
water patterns, 180–6
flooding, 12, 105, 155–6, 187–8
Florence, 283, 298
flow of water, 22, 24, 30, 113, 165, 175
flowering of wells, 256
Forcheim, 247
fords, 303–5, 341
forestry, 14
Forncett Meadows, 95
fortifications *see* defences
Foss Dyke, 19, 255
Fowlmere, 95
Foxton, 62–3
fragmentation, 260, 265, 268–70, 279
free-floating species, 176
Friedbergerau, 17
fringing herbs, 46, 162, 163, 168, 170–1, 172

geographic distribution of river plants, 46
Gerald of Wales, 224–5
Ghasel, 209, 210
Ghasel, river, 209
Girgenti, 295

glacial drift, 54
Glastonbury, 187
global warming, 279
Godmanchester, 293, 336
Godstow, 337
Golo, River, 77–81
Gozo
and tourism, 271, 273
changes in, 270–4
defences, 296, 331
environmental flows, 270
farming, 271, 272
riverscape, 242
socio-economic forces, 271, 272–3
wealth and mobility, 273
see also Malta
Grahame, Kenneth, 11
Granta, River, 62
grasslands, wet, 228–30
gravel, extraction, 231, 235
Great Gorge
Great Ouse, River, 64–5, 298
Grenoble, 320
groundwater-dependent wetlands, 195–6
Gunzburg, 247

habitat-species interpretation, 130
Hadrian's Wall, 331
Halladale, river, 207–9
Hammerfest, 324
Hampton Court palace, 344
Hardwick Hall, 227
harshness, 308–9
hedges, 249, 250, 257
Helmond, 283
hemp, 227
Henley, 343
heterogeneity, 151, 152
Hiz, River, 261

Hobson, Tobias, 353
Hoe Meadow, 95
Holme Fen, 65
horizontal patterns, 111
humans and rivers, 19–22, 282
humid grassland, 191, 199
Hungary, 142–3, 144, 176, 355
   see also Eger, River
Huntingdon, 293
Huy, 294, 336

Iceland, 43, 123, 323–4
Icklingham Poors' Fen, 95, 263, 275, 276
Inchnadamph, 319
industry, 293–4
inns, 293
Irchen, River, 42
irrigation, 12, 103, 243
Isère, River, 320
Isle of Ely, 308
Isqof, River, 68
is-Simlija, 364
Itchen, River, 112, 135, 137–8
Itzehoe, 336

Karlsruhe, 293
Kbir, River, 67–77, 98, 297
Kellinghauser, 336
Kings Fen, 214
King's Lynn, 65, 298
Kingsley, Charles, 294
Kintore, 81
Kinzig, River, 261–2

Lady of the Fountain, 295
Lake District, 308, 328
Landsberg, 247
Landscape Description Units, 244

landscape features, classification, 240
landscape planning, for water purification, 234
landscape, scale of, 257
Lark, River, 20, 203–7, 275
layers, of riverscape, 54
Lech, River, 247
Les Roches, 336
Lincoln, 255, 287
Littleport, 64
livestock farming, 295, 320
Living Landscapes Project, 244–5
Lochem, 289, 336
locks, 64, 292
Lofoten Islands, 324
Loing, River, 112
London, 247, 293, 344
longitudinal variation, 25–30
Lonsdale Moor, 277
Lopham Fens, 95
loss of species, Malta, 75
loss of vegetation, 47–50
Lourdes, 296
Lowther, River, 126
Lydwell, 341
Lyon, 289, 335
Lyvenet, River, 126

Madeira, 299, 326–7
Maes Brook, 125
Magnocaricatum, 198
Maidenhead, 343
Main, River, 247, 293
Mainz, 283
Malta, 94–9
   aquifers, 87
   boreholes, 96
   bridges, 305–6
   communications, 74, 76
   corridors, 266
   dams, 98

   defences, 76, 297
   farming, 76, 243, 363–4
   flooding, 139
   flora, 73
   galleries, 96
   geology, 240–3
   Great Gorges, 73
   Great Plateau, 67–77
   habitat destruction, 268–9
   irrigation, 97
   landscape, 240–3
   marshes, 74, 97, 108
   population, 309
   recreation, 77
   river patterns, 123
   river vegetation, 74
   riverscapes, 108–9, 110, 144
   species loss, 75
   tanks, 97
   terracing, 67
   water abstraction, 74, 99
   water sources, 96–8
   wells, 97
   see also Gozo
Market Harborough, 114
Marsa, 74
marshes, 108
Massif Central, 123
Maasland, 336
matrices, 150, 274
Mdina, 15, 297, 305, 365
meadows, 229–30, 245–7, 309, 319, 337
meanders, 110
Megève, 294, 320
Melton Valley Park, 235
Meuse, River, 247
Mildenhall, 204
mills, 290
   see also water mills
minerals, extraction, 231, 235

Mississippi, River, 7
morphological resistance, 278
mosaics, 30, 43, 45, 139–40, 147, 154, 156, 262–4
    boundaries, 266
    on Gozo, 270
Moselle, River, 123, 194
Mown Fen, 214–15

Nadder, River, 117, 119
Namur, 247, 293, 336
Nar Meadow, 342
natural capital, 8, 141
Natural England, 243–4
naturalness, 16–19
Navaccia, River, 78, 80
Nene, River, 308
Neolithic era, 55, 334
Netherlands, 49, 264
Norrland, 313–14
North America and Europe
    geochemical differences, 27
    plants compared, 168, 169
North Sea fishing, 84
Norway, northern, 324
Norwich, 283, 298

ochre pollution, diagnostic plants, 40
olives, 243
organisation of landscape, 150–1
Orlando, water purification, 232
oval-tailed plants, 31, 46, 158, 168, 169, 176–7
ox-bow lakes, 179
Oxford, 343
Oxmoor, 328

Pappenheim, 293
Paris, 336
Parvocaricatum, 198
patches, 139, 140, 147–8, 150
Patrick, Saint, 295
patterns, 6, 111, 147–9
    and Drainage Order, 121–4
    streams, 89
    vegetation, 127–9
Peak District, 123, 133, 139, 147
pearls, 225
peat
    as resource, 230–1
    extraction of, 14, 356
    history of, 277
Piddle, River, 49
pilgrim routes, 295–6
Pisa, 283
planned countryside, 246
plateaux, 261–2
Po, River, 180, 227
poets, 11
pollards, 154
pollution, 25, 44, 47, 48, 49, 114, 232–5
    diagnostic plants, 40–1
    in France, 49
    industrial, 294
    in Ireland, 47, 49
    of wetlands, 232
ponds, 63
    as landscapes, 354–7
    numbers of, 101
    origin, 356
    watercress, 355
pools, 110
population changes, 308–9, 319
Port Meadows (Oxford), 337
Potter, Beatrix, 11, 308
pristine, riverscapes, 17

pristine vegetation, 22
processes, 148, 150
profiles, 110
Programmes of Measures, 88
purification of water, 232–3, 235
Pyrenees, river patterns, 123

Qormi, 74
quality of water, 13, 21
Quantock Hills, 293

rainfall, 110
raised bogs, 189, 200
Rambla del Estrecho, 314–18
Ransome, Arthur, 11
Ranworth, 215, 277
Rastatt, 293
Reach, 64
Reading, 344
recreation, 15, 235, 236
    River Thames, 344
    and navigation, 336
Redgrave Fen, 95
reedswamps, 189–90, 198
Reedham Marshes, 215
reeds, uses, 228
regulation of rivers, 105
resistance to change, 278
resources, 217
restoration, 22, 50–2
Rhee, River, 62
Rhine, River, 8, 186, 187, 297
Rhône, River, 104, 320
Ribe (Denmark), 247, 294
Ribe, River, 17, 247
rice, 40, 227
riffles, 110
Rihana, River, 10
riparian ecosystems, values of, 218
river basin, definition, 88

rivers
    common species, 31–4, 120, 129
    definition, 1
riverscape
    definition, 1
    elements, 5–6, 257–8, 264–5
    layers, 54
    scale of, 110, 245
    settlement, 239
    topography, 239
    views of, 239
rock types, 25, 27, 29, 30, 108
Roman Empire, 19, 55
Rome, siting, 247
rooted floating plants, 167, 168, 176–7
rosettes, 162, 167, 177
Ruhr, River, 293, 363
run-off, 115
rushes, 162, 163, 171, 177, 227

sacred riverscapes, 256, 295–6
sacred springs, Malta, 365
saeters, 313, 314
    see also sheilings
Saffron Walden, 63, 336
San Gorg, River, 84
sand, extraction, 231, 235
sandstone streams, 38
Sara, River, 242
Scale
    of landscape elements, 260
    of riverscapes, 110, 245
Scorse, River, 17
Scottish Highlands, 318–20
Scottish-English border, 329–31
scramblers, 168, 169
sedge swamps, 189–90, 198

self-sufficient production, 292
sense of place, 6, 144–7
sensitivity, 34–6, 115–16, 277–8
settlements, 247–8, 258, 281–91
    Malta, 109
    River Eger, 143
    see also cities; towns; villages
Severn, River, 180
shading, 40, 165, 166, 171, 173–4
shallowing, 30, 48
sheet flow, 86
sheiling, 323
    see also saeters
short herbs, 171
Siggiewi, 74, 77, 295
Silkeborg, 50
Silsoe, 50
silt, 160
sizes of rivers, 113
Skåne, 309–14
skewing, 47
smiling landscape, 334, 346
snow melt, 111
Soham, 187
Somerset Levels, 8, 187, 328
source marshes, 195
Southend-on-Sea, 345
species-habitat interpretation, 130
Spoon-leaved herbs, 46, 162, 168
sport *see* recreation
springs, 96, 108, 191, 198
Standon, 289, 294
Stanton Harcourt, 343
status, ecological, 88
stepping stones, 303

Stoke-by-Nayland, 336
Storjen, 314
storm flows, 16, 129
Stour, River, 261, 339
strap-leaved plants, 46, 162, 168, 169, 176
Strasbourg, 335
structural resistance, 278
structure, 157
submerged plants, 167
subsistence farming, 324
supply of water, 300
Sussex Weald, flooding, 139
Sutton Broad Fen, 215
Swabian Alps, 23
Sweden, 309–14
    and Alps, 321–3
    defences, 323
    landscape elements, 245–7
    meadows, 245–7, 309
    river conservation, 49

Ta'Baldu, 359–66
tall herb communities, 191–2, 196, 199
tall monocotyledons, 158, 161, 162, 168–70
    Europe and North America compared, 168
    as fringe vegetation, 172
    geographic distribution, 46
    habitats, 163, 164
    River Don, 36
    shading by, 171–3
Tanat, River, 124
Tapio, River, 351–3
Teddington Lock, 344
tempered landscape, 334, 346
terraces, 67, 262

Thames, River, 337
    flood plain, 179–216
    landscape, 336–46
    navigation, 339
    settlements, 247
    tributaries, 261
Thingvellir, 7
Thorpe Marshes, 215
Tiber, River, 247
Till, River, 118
time changes, 116–20
Tower of London, 345
Towns
    canal-side, 287
    riverside, 281–3, 287, 289–90
    siting, 247
    trading, 335–6, 341
    traditional rivers, 17, 30
    traditional vegetation, 22
    transition mires, 191, 198
    transition resistance, 278
transport, 63, 288–9, 293
    Alps, 323
    Sweden, 323
trees, 154, 250–1
    and flash foods, 251
    and flood plains, 200, 227–8
    and riverbanks, 174
    in Europe and North America, 168
    for water purification, 235
    riverside, 154
Trent, River, 255
Treutlingen, 293
tributary rivers, 261, 345–6
Twenthe Kanaal, 336
types, 5

Ulm, 247
Uppsala, 247, 296, 297
upstream-downstream variation *see* downstream development
Upware, 187
urban dwellers, requirements, 252–3

valleys, 2
values of riverscape, 8–15
vegetation, 239
    classification of, 197
    conservation value, 22
    ethical value, 22
    habit, 22
    loss of, 47–50
    mountain streams, 22
vertical patterns, 111, 166
Victoria, 242
Vikings, 283, 298
villages, 247, 287, 288–9
    ponds, 356
vineyards, 295
Volga, River, 267
vulnerability, 12
Vyrnwy, River, 124–5

Waccasassa River, 56–8
Wallingford, 343
warfare, 329–31
    see also defences
wash-out, 170
Water Framework Directive, 213
water meadows *see* meadows
water mills, 19, 103, 148, 194, 292, 293
    diversions for, 298–9

water-supported plants, 162, 165, 168, 169, 175–7
weirs, 43
wells, 63, 289, 295–6
Welsh Marches, 331
Westminster, 293, 344
Westminster, Duke of, 320
wetlands, classification, 189–93
    commercial value, 226
    draining, 197
    for water purification, 232
    harshness, 328–9
    impacts, 181
    Norfolk, 327
    river-fed, 196
wetness of land, 87
wharves, 289, 352
whole catchment planning, 105
Wicken Fen, 64, 65, 186
wide-leaved herbs, 163
width of rivers, 167
Wigan, 101
Windsor Castle, 345
Winifrid's Well, Saint, 296
winterbournes, 43
Wisbech, 65, 219, 298
Witham, River, 255
Woman of the Wells, 295
Woodwalton Fen, 65
writers, 11
Wylye, River, 109, 117, 118, 136–7
Wynbury Moss, 234

Yare, River, 21
York, 298

Zebbug, 68, 74, 76
Zutphen, 336